The Dog Trainer's Resource 2

The APDT Chronicle of the Dog Collection

Mychelle Blake, Editor

Publishing

Wenatchee, Washington U.S.A.

The Dog Trainer's Resource 2. The APDT Chronicle of the Dog Collection
Mychelle Blake, Editor

Dogwise Publishing
A Division of Direct Book Service, Inc.
403 S Mission
Wenatchee, Washington 9880
1-509-663-9115, 1-800-776-2665
website: www.dogwisepublishing.com
email: info@dogwisepublshing.com

Indexing: Cheryl Smith

Limits of Liability and Disclaimer of Warranty:
The author and publisher shall not be liable in the event of incidental or consequential damages in connection with, or arising out of, the furnishing, performance, or use of the instructions and suggestions contained in this book.

Library of Congress Cataloging-in-Publication Data:
The dog trainer's resource 2 : the APDT chronicle of the dog collection / Mychelle E. Blake, editor.
p. cm.
ISBN 978-1-929242-57-3
1. Dogs--Training. 2. Dogs--Behavior. 3. Small business. I. Blake, Mychelle. II. Association of Pet Dog Trainers.
SF431.D664 2008
636.7'0835--dc22
2008021476

ISBN: 978-1-929242-57-3

Printed in the U.S.A.

Contents

v

From the President of APDT

In an ever-evolving discipline like dog training, there are no absolutes. Thanks to ongoing research we are constantly learning more and more about dog behavior and training. In fact, if you meet someone who claims to know all there is to know about training dogs, run...fast!

All of the new information has led to quite a revolution in the last few decades. More and more professional dog trainers recognize there is a science to behavior and that there are effective and gentle methods of training.

Dogs are also being held to new standards in our homes and in our society. Today family dogs are brought along on vacations, for regular outings to dog parks & even out to dinner at restaurants. Along with all of this integration into our families and communities has come the challenge of training our pooches to be well behaved, social citizens. Enter the dog trainer—or to be more specific the pet dog trainer.

Pet dog trainers teach so much more than the basics of sit, down and stay. We influence and assist in the relationships between people and their pets!

I'm excited about dog training in general, and about the future of our pet profession. But as I noted earlier, there's still so much for everyone to learn...including experienced trainers. *The Dog Trainer's Resource, 2. The APDT Chronicle of the Dog* Collection provides yet another practical, easy-to-use reference guide from newbies to nearly retired. These articles are written by the pinnacles in our profession. They've been there, done that and have the additional gift of being able to pass along knowledge to you via these brilliant articles.

These great articles are straight out of *The APDT Chronicle Of The Dog*. I'd like to extend a special thank-you to Mychelle Blake, our supreme editor, for her efforts in compiling this book and to all of the contributing experts who generously provided this material which will give you great insights into all of the elements of dog training including training techniques, learning theory, suggestions for your curriculum, business strategies and more. And a sincere thank-you to Dogwise for publishing yet another valuable resource for trainers to sink their teeth into.

This book should provide you with easy access to information that will enhance the relationships that you have with your clients and with your own pets. On behalf of the APDT, I encourage you to continue to educate yourself and others in our pursuit of a more dog friendly world!

Kellyann Conway, CABC
APDT President 2008

Puppy Training

All dog trainers know that the key to creating a healthy, happy, and behaviorally sound adult dog is to nurture a puppy in its formative first few weeks and months of life. The articles in this section focus on the importance of socialization and the various ways in which the "community"—trainers, veterinarians, breeders, and owners—can cultivate and enrich a puppy's developmental experiences. From how one chooses a puppy's first class, to how one acclimates a puppy to grooming, to learning how to accept each puppy as an unique individual compared to past dogs owned, can all significantly impact the health and well being of the adult dog to be for years to come.

Puppy Socialization: How to Build a Foundation for a Relationship

Trish O'Connor, May/June 2006

Puppy classes have become more popular and with good reason—trainers are beginning to really understand the need for socialization and training that goes along with raising a puppy. The window of development for a puppy is relatively short, so getting them started out on the right "paw" with a well run class is important. The experiences of the puppy and their owners influence how they are going to handle their dog in the future. A poorly managed puppy class will not help that puppy later in life and may even cause harm.

As trainers, we can assist new puppy owners with the socialization that puppies need. For a puppy, socializing is meeting new people and dogs of all ages and getting to experience new places and objects every day. At the Dumb Friends League animal shelter, our puppy classes originated as a socialization class with little training for the owners or their puppies. Puppy owners attended the two classes we held each week because they wanted a tired puppy. We were doing that very well, but it was feeling too much like running a supervised dog park. So we decided it was time for a change.

In January 2005 we made a change to our puppy classes. Change is a hard thing to accomplish with an established program, but we turned it on its floppy puppy ear and now our classes are three times more popular than in previous years. We started with a name change from Puppy Club to Puppy Preschool. There are many puppy preschool classes out there, but in our case it describes exactly what our clients are getting—introductory training to prepare their puppies for the group class they are going to take as adolescents. Even if clients and their puppy don't take any classes beyond Puppy Preschool, they have learned many great tips, training, and suggestions to help them along.

In order to make our class stand out from other puppy classes in the area, we chose to focus not only on the socialization of the puppies to people and other pups, but on relationship building between pup and owner. Currently, our class is about 50% off-lead play and 50% training puppies and owners. Clients walk away learning more than just what the person sitting next to them did last week.

Set Up

The Dumb Friends League puppy classes are run as an on going drop-in style class. Although this throws together puppies at different levels of training, it allows them to socialize with new puppies every week. This gives them a chance to interact with different play partners and experience different play styles, as well as get the chance to meet new people each week. We hold seven Puppy Preschools each week between our two locations. Clients can attend as many or as few of the classes as they feel their puppies need before they reach six months of age. Clients have the option of paying as they go or purchasing a punch card for six classes. The punch cards have proven to be the popular option.

Since we have many puppies at different levels, we set up a transition area to help the new ones adjust to the room. The first time attending a class can be frightening for a less confident puppy. We allow puppies that have good play skills to go in one-on-one with the new puppies to help acclimate them to the room. We rotate the puppies throughout the class so the new puppies get a chance to socialize with a variety of puppies. Most pups graduate out of the transition area by their second or third time in class.

Safety

To make sure we are offering a wonderful experience, one of our priorities is keeping puppies, clients, and staff safe. This means that we limit the number of puppies that attend each class. From our experiences, six puppies per staff member are about all we can keep an eye on. We also ask the owners to keep an eye on their own dog. By having them participate in watching the interactions of their puppy, we help them learn skills that will help them when they eventually go to a dog park. We explain to owners about puppy interactions during the play times. As the instructors travel around the room, they talk about what they are seeing during play.

The instructors work to redirect rough play. One method we use during these play times is splitting—walking between the puppies and so redirecting their play off each other. Another method of redirecting rough play is to use a water squirt bottle. The water bottles are used minimally, but are essential because we do not allow the puppies to wear collars during playtime. This is a safety issue for the puppies because they can get caught on another pup's collar.

We have also been using an adult dog in one of our play groups. This adult dog has been great at keeping the room calm by splitting rough play and giving off calming signals. Finding the right adult dog is not an easy task. You want to look for a dog that can handle the puppies and is a "mentor" to the younger dogs.

Training: Building the Relationship

Now that everyone feels safe, we can focus on the relationship training that goes into each of our Puppy Preschools. A majority of our clients are coming to socialize their puppies, but this is our chance to get them involved in the training of their new dog. Since we have puppies of all different training levels, we developed 26 lesson plans for the instructors to follow. We divided the lesson plans into topics that last two to four weeks, such as polite walking, coming when called, and normal puppy behaviors (like puppy nipping and chewing). Having lesson plans gives the puppies and owners some consistency in their training and they know what to expect each time they attend.

We are able to incorporate two 15-minute training times in each lesson plan. These include lectures, demonstrations, and practice time on the major topic, such as polite walking. The second training time may include a topic that relates to the major topic, or we may get the group involved in a game or socialization exercise that relates to items we talked about this week like "pass the puppy" or another training game. For example, we may work on "penalty yards" in the first training segment. The second segment will be a related topic like "leave it," an important command to have when out for a walk.

But building the relationship does not just mean training the puppies to sit or down when asked. It is also an opportunity to educate the owners that their puppy's middle name is not "no, no, bad dog." Once they step through the class door, they are immersed in positive training. We are able to enlighten the owners and they become involved in their puppies' lives. With the example of "penalty yards," we teach the owners to talk and treat their dogs while walking them instead of jerking on the leash because the puppy is pulling. Or if the puppy is chewing everything in sight, we can explain the benefits of management and why it works. We are able to answer questions and give them direction that they may not get at other places.

By offering a drop-in class with structure, you can give your puppy owners a great foundation in positive reinforcement and relationship building. Our Puppy Preschool seems to be ever evolving as we learn about the puppies that attend and what the owners need to make raising a puppy fun and exciting. ❖

Striving for Puppy Wellness: Are Early Socialization and Infectious Disease Prevention Incompatible?

Jennifer Messer, Edited by Terry Long, November/December 2006

What is Puppy Wellness?

Wellness is more than simply freedom from disease; it is an overall state of physical and mental well-being. Puppy wellness depends on many factors, including genetics, nutrition, protection from parasites and infectious diseases, grooming, intellectual stimulation, exercise, socialization, and a loving and safe environment. When a puppy is both physically and behaviorally well, he is more likely to meet the expectations of his human family and is at decreased risk of re-homing or euthanasia.

One of the dilemmas in the pursuit of puppy wellness is balancing the need for early socialization with the need for protection from infectious disease. Traditionally, the puppy owner has been advised to restrict the puppy to the house and the yard, until completion of his vaccination series. The idea was to protect him from infectious diseases until he was well immunized, which can mean virtual isolation from the outside world until over four months of age. However, the window of opportunity to most effectively socialize a puppy usually closes before the puppy is fully vaccinated, and delaying vital socialization often has negative long-term behavioral consequences. Research shows that lack of early socialization increases the likelihood of behavior problems such as fear and aggression.

But is this degree of precaution still necessary? This "traditional" approach is based on the limitations of vaccines being used two decades ago. Vaccines have improved significantly in the last 15 years, as has our understanding of the importance of early socialization. Let us then re-examine traditional recommendations in the light of modern advances in immunology and insight into canine behavioral development.

This article will examine puppy socialization needs and the role of vaccination in the prevention of infectious disease, and explore the actual risk associated with socializing puppies before completion of their puppy vaccination series.

The Value of Early Socialization

Mother Nature designed dogs to be especially receptive to interactions with novel people, dogs, places, and new experiences while very young, so that they grow up to be comfortable with the everyday elements of their environment.[1] This prevents them from wasting energy by responding fearfully to the common events and encounters of their day-to-day life.

Puppies are programmed to be most accepting of new experiences until the age of about 12 weeks.[2,3,4,5,6] Mother Nature decrees that anything the puppy hasn't encountered by 12 weeks old is odd enough to warrant caution! The period from three to approximately 12 weeks old is called the "sensitive period," whereby puppies are most able to easily acclimatize to novel stimuli. From 12 to 18 weeks old the window of opportunity to socialize the puppy closes rapidly, such that with each passing week it becomes increasingly difficult to successfully socialize a dog. Once the dog reaches 18 weeks of age the window of socialization closes and it is then much harder—and sometimes impossible—to train a dog to like something new or acclimatize him to something that he finds frightening. Poorly socialized dogs are at much greater risk for responding fearfully to unfamiliar people, dogs, and experiences.[2,4,6,7]

Socialization[8] is a big project: it requires exposure to people, dogs, other pets, places, sounds and experiences they will be subjected to in the life they share with us. Depending on the owner's lifestyle, this might include trains, garbage trucks, school-yards of screaming children, crowds, cats, crying infants, and much more. Most puppies will be subjected to people of both sexes, various ages and appearances, handling for routine grooming, and the noises of a variety of household appliances in their day-to-day life with us.[9] While it is impossible to expose a young puppy to absolutely everything he will ever encounter in life, the more bases that are covered while the window of socialization is open, the greater the chance that the puppy will be able to generalize from his prior experiences and find something reassuringly familiar in a new situation.

One way to promote socialization is through "puppy classes."

Puppy Classes

Puppy classes—the brainchild of Dr. Ian Dunbar—were developed as a way of enabling puppy socialization and training in a friendly and safe environment. In a typical puppy class, off-leash play and play-fighting helps socialize puppies to other dogs and allows them to learn to be gentle with their jaws, handling exercises acclimatize them to being touched by strangers, and exposure to odd sights and sounds (using props, CDs, and theatrics) accustoms them to a wide range of life experiences. Between socialization activities, topics such as housetraining, exercise, and environmental stimulation are addressed with owners and the puppies are taught some basic obedience skills.

Puppy classes help puppies achieve wellness by facilitating socialization and by teaching the puppies' guardians how to assist the puppies in acquiring skills that are expected of them in order for them to be cherished members of their human family and of society. Since puppy classes are so important to the lifelong well-being of puppies, it is crucial that as many puppies as possible attend them. Despite this, many owners are discouraged from enrolling their dog because of recommendations from breeders or veterinarians who argue that puppies should not be exposed to other dogs until their full vaccination schedule is complete, something that doesn't occur until after the puppy is 12 weeks old, when his peak socialization period has already passed.

Puppy owners, faced with balancing the very real threat of their puppy becoming seriously ill against what may seem to them to be the nebulous benefits of puppy classes, cannot be blamed for choosing to keep their puppies at home. Yet, the relative risks have changed with improvements in vaccines. Although vaccination does not guarantee protection from disease, newer vaccines allow more reliable protection at a younger age.

Vaccines and How They Work (and Don't Work): Immunology 101

The diseases against which a puppy is vaccinated depends on the environment that he lives in, his lifestyle, and his health status. Puppies in North America are generally vaccinated against at least five infectious diseases: distemper, hepatitis, parvovirus, parainfluenza (these four are often administered as one combination vaccine), and rabies. Depending on their risk of exposure, some puppies are also vaccinated against leptopsirosis,10 Bordetella (kennel cough), Borellia burgdorferi (Lyme disease), and other disease agents. Of these, the disease that is usually of greatest concern when considering early exposure to other dogs is parvovirus. The reason for this is threefold: the virus is incredibly resilient in the environment, the disease is severe, and the older vaccines were not very reliable at providing protection in young puppies.

To understand why the older vaccines were less reliable, you must first understand something of how vaccines work.

Antibodies

Antibodies are special proteins made by the body to neutralize disease before they can cause harm. A puppy gets maternal antibodies from his mother, partially through their shared blood supply while the puppy is still a fetus, but mostly through the milk he suckles from her after birth. The type and amount of maternal antibodies a puppy gets depends on his mother's immune system, i.e., what diseases and vaccines she's been exposed to in her life. Maternal antibodies are temporary; they gradually break down and disappear completely by the time he is about four months old.

In order to have lasting immune protection, the puppy's immune system needs to make its own antibodies. The puppy's immune system can be stimulated to make antibodies in one of two ways: the puppy can be exposed to the disease and risk getting very ill, or he can be vaccinated against the disease. Vaccines are made with weakened, altered, or killed disease agents—still close enough to "the real thing" to stimulate the production of antibodies, but not capable of causing the disease itself.

The first time the body meets either the real disease or the vaccine against a disease it makes some antibodies, and the cells of the immune system register that they have encountered that particular disease intruder. When the puppy gets his next dose of the vaccine a few weeks later, his body makes many more antibodies even faster and an army of memory cells is made, ready to fight the disease at the drop of a hat if needed in the future. At this point, there is long-lasting immunity—up to a year for some disease agents, much longer for others.

Maternal Antibody Interference

Maternal antibodies are especially important in the first six weeks of life when the puppy's immune system is too immature to make its own antibodies in response to either vaccination or a real disease encounter. The downside of maternal antibodies is they can also interfere with the effectiveness of vaccines. This problem is called "maternal antibody interference."

Since a vaccine is like a fake disease, the maternal antibodies neutralize it as if it was the disease itself, sometimes so well that the puppy's immune system isn't stimulated enough by the vaccine, and not enough antibodies are made. This is one of the reasons why we vaccinate puppies every few weeks: for a given puppy we don't know exactly when the maternal antibody level is low enough for the vaccine to work properly. Because of the possibility of maternal antibody interference, there can be periods when the puppy has neither enough maternal antibodies nor enough of his own antibodies to fight off real disease if he encounters it. These periods are called "windows of vulnerability."

How Vaccines and Vaccination Schedules Have Changed

The windows of vulnerability used to pose a huge problem with regards to parvovirus in puppies. In recent years these windows have become much smaller and, therefore, less problematic, because the newer vaccines are much better at stimulating the immune system even while the puppy still has maternal antibodies in his system. These newer vaccines are called "high-titer, low-passage" vaccines because the disease substance used in making the vaccine is put through fewer "passages" to weaken it and, therefore, the vaccine product is capable of stimulating the immune system better, resulting in more antibodies being made (measured as a "titer"). Even breeds that have historically been more susceptible to parvovirus, such as the black-and-tan-coated breeds, don't seem to be at increased risk anymore when the newer, "stronger" vaccines are used.

Before the "high-titer, low-passage" vaccines[11] were introduced, the likelihood of maternal antibody interference in young puppies was much greater, and it was quite common for puppies to receive vaccinations at 8, 12, and 16 weeks of age and, sometimes, even a final booster at 18 to 20 weeks of age for puppies at increased risk.

Both manufacturers of the newer vaccines and independent investigators have demonstrated that three doses of the high-titer, low-passage vaccines given at six, nine, and 12 weeks of age are at least as effective at immunizing a puppy as were the older vaccines given at three-week intervals until the puppy was 18 to 20 weeks old.[12] This is reflected in the American Animal Health Association 2006 Vaccine Guidelines[13], which now recommends vaccinating puppies starting at six to eight weeks of age and revaccinating every three to four weeks[14] until the last dose of vaccine is given at 12 weeks of age or older. [15]

With an accelerated schedule (starting at six rather than eight weeks of age) using the newer vaccines (high-titer, low-passage), puppies can now be effectively vaccinated at an earlier age. While this should have paved the road to getting puppies into socialization classes while the window of socialization is still wide open, there still is great hesitation in the veterinary, breeder, and training community to encourage the attendance of puppies under 12 weeks of age in these classes.

Expert Opinion on the Relative-Risk Dilemma

While it has long been recognized that behavioral illness kills more dogs than infectious disease, the first veterinary expert to promote getting puppies into socialization classes after a minimum of one vaccination was Dr. R.K. Anderson, a veterinarian, board certified in both population medicine and behavior. In an open letter to his colleagues titled "Puppy Vaccination and Socialization Should Go Together,"[16] he emphasized that we have a responsibility to enable early learning and socialization in young puppies, and that they should be enrolled in a socialization program as a key part of any preventive medicine program.

Dr. Anderson recommends that puppies start puppy class at eight to nine weeks of age, with a minimum of one vaccination. He further argues that:

> Experience and epidemiologic data support the relative safety and lack of transmission of disease in these puppy socialization classes over the past 10 years in many parts of the United States. In fact, the risk of a dog dying because of infection with distemper or parvo[virus] disease is far less than the much higher risk of a dog dying (euthanasia) because of a behavior problem.

Dr. Anderson concludes by stating that 10 years of good experience and data with few exceptions allows veterinarians to generally recommend early socialization and training classes, beginning when puppies are eight to nine weeks of age.

The University of Minnesota[17] (where Dr. Anderson is a Professor Emeritus[18]) is not the only veterinary school starting puppies in class after one vaccination. At the Purdue University School of Veterinary Medicine, puppies between 7 and 14 weeks of age can start class so long as they have been administered their first vaccination against distemper, parvovirus, and Bordetella at six weeks of age or older, and at least ten days before class. Dr. Andrew Leuscher, veterinary behaviorist and director of the Animal Behavior Clinic at Purdue University, and Steve Thompson, APBV, director of the Pet Wellness Clinic at Purdue University, state in their open letter to the public that many more puppies currently lose their homes due to behavior reasons than die of viral diseases, and that they are not aware of any parvovirus problems in puppy classes since the high-titer vaccines gained mainstream use in 1995. They state that:

> There have been no puppy class participants infected with Parvovirus in any puppy classes offered at Ohio State [where puppies 8 to 16 weeks can enroll] or Purdue University, and these are both facilities that treat high humane society caseloads and numerous Parvo[virus] cases annually.[19]

For over ten years at Montessaurus Puppy School in Guelph, Ontario, Canada, we have been accepting puppies from eight weeks of age with a minimum of one vaccination against parvovirus and distemper. The additional precautions we take are simple: owners are asked to keep their pup at home if he is unwell or has diarrhea, and the floor is cleaned with a dilute bleach solution if a puppy defecates in class. We have not had a single incident of suspected infectious disease transmission to this day.

Socialization and Infectious Disease Prevention Work Hand in Hand for Puppy Wellness

There is a growing consensus that puppies are NOT getting ill in puppy classes that enroll puppies who are seven weeks and older and who have been vaccinated at least seven to ten days before starting class. However, this is not to suggest that young puppies should be exposed indiscriminately to other dogs and outdoor areas. It is still prudent to avoid exposing a puppy to dogs of unknown health status, or to parks and other areas likely contaminated with dog feces until the puppy is fully vaccinated. In regions where parvovirus is rampant,[20] or where other infectious disease agents may be present,[21] it may even be warranted to keep the puppy from walking on public property until fully vaccinated. Keep in mind that socialization to dogs is but one aspect of socialization, and that puppies can be safely exposed to people, places, sights, smells, and sounds without significant risk of exposure to infectious disease (see "Safe" Socialization "Do's" below).

Puppyhood remains the single greatest opportunity to positively influence a dog's behavioral development. Since more dogs are euthanized for behavioral reasons than for all medical causes combined,[2,7] it would be unwise to allow unfounded fear of exposure to infectious disease to interfere with efforts towards early socialization. Advising puppy owners to wait until the puppy is over 12 weeks of age before exposing him to the world he will be living in might have been appropriate a decade ago, but is now clearly outdated. In striving towards puppy wellness, socialization and infectious disease prevention must go hand in hand.

This article is intended to provide general information on the topic of vaccination of puppies, socialization of puppies, and the relative risks of behavioral illness and infectious disease when puppies are exposed to other dogs before the completion of their vaccination series. The information contained within is not intended as veterinary recommendations, and should not replace the advice of your veterinarian.

"Safe" Socialization "Do's"

- Drive to a busy mall and hang out with your pup on a mat at the entrance. Strangers will flock to you, manhandle your pup, and willingly feed him treats.

- Host a puppy party: invite friends and family over, play some music, toss some streamers, and pass your pup around.

- Bring your puppy to indoor Scouts or Brownies meetings. Supervise children interacting with him.

- Play sound-desensitization CDs or cassettes. A whole range of everyday noises such as sounds of motorcycles, stormy weather, and crying infants are available. Feed lots of treats for scary noises.

- Park yourself with your puppy at an outdoor café along a busy street. The puppy can rest on a pillow/bed at your feet. Allow strangers to pet your dog, and offer him biscuits.

- Take drives to different parts of town and country with your pup safely seat-belted in the back seat. Visit countryside, different neighborhoods with people of various ethnicities, and go through the carwash and some drive-thrus. Have the window open so that he can take in all of the sights and sounds and smells (car wash excepted!).

- Take your puppy for long strolls tethered in a wagon, stroller, or body sling (depending on size/weight!). ❖

References

[1] While the focus of this article is on the "nurture" aspect of socialization, both "nature" (genetics) and "nurture" (environment) influence the socialization process. The extent to which environment affects behavior is determined by genetics, which cannot be influenced after conception.

[2] Landsberg, G., Hunthausen W. & Ackerman L. *Handbook of Behavior Problems of the Dog and Cat, 2nd Ed.*, Elsevier Saunders, 2003.

[3] Horwitz, D., Mills, D., & Heath, S., eds. *British Small Animal Veterinary Association Manual of Canine and Feline Behavioural Medicine, British Small Animal Veterinary Association*, 2002.

[4] Lindsay, S.R. *Applied Dog Behavior and Training, Volume 2: Etiology and Assessment of Behavior Problems*, Iowa State University Press, 2001.

[5] Beaver, B.V. *Canine Behavior: A Guide for Veterinarians*, W.B. Saunders Company, 1999.

[6] Scott, J.P. & Fuller, J.L. *Genetics and the Social Behavior of the Dog*, University of Chicago Press, 1965.

[7] Seskel, K. "Puppy socialization classes. progress in companion animal behavior." *Veterinary Clinics of North America: Small Animal Practice*. 27(3):465-477.

[8] Formal use of the term "socialization" does not actually extend to non-social attachments. For the purpose of this article I have included localization (attachment

to non-living parts of the environment) when referring to socialization, as it is thought to represent the same process, but applied to different objects. The similarity between socialization and localization is addressed in the chapter titled "Early Experience and the Development of Behavior" by James Serpell and J.A. Jagoe in *The Domestic Dog: Its Evolution, Behavior and Interactions With People* edited by James Serpell, (1995) Cambridge University Press.

[9] Socialization hit lists are available on many Web sites and in many books including: www.dogpact.com; *The Kinderpuppy Course: A Curriculum Manual for Instructors* by Dr. Jennifer Messer; *After You Get Your Puppy* by Dr. Ian Dunbar; *The Culture Clash* by Jean Donaldson; and *Handbook of Behavior Problems of the Dog and Cat* by G. Landsberg, W. Hunthausen, and L. Ackerman.

[10] Puppies under nine weeks of age are not routinely vaccinated for leptospirosis due to the higher risk of adverse reactions in younger puppies.

[11] "Vaccines" in this section refers to distemper, hepatitis, parvovirus, and parainfluenza (usually administered as one combination vaccine).

[12] Smith-Carr, S., Macintire DK, & Swango, LJ. "Canine parvovirus. Part I. Pathogenesis and vaccination." *Compen Contin Educ Pract Vet* 19(2):125-133, 1997.

[13] 2006 American Animal Health Association Canine Vaccine Guidelines available at www.aahanet.org.

[14] I consider it worthwhile to point out that although the immune system responds to boosters in the same way, regardless of whether they are done ten days apart or four weeks apart, the vaccine manufacturer will make a recommendation on the period between boosters for their product based on the research conducted in the process of having their vaccine product approved [personal communications with vaccine manufacturers]. Veterinarians will generally want to follow these recommendations. This is why some vaccines are boostered at two to four week intervals, and others at three to four week intervals.

[15] Rabies is administered only once to puppies at least 12 weeks of age. Because of the risk of rabies to humans, the rabies vaccine is made to be so strong that the puppy only needs one exposure to it.

[16] Open letter by Dr. R.K. Anderson posted on many Internet sites, including www.apdt.com, and available upon request through the University of Minnesota; phone (612) 644-7400.

[17] www.cvm.umn.edu/newsandevents/events/puppy_classes/home.html.

[18] Dr. R.K. Anderson, DVM, DACVPM, DACVB is a professor Emeritus, College of Veterinary Medicine; Past Director, Animal Behavior Service of the College of Veterinary Medicine and Current Director, Center to Study Human Animal Relationships and Environments, University of Minnesota.

[19] www.vet.purdue.edu/animalbehaviour.

[20] Your veterinarian can advise you of the incidence of parvovirus in your area.

[21] For example, leptospirosis is transmitted through the urine of an infected animal and can be ingested through contaminated water.

This article was nominated for a DWAA Maxwell Award for the 2007 Writing Competition.

Raising "Kane"

Jodi Brunson, January/February 2005

If you ask 15 different breeders for their opinion on how to raise a litter, you will get 15 different answers. When it comes to picking a puppy, those 15 different opinions can make you feel like you are playing a game of "pin the tail on the donkey!" I have had the wonderful, albeit frustrating, opportunity to be on both ends of the spectrum. Over the past two decades I have raised numerous litters and I have also procured many dogs from other breeders. In my evolution as a breeder, I feel I have come upon several practices that give both the puppy and their future owners a foundation that will make building a relationship significantly easier.

Puppies need to be born and raised in the house, right in the middle of everyday life. They need to hear the TV, the doorbell, the phone ringing, children playing, other dogs barking, dropping pots and pans, doors slamming, and all of those everyday noises which will be a part of their environment for the rest of their life. I have seen so many puppies that have come from breeders who isolate the litter. These puppies are so traumatized when they go to their new homes that it makes it difficult for the new owner to overcome the environmental sensitivities which have been created. I love to start taking my puppies out at six weeks. This gets them used to riding in a car and arriving at a new place where fun things happen. I am careful to take them to places where they will be unlikely to come into contact with any viruses. Fortunately I have many friends with kids and other dogs who love to have puppies come and visit!

Since I would not breed a litter without having at least 75% of the litter sold, the new owners are called the moment the puppies are born. I want my buyers to be frequent visitors. Even though the puppies' eyes and ears are not functioning, their noses are. I want them to know the smell of their new owners from birth. I want the new owners to be able to hold them and touch them long before the puppy comes home.

I also want them to be able to watch the puppies at different phases. The socialization benefits of having the owners, their friends, and families visit on a regular basis is invaluable. I can hear many of you gasping, "what about disease?" While I do ask that no one come directly from the local shelter or humane society, I actually believe that it is a benefit to the puppies' immune system to be exposed to low doses of antibodies shed by other pets and the common bacteria that people carry around. Having the opportunity to be exposed to a myriad of different germs and bacteria give the puppies' immune systems the ability to build resistance naturally to various ailments.

The most important aspect of raising a litter is weaning. Puppies who are weaned by their mothers learn many traits that are not possible to learn from their littermates or humans. First they learn bite inhibition. Mom does not tolerate mouthy puppies, littermates and humans do. This diminishes the problem of puppy biting. Second, they learn "self-imposed self control." They learn when things are available and when they are not. Mom lets them know when she is available and when she is not! As a result, they learn the third important lesson: "How to read other dogs." I have watched puppy after puppy raised in this manner come into a new group of dogs and accurately read these dogs. They do not come barging in assuming everyone will accept them. This makes for a much more pleasant dog. (For more in-depth information, please see "Whelping and Weaning." *The Dog Trainer's Resource. The APDT Chronicle of the Dog.*)

I begin crate training as soon as the puppies are up and mobile, which is usually when they are about four weeks old. I put a crate without the door in the whelping box. The puppies naturally gravitate to sleeping in it. Once the puppies are well on the road to being weaned, I begin to separate the litter into crates at night, at first with two or three puppies to a crate. As they become accustomed to being confined I will put them in individual crates. This makes sending the puppy home so much easier for the new owners as the crate is something the puppy is already familiar with. I always send the puppy home with a stuffed animal that has been in with the whole litter. I have found that having something that smells familiar to put in their crate in their new home is comforting to the puppy.

I am a firm believer in temperament testing the litter. Temperament testing is a rather controversial topic. It is my belief that temperament testing will show you only extremes within the litter. It will not predict what a puppy will be like when it is grown. Depending on how often and over what time period the bitch was bred, I may test the puppies over a two week period. Gestational age may differ from actual birth age. A puppy may have been conceived a week earlier than its littermate which may affect their developmental age.

At this time I will be looking to see which puppies are bold with investigative traits which lead me to believe the puppy is self-confident. I want to see which puppies' reaction to novel stimuli is cautious but confident. I want to see which puppies startle and recover quickly. I want to know which puppies are a bull in a china shop and I want to know which puppies are reluctant to venture outside of their comfort zone. Again I am looking for extremes or red flags so that when a puppy goes home I am better able to counsel the owners in the best way to manage their new puppy.

The test I have come up with consists of several different aspects. First would be just putting the puppy down and seeing how they react to a strange environment: are they bold, confident, and curious, or are they overwhelmed? I assess how willing the puppy is to follow me: are they under my feet or off on their own agenda? I ask the puppy to come several times when he is distracted. How interested is the puppy in me? I roll out a plastic jar with pennies in it to see how curious they are. I test for a natural retrieve: do they recognize a pattern, do they steal it and take off, or do they ignore it completely? I ask the puppy to chase a toy and see whether they will play tug: how willing are they to interact with me? I look for noise sensitivity. I am not looking so much for a puppy that is not noise sensitive, but more at how the puppy reacts after the sound. I like to see the puppy startle and either investigate the source of the sound, or as my Jack Russell Terrier puppies generally do, acknowledge the sound and return to what they were doing. Since I do not use force in my training program, I am not too concerned with pain sensitivity, but I don't want to place a puppy that is very pain sensitive in a family with small children. I do however administer the elevation test, supporting the puppy an inch or two off the floor. This gives me an idea of how patient the puppy is: does the puppy hang there or does he struggle and fight to get away? Is the struggle out of boredom or fear? When I place the puppy on its back, I do not pin it to the floor and hold it there. I gently turn the puppy over and lay him in my lap, in the groove between my legs. I want the puppy to feel safe. I gently restrain him for 30 seconds or so, always taking my cue from the puppy. If they exhibit any fear, I do not continue. I do this differently than most and I do it for very different reasons. I do not believe in rank among dogs, nor do I believe in "dominance." When I perform these two tests, I am looking for degrees of patience and how much eye contact the puppy will offer. If I am placing a pet with children, I want a very patient puppy. If I am looking for a puppy for myself, I want a nice balance between passive and totally impatient.

I also have the male puppies neutered between six and eight weeks of age. Many veterinarians are unwilling to neuter at a young age. Performing this procedure before they go home ensures that it is accomplished with as little stress as possible. I have a wonderful working relationship with my vet and I am able to take all the boys in at the same time. This keeps the stress level very low. They have each other, which is comforting, and they have me holding them while they are anesthetized and holding them when they wake up. They can then return home without having to stay in the clinic which can be a very scary place.

Bringing Puppy Home!

I try to arm my puppy buyers with as much information as I possibly can. I furnish them with a copy of Jean Donaldson's *The Culture Clash* and several handouts that I have prepared covering everything from housebreaking to vaccination schedules. All of this information is provided the first time they come to visit the puppies, giving them ample time to study and read before the puppy comes home.

What is the optimum age to send a puppy home? I used to say seven weeks, and while I still believe that it can be an appropriate age, I now prefer to send them home a few days shy of nine weeks. By allowing the bitch to wean the puppies, she spends as much time as she wants with them right up until the day they go home. The extra few weeks gives her more time to teach them the lessons only she is able to.

The fear imprint phase begins at about nine weeks of age. This period can be a very defining stage of a puppy's life, one that may have long term ramifications, positive or negative. Being aware of this period gives you the ability to protect your puppy from those situations that may create a life long fear. It also is a wonderful opportunity to ingrain your recall and other positive behaviors! During this period, I attempt to avoid anything negative. I go to the vet only to visit, unless it is absolutely necessary. The puppy and I attend classes, being careful to avoid any dog that may threaten or intimidate my puppy. We visit as many new and positive places as I can find. I am always on the puppy's program. If it frightens the puppy, we are out of there. I will never ask my dog to cope. If they are afraid, they have good reason and who am I to question it? I may come back in a week and that fear will have resolved itself. If I push, I am more likely to create a permanent phobia.

During the fear imprint phase, the puppy is just beginning to venture out on his own. He is learning what is safe and what is dangerous in his environment. Read that sentence again! By taking this statement to heart, you have the ability to prevent your puppy from making the association between someone or something which he may perceive as dangerous for the rest of his life. On the other hand, it is also a wonderful time to allow him to make associations that are wonderful and reinforcing. This is the perfect time to create a dog that, when off lead, constantly checks back.

Playing the Hide and Seek Game

This is wonderful game which will help you instill a good recall and create a dog who is constantly aware of where you are. Does it always work? Of course not! But I would say most of the time it does.

First take the puppy to an unfamiliar, safe place. I live near many state and local parks where I can play this game. The only requirement is that you have a place to hide where you are still able to see the puppy. Put the puppy down, wait for him to get distracted and then step behind the corner of a building or behind a tree. Make sure that you can observe the puppy! Wait until he begins to show concern. His tail goes down, his ears flatten, he may even start to whine, but wait just a little longer. Then pop out with an exuberant "Puppy, Puppy, Puppy!" and lots of the puppy's favorite treats or ball. Relief is probably one of the strongest reinforcers you can use. I will continue to play this game until the puppy is at least 12 weeks old. Occasionally I play it with my adult dogs just to keep them on their toes. There are two extremes that you may run into. The puppy who never lets you out of his sight long enough to hide is the puppy that you probably won't have to worry about. Continue to try and play the game, and you may find that he is just a late bloomer and will be more adventurous later. Then there is the self sufficient puppy who just never gets worried. These are what we used to call "independent" dogs. I no longer use that term as I feel it is derogatory. I now refer to them as self-sufficient. These are the dogs that just really don't need us, they are perfectly happy doing their own thing. This is a trait that is usually picked up during temperament testing and I would be very diligent in making sure that the new owners of this puppy micro-manage his.

Raising puppies is time consuming, expensive, tiring, and incredibly rewarding. It is such a joy to see one of your puppies 10 or 15 years later and realize what a wonderful companion they have been over the years. I raise my puppies the way I would want a breeder to raise a puppy that I was buying. Put your heart and soul into these little creatures! Give them the best start you possibly can. Sometimes that start is interfering with Mother Nature as little as possible. Mother really does know best! ❖

Great Expectations

Teoti Anderson, January/February 2005

"You've got to help me, or I'm afraid we're just going to have to get rid of this dog," the woman complained, clearly upset.

My grip on the phone tightened as I asked, "What seems to be the problem?"

"She's peeing everywhere!" she exclaimed. "We've tried one of those cages, but it didn't work. We take her out all the time and she still comes right in and pees on the carpet. We tried those pads, and newspapers … well, it's just not working. She just doesn't get it!"

"How old is your dog?" I asked.

"10 weeks. You'd think she'd figure it out by now!"

Sigh. Another phone call, another lease running out on a poor puppy with an owner who has unrealistic expectations. How do you keep your cool when dealing with these types of clients?

It's important to remember that as trainers, we have a completely different perspective on puppies. A trainer waltzes into a room full of wiggling puppies and sees possibilities. Border Collie flipping somersaults at the end of the leash? Potential agility superstar! Labrador dragging his owner across the room, combing for treats? Tracking champ! Mixed breed happily jumping on her owner, trying to kiss her face? How affectionate, perhaps a therapy dog lurks inside!

Trainers see a wide variety of puppies. We learn what normal behavior is for different ages and different breeds. It's our job. Our students, however, do not have this wealth of knowledge to draw upon. Just as we practice patience with puppies, practicing patience with your clients will help them better understand that foreign canine creature chewing the end of their leashes.

Let's look at some common complaints from puppy owners, and some suggestions for how to address them.

"He's always carrying something in his mouth!" (Retriever) or "He's always sniffing the ground!" (Hound) or "She's always chasing the children!" (Herding breed)

Most trainers are gluttons for knowledge. We attend conferences, spend a small fortune on books and videos, and soak up everything we can about dogs. We learn the nuances between a Nova Scotia Duck Tolling Retriever and a Petit Basset Griffon Vendéen.

Our clients? Many choose their dog based on a TV show, what was cute at the local pet store, or from a litter their neighbors had. Not all clients, of course! But the ones who have the above complaints are often those who didn't completely research the breed, or combination of breeds, they brought home.

While it's tempting to lecture them on what they should have done, that's not the best way to teach them. Instead, share your knowledge of their breeds and help them channel traits into acceptable behaviors—"Retriever putting everything in his mouth? Oh that's what they're good at. I taught mine to bring in the groceries!"

"This puppy is so hyper! He jumps on everyone, he's constantly biting me, and now the kids are afraid of him!"

You're thinking this sounds like a perfectly normal puppy. But many clients have no idea what normal puppy behavior is. Sure, you know that puppies constantly use their little needle teeth. But often, clients fear they may have brought home an aggressive dog. To a trainer, a puppy that jumps up wants attention. But some parents may be frightened when they see their child knocked over by an exuberant canine greeting.

I've found many clients are relieved just to understand their puppies are not mutants. By explaining normal puppy behavior and why they do what they do, you could set your clients' concerns to rest. Many owners also don't realize just how much exercise puppies need each day. Give them concrete examples of how to safely exercise their puppies to expend some of that energy. And then help them teach their puppies alternate behaviors they like better!

"Why is it taking so long to housetrain this puppy?!"

Trainers know all about setting up routine feeding schedules and potty breaks. We recommend confinement and hawk-like supervision. We emphasize the importance of going outside with puppies in order to praise them the second they potty outdoors, which is all well and good advice. But to a new puppy owner, all of these instructions are a challenge when balancing families, careers, and buckets of enzymatic cleaner!

Try giving your clients set goals. It may help to offer some sample written schedules of exactly when their puppy will need to eat, sleep, exercise, play, and potty. Gently remind them that puppies are just babies. And give them the light at the end of the tunnel. Explain that if they put forth a major effort now, it will get easier down the road!

"My old dog was never like this."

Sometimes referred to as the "Old Shep Syndrome," having a previous dog achieve the status of sainthood can often cloud a puppy's entrance into a family. As we spend years with a dog ... learn his quirks and charms ... we become more familiar with each other's routines. We fall into place together, like comfy shoes. When that old friend has passed on, it leaves a terrible hole behind ... one that some try to fill with a new puppy. But that peg rarely fits the same way.

Whereas an older dog needed to go outside a couple times a day, puppies need to go all the time. The older dog may have kept the same bone for a decade, but the new puppy is going through chew bones by the boatload! Older dogs curl up for naps ... puppies gleefully attack your pillows. A previous dog may have loved going for a swim, but the new puppy is afraid of the water. The puppy, of course, can never replace the older dog.

Intellectually, your clients probably know this. But trying to fill a void in a heart is not always so rational! Some reassurances from you may help ease their transition. By acknowledging that Old Shep was, indeed, one of a kind, you're validating your client's memory of their beloved pet. You might try asking them to write or tell you special things about their new puppy. Point out a few positive points yourself, to get them started!

How long has it been since you got a new puppy? For example, I went eight years in between pups. Even though I work with puppies every week, I had forgotten what it was like to live with one. I was exhausted the first day! By sharing some of my stories with my clients, I've found they feel better about their own frustration. Reassure them that just as we have different friends throughout our lives, they can form special relationships with this new puppy as well. If they give him a chance, and appreciate him for who he is, he could prove to be another cherished "Old Shep" for a future puppy to follow! ❖

Adventures in Raising a Singleton Puppy

Stacey La Forge, January/February 2005

Raising a singleton puppy presents different challenges compared to raising a traditional litter of multiple puppies. Having reared multiple singleton puppies, I have learned that the path to raising a well adjusted singleton is rewarding, but it is not an easy journey.

Potential issues can arise even before the puppy's birth. Singletons are often larger than average which may lead to difficulty in the birthing process if the puppy is too large to pass through the birth canal, or uterine inertia sets in. Sometimes a C-section before the dam is in full blown labor is the safest option for mother and pup. Unfortunately, if a dog has not started labor, certain hormones which help facilitate the "mothering instinct" have not been released. In the case of a mother that previously raised a litter, this may not pose problems since she may "know" what to do based on prior experience. It is common for a first time mother, however, waking and groggy from anesthesia, to not recognize the squirming thing that keeps sucking and pawing near her incision. Disturbingly, many new mothers in similar situations totally reject their puppies. It is critical for a puppy to get "first milk" from its mother, as the colostrum conveys immunity to the puppy. When my dog delivered a singleton by C-section, the veterinarian suggested to "hold mom down if need be" so that the puppy could nurse, at least for the first day. This is where prior training can be advantageous; if a new mother is not inclined to allow a puppy to nurse, a solid down stay may allow an owner to latch the puppy on during feeding times. An added benefit of nursing is in triggering the "mothering" hormones which may be lacking.

Puppies cannot urinate or defecate on their own for the first few weeks of their lives. The dam normally facilitates this process by licking the pup. If this instinct does not kick in, an owner can accomplish this by using a moist cotton ball or baby wipe to stimulate the puppy. For my singleton, I actually slathered him with butter. I encouraged the dam to lick off the butter and thereby stimulate the puppy; eventually this task became second nature, and the butter was no longer needed.

Newborn puppies can not regulate their temperatures for the first two weeks. In multiple puppy litters, puppies huddle together in a pile and with mom to keep warm. A singleton does not have littermates with which to "pile" and may not have the mother available to provide warmth if the dam is recovering from surgery or is not comfortable staying with her puppy. Although a heating unit can be beneficial, with my singletons, I use a "stand-in sibling," a stuffed animal with a warm pack inserted along with a device mimicking a heartbeat. For the first two weeks, my singletons spend most of their time cuddling on top or laying underneath their stuffed sibling, especially when the mother is not present.

Singleton puppies are notorious for growing up to be very people oriented, but uncomfortable with other dogs since they lack early littermate socialization. In some ways, life can be a little too easy for a singleton as there is little competition for resources and a singleton does not encounter the same stresses that occur amongst a larger litter. Not surprisingly, some breeders note that their singletons grow up to be overly assertive, and have difficulty coping with frustrating situations. Sometimes the best option is to allow another mother with a litter of the same age to raise the puppy and provide normal litter interaction. If a foster family is not available, an owner must provide as much simulated littermate interaction as possible. I mimic intra-litter competition by momentarily restraining the puppy from nursing, pushing the puppy as a littermate would, and putting soft toys in the pup's path to climb over. The stuffed sibling is also useful when a singleton opens its eyes and starts to interact with the world. The stuffed sibling can act as a puppet to teach "doglike" interaction: encouraging the puppy to play, holding the puppy down, letting the puppy hold the toy down, "running" up to the puppy, retreating, simulating play bows, etc. Without littermates, the human becomes the main outlet for endless puppy energy.

The dam also teaches a singleton many life lessons, especially in dealing with frustration at weaning. One may want to encourage the dam to stay with a singleton longer than normal to take advantage of her tutelage. Once the singleton is old enough, other friendly, family dogs can aid in schooling the singleton in such areas as bite inhibition, a very important and sometimes difficult lesson for the singleton. Exposure to others dogs at an early age (generally around four weeks in my household) helps the puppy to recognize and respond to dog body language. I have very shaggy dogs, and have noted that their eye movements and, to a lesser extent, body movements can be obscured under their hair. In order to facilitate a singleton's observation of body language, I have resorted to shaving an adult dog skilled in inter-dog communication. However, in addition to adult interaction, the singleton pup needs to learn to be comfortable with puppy behavior. As soon as possible, one should consider enrolling the singleton in at least one, if not multiple, puppy kindergarten classes. From my experience, this is often a difficult transition even if a puppy plays well with older dogs. However, with time, patience and a lot of work, singleton puppies can develop into well adjusted, sociable adults. ❖

Handling Exercises for Veterinary Exams & Grooming—A Special APDT Chronicle of the Dog Student Handout

Terry Long, January/February 2005

One of the saddest things to see is a puppy or older dog be absolutely terrified of something as simple as a nail trim. Some dogs lose control of bodily functions, scream in terror, struggle violently, and bite and scratch in their frantic attempts to avoid having their nails trimmed. Some dogs have to be sedated or even anesthetized for this simple procedure. Others go without nail trims, which often results in dangerously long nails that can get caught in carpeting and can also cause the dog to adopt an unnatural gait, which can cause joint discomfort. It doesn't have to be this way. All dogs will eventually have to be groomed, vaccinated, examined, restrained, etc., so it's best to teach your dog, early in its life to, if not enjoy these procedures, to tolerate them.

Tools you will need . . .

- Cotton balls or plain cleansing pads
- Nail trimmers and short, wooden match sticks
- Yummy treats

The following procedures apply equally to older dogs as well as puppies. In no case should these procedures turn into a wrestling match or a test of who is "dominant." It is a natural reaction for animals to resist being restrained. It is not a show of dominance! It's scary to be restrained and fight they will—they are hard-wired to do so.

Please note: Owners of dogs and puppies that have a severe reaction to having their nails trimmed should ask their veterinarian about sedating the dog for nail trims until the desensitization process is completed. They can also consider the old tactic of walking their dogs on sidewalks in an attempt to wear the nails down naturally.

Restraint

Start by getting some yummy treats handy. Hold your dog comfortably in your lap. Gently place your hands over the dog's shoulders with the heels of your hands on the top and your fingers wrapping around toward the chest. Briefly (no more than a second or two) apply a small amount of pressure, say "Yes!" for the dog not reacting (if the dog reacts, you are using too much pressure or doing it for too long—back up), and give the dog a treat and pet and praise him. Gradually build up until you can exert a little more pressure and/or for longer periods of time without your dog resisting. Reward profusely each time.

When your dog is accustomed to having his shoulders held, use the same gradual process to accustom him to:

- Having his foot held.

- Having his leg held (each one, one at a time).

- Having his shoulders held.

- Having his hips held between your hands.

- Having his head held between your hands.

- Having his entire body held (tucked against your side, with the front end held by your hand and the hips tucked in by your elbow).

- Having his head held in the crook of your arm (do this only if you have successfully performed all of the above, and be sure to keep your face away from the dog's mouth).

If your dog fights, struggles, growls, or bites during the beginning stages of these exercises, obtain the services of a positive reinforcement trainer to help you.

Accustom your dog to a variety of "mock examinations"

- **Mouth**: Gently open your dog's mouth an inch or so. Say "Yes!" for the dog not reacting (if he reacts, you need to back up and just briefly touch the dog's lips or open the mouth less), and give the dog a treat and pet and praise him. Gradually build up until you can open the mouth wider, move your fingers around the lips, and gently press down on the tongue. Reward profusely each time. One trick that works well after the dog is accustomed to having you handle his lips and mouth is to open your dog's mouth and press a treat down on his tongue for him to eat. Surprise!

- **Ears**: Lift or touch the flap of one of the dog's ears and gently and briefly touch the skin around the ear. Say "Yes!" for the dog not reacting, give the dog a treat and pet and praise him. Gradually build up until you can touch all areas on the outside of the ear and eventually press a finger-tip into the inside of the ear (don't poke down into the ear canal, just the surface outside it). Reward profusely each time. Next, take a cotton ball or plain cotton pad (sold in stores as face cleansers), and gently wipe the ear flap and the area just outside the ear canal. Reward profusely each time!

- **Feet and Toes**: Gently hold your dog's paw in your hand and reward him for letting you hold it for longer and longer periods of time. Gradually apply a little bit of pressure to the paw. Gradually build up to the point where you are touching each toe and exerting mild pressure on each toe to the point where the nail is lifted. Go slowly; this is the foundation of a nail trim and for checking between toes for those nasty foxtails (plant seeds that cause pain and abscesses).

- **Nail Trims**: Here is a great exercise from British trainer John Rogerson. In separate handling exercises, accustom your dog to the sight and sound of nail clippers by placing them on the floor for the dog to sniff. Reward for any curiosity or interaction with the clippers. Next, pick up the clippers and flex them in your hands so the dog gets used to them in your hands, both the sight and the sounds. Take a wooden matchstick, and clip the matchstick into several pieces, tossing the dog a treat each time you clip. Clipping the matchstick sounds very similar to the sound made by trimming a dog's nails!

  Only when your dog thoroughly enjoys having his feet and toes handled and is accustomed to the sound of the clippers clipping the matchstick do you go to the next stage: fake clipping of the nails. Pick up the dog's foot and place a matchstick under the foot and clip the matchstick while it is in the same hand as the dog's foot. Reward, repeat, reward. When your dog is used to this, trim the very tip only of one of the dog's nails. Reward profusely. Stop. Do additional nails in several other separate sessions and only gradually build up until you can trim several nails in one session.

The gradual process of desensitization described above will help your dog throughout his life. ❖

The Veterinarian's Role in Puppy Development

Lore I. Haug, January/February 2005

Veterinarians play a unique and important role in a puppy's life. Once a puppy leaves the breeder's home, the veterinarian is typically the first, and sometimes the only, professional to have contact with the puppy and its new owner over the next several weeks or months. Veterinarians are in a unique position to assist new puppy owners since they have several contacts with a puppy over the first four to eight months of the puppy's life. Once a puppy owner makes contact with their veterinarian for the puppy's first visit, the veterinarian has several important responsibilities: 1) to establish an appropriate vaccination schedule to maximize protection against communicable disease yet minimize adverse reactions; 2) to ensure the puppy has as positive an experience as possible during each visit; 3) to educate the owner about general health care, disease conditions, and behavioral traits that may be specific to the chosen breed; 4) to educate the owner about the importance of socialization and early training; and 5) to help the owner recognize potential behavior problems early and seek appropriate intervention.

Puppies are typically presented for their first veterinary visit between five and nine weeks of age. The first vaccination is generally given between six and eight weeks of age. A minimum of two vaccinations is required to establish some degree of long lasting immunity. Because the exact age when maternal antibody interference ends varies with the individual puppy and the disease, vaccinations are typically given every three to four weeks up until 15-17 weeks of age. This means the veterinarian will see each puppy from two to five times during the course of its vaccination series and possibly again if the animal is spayed or neutered as an adolescent.

The first or second vaccination visit often occurs during what is often called the first "fear period." This means a traumatic experience during the visit can have a lasting effect on the puppy's behavior. If the vaccination visit is frightening or otherwise overwhelming, the puppy may make negative associations to any variety of stimuli present: the personnel, the clinic, the room, certain odors, instruments, restraint, etc. These associations will vary from puppy to puppy and impact whether this experience generalizes outside the clinic (e.g., to other "strangers"). If the vaccination visits are the puppy's only contact with strangers outside the owner's home during the sensitive period, the puppy could easily generalize this fear to all strangers.

Puppy visits should be choreographed with the puppy's physical and psychological well-being in mind. At our clinic, owners are encouraged to bring in fecal samples rather than subjecting the puppy to the stress of acquiring one at the clinic. The temperature is one of the last parts of the physical exam performed rather than the first as is so often done in general clinics. (It's rather invasive and scary!) The puppy is encouraged to play and food is used liberally as a distraction and reward. Restraint is minimal during all procedures. Within the bounds of good medicine, I alter diagnostic procedures and schedules as much as possible to limit potentially traumatic experiences. The puppy's reaction during subsequent visits is our report card on how well we did during the previous ones.

During the first couple visits, the veterinarian also has the opportunity to discuss general health issues including diseases that may be specific to the breed. Similarly, behavioral characteristics can be discussed as well. Unfortunately, many owners buy puppies on impulse or by "fad factor;" they often have little or no knowledge about the behavioral characteristics or requirements of the breed they have chosen. These first visits are a perfect opportunity to begin educating the owner and encouraging the owner to seek further information on the puppy—before trouble begins.

It is also extremely important to discuss socialization during the very first visit. Since most puppies are presented at six to eight weeks of age, and the sensitive socialization period only extends up to 12-14 weeks of age, this is not a process that can be postponed. *By no means should socialization be delayed until after the puppy vaccination series is complete!* Far more puppies will be lost from their homes from behavioral issues than from dying from a puppy-hood disease. In my experience, pre- and postnatal health are the largest factors in disease susceptibility in puppies. Puppies from litters with good pre- and postnatal health rarely contract parvovirus during socialization outings, yet I have seen puppies from litters with poor health contract parvovirus without even leaving their homes. Certainly it is the veterinarian's job to help the owner balance necessary socialization outings with unnecessary exposure to areas with potentially concentrated sources of viral spores (e.g. dog parks). Well run puppy classes are a great socialization experience and typically safe.

Serial puppy visits allow the veterinarian to track the puppy's behavioral development. The veterinarian can assess whether the puppy seems to be receiving sufficient and appropriate socialization or whether warning signs of a problem are becoming apparent. The owner can be directed to resources, including a professional trainer, to aid him or her in dealing with the problem promptly.

Veterinarians should discuss spaying and neutering with the owner. Puppies are typically altered around four to eight months of age. Spaying and neutering frequently occur during the "second fear period" which can begin around six months of age. A number of behavioral changes can abruptly occur in dogs during this time. Owners often blame the surgical procedure for these changes and the veterinarian should warn owners that this is generally a coincidence, not a cause. Having said this, again it is the veterinarian's responsibility to ensure the animal is handled humanely to prevent a negative association during this impressionable time. It is also important that the veterinarian educate the owner about the realistic effects of spaying and neutering. These procedures do have health benefits for dogs. However, owners should understand that spaying and neutering do not prevent behavioral problems, nor do those surgical procedures generally fix them. Surgical alteration can affect some sexually dimorphic behaviors (mounting, roaming, marking), but it tends to have minimal effect on other behavior problems—it is not a substitute for appropriate management and training. ❖

Preparing a Puppy for Grooming

Nikki Myers, January/February 2005

Grooming is a large part of life for many dogs. Regular baths and haircuts are necessary for any cute little fluffy dog so that she can stay a cherished, clean member of the house. For some puppies this can be a traumatic experience. Though much of a pup's experience depends largely on the groomer the owner eventually chooses, there are a few quick training steps that can be taken with a dog to make grooming easier.

Socialization to grooming should start very early. If your clients wait until grooming is needed before taking any steps to see a groomer, the puppy can be nearly six months old and very unruly for handling. Daily grooming training can be done in just a few minutes a day. Here are some of the sights, sounds, and sensations that a puppy will experience in their grooming lifetime. Using a few suggested exercises, paired with a complete handling desensitization program, you can help make grooming more enjoyable when the time comes.

Sights

The sights experienced on a trip to the groomer range from other dogs and cats to large equipment. Aside from the shop environment itself, the process of being groomed can include all of the following:

- **Shiny and long objects in a person's hand**. Scissors for trimming and hemostats for hair plucking can be scary for a shy dog. Condition a positive association to objects picked up and moved towards the puppy.

- **Brushes and blow dryers moving quickly towards the body and head**. Brushes come in many shapes and sizes. Blow dryers are strangely shaped. Add them to the classical conditioning sessions.

- **The groomer's face very close to the puppy's face**. For some breeds, and their mixes, very detailed clipping and scissoring is needed on the head and face.

- **Height**. The view from up on a table is very different. A puppy needs to realize there are edges to the table. One easy way to show them this is to place the puppy on a table (place a rubber backed bath mat on the table for traction) and lure the puppy slowly to the edge. Lower the treat below the edge, as if you were luring a down. The puppy will lie down with her feet over the edge and reach for the treat. Do this at each edge.

Sounds

Grooming shops can be very noisy. Not all the sounds will be new to a puppy, but the constant noise and so many at one time can be stressful.

- **Noisy equipment such as clippers and blow dryers**. Clients rarely have clippers of their own, but almost every household has a blow dryer. Describe a gradual desensitization program and get them started right away.

- **Running water**. The sound of a wide-open faucet is very noisy and a blast of water in conjunction with it makes the sound a predictor of bad things. The same kind of desensitization program used with the blow dryer will work with water.

- **Scissors opening and closing**. This is a very distinct sound, like that of nails being clipped. It is quick and sharp and may be very close to the ear. Open and close any household scissors all around the puppy's body without actually making contact. Work with the puppy until she accepts hands around the muzzle and the scissors rubbed along the head, cheeks, and between the eyes.

- **Items dropped on the floor**. It happens. It doesn't happen on purpose, but it happens. And if a groomer drops scissors or clippers, loud expletives may follow.

Sensations

If you look at the handling a dog gets during grooming, groomers do some very rude things. A comprehensive handling desensitization program will get puppies used to the grabbing and the holding. Here are a few to be sure to add for grooming preparation.

- **Brushing**. Gentle brushing should be a part of a puppy's everyday life. Hair should be gently brushed against natural growth as well as with the growth of the hair.

- **Wet feet, hair, and skin**. Water all over the body is a very new sensation. When first introduced, cup warm water from an already filled source (so the sound of running water and the strange new sensation are not paired). To avoid unpleasant sensations, fold the little ears so water does not go down into the ear and don't tip the head straight up or water may run into the pup's nose.

- **Slippery surfaces**. A good groomer will have non-slip surfaces in the bath tubs and on the grooming tables, but one slip in a home tub or sink can create a bad memory that goes with the puppy to the grooming shop for the first time.

- **Vibrations on the body**. Clippers can tickle or simply frighten a dog when the vibrations of the motor come into contact with her body. Desensitization to this sensation may have to include a trip to a grooming shop.

- **Hair pulling**. Plucking and hand-stripping involves pulling out dead or shedding hair and it is done on most terrier breeds. Also, many breeds need to have hair plucked from the ear canal to keep good airflow and prevent yeast and bacteria buildup. Stroke the puppy's hair between two fingers so that there is some tension on the hair. Feed the puppy during this procedure. More pressure can gradually be added, but no hair should be pulled out yet. Owners unfamiliar with the hair that needs to be removed might make the mistake of pulling out live hair. Ouch!

- **Blowing on the body and in face**. Most groomers who trim the head with scissors will cut a little, and blow the clipped hair away before starting to trim again. (I did it all the time.) Discourage play at home that involves blowing at the dog to stir them up or tease them. Likewise, hair "tickling" to make them jump should be avoided. Of course the context is different. A groomer handling the head with scissors and the owner rolling on the floor chasing the puppy are very different. But a puppy sensitized to air blowing can find such a thing uncomfortable from a groomer.

Encourage your clients to find a groomer as early as possible. They should go observe not only to be sure the groomers are gentle, but also to see what type of handling and equipment will be used with their dog. They will get a better idea of what to put in their puppy's grooming prep program at home. Early trips to the groomer do not have to include a body clip and a huge change in the puppy's look. Baths, ear cleaning, and feet trims are simple and get the puppy used to the environment of a busy salon. ❖

The Perfect Puppy Class? Walk Before You Run!

Pia Silvani, January/February 2005

What does it take to conduct a first-rate puppy class? Dr. Ian Dunbar was among the first to promote the idea of puppy classes years ago. Puppy classes are designed to ensure pups would have positive experiences with dogs, people, and novel stimuli, in a clean and safe environment, under the watchful guidance of an educated and experienced dog trainer.

A well-planned puppy class can improve the quality of life for both dog and owner, assisting them in avoiding potential future problems. Puppy owners see an endless trail of troubles, from shredded paper, torn clothing, soiled carpets, and more. Your goal should be to help owners understand their dogs so they can achieve better management techniques, as well as the benefits of having a well-socialized, well-mannered, trained dog as an adult.

In the past 18 years of teaching classes, I have found the following factors to be crucial to the success of puppy programs.

Age group

The pups should be between eight to 16 weeks at the beginning of class. Kersti Seksel's study (1997) showed "the closer the puppies are in age to each other, the better." Permitting puppies five months or older into class can cause problems.

Vaccination Policy?

We allow puppies into class after their first set of vaccinations. We feel confident that this is sufficient since our grounds and classrooms are kept clean and free of disease. During our busy season, we can train 800-900 dogs each week. We have never had a situation where a puppy became ill. However, we must be careful not to challenge veterinarians' recommendations. Any confrontation runs the risk of alienating the client, the veterinarians, and potential future referrals.

Class Size

A 40 by 40 foot area can adequately hold 10 to 12 puppies with an instructor and assistant. Have enough gates and pens available so you can divide the room up for playtime and safe havens should this prove necessary.

Puppy Playtime Parameters

- All pups should enjoy play and there should be give and take between playmates.
- Keep play sessions short. Long, uninterrupted sessions cause pups to become rough or boisterous.
- Stop play if a puppy is getting too aroused or if there is excessive vocalization.

- Pair up pups that have similar play styles and are similar in age.

- Puppies should be taught to check in with their owners during play. If a puppy can't look to the owner in the presence of other puppies, he shouldn't be permitted off leash.

- Pups should not leave class thinking it's all about dogs. They will be far more difficult to control later on in life. Puppies should be given two to three minutes of puppy playtime before the owners go to their pups and ask for a behavior. Once the pup complies, he may return to play as his reward.

What to Teach?

Today's society tends to focus on what is wrong, who is to blame, and how we can fix it. Our job should be to help educate families about how to prevent bad habits from starting. Puppies are like sponges and learn very quickly about what works and doesn't. Rather than punish inappropriate behaviors, owners should teach their pups what is expected. I do feel that we need to teach owners about punishment. They will do it anyway—and do it wrong, too often, too late, or too harshly. Punishment need not be painful, but reprimands are in line when a pup is over the top. Keep in mind, the more discipline is provided, the less punishment will be needed.

Our curriculum is geared toward socialization, problem prevention, and helping owners become good "dog trainers." We focus on restraint exercises, handling and touching, grooming, greeting, impulse control, bite inhibition, proper chew toys, and how to play with other dogs. Students need to be reminded that training isn't complete after six to eight weeks, nor should they expect perfection from their immature dogs.

What Method Will You Use?

I like to train with positive reinforcement. Not only does it improve the pup's behavior, it also teaches the puppy to enjoy training as well as developing a high reinforcement history for each behavior. Using a combination of classical and operant techniques are the best. However, you should use a method you like and are good at, but remain flexible and consider the ability of the owner, e.g., you may get owners who are resistant to using food, clickers, head collars, etc. Remember to teach people how to wean the pup off food lures as soon as possible so they are not dependent upon the treat. How many times have you heard "he only does it when I have a treat in my hand?"

Graduation Lecture

Don't lose them now! Educate them about their future. The juvenile stage begins at about 84 days followed by sexual (about six months) and behavioral maturity (one to two years). Their dog's behavior will change from immature to mature, and will fluctuate. This can be quite perplexing and frustrating to clients. Outline for the owners the developmental changes they can expect:

- **Increase in independence**. Clients can expect their dogs to be more confident and willing to explore the world at greater distances. They may exhibit *characteristics* of a rebellious teenager.

- **Sexual maturity**. Most dogs will develop a greater interest in other dogs leaving the owner feeling like second fiddle. Assure owners that continuing training will help to develop the human/dog relationship during this difficult time.

- **Threats/Aggressive actions**. Threats or aggression typically surface during this stage. Hopefully, these behaviors haven't already developed, although some pups may have been subtly signaling before now, unbeknownst to the family. For example, eating faster when approached, or taking bones into a safe haven to chew. If we educate owners early on about potential behavior problems, we may be able to help them "beat the bite!" Many owners think the behaviors "will go away with age" or that "it is just a stage." We know better!

- **A mind of his own**. Behavior patterns will be variable. They may exhibit exuberance for training one day and shy away the next. Don't let them feel that puppy class failed because their dog is no longer listening. As Drs. Scott Line and R.K. Anderson wrote, "dogs stop learning when we stop teaching them." Explain why owners should not lower their standards. Consistency with rules and training throughout the dog's developmental phases is the key to a well-behaved and beloved pet.

In other words, "Juvenile dogs are unpredictable, undependable, and untrustworthy. But we love them anyway!"

Benefits to You

By conducting a first-rate puppy class, you will be sending more pups out into the world that are friendly, confident, and well-behaved. You will create more responsible owners, build long-term relationships with clients, and improve pups' personalities which, in turn, will help veterinarians. By supporting and educating owners, more pups will remain in their original homes. Owners will be happy and refer future clients to you. Last, but not least, the combination of good socialization and early training will help build strong bonds between the dog and her family. ❖

References and Recommended Reading

Puotinen C.J. "The case for kindergarten." *The Whole Dog Journal.* April: 3-7, 2001.

Seksel K. "Puppy socialization classes." *Veterinary Clinics of North America: Small Animal Practice.* 27(3), 1997.

Line S.W., Anderson, R.K. "Use of motivation, restraint, and punishment." Animal Humane Society of Hennepin County, 1996.

London, K. Frolicking Fidos Workshop, April 2003.

Silvani, P. *Kindergarten Puppy Training, an Owner's Manual.* St. Hubert's Animal Welfare Center, Madison, NJ, www.sthuberts.org.

Learning Theory and Training Applications

Understanding how dogs learn and what motivates them to act allows trainers to communicate more effectively and humanely with our canine charges. Operant and classical conditioning and schedules of reinforcement are central learning theory concepts that help to define the science behind animal training. The articles in this section take both a constructive and critical view of applied learning theory in present-day dog training. The first series of articles present the practical use of varying reinforcements and controlling antecedent events, followed by thoughtful discussions of anthropomorphism and the role social psychology plays in owner interpretations of the behavior of their pets. The final selection evaluates lure-reward training and free shaping training techniques.

Shake It Up, Baby: The Dynamics of Reinforcement

Merope Pavlides, July/August 2006

Beatrice, my Husky/Beagle mix, is giving me the hairy eyeball. There are three dogs in her front yard, and she would really like to go tell them a thing or two. I, however, am insisting that she sit quietly by my side and control that urge. She does, and when the dogs have gone, she trots off to find a tennis ball. I owe her a game of fetch. A cookie or some petting instead? Not good enough! You get what you pay for.

One of the biggest stumbling blocks for pet dog owners can be frustration at lack of reinforcer efficacy, as compared to the apparent effectiveness of punishers. The impact of a punisher can be so immediate and so dramatic that compulsory training can seem easier and more accessible. As positive trainers, however, it behooves us to help clients understand the complexities of well-utilized reinforcement techniques. It's easy to become complacent with reinforcers, however, especially if your case load is made up of a large number of chow hounds. Yet it can be very useful to think outside the "cookie jar."

Reinforcement Variety

The term "variety" is used here to delineate categories of reinforcement: edible, sensory, or social. Edible reinforcers are, for many dogs, the favorite kind. These are easy to procure and utilize—fill the bait bag with yummies and off we go. There are many reasons, however, to explore the full spectrum of possible reinforcement techniques available, and to urge clients to do the same. For the dog, access to different types of reinforcement expands reliability of target behaviors, as reinforcement can be delivered whether treats are available or not. Think of it this way: you might train dogs because people pay you to do so. But most of us also receive positive reinforcement when clients exclaim their pleasure at their dog's progress and at watching "light-bulb" moments for the dogs. We enjoy the interaction with the dogs themselves—the tail wags when we approach. The paychecks keep us working when we're frustrated, tired, or bored, or dealing with a challenging dog and/or owner. But the social reinforcement (and even sensory reinforcement—petting a dog is enjoyable for humans as well as dogs!) makes us stay after class to answer questions, compels us to do pro bono and volunteer work, and propels us to train and compete with our own dogs.

Dogs are social creatures—how often do we talk with our clients about problem behaviors that stem from lack of appropriate social skills on the part of dogs? The need that often drives challenging behaviors can be the source of reinforcement as well. It's not always easy to convince clients, who desire nothing more than closeness with their canine companions, to utilize attention as well as reinforcement. But once they understand that interaction in the form of games, outings, or just "hanging out" with their dogs can be a valuable training tool when doled out for target behaviors, they ultimately find the time spent with their dogs is more enjoyable. This then, becomes reinforcement for them, and will result in increased usage of social reinforcers. A simple example of this might be the training of a retrieve with a ball placed in the owner's hand. If the ball isn't thrown until placed politely in the hand (and the dog wants the ball to be thrown), the polite ball return will increase. Playing ball this way is often much more pleasant for the human, who can now sit on a lawn chair with a beverage and "play fetch." So playing fetch becomes a more common occurrence.

Not only are dogs highly social, they are highly sensory. Doesn't it make good sense to utilize this to our advantage as trainers? Although many pet dog owners recognize that their dogs like to receive petting, they often don't explore sensory reinforcement beyond providing a few scratches behind the ear. Teaching the fundamentals of canine massage can be a great way to urge clients to vary the kinds of touch they offer in exchange for target behaviors. (And can often teach them to be more attuned to the types of touch dogs don't like!) Allowing dogs to sniff as reinforcement—whether informally or as a structured game of "hide and seek," can be an extremely useful tool. Access to a window to watch outdoor comings and going—as long as arousal level doesn't get out of hand—can be a great reward and "brain-break" for some dogs. We all know a dog or two who would do circus tricks for a chance to ride in a car. This activity can be a tremendous tool—offering both a sensory "high" and social interaction as well.

One of the other wonderful aspects of prodding clients to think across this reinforcement spectrum is that dog owners become more creative in their approaches to positive training. We cherish creativity in our dogs, and bringing that same spark to training helps foster an exciting and interactive relationship between dogs and their humans. If training sessions are fun for all, they will be more likely to occur, resulting in a dog more fluent in appropriate behaviors, and an owner more aware of dog responses.

Reinforcement is Unique to the Individual

Not only do we need to remember that variety is truly the spice of life, we also need to keep in mind that one dog's trash is another's treasure. Clients often ask trainers to recommend treats and toys. We all have our favorites, items chosen because they seem popular with the furry set. But we need to encourage owners to really investigate the preferences of each individual dog, both across the spectrum of reinforcers, and within each category. It's not too much to ask clients to engage in some informal "reinforcer sampling." Does Fido prefer treats or toys? Petting or games? Do hot dogs trump liver treats? Ball chase beat tug? Belly rubs better than chin tickles? Knowing the answers to questions like these help fill the trainer toolbox. Humans who preside over multi-dog households may also need reminding that no two dogs will respond the same way to a reinforcer. While a woman and her sister might both be chocoholics, one might prefer chocolate-covered cherries, the other nut clusters. Good information for a husband to know! The closer the reinforcer is to specific preference, the more powerful it will be. Sometimes we sell our clients short, assuming that they aren't able or willing to think about reinforcement in detail. Make a game in class out of reinforcer sampling—the owner who returns the following week with the most examples of specific, varied reinforcements for his/her dog wins a prize.

Reinforcement Changes

Very few things in life are static, including reinforcer preferences. The power of any individual reinforcer changes over time and environment. As a puppy, Rover may have loved playing tug. As a mature adult, however, the game may hold little interest. Scratches at the base of the tail may no longer feel good to the dog with aging hips. Paw touch may only be pleasurable at the end of the day when Rover is relaxed. Attention to evolution of reinforcement over the course of the dog's day, year, or life will help keep variety fresh. Remember eating smores by the campfire? Try one again in your kitchen and see if it's as wonderful.

Reinforcer efficacy in differing environments can often confound dog owners. Nice sit-stays for treats at home disappear at the park. Interested in a toy as a stranger approaches? You've got to be kidding! All too often, an event in which a dog doesn't respond to the reinforcement offered causes the owner to doubt the usefulness of a reinforcement-based approach to training. Helping them understand how fluid reinforcement can be, may make them more likely to commit globally to positive training.

Automatically Reinforcing Behaviors

When previously favored reinforcers fail to increase behaviors in certain environments, it is often because the environment is providing other, stronger reinforcement. On a walk in the park, for instance, barking and lunging may make strangers back away. Access to distance from the stranger is more reinforcing than the treat offered for a polite sit. Conversely, jumping up on a stranger may provide attention, which may also be more coveted at this moment than a treat. Sometimes, however, the reinforcement seems more mysterious. Access to liver might not be nearly as wonderful as smelling another dog's pee-mail. Certain behaviors are inherently reinforcing for the dog. Barking, sniffing, licking, tail-chasing, chewing, can all be automatically reinforcing. The dog may receive sensory reinforcement from the behavior. Arousal levels may be heightened by engaging in the behavior, and at some point, being aroused simply feels good.

Figuring out why a dog is engaging in a self-reinforcing behavior may be, however, an exercise in futility. And it doesn't really matter. What's important is understanding the behavior's power. Then the behavior can be used to the trainer's advantage, or the trainer can attempt to counter-condition so the behavior doesn't occur. We're all familiar with the Premack Principle: a higher probability behavior can be used to reinforce a lower probability behavior. Behaviors that are intrinsically reinforced are certainly as likely to occur as those that are reinforced by us. Why not add them to our reinforcer inventory? Beatrice, for example, loves to bark at jet skis. This isn't a problematic behavior, because a jet ski is much louder than she is! She is first asked for a recall and a sit, then released to bark at the noisy intruder. The strength of the barking as reinforcement increases her willingness to offer a quick recall lakeside.

Schedules of Reinforcement

Not only is it helpful to "shake it up" in terms of reinforcer variety, it is crucial to keep in mind that schedules of reinforcement delivery can be key in increasing desired behaviors. Owners sometimes need to be reminded that behaviors on acquisition are best mastered by continuous reinforcement—so keep those treats handy! However, understanding schedules of reinforcement often will help assure them that their dog will learn to "work for them." Intermittent reinforcement schedules can be broken into two types: ratio schedules (based on number of responses) and interval schedules (based on length of time between responses). Ratio schedules are most common, whether fixed-ratio or variable-ratio. A fixed-ratio schedule is one in which the dog is reinforced after a certain number of responses. A treat after every third hurdle jump, for instance, while a variable ratio schedule means that a reinforcer is delivered after a random number of responses. A variable ratio schedule can contribute greatly to proofing target behavior, and clients should be instructed in implementing this. Describing this schedule in terms of slot machine payout is an easily understood illustration.

Interval schedules, either fixed or variable, can be used to train duration behaviors. In training loose-leash walking for example, a reinforcer might be delivered based on amount of time spent walking nicely. As with ratio schedules, a variable interval schedule will ultimately prove more effective than a fixed interval schedule. To help clients become fluent with this notion, it may help to walk in tandem with them and prompt for reinforcement, until they discover a personal rhythm.

Not Just for Dogs

For many trainers, a disconnect exists between training ability and teaching ability. As solid as our dog handling skills might be, their value lies in our abilities to transfer them to pet parents. Positive training means utilizing positive reinforcement methods with humans as well as dogs. Dole out praise, prizes, and social interaction. Dog owners come to us not only to learn how to train behaviors, but to access an active listener where their dogs are concerned. Remember to target and mark human behavior as it happens and reward it. "Mary, look at how well Snooky is heeling for you, keep it up!" And afterwards, "You two had a great class tonight, I can't wait to see what you accomplish by next week." For clients, most reinforcement will be social—but the occasional human treat or game doesn't hurt either. Reinforcement for children involved in training should be immediate and of value to them. At the end of a class or training session, always leave both dogs and humans wanting more! ❖

Antecedent Events - Looking Past the Cue

Wendy van Kerkhove, March/April 2005

Most trainers are introduced to the antecedent in the A–B–C three term contingency model as the "cue" or the discriminative stimulus S^D. We are taught the central thesis of operant conditioning is that behavior occurs as a function of its consequences and the most efficient way to produce changes in behavior is to manipulate consequences (Smith & Iwata, 1997). However, the category of antecedents and their influence on behavior is a topic that has received little attention in the dog training community, yet should be examined more closely.

A discussion about antecedent processes and procedures must be preceded by an explanation of functional behavior assessment (FBA). FBA is a procedure that uses techniques such as direct observation, careful questioning of caregivers, and the direct manipulation of possible controlling stimuli. The goal of a FBA is to identify the stimuli occurring in a training setting and then answer the question: Which stimuli is this behavior a function of (Miltenberger, 1998 as cited in Luiselli, 1998)? Behavior can be as functionally related to antecedents as it can be to consequences. This fact can help explain why some behaviors seem to be impervious to changes in consequences. If the behavior is a function of an antecedent, then it is that which will need to be changed in order to bring about a change in behavior. Conducting a FBA is tedious, complicated, and often time consuming. The description offered here is highly simplified. However, it is important to note that scientific procedures are used to identify the stimuli to be discussed throughout this article.

An antecedent is a stimulus that occurs before the target behavior that plays a role in "triggering" the specific behavior. The three general classes of antecedents are: Discriminative Stimuli S^D's, Establishing Operations EO's, and Setting Events (Miltenberger, 1998 as cited in Luiselli, 1998). Each of these fit the criteria as stated above, but their processes are different. There is not widespread agreement on the exact definitions and distinctions between and among establishing operations and setting events. They are both antecedents of consequence and as such, can be functionally related to behavior. What is important to understand is the influence they can have on behavior, not the precise definitions and categories they fall into.

The S^D predicts the availability of reinforcement for the performance of a particular behavior based on a history of the repeated availability of reinforcement for performing that behavior. As a result of this predictive relationship, the S^D controls responding. A behavior has come under stimulus control when it is offered predictably after the presentation of the S^D and is not offered in its absence (Smith & Iwata, 1997).

The use of the word "operation" in "Establishing Operation" implies that an act or action has been deliberately engaged in (McGill, 1999). A clear example of an EO is food deprivation. Withholding food is an "operation" that the trainer performs prior to a training session in order to "establish" food as an effective reinforcer. There are two criteria that a procedure must meet in order to be considered an EO. First, the operation must alter the value of the reinforcer by making it either more, or less, reinforcing. Next, there must be a corresponding alteration in the frequency of all behaviors that have been reinforced by that stimulus (Michael, 2000).

A dog denied food for 24 hours will be in a state of deprivation. The value of food as reinforcement is increased by this state. All behaviors previously reinforced by food will likely increase as a result of this state of deprivation. Thus, each of the criteria is met in the example given. EO's tend to be related to operations of satiation and deprivation and can enhance and improve responding or diminish and deteriorate responding.

The term Setting Event refers mainly to external or environmental conditions occurring at the time that training occurs that can affect behavior. Examples such as time of day, ambient lighting, sleeping habits, eating routines, diet, daily activities, room temperature, and other conditions can serve as setting events (Carr, E.G., Carlson, J.I., Langdon, N.A., Magito-McLaughlin, D. & Yarbrough, S.C. 1998 as cited in Luiselli 1998).

Consider the trainer attempting to train a Chinese Crested dog in a room whose ambient temperature is 50 degrees. The cold temperature is a setting event for shivering and "keeping warm" behavior and could interfere with the presentation of the S^D setting the occasion for the performance of the behavior. However, at 75 degrees, with the state of "coldness" no longer present, the presentation of the discriminative stimuli will set the occasion for responding as usual. Setting events can enhance and improve responding or can diminish and deteriorate responding. Early morning is a setting event for performing specific behaviors such as showering and getting dressed. Late evening is a setting event for "getting ready for bed" behaviors. Late evening, however, is not a setting event for getting dressed for work.

Adults and children with severe developmental disabilities are often non-communicative. These individuals can present challenging behavior, but cannot articulate its cause. This scenario can present serious problems to their care givers. Research in the field of antecedent intervention strategies has helped to mitigate the behavior problems these caregivers often face (Luiselli, 1998). These intervention strategies can also be used when modifying the behavior of animals.

The most common antecedent intervention strategies include: 1) eliminate or modify the conditions that provoke the behavior; 2) introduce a preemptive procedure that prevents the behavior from occurring; 3) develop a fading (transfer-of-stimulus) model; 4) introduce procedures that alter reinforcer effectiveness (Smith & Iwata, 1997; Luiselli, 1998); and 5) create a behavioral momentum paradigm (McGill, 1999).

Eliminate the Conditions That Provoke the Behavior

This approach involves changing the context/condition in which the undesirable behavior occurs as a method of eliminating the behavior (Luiselli, 1998).

Consider Mary, a 23-year-old woman with mental retardation residing at a community residence. The staff reported that Mary "tantrummed" every morning when she was instructed to take her shower. They had tried to modify her behavior by using positive reinforcement for approximations leading to the act of showering, and used negative punishment when she presented challenging behavior. None of these techniques worked. A FBA was conducted and it was noted that, with the exception of the morning shower ritual, Mary was relatively engaged and compliant to staff demands during the day. Another finding was that Mary did not seem to be a morning person; she needed extra help to wake up and was less energetic during this time of day. A recommendation was made that staff shift Mary's shower request to the evening from the morning. Within two days, Mary's agitation and tantrums ended (Luiselli, 1998).

A dog with separation anxiety might be more agitated in the morning than in the evening because he associates morning with his owners impending absence. A goal in SA training is to reduce the dog's anxiety around pre-departure cues. Starting the desensitization program in the evening might give the trainer a definite advantage if the dog's state of agitation is lower at this time.

Antecedent physical exercise can be used to improve loose leash walking. Being crated all day is a setting event for "super activity" when the dog is let out. This state will predispose the dog to pull when taken for a walk. Typical methods for reducing this behavior (stop and "be a tree") may not be effective due to the dog's physical state. Instead, exercising the dog in the yard prior to a walk will reduce the dog's energy level. With that condition changed, the dog will mostly likely engage in loose leash walking on his own and if not, will probably be more amenable to slowing down as a result of the consequences for pulling.

Introduce Preemptive Procedures

This strategy involves changing the antecedent conditions so that the individual is inclined to respond with behaviors that are incompatible with the problem behavior before the problem behavior occurs. The goal is to have the appropriate, incompatible behavior "crowd out" the challenging behavior (Luiselli, 1998).

Luiselli (1998) describes a 10- year-old girl with severe neurological impairment. She exhibited "compulsive like" object grabbing and object mouthing when in the classroom. These behaviors interfered with her learning. A FBA was conducted and suggested that the behavior was reinforced by the pleasurable consequences of tactile and oral stimulation. The clinicians designed a plan that allowed the girl access to acceptable oral/tactile stimulus and, as a result, the frequency of the inappropriate object grabbing and mouthing decreased significantly and her learning improved.

Giving a young pup something to hold in his mouth when on a leash walk will often keep him from grabbing the leash with his mouth and dragging his owner around. My parrot, Hedwig, will yell for me when I leave the room. However, if I give her a treat to eat and turn on the music before I leave the room, this behavior does not occur.

The reduction of stereotypic behaviors such as tail chasing or obsessive licking might be reduced using a preemptive procedure. If the antecedent stimuli that lead to these behaviors can be identified (such as presence of houseguests) and the dog is given access to a highly desirable item such as a bone prior to the introduction of the antecedent, the problem might be mitigated by the fact that the dog is engaged with the bone. Again, this strategy would be used in conjunction with other behavior modification tools such as the use of medicine that reduces the behavior.

Develop a Fading (Transfer of Stimulus) Procedure

This method involves first eliminating the stimulus that is triggering the problem behavior, then establishing a protocol whereby the individual's behavior is under stimulus control and then slowly fading in the stimulus that originally caused the problem (Luiselli, 1998).

Consider this example: A child with developmental disabilities was compliant for the classroom teacher, but acted out with her speech teacher. Identical intervention tactics were used by each teacher, but during speech class the child's challenging behaviors persisted. The stimulus fading strategy involved the speech teacher sitting quietly in the room while the classroom teacher conducted the speech lessons. As the child's behavior improved, the speech teacher gradually began sitting closer to the child and then finally began to conduct the training sessions while the classroom teacher stayed in the room. The child's behavior improved; the classroom teacher was eventually faded out. Over a 45-week evaluation the child's improved behavior continued (Luiselli, 1998).

The use of a fading procedure is very effective for eliminating the need for the Gentle Leader™. The Gentle Leader is used until the dog's leash walking involves no pulling. The procedure would begin by clipping the leash on to the buckle collar towards the end of a long walk while keeping the Gentle Leader on. Next, the leash will be placed on the buckle collar earlier in the walk while the Gentle Leader stays on. Later, the nose loop of the Gentle Leader will be taken off while the leash is on the buckle collar and then finally the Gentle Leader will be removed completely.

Introduce Procedures That Alter Reinforcer Effectiveness

This refers to creating a state of deprivation or satiation (Smith & Iwata, 1997; Michael, 2000; McGill 1999). There are instances when deliberate operations are used to create these states and times when these states occur as a result of other events. For example, physical illness can diminish the value of food as a reinforcer; it might also diminish Frisbee™ catching (physical activity) as a reinforcer. Diabetes, however, can increase the value of water as a reinforcer. Medication can suppress or increase appetite making food more or less reinforcing.

Self-injurious and other problem behaviors often occur in institutional environments in which little or no direct attention is given to patients. These patients discover that behaving inappropriately gains them significant staff attention. The staff's attempt at stopping the "bad" behavior inadvertently rewards it (they come running over) and the patients learn that reinforcement is contingent upon staff presence. However, several studies have demonstrated that giving increased attention across the board to these patients even while they are engaging in challenging behavior leads to a diminishment of the "bad" behavior. The reinforcement is offered non-contingent upon any given "good" or "bad" behavior. Offering a dense schedule of non-contingent reinforcement can reduce unwanted behavior as equally effectively as the differential reinforcement of another behavior (Wilder & Carr, 1998; McGill, 1999; Iwata & Smith, 2000).

This fact completely turns upside down the notion that crated dogs should not be given attention or allowed out when barking. Using a dense schedule of non-contingent reinforcement during the time that the dog is crated will, in fact, lead to a diminishment of the barking due to the elimination of the state of attention deprivation.

Create Behavioral Momentum

This technique is based on the principle that when you want an individual to engage in a behavior that has a low probability of occurring, the request for that behavior should be inserted in between a number of requests for behaviors that have a high probability of occurring. This technique increases the likelihood of the target, low probability behavior being offered (Smith & Iwata, 1997; McGill 1999).

If a child refuses to take a walk, the caregiver might ask the child to do a number of behaviors that are likely to be accomplished (e.g., "tie your shoes," "put on your coat"), provide reinforcement following the completion of each task and then make the low probability request ("come with me"), and reward the child when the task is completed. This procedure creates "momentum" as each task is completed and rewarded. Interspersing "high probability" requests with a low probability request creates a setting event for the opportunity to earn high levels of reinforcement. This change in events results in the child achieving repeated success and increased reinforcement and "builds momentum" for improved responding to all demands (Koegel, Cater & Koegel as cited in Luiselli 1998; *Behavioral Momentum*, n.d.).

Consider the dog that is already comfortable with four known men in the family. The trainer could have one unknown man inserted amongst the known men. The dog will be instructed to go to each man to get a treat one after another. If the dog knows the first three men, and gets treats from them, there may be enough behavioral momentum to get him to approach the fourth (unknown) man.

We humans can articulate that we are tired, cold, or cranky. If we are on medications or ill, it is understandable that our behavior might be affected by these conditions. Considering the numerous antecedents at play during any given moment, it is not hard to understand why our productivity, mood, and behavior can change frequently. The dogs we train are affected by these same types of antecedents, but we are not always (or ever) aware of the specific stimuli affecting them. An understanding of antecedent processes and procedures gives trainers a new set of tools in which to evaluate and modify behavior. Manipulating antecedents can play a crucial role in resolving unwanted behavior problems that are not easily resolved by making changes in consequences. This tactic does not preclude the use of other training protocols such as altering consequences, using medication, or engaging in a systematic desensitization program and should be considered a vital tool in the trainer's toolbox.

The author wishes to thank Dr. Gail Peterson and Dr. Susan Friedman for their support, suggestions and careful editing. ❖

References

Behavioral Momentum. (n.d.). Retrieved July 21, 2004, from http://www.mvesc.k12. oh.us/psychology/PsychBulletins/2_93.htm.

Carr, E.G., Carlson, J.I., Langdon, N.A., Magito-McLaughlin, D. & Yarbrough, S.C. "Two perspectives on antecedent control: Molecular and molar." In J.K. Luiselli & M. J. Cameron (Eds.), *Antecedent Control: Innovative Approaches to Behavioral Support* (pp. 3–28). Baltimore, MD: Paul H. Brookes Publishing Co, 1998.

Iwata, B.A., Smith, R. G. & Michel, J. "Current research on the influence of establishing operations on behavior in applied settings." *J Appl Behav Anal*, 33, 411–418, 2000.

Kennedy, C.H. & Meyer, K.A. "Establishing operations and the motivation of challenging behavior." In J.K. Luiselli & M. J. Cameron (Eds.), *Antecedent Control: Innovative Approaches to Behavioral Support* (pp. 329–346). Baltimore, MD: Paul H. Brookes Publishing Co, 1998.

Koegel, R.L., Carter, C.M., Koegel, L.K. "Setting events to improve parent-teacher coordination and motivation for children with autism." In J.K. Luiselli & M. J. Cameron (Eds.), *Antecedent Control: Innovative Approaches to Behavioral Support* (pp. 167–186). Baltimore: Paul H. Brookes Publishing Co, 1998.

Luiselli, J.K. "Intervention conceptualization and formulation." In J.K. Luiselli & M. J. Cameron (Eds.), *Antecedent Control: Innovative Approaches to Behavioral Support* (pp. 29–44). Baltimore: Paul H. Brookes Publishing Co, 1998.

Michael, J. "Implications and refinements of the establishing operation concept." *J Appl Behav Anal*, 33, 401–410, 2000.

McGill, P. "Establishing operations: Implications for the assessment, treatment and prevention of problem behavior." *J Appl Behav Anal*, 32, 393–418, 1999.

Miltenberger, R.G. "Methods for assessing antecedent influences on challenging behavior." In J.K. Luiselli & M. J. Cameron (Eds.), *Antecedent Control: Innovative Approaches to Behavioral Support* (pp. 47–65). Baltimore, MD: Paul H. Brookes Publishing Co, 1998.

Smith, R. G. & Iwata, B.A. "Antecedent influences on behavior disorders." *J Appl Behav Anal*, 30, 343–375, 1997.

Wilder, D.A. & Carr, J.E. "Recent advances in the modification of establishing operations to reduce aberrant behavior." *Behavioral Interventions*, 13, 43–59, 1998.

Critical Anthropomorphism Vs. "Classical" Anthropomorphism: Two Sides of the Same Coin? Not!

Wendy van Kerkhove, July/August 2005

Anthropomorphism is the expression of human feelings and motivations to non-human entities. According to Spada (1997), the negative connotations of the term can be traced back to 570 B.C. when Xenophanes criticized the idea that deities had human form. He writes:

> But if oxen (and horses) and lions had hands or could draw with hands and create works of art like those made by men, horses would draw pictures of gods like horses, and oxen of gods like oxen and they would make the bodies (of their gods) in accordance with the form that each species itself possesses (Freeman, 1948, p.22).

Anthropomorphism is so pervasive among dog trainers and scientific researchers that it is worth considering why we do it. A suitable explanation seems to be that, since most of the universe is not understandable to us as humans, we tend to transfer to every object those qualities with which we are familiar with (Guthrie, 1997). In essence, the only way we have in which to interpret the world around us is through our own consciousness.

The term "theory of mind" is the notion that one individual can know and understand what is going on in the mind of another individual and that each individual has self awareness (Wynne, 2001). We have limited ability to have theory of mind with other humans. Consider how hard it is to try and figure out what someone else is thinking and feeling in any given situation. However, our ability to have theory of mind with another species is virtually impossible. The "private experiences" of animals are not available to us for viewing.

In an attempt to avoid the use of anthropomorphism, behaviorists proposed a method which involved the use of objective and descriptive language to describe only those behaviors which were observable. Additionally, for years the use of parsimony has been the accepted criterion used in behaviorism for deciding among scientific theories or explanations. It dictates that one should always choose the simplest explanation of a phenomenon, the one that requires the fewest leaps of logic. Explanations such as "X behavior is a conditioned response to Y stimulus" are considered more parsimonious than "X behavior is a result of intentional deception by the animal."

Recently, however, the growing field of cognitive ethology has lead to a resurgence of anthropomorphism. Founded by Donald Griffin, cognitive ethology attempts to study animal cognition or the mental experiences in animals (Beer, 1991). Griffin believes that it is likely that animals have mental experiences and that these experiences can have an effect on their behavior. He suggests that the complexity of animal behavior implies conscious beliefs and desires, and that an anthropomorphic explanation can be more parsimonious than one built solely on behavioral laws (Wynne, 2004).

Gordon Burghardt, (1991) a contemporary of Griffin, also believes there is enough evidence to imply that some of the behaviors observed in animals are a result of cognitive processes. Burghardt (1994) argues that despite the fact that scientists could not "see" electrons, molecules, and genes, this fact did not stop them from making assumptions about them, forming hypothesis, and then testing them. This method gave us considerable understanding of these phenomena long before we could directly observe them.

The field of cognitive ethology, however, presents serious challenges to those researchers studying it. Consider how complex it might be to investigate consciousness, let alone conscious deliberation, in animals. Rivas (2002) calls for such an investigation and thinks that understanding the private experience of others should be added to the traditional four aims of ethological endeavors—proximate causation, function, development, and evolution. He sanctions the use of many methods including anthropomorphism, anecdotes, and empathy to begin the study of animal consciousness, but insists that researchers be critical in their interpretations, emphasizing plausibility and empirical investigation of predictions (Mitchell, Thompson, & Miles, 1997).

Burghardt (2004) developed the concept of critical anthropomorphism in order to establish ground rules for dealing with the anthropomorphic tendencies that we, as humans, confront when trying to understand the behavior of other species. Critical anthropomorphism involves not only careful replicable observation, but also knowledge of the natural history, ecology, and sensory and neural systems of animals as well.

Melissa Kaplan, (2000) herpetologist and author of *Iguanas for Dummies*, illustrates the difference between anthropomorphism (what she refers to as "classical" anthropomorphism) and critical anthropomorphism in the example below:

Classical Anthropomorphism. My iguana loves his hot rock. I know this because he lays on it most of the day and most of the night. Iguanas don't feel pain, so that's why he stays on there even though the skin on his tummy is all blistered and oozy.

Critical Anthropomorphism. Iguanas, like all reptiles, have a specific thermal range they require to enable them to regulate their core body temperature by moving back and forth throughout the thermal gradient. Iguanas, like many reptiles, evolved as sun-baskers (heliotherms), needing to be surrounded by air of a certain temperature in order to raise their core body temperature. They then thermo-regulate by moving back and forth between areas of warmer and cooler air temperatures. When heliotherms are presented with only thermal options, i.e., a hot rock and cool air, they remain on the hot rock until their body signals that their core body temperature has been reached and so triggers a move to a cooler area. The reason the needed signal is not generated is because the blood warmed when flowing under the skin plastered to the hot rock circulates through the rest of the body which is not in contact with the hot rock, it rapidly cools down, so the internal organs and bulk of the blood never get warm enough to trigger the move. Reptiles do indeed feel pain, but their instinct to try to get warm enough may override the pain messages sent by the damaged nerves, and so they remain on the hot rock, vainly waiting to get warm enough to move.

It is clear, by this example, that there exists a major difference between the two distinct types of anthropomorphism. It is interesting to note that although the use of critical anthropomorphism is viewed by proponents of cognitive ethology as one acceptable tool to generate hypothesis, the "classical" type of anthropomorphism that is rampant in our dog training community is frowned upon as much by these proponents as it is by behaviorists.

Referring to Marshall Thomas's *The Hidden Life of Dogs*, da Waal (1997), a proponent of cognitive ethology, states the following:

> There is quite a difference between the use of anthropomorphism for communicatory reasons, or as a tool to generate hypothesis, and anthropomorphism that does little else than project human emotions and intentions onto animals without an attempt at justification, explanation, or serious investigation. The uncritical anthropomorphism of Marshall Thomas is precisely what has given the practice a bad name, and has led critics to oppose it in all forms and disguises. (p. xvi)

Rivas and Burghardt (2002) agree that anthropomorphism can be harmful when it is unacknowledged, unrecognized, or used in a way that accepts conclusions by eliminating the need to actually test them. They point to numerous scientific studies on animals (including their own) whereby the researchers fail to put themselves in the shoes of the animals they are studying and as a result come to erroneous conclusions.

The take home message is one of warning: Don't be fooled by the use of the term critical anthropomorphism as a "legal" way in which to use the "classical" anthropomorphism that is so prevalent in our dog training circles today. Critical anthropomorphism is a completely different animal and one that warrants serious consideration by trainers and researchers alike. "Classical" anthropomorphism should be avoided at all costs. ❖

References

Guthrie, S.E. "Anthropomorphism: A Definition and a Theory." In Mitchell, R.W., Thompson, N.S.& Miles, H.L. (Eds.), *Anthropomorphism, Anecdotes and Animals* (pp. 51–58). State University of New York Press, NY, 1997.

Kaplan, M. *Ethology, Ecology and Critical Anthropomorphism.* Melissa Kaplan's Herp Care Collection, 2000. Retrieved December 1, 2004 from the World Wide Web: www.anapsid.org/ethology.html.

Mitchell, R.W., Thompson, N. S., & Miles, H.L. "Taking Anthropomorphism and Anecdotes Seriously." R.W. Mitchell, N.S. Thompson, & Miles, H.L. (Eds.), *Anthropomorphism, Anecdotes and Animals* (pp. 37–49). State University of New York Press, NY, 1997.

Rivas, J.A. & G. M. Burghardt. "Crotalomorphism: A metaphor to understand anthropomorphism by omission." In M. Bekoff, A. Colin, & G.M. Burghardt (Eds.), *The Cognitive Animal: Empirical and Theoretical Perspectives on Animal Cognition* (pp. 9–17). Cambridge, MA: MIT Press, 2002.

Spada, E.C. "Amorphism, Mechanomorphism and Anthropomorphism." In R.W. Mitchell, N.S. Thompson, & H.L. Miles (Eds.), *Anthropomorphism, Anecdotes and Animals* (pp. 37–49). State University of New York Press, NY, 1997.

Wynne, C. D. L. *Animal Cognition: The Mental Lives of Animals.* Basingstoke, Hampshire, England; New York, NY: Palgrave, 2001.

Wynne, C.D. "The perils of anthropomorphism." *Nature* (428) 606, 2004.

Blame and Social Psychology: Understanding Owner Interpretations of Dog Behavior

Eve Marschark, January/February 2007

Because humans and dogs engage in social relationships, it is reasonable to look to Social Psychology to further our understanding of how we interact. Owner-interpretations of dog behavior are often anthropomorphic and inaccurate. When trying to find the cause of a behavior, many owners are quick to attribute cause to an underlying personality or character flaw instead of identifying an environmental cause of the event. In this article, we will take a look at some basic principles of Social Psychology that can be useful in understanding why we humans tend to make these assumptions.

Carlson and Buskist (1997) define social psychology as, "the branch of psychology that studies our social nature—how the actual, imagined, or implied presence of others influences our thoughts, feelings, and behaviors." Every day we interpret the acts of those around us and use these interpretations to help us interact effectively. We make assessments of personality characteristics in order to predict how each individual might act in the future and we are just as concerned about how we appear to others. In order to simplify this complex task we use schema (mental framework or body of knowledge) to organize information about a person, place or thing. But, much like prejudice, this generalizing or short cutting often leads us to error.

When we are trying to understand why someone acted the way they did, we are looking to "attribute" causation. Social psychologists classify causation (Heider, 1958) as either due to situational factors (stimuli in the environment; Kelley, 1967 proposed these to be "external") or to dispositional factors (personality characteristics; Kelley proposed these to be "internal"). We will use these terms to discuss our problem of jumping to conclusions regarding dog behavior.

There are two concepts in social psychology that bias our ability to explain behavior. They are the Fundamental Attribution Error and the Actor-Observer Effect. The Fundamental Attribution Error is defined as "the tendency to over-estimate the significance of dispositional factors and under-estimate the significance of situational factors in explaining other people's behavior." (Carlson & Buskist, p. 488). An example of this can be seen in a typical client interpretation of house-soiling. "He is being spiteful. He did this because he is getting back at me for leaving him alone all day." The client is probably feeling guilty about the absence and sees the dog as justifiably being an angry, malevolent individual. It does not occur to the client that the dog's basic house-training may have been incomplete or hurried, which would be an "external" cause. The client does not see that managing the environment so that the dog cannot have an accident is the best solution. Examples of managing the environment are: hiring a dog walker so he is let out multiple times a day; keeping him in a small space (i.e., crate) which he is less likely to soil; using an enzyme cleaner to remove any odors that may trigger marking behavior, etc.

Even after a complete explanation of how to fix the problem, our client is likely to reply. "Yes, but why is he like this? I love him and he seems to love me. I can't understand why he would be so defiant." Our client is attributing the dog's behavior to internal factors (i.e., some nebulous mind-state of defiance, anger, or spite) when she should be focusing on the environmental factors (i.e., cues from and personal history of interacting with his environment) to explain his behavior.

The second bias is The Actor-Observer Effect, which is "the tendency to attribute one's own behavior to situational factors, but others' behavior to dispositional factors" (Carlson & Buskist, p. 489). Because we are aware of our behavior in direct response to things in the environment, we do not make The Fundamental Attribution Error regarding our own actions (Sande, Goethals, & Radloff, 1988). Instead we see our own behavior as adaptable, flexible, and not fixed. When we make a mistake during training, we quickly can identify distractions or reasons (external/situational) for our failing. "The tunnel was curved and I didn't see the corner, so that is why I tripped over it." Other students (observers) in the agility class might conclude that I am a clumsy person (internal characteristic/ dispositional). If I am slow to deliver a click or a treat, or have delayed timing in signaling, other class participants (observers) might conclude that I am not a very gifted trainer.

They are assessing the cause of my behavior to long-lasting, dispositional factors of my personality. I (actor) would be more likely to explain my own behavior as due to feeling tired or stressed (both temporary characteristics that were caused by external factors). When viewing other's behavior, however, we are not as aware of the environmental factors that may be influencing their responding and so we conclude that their behavior is stable and due to some long-lasting, consistent "personal disposition."

A real problem with the Actor-Observer Effect is that a dog is always an actor. He cannot verbally convince us that there were environmental factors that may have contributed to his behavior. So we are free to continue attributing his behavior to internal, stable, and consistent factors.

If an owner believes his dog to have a dysfunctional personality, this can make it difficult for the client to comply with behavioral modification protocols. If the assumption is that an individual is always manipulative, spiteful or contrary, a client will have little hope of changing this permanent condition. If, however, the client can be helped to identify environmental causes (cues, etc.) that may be contributing to the behavior, then she/he can feel empowered to control the situation and re-train the dog.

Perhaps we could help owners to understand that these biases are something we all do and need to be aware of. It is a normal, universal human tendency to want to assign cause to the behavior of another and, knowing this, we can view our tendency as an evolutionary trick that our minds play on us. This takes the blame away from the animal and gives back control to the owner. Often knowing that we are likely to behave in a certain way gives us the power to change our thinking from a mindless response to a mindful approach. ❖

References

Carlson, N. & Buskist, W. *Psychology: The Science of Behavior*, 5th ed. Londong: Allyn and Bacon, 1997.

Heider, E.R. *The Psychology of Interpersonal Relations*. New York: John Wiley & Sons, 1958.

Kelley H.H. "Attribution theory and research." *An Rev Psych*, 37, 457-501, 1967.

Sande, G.N., Goethals, G.R., & Radloff, C.E. "Perceiving one's own traits and others: The multifaceted self." *J Person Soc Psych*, 54, 13-20, 1988.

Are "Free-Shaped" Dogs Better Problem Solvers?
A Look at the Criticisms of Lure-Reward Training

Pamela Buitrago, July/August 2005

Over the past several years, most professional dog trainers have heard or read about criticisms of lure-reward training. These criticisms have been made along with enthusiastic claims about the superiority of free-shaped (unprompted, trial-and-error) clicker training. Those of us who use free-shaping understand the enthusiasm. It's challenging and exciting to communicate with dogs in such a free-form way, developing a new behavior one small increment at a time.

As technicians of scientific procedures, however, it's important that we take a collective, critical look at what's being said. Are these criticisms and claims supported at all by empirical studies? Do they represent the cutting edge of what's happening in dog training, or is it a piece of history repeating itself? Has some objectivity been lost as one reward-based operant technology is criticized and another is lauded?

It would be a shame to allow misunderstandings to drive a wedge between our fledgling ranks, as we all work to convince our clients of the powers of positive reinforcement. Fortunately, humane, no-force trainers share much common ground.

Following are some key criticisms and claims, and some explanation of the history and uses, and the strengths and pitfalls, of these training technologies, based on scientific texts and literature in applied behavior analysis and learning theory.

"Luring isn't training. It implies doubt in the laws of learning."

A lure is one kind of orienting prompt (sticks and balls are others) that is used to guide a dog into a desired behavior (Lindsay, 2000). These prompts are antecedents, i.e., stimuli that come before a behavior. See van Kerkhove's article (2005) for definitions of antecedents. Since the three-term contingency of A-B-C (antecedent-behavior-consequence) is the basic unit of analysis in learning theory, we can't just dismiss A.

Like other prompts—including verbal ones like high-pitched noises, gestural ones like clapping or crouching, or environmental ones like using a wall to get a straight heel position—a lure is used to get the desired behavior during the early part of training and then is gradually eliminated after the behavior has been strengthened through reinforcement. Since fading is the technology for eliminating the prompt, prompting and fading go hand in hand.

Prompting-fading and shaping have distinct purposes. Fading is about stimulus control, the A part of A-B-C. It typically begins with a behavior that's already in the animal's repertoire and gradually changes what controls (or evokes) it. So a sit is first evoked with a lure, and over several repetitions the lure is faded out as a gestural or verbal cue is faded in. Whether we're shapers or prompters or both, we all use fading when installing verbal cues.

In contrast, shaping is about developing a behavior that's not yet in the animal's repertoire, the B part of A-B-C. Shaping begins with an approximation of the final desired behavior and gradually develops it into the final one. In short, fading changes the controlling stimuli of an existing behavior whereas shaping develops new behavior. Both techniques rely on the C part of A-B-C, reinforcement, to strengthen or maintain behavior.

In the real world, though, the distinction isn't drawn so neatly, since the two procedures are often used together. We use prompts during shaping (e.g., to teach rollover or spin) and some successive approximations during luring (e.g., getting a full down). And in both lure-reward training and shaping, clickers can be used.

Also known as "errorless learning," prompting-fading has been around since Skinner's, Terrace's, and others' work in the 1930s to 1960s, which showed that, with sufficient care, a discrimination could be learned with few or no errors (Skinner, 1938; Schlosberg & Solomon, 1943; Terrace, 1963, 1966). Skinner and Terrace both believed that errors resulting from "trial and error" discrimination training (i.e., shaping) were aversive and harmful. With children and animals, shaping often provoked problem behaviors when subjects made mistakes and lost reinforcement. Aggression, self-injury, tantrums, frustration, apathy and escape behaviors were all cited as direct consequences of shaping (Touchette & Howard, 1984).

So errorless techniques were developed to get behaviors more efficiently, with a steady rate of reinforcement, and less wear and tear on the learner. At the time, this caused quite a paradigm shift since it was widely assumed that errors were necessary for learning. A considerable body of evidence has since accumulated that errorless techniques are successful with human and nonhuman animals (Schroeder, 1997).

The notion that "prompting isn't training" is somewhat understandable since we know that consequences, not antecedents, determine behavior. We all strive to focus our clients on consequences rather than antecedents. Although antecedents don't cause behavior to occur, they increase the likelihood of behavior if their presence has been associated with past reinforcement of the behavior. In short, B is a function of C in the presence of A.

So a dog learns that in the presence of antecedent X (mom), sits are noticed and reinforced, but in the presence of antecedent Y (child), sits are not reinforced. Sits become much more likely in front of mom, who is the discriminative stimulus (SD) for reinforcement for sits.

"Luring is coercive."

Interestingly, this same criticism was leveled at all operant conditioning during Skinner's career. Whether used in fading or shaping, reinforcement was perceived as manipulative. The power that reinforcement demonstrated to change behavior—including human behavior—made people uncomfortable. It ran counter to strong beliefs about human free will and superiority over animals. Today's critics have focused on one operant technique, using food as an orienting prompt, but perhaps a part of history is replaying today.

Furthermore, it seems inconsistent for luring critics to acknowledge the truth that reinforcement is the power of operant conditioning, yet say that antecedent lures are so powerful they render animals helpless. The fact is, positive reinforcement (R+)—after the behavior not before—is so powerful that any operant technology that uses it can produce self-injurious behavior.

Rasey & Iverson (1993) shaped rats, using food reinforcers, to lean so far over a ledge that they fell off. (They were saved by a net.) Schaefer (1970) shaped self-injurious head banging in Rhesus monkeys. Learning textbooks usually supply several examples of parents inadvertently shaping obnoxious, even self-injurious behavior in their children by ignoring (and subsequently paying attention to) increasing levels of destructive behavior like screaming or head-banging.

We've all seen the cartoon in an ad in *The APDT Chronicle of the Dog* of a hapless dog appearing before a judge, protesting "But I was lured!" The dog could just as truthfully say, "But I was shaped!" In reality, neither luring nor shaping is "coercive," but both methods powerfully determine behavior through reinforcement. Murray Sidman's (1989) definition may help alleviate confusion about what learning theorists consider coercive: "To be coerced is to be compelled under duress or threat to do something 'against our will…' Control by positive reinforcement is non-coercive; coercion enters the picture when our actions are controlled by negative reinforcement or punishment." (pp. 31–32)

Perhaps a more accurate word to capture some trainers' concerns about lures is "intrusive." This term is used in textbooks to describe stronger prompts like physical guidance or force. Because of a treat's salience, we could construe it as intrusive. Of course, the "intrusiveness" of physical force is light years away from the intrusiveness of a hot dog morsel. Both are quite salient to the animal, but force is aversive and food is deliriously enticing. It's easy to make food lures less salient or intrusive by lowering their value. As Karen Overall points out (1997), dog biscuits are generally not sufficient motivation, but some foods are so desirable that the dog becomes too stimulated or distracted by them. Something between these two extremes is preferred.

"Luring produces passive dogs. Shaping produces 'creative' ones."

To unravel these claims, we first have to ground them in precise definitions of observable behaviors. What does "creative" mean? What behaviors constitute creativity? Behavioral (operational) definitions are key to the scientific process, because they recast fuzzy concepts or labels into specific behaviors that two or more people can agree on, observe, and count.

A term commonly used in the literature that encompasses the concepts of creativity and problem-solving is response generalization or response variation. Variation can be measured along dimensions such as speed, topography, latency, intensity, position, and duration. It means that a variety of behaviors (or variations of one behavior) occur in the presence of a stimulus or situation. One reason they occur is that they are all functionally equivalent, i.e., achieve the same consequence. A dog with a food toy, for example, quickly learns that pawing, nosing, licking, and biting are all helpful in getting some food.

So does shaping produce more response variability than prompting? This question hasn't been directly studied in the literature, so we have to glean our answers indirectly.

First, two caveats are in order:

• We should remember that all animals are adapted problem solvers. They are biological learning machines that interact with the environment and have their behavior shaped (selected) by its consequences (Pierce & Epling, 1999). In fact, Skinner (1990) said that evolution and operant learning operate by the same processes: trying or producing new things (variation) and discarding what doesn't work (selection). No operant technique can undo what thousands of years of evolution has produced.

• Behavior is naturally variable. But in the absence of explicit reinforcement for variability, responding becomes more stereotyped (repetitive) and less variable with continued operant conditioning (Domjan, 2003). By definition, shaping narrows the range of behaviors as we select the behaviors we want and extinguish the ones we don't.

Two key procedures that involve shaping, however, have resulted in increased response variation: 1) extinction; and 2) explicitly reinforcing variation or novelty, as Pryor did with a porpoise (Pryor, Haag, & O'Reilly, 1969) and as she has taught with her well known "101 things to do with a box" game (Pryor, 1999).

In the first procedure, pure extinction (when a behavior that was previously reinforced is no longer reinforced), behavior can increase or become more variable in frequency, duration, topography, and intensity. In addition, extinction bursts can briefly produce novel behaviors, ones that haven't occurred in that situation (Miltenberger, 2004). For example, when a child's parents no longer reinforce the child's night-time crying, he cries louder and longer (increased intensity and duration) and screams and hits the pillow (novel behaviors).

However, the evidence of increased variability with partial extinction, when reinforcement isn't reduced to zero (as is the case with shaping), is mixed. Some studies report increased variability, but others show small or no effects (Grunow & Neuringer, 2002).

Another route to increased variability is when variability is made the explicit criterion for reinforcement, as in Pryor's study and her box game. Much research since then has shown that varying and repeating behaviors are in part operant skills under the control of reinforcing consequences (e.g., Neuringer, Deiss, & Olson, 2000; Stokes, Mechner, & Balsam, 1999). In other words, if a stereotypy is reinforced, it will increase, and if variability is reinforced, that will increase.

One study with preschoolers showed that the frequency of children's creative play with building blocks could be increased through praise from the teacher (Goetz & Baer, 1973).

Variability as an operant has considerable applied potential when attempting to train an animal or person to solve problems. A study with rats as a model (Arnesen, 2000) showed that prior reinforcements of response variations increased the rats' exploration of novel objects and discovery of reinforcers (i.e., problem solving), even in a novel environment.

Nevertheless, researchers who study creativity debate whether reinforcement facilitates or impedes it. There is some support for the facilitation hypotheses, but also a "body of literature" that indicates that reinforcement interferes with creativity (Neuringer, 2004). If the latter is true, interference would occur with both lure-reward training and shaping, since both use reinforcement.

One way to look at the issue is to consider that some problems require flexibility and others require rigidity. Variability is reinforced when writing a poem. But rote repetition is reinforced when solving long division problems. Similarly, in assistance or scent work, a dog's variability on some tasks would more likely be reinforced whereas in a pet owner's home a more rigid obedience might be.

Turning back to prompting-fading techniques, what does the research say about their limitations? There may be some truth to the criticisms we've heard, but again the evidence is mixed. Terrace's 1960s studies and many since then (e.g., Dorry & Zeaman, 1973; Fields, 1980; Robinson & Storm, 1978) have directly compared errorless techniques with trial-and-error and have shown errorless to be superior with developmentally disabled children and animals. These researchers have concluded that animals and people learn complex discriminations more readily using errorless training (prompting-fading) than trial-and-error (shaping) (Klein, 1987).

But others, citing different studies, have concluded the opposite. They say that although trial-and-error has more adverse side effects compared to errorless training, it also results in greater flexibility when what is learned has to be modified later. These studies have shown that fading narrows attention to specific features of the prompt stimulus, which can impede learning in situations where the correct responses are changed or controlled by multiple cues (Marsh & Johnson, 1968; Gollin & Savoy, 1968; Jones & Eayrs, 1992).

One study these researchers cite taught one group of pigeons an errorless discrimination and another group a trial-and-error discrimination. The errorless group had extreme difficulty changing their behavior when the discrimination was reversed compared to the trial-and-error group, which handled the reversal well (Marsh & Johnson, 1968).

Another issue with fading cited in the literature is that research has not yet determined exactly how to produce a successful transfer from prompted to unprompted responding. There are six classes of prompts and three types of fading, and which of these combinations is optimal, and for which participants or behaviors, isn't known.

The same is true for shaping however. Research hasn't determined exactly how many successive steps, what size of steps, or how many trials at each step are optimal. In fading, prompt dependence can occur if prompts are offered too long, and premature removal of prompts can lead to persistent errors. Similarly, in shaping, the learner can get stuck on one approximation if it is reinforced too long, or lose the approximation if it's reinforced too briefly. So both methods are presented in textbooks as a bit of an art, involving planned and impromptu judgment calls depending on the trainer, the learner, and the situation (Martin & Pear, 2003).

Some researchers believe that errorless procedures are best suited for the learning of basic facts—like arithmetic and spelling—things that won't change. In contrast, since trial-and-error learning may produce more flexibility in responding, it may be more appropriate in problem solving situations or those in which the contingencies could change (Pierce & Epling, 1999).

Presuming these limitations with errorless methods do exist, dog trainers should nevertheless resist casting operant techniques in categorical good-bad roles, and accept that fading and shaping each has its distinct advantages, pitfalls, and unique areas of most effective application.

If shaping does produce greater flexibility, and fading does produce more fixed learning, we shouldn't assume that one outcome is a virtue and the other a vice. Many pet owners and handlers of working dogs would likely prefer strict compliance and not an ounce of variability. On the other hand, many trainers probably prefer more variability.

There doesn't seem to be a preponderance of evidence yet to decide the issue. That can be frustrating, because it leaves us without quick, clear-cut answers. Instead, we have to think like scientists, weigh the evidence, and keep an open mind. This issue challenges all trainers to continue learning and sharpening our skills in practicing and teaching all noncoercive operant techniques, and to keep our training as flexible and individualized as possible. ❖

References

Domjan, M. *The Principles of Learning and Behavior*. Belmont, CA, Wadsworth/ Thomson Learning, 2003.

Dorry, G. W. & Zeaman, D. "The use of a fading technique in paried-associate teaching of a reading vocabulary with retardates." *Mental Retardation*, 11, 3–6, 1973.

Fields, L. "Enhanced learning of new discriminations after stimulus fading." *Bulletin of the Psychonomic Society*, 15, 327–330, 1980.

Goetz, E. & Baer, D. "Social control of form diversity and the emergence of new forms in children's blockbuilding." *J Appl Behav Anal*, 6, 209–217, 1973.

Gollin, E. S. & Savoy, P. "Fading procedures and conditional discrimination in children." *J Exp Anal Behav*, 11, 443–451, 1969.

Grunow, A. & Neuringer, A. "Learning to vary and varying to learn." *Psychon B Rev*, 9, 250–258, 2002.

Jones, R. & Eayrs, C. B. "The use of errorless learning procedures in teaching people with a learning disability: A critical review." *Mental Hand Res*, 5, 204–210, 1992.

Klein, S. B. *Learning: Principles and Applications*. New York, McGraw Hill Book Company, 1987.

Lindsay, S. R. *Handbook of Applied Dog Behavior and Training: Adaptation and Learning*, Vol 1. Ames, IO, Iowa State Press, 2000.

Marsh, G. & Johnson, R. "Discrimination reversal following learning without 'errors.'" *Psychono Sci*, 10, 261–262, 1968.

Martin, G. & Pear, J. *Behavior Modification: What It Is and How to Do It*. Upper Saddle River, NJ, Prentice-Hall, 2003.

Miltenberger, R. G. *Behavior Modification: Principles and Procedures*. Belmont, CA, Wadsworth/Thompson Learning, 2004.

Neuringer, A. "Reinforced variability in animals and people." *American Psychologist*, 59, 891–906, 2004.

Neuringer, A., Deiss, C. & Olson, G. "Reinforced variability and operant learning." *J Exper Psych*, 26, 98–111, 2000.

Overall, K. *Clinical Behavioral Medicine for Small Animals*. St. Louis, MO, Mosby, Inc., 1997.

Pierce, W. D. & Epling, W. F. *Behavior Analysis and Learning*. Upper Saddle River, NJ, Prentice-Hall, Inc., 1999.

Pryor, K. *Don't Shoot the Dog! The New Art of Teaching and Training*. NY, Bantam Books, 1999.

Pryor, K., Haag, R. & O'Reilly, J. "The creative porpoise: training for novel behavior." *J Exper Anal Beh*, 12, 653–661, 1969.

Rasey, H. W. "An experimental acquisition of maladaptive behavior by shaping." *J Behav Ther Exper Psy*, 24, 34–43, 1993.

Robinson, P. W. & Storm, R. H. "Effects of error and errorless discrimination acquisition on reversal learning." *J Exper Anal Behav*, 29, 517–525, 1978.

Schaefer, H. H. "Self-injurious behavior: Shaping "head banging" in monkeys." *J Appl Behav Anal*, 3, 111–116, 1970.

Schlosberg, H., & Solomon, R. L. "Latency of response in a choice discrimination." *J Exper Psy*, 33, 22–39, 1943.

Schroeder, S. Selective eye fixations during transfer of discriminative stimulus control. In D. M. Baer & E. M. Pinkston (Eds.), *Environment and Behavior*. Boulder, CO, Westview Press, 1997.

Sidman, M. *Coercion and Its Fallout*. Boston, MA, Authors Cooperative, 1989.

Skinner, B. F. "Can psychology be a science of mind?" *American Psychologist*, 45, 1206–1210, 1990.

Stokes, P. D., Mechner, F. & Balsam, P. D. "Effects of different acquisition procedures on response variability." *Animal Learning & Behavior*, 27, 28–41, 1999.

Terrace, H. S. "Errorless transfer of a discrimination across two continua." *J Exper Anal Behav*, 6, 223–232, 1963.

Terrace, H.S. "Stimulus control." In W. K. Honig (Ed.), *Operant Behavior: Areas of Research and Application*. NY, Appleton-Century-Crofts, 1966.

Touchette, P. E., & Howard, J. S. "Errorless learning: reinforcement contingencies and stimulus control transfer in delayed prompting." *J Appl Behav Anal*, 17, 175–188, 1984.

ASSOCIATION of PET DOG TRAINERS

Dog Behavior, Training, and Modification

Trainers and behavior consultants can experience a wide range of challenges when working with dogs and their owners. The articles in this section illustrate the numerous behavioral problems and training conundrums that can exist in one's practice. Several articles discuss real-life case studies of dogs with issues such as human-directed aggression, hyperactivity, resource guarding, separation anxiety, fear, and intra-dog intra-household aggression. Another series of articles presents the relatively new sport of Rally and how to get you, and your clients, involved in this fun new twist on competitive obedience. A variety of specialty training topics is presented in articles about field sports, herding, deaf dogs, special needs dogs, and even working with cats! The importance of understanding the impact of medicine on dog behavior is highlighted in articles about the use of behavior-modifying drugs and the impact of medical problems on a dog's behavior.

The Magic of Free-Shaping

Pamela S. Dennison, November/December 2006

In my article in the Jul/Aug 2005 issue of *The APDT Chronicle of the Dog*, I spoke a great deal about the importance of teaching aggressive dogs core/foundation behaviors before working on the systematic desensitization process. There is another aspect of a solid foundation—the dog's "inner" foundation, if you will. What I mean by that is self-assurance, ability to cope or lack thereof, and the motivation to act in certain ways. We all know dogs, even those from the same litter or raised in the same environment, that act differently from one another. Some are bold, some shy, some are fearful, some unflappable no matter what comes down the pike, and others freak out at the slightest change. So how does one tap into a dog's "inner" foundation?

Many years ago, when I first heard about free-shaping, I thought it was silly and a waste of time. Why not just lure or tell the dog what you want him to do? Then a friend of mine showed me what she had taught her dogs to do by free-shaping and I was suitably impressed. I tried it out on my own dogs to teach weave poles and other agility tasks and was completely hooked (as were my Border Collies). Beau was terrified of the agility equipment and free-shaping helped him get over his fear of the contact obstacles. Before free-shaping, even the sight of a teeter or "A" frame would send him running away in abject fear.

I wanted to try it with my Sheltie Cody, but was a little concerned that he wouldn't offer me anything. I had started his training using traditional methods, which most certainly doesn't allow for independent thinking. Although at the time I hadn't used aversives with Cody in seven years, he was reluctant to offer anything. If he made a mistake, he would frequently freak out (as in run away from me) or shut down (stand in an awkward position, freeze, and stare off into space), even if I gave him a treat for "failing." (I wanted to show him it was okay to fail sometimes—that I wasn't going to hurt him anymore.) I was determined to try free shaping with him anyway. I sat down on the floor with a bucket of food, a clicker, a smile, and an expectant look on my face. No matter what he gave me—an ear flick, bark, head turn, eye blink—anything whatsoever, he got a click and treat. Because it didn't matter what he offered me, there was no way he could be wrong. He picked up the concept in about 10 minutes and we ended the session with him pawing the ground. With that one initial session, I was able to wipe the fear off his face and regain the trust I had lost so long ago.

One day I was working on teaching some core behaviors with an aggressive dog and decided to see if she would free-shape for us. I picked something simple—"put your front feet in the car tire that was lying flat on the ground." Within minutes, she had done it! I then decided to teach her to ride a skateboard. Again, within minutes she had put her front feet on the board and moved it an inch or so and seemed quite pleased with herself.

At this point, I thought, "Wow, this is pretty cool. This dog is really smart. I wonder if the other aggressive dogs I am working with could benefit from this?" So I tried it, and each and every aggressive dog became quite proficient at free-shaping. It didn't matter what we taught the dog to do—they picked it up very quickly.

One very stormy, freezing morning at my aggressive dog class, we decided to work inside my building (because it is only 1700 square feet, we normally work outside). There isn't much room to safely heel around or do other moving types of behaviors—not with two aggressive dogs that need a great deal of room to be comfortable. (I only work two dogs at a time inside.) So, I divided the room in half using baby gates (more for a visual separation than a real protected contact situation) and set up the skateboard on one side and the tire on the other side. I had the dogs come in and the owners were instructed to work on their "task" of free-shaping. I have to say, we were all pretty nervous about this context. The dogs had never been in my building before with another dog there and I wasn't really sure how this would work out. They were all told, "Whatever happens, don't drop the leash!!"

A very interesting and fascinating phenomena occurred. Neither dog aggressed at each other or at the rest of us standing around watching. They were quite engrossed in the task at hand and much too busy to bother with us. Even when we applauded and loudly cheered their successful efforts (we were so excited that we forgot we were watching aggressive dogs!), the only reaction we got was a calm look, a relaxed facial expression and a gentle tail wag. When the next two dogs came in the building, we tried it again and got the same results—two very excited working dogs that exhibited no aggression.

Over and over again, with each class, (indoors or outdoors) we did more and more free-shaping. Over and over again, the dogs remained calm and focused. The more complicated the task, the more unperturbed the dogs became with their provoking stimuli close by (and in fact, their provoking stimuli were much closer than they had ever been before). Not once did the dogs aggress during a free-shaping session.

I started to think about what was really going on. What was it about free-shaping that caused the dogs to not only focus on their owners, but make the sight of their provoking stimuli a non-issue? I think it is more than just attention to their owners and more than the core behaviors.

Free-shaping is a multi-faceted "methodology," for lack of a better word. It teaches the owner how to teach and become quite surgical in the precision of clicking and food delivery. It teaches them how to break behaviors down into very small approximations and to be quiet to allow the dogs the opportunity to think.

Free-shaping adds another aspect to the learning process, and what the click really means. Many dogs are clicker trained, but they still have a tendency to wait for the handler to tell them what to do. Free-shaping teaches them that their behavior actually makes you click. It teaches the dog that it's okay to problem solve and offer behaviors. The great thing about having a dog that now offers behaviors willingly, is that the dog can learn that he can influence his environment which can lead to more positive behavior outcomes.

Many dogs start out being aggressive because they are afraid. Some may have been going through a fear period and it was handled incorrectly. Some dogs may have been attacked by other dogs, creating a fearful or aggressive dog. Some may have been inadvertently reinforced for aggressing. Whatever the reason, the result is quite often a dog that lacks confidence and appropriate coping skills (or we don't like the way they are utilizing their coping devices—such as active aggression/lunging/biting).

So now put together all of the great benefits of free-shaping and add those to working with an aggressive dog. Just seeing their aggressive dogs learn to solve these mental puzzles is quite exciting for the handlers. They often start to think, "Maybe my dog really can learn to be more like other 'normal' dogs." They become immersed in the free-shaping process and extremely tuned into their dog. The growing connection between dog and handler is a beauty to behold. The handler also gains enthusiasm and dedication to stick with the long haul of the systematic desensitization process.

The dogs I have worked with appear to become totally engaged in the learning process with free-shaping. Once they understand the concept, they start to pick up all new behaviors faster and faster. Free-shaping in the presence of other dogs that are also busy free-shaping creates a wonderful climate of concentrated attention to their owners and they are not reacting to their provoking stimuli. The dogs are well aware of the other dogs in close proximity and they choose not to aggress. Even if we are not working on free-shaping for a particular session, the dogs give the owners much more attention then they did before learning how to free-shape.

This is a short story to help illustrate how free-shaping can help an aggressive dog; I am working with an aggressive Neapolitan Mastiff mix named Moby and his owner, Trish. Although we put no pressure on him whatsoever (we just let him roam the room with treats scattered all over and if he went up to Trish, he got extra treats), he would often shut down and just lay on the floor in a lump. After he had learned some basic skills, I just had this gut feeling that he was exceedingly insecure and decided the time was right for free-shaping. Very slowly and carefully, we taught him to free-shape putting his front feet in the tire. This first behavior was quite hard for him. Once he understood the concept of offering behaviors, he became a free-shaping fiend. In just a few weeks we taught Moby to balance on a Buja Board (a piece of plywood with a ball screwed in underneath—the dog steps on it and it tips in all different directions, pretty scary for a fearful dog!), put his front feet up on a chair, ride the skateboard, nose target a yogurt container lid, close a door, shake paw, and wave. Each time we added in a new behavior, we were astonished at how fast he learned his new task. Trish was on her way to becoming a very good trainer and starting to look at Moby in a new and positive light.

Because of the fun, and yes, mostly useless stuff he was learning to do, he became quite comfortable with me (less signs of stress) and started to come up to me in a happy and relaxed manner. He took food gently from me and would do simple behaviors when I asked him to. The look in his eyes went from a hard stare with huge pupils (pretty scary!) to a nice relaxed and softened look. Sometimes, Moby would roll around on the floor, scratching his back and exposing his substantial belly to our accompanying giggles.

One day, I wanted to try free-shaping another behavior (doing a figure eight around two cones with no luring). It was too hard to explain to Trish, so I picked up the clicker and some treats and started to free-shape Moby myself. He was a little nervous at first (his body and face stiffened slightly, tail was tucked) and so I gave him some extra treats, just for thinking (and not biting me…). We worked on that one behavior for a few minutes and he learned to go around one cone. I decided to end the session and go for a walk. We all went out into the 100-acre field next to my building and got the thrill of our lives. Moby started racing around like a puppy, play bowing to me, then rolling over on his back, then back up, repeating the process a few times while we were cheering, clapping, and laughing.

The following week, after a few minutes of me free-shaping Moby to do the weave poles, we decided to see if we could interest him in a toy. For the first time since Trish had rescued him, he played with a toy—shook it, flung it up in the air, chased it, and brought it back. Free-shaping did not miraculously cause Moby to spontaneously play with a toy, however, it did cause him to be more relaxed and less stressed. (Many dogs won't play with toys if they are stressed.) With the advent of free-shaping, Trish observed that Moby's behavior in "real life" was becoming much more relaxed. He was now not stressed in situations where he had previously reacted.

Perhaps this can all be explained by the fact that the owners of these aggressive dogs are becoming better trainers with better teaching skills and more confident people overall. Perhaps it is because we are teaching the dogs tons of useless (and useful) behaviors in a more fun and exciting manner. Perhaps dogs can learn more effectively with free-shaping, rather than using other methods such as lure and reward or "traditional" training. It can enable the dog to develop a relationship with his owner that would not likely be possible outside of using the free shaping process.

If, in the past, aversives were used to "correct" a behavior or the aggression issue, this can greatly suppress the dog's behavioral repertoire, and add the stress of the punishment into the mix. Free-shaping is a great way to develop a dog that is more likely to problem solve by trying new and different things and this can lead to learning alternate and incompatible behaviors faster. With that, coupled with the desensitization process, they will then learn to react in a more appropriate manner for our human society. By learning new behaviors, the dog can develop a new behavioral relationship with his owner that can lead to more effective learning and communication between them. With this comes the ability to accept what was once scary. Most certainly we can't know exactly what our dogs are thinking; however, we can observe a change in overall behavior. And most certainly I will not be abandoning teaching the core behaviors, but with the addition of the element of free-shaping, the aggressive dogs I work with continue to make faster progress in the systematic desensitization process. ❖

Leashes? We Don't Need No Stinkin' Leashes!

Wendy van Kerkhove, January/February 2007

First and foremost, it is important to understand that by offering this class, we in no way endorse throwing leashes away. We make it clear that despite how well our clients' dogs have done in class, they must be leashed for safety outside of class.

For the past year all of my basic and advanced training classes have been run without the use of leashes. This means that from the time the dogs enter the training area until they leave, they cannot be controlled by anything other than a steady stream of reinforcements that trump the dog's desire to sniff the butt of the dog on the other side of the room.

I started offering off-leash classes for one major reason: training a dog on leash does not prepare the owner to deal with the problems that arise when the dog is in the home or in the backyard and off leash. I decided that I would serve my clients better if I taught them how to gain and keep control of their dogs when they were off-leash and out of reach.

Our basic training class is offered to dogs over five months that have no real obedience skills and to dogs that have the basic skills down, but would be challenged by distractions while off-leash. Our advanced class is for dogs with a solid foundation of basic obedience.

To date we have had no fights, no bites, and no real altercations since we have been running these classes. Each dog is carefully screened (questionnaire) for aggression and resource guarding. The dogs do not have to be playful to take the class, but they must not be reactive. The trainers all have experience with dog-on-dog aggression issues.

The standard ratio of dogs to trainers is four-to-one and it is typical for us to have 12 to 15 dogs in the training center with four trainers running the class. We often have a mix of small dogs and large dogs. In our last class we had four small dogs, a Great Dane, a young Pit Bull, and a very large, exuberant Boxer. With 12 to 15 dogs of various sizes, energy levels, and play styles it is critical that all dogs have a positive experience and do not get overwhelmed.

The role of the trainers is to manage the dogs and to provide lots of hands-on coaching and cheerleading. In order to make things run smoothly, each trainer is assigned three to four dogs (and owners) to instruct and keep track of. Each of us has a keen eye for potential conflict and we feel comfortable diffusing a tense situation. We all have Direct Stop™ in case of an emergency.

The first week of class is an orientation for humans only. During this time we review the training methods that we use (lure–reward), and explain how dogs learn. A large amount of time is devoted to discussing the nature of reinforcements. We challenge the clients to come up with a list of reinforcers that they think will most motivate their dogs and to bring at least two different types (i.e., treats and tug toy). As far as treats, the owners are instructed to bring a minimum of three different types of treats in separate baggies. They must pick food that they know their dogs will go nuts for. If someone chooses inappropriate treats (i.e., the dog is not crazy about them) or if they don't have enough variety, they will quickly lose control of their dog.

We also review the importance of the rate of reinforcement. For the most part, this lecture goes in one ear and out the other, but hits clients like a large truck during the first class with dogs. They quickly learn that if they don't deliver a steady stream of reinforcements, they will lose complete control of their dogs.

The advice to bring a tired, hungry dog to class is common, but in an off-leash class it is vital that the dog be rather exhausted and very hungry. We often suggest that the owners take their dog to an off-leash dog park for a run, or engage in a long game of fetch. Our motto is, "A tired dog is a good dog."

During the orientation we ask each person to introduce themselves and to say a few words about his or her dog. We do this so the owners can get to know one another, but also because it gives us the opportunity to get more information about the dog. I view this as an opportunity to inquire one more time about the dog's social skills.

We also stress the importance of coming to class on time because coming late will cause a disruption. If a dog goes for a party ride, owners are instructed to immediately get their dog's attention and hold it by delivering a steady stream of treats. The only restriction given to owners is to not give treats to any dog except for their own. Finally, we instruct the owners to come into the space and immediately take their dog off the leash during the next class. For the first five minutes of class we have a total play free-for-all.

Homework for the first week includes figuring out the best reinforcers for their dog and working on the "name game" exercise. The goal of the "name game" is to get the dogs to spin on a dime when they hear their name. It is the foundation on which the class is built.

The exercises covered in the basic class are similar to the exercises that would be offered in any other basic class. They include sit, down, stay, come, no-leash walking, leave it, etc. What differentiates this class from any other on-leash class has less to do with the exercises that we cover and more to do with the management of the dogs.

During week two, each owner enters the room and lets their dog off-leash. As at the dog park, as each new dog enters the space, all of the dogs come running to say hello. We allow these interactions to take place until a few minutes after the last dog enters the room. To end the play session we get everyone's attention and instruct each owner to not call their dog, but rather to approach him, put a very good treat under his nose, and lure him back to the designated spot where training will begin. Later, after we have taught come, we instruct owners to use the word and only lure the dog if the dog does not respond to the word.

During the first two weeks with dogs, a large amount of time is spent coaching owners through the process of getting their dog back once they have lost his attention and he is making a bee line for the dog next to him. Despite our constant reminders, the owners continue to yell their dog's name (or come) as though that might work!

The Dog Trainer's Resource 2

There are two hurdles to overcome in this scenario: First, we have to get the owner to react quickly when his or her dog goes for a joy ride (often times they just stand there, checked out, watching it happen); and second we must inhibit an owner from calling his or her dog and get the owner instead to say nothing, run up to his or her dog, and lure him back with food.

The pace of an off-leash class has to be fast. If it takes longer than two-and-a-half minutes to explain and demo the next exercise, the class will deteriorate into chaos. Additionally, it is important to structure the lessons such that moving exercises are interspersed between standing exercises. For example, we'll work on down and leave it and then we'll work on no-leash walking. Usually we'll work on three exercises and then have a play break for five minutes.

By the end of week, three of the owners have much better control of their dogs and the classes start to run smoothly. We still have the dogs that go for joy rides, but it is much less frequent and the owner can usually get the dog back quickly. In general we do much less damage control (getting dogs to come back) at this point and the responsibility for keeping the dog's attention falls more upon the owner than on the trainers.

There are a few situations when we will use leashes. During a lecture, if there is a dog in class that habitually runs around and is not responding to the "alleged" reinforcements despite our best efforts, we will put the dog on-leash and tether him to a stationary object for the duration of the lecture. There are some exercises that require leashes. For example when we teach sit politely for petting (or greeting) the dogs must be leashed so that if they jump we can turn and walk away and they can't follow us while continuing to jump.

There is no question, running an off-leash class takes a huge amount of mental and physical energy. But there are distinct benefits that cannot be gained by doing on-leash classes. First, the owners are often skeptical that their dog will do well in the class and are amazed to see what kind of verbal control they can actually achieve. Since we focus on recalls and no-leash walking, these behaviors tend to improve significantly. One of the benefits of allowing the dogs to play is that we have a fantastic opportunity to teach the dogs how to come away from play.

Most importantly, the owners leave the class with a very good understanding of how to control their dog when it is off-leash and out of reach. The feedback from our clients has been great and our attrition rate is extremely low. We all have great fun. I'll never go back to leashed classes! ❖

The Environmental Cue: A Valuable In-Home Training Tool

Nicole Wilde, May/June 2007

The cue for a dog to perform a desired behavior normally comes directly from a person, in the form of a verbal request, a hand signal, or both. An "environmental cue" comes from something in the environment. For example, the ring of a doorbell is the cue for a dog to go lay on his bed. Of course, dogs are not born knowing that a doorbell is a signal to go to bed—in fact, most seem to believe it is a cue to run to the door, then jump and bark like a maniac! Dogs must be taught to understand what a specific environmental cue means and exactly how to respond.

It is simple enough to teach an environmental cue, but first the dog must understand and reliably perform the desired behavior. In the doorbell example, the dog would first have to understand and reliably perform the behavior "go to bed"—consisting of going to the bed, lying down, and staying until released—when requested. Assuming the owner normally used a verbal cue to elicit the behavior, the sound of the doorbell would be introduced, followed by the owner's cue. Once the doorbell-verbal cue pattern had been repeated enough times, the dog would hear the doorbell, anticipate the verbal cue, and go to bed at the sound of the doorbell alone. (An alternative cue would be the owner reaching for the doorknob; this can be useful to keep dogs from door-darting not only when guests arrive, but when a family member exits.)

Why use environmental cues? For one thing, they can be extremely useful for solving behavior issues, and can be used in creative ways. And when your client sees their dog respond to an environmental cue alone, they will think you are brilliant! They will also see that the dog is capable of much more than they believed possible. Also, when a client is training something that is perceived as fun and interesting, their attitude is likely to be light and happy. Light and happy equals motivation to practice.

Let's focus on the value of environmental cues in solving behavior issues, especially those in the home environment. This is where our clients complain about things like the dog being a pest at dinnertime, demanding attention from visitors, and a host of other behaviors that fall under the umbrella of "house manners." If an owner's only response to an unwanted behavior is to ineffectively reprimand the dog, the result is likely to be a lot of back-and-forth, non-productive communication that can escalate into far bigger problems. For example, the dog jumps and mouths the owner; the owner says, "No!" and pushes the dog down. In many cases, the dog will simply jump up again (and we all know what a great game that is for dogs), perhaps with greater enthusiasm, and the pattern continues. In some cases, this scenario can boil over into aggression. At the very least, it doesn't solve the problem.

Another problem with simply reprimanding a dog for an unwanted behavior is that the dog still learns that the behavior can be successful in specific contexts.

For example, in the pestering-during-dinner scenario, the dog might learn to try it only when the five-year-old son is present, because it sometimes results in food being slipped to her. Or a dog might learn that if he persists long enough, mom will reprimand a time or two and then give in.

Teaching a dog an alternate behavior is always a good solution, and environmental cues take the concept a step further. In the dinnertime scenario, the dog could be taught to go to his bed and lie down during meals. Pick a cue such as someone sitting down at the table. (An alternate cue would be the pulling out of a chair.) Assuming the dog already knows go to bed, have the person sit down and then send the dog to bed. Work toward the dog going to the bed as soon as the person sits. Have the family practice reinforcing the dog for remaining on the bed during the meal by tossing treats and praising, generously at first and then more sporadically. The eventual outcome could be that the dog is given one treat after the family has finished the meal; or that the treats are eventually phased out completely and the dog learns to go to bed and relax during the family's mealtimes.

The use of environmental cues is limited only by your own creativity. I have used the opening of the dishwasher door as a cue for my dogs to go lie down—otherwise, Mojo is the pre-wash cycle. I had a client recently whose Jack Russell Terrier was certain that mom picking up the phone was his cue to find the nearest forbidden object and run around the house with it. Predictably, mom would pay attention to him. So we taught him instead that a phone being picked up was his cue to lie down and stay. I used the same cue with a family whose sixteen-year-old daughter chatted on the phone a lot (imagine that!) and whose Beagle mix would start barking each time the daughter picked up the phone. Since the dog wouldn't bark while in a down, the down-stay neatly solved the problem.

A trainer friend likes to use the cue of anything being placed on the kitchen counter as a cue to go lie down and stay by the kitchen door. Before my German Shepherd Soko passed in April, she and Mojo both knew that whenever I opened a treat roll to slice it up, that was their cue to lie down and stay. In fact, they got to the point that they would lie down as soon as the cutting board came out, which preceded the appearance of the roll—that was thanks to my being domestically challenged, and the cutting board never being used for anything else. Of course, they would get slices tossed to them periodically.

Lying down and staying is a convenient behavior to pair with environmental cues, but it is certainly not the only one. Dogs can be taught that when in the yard, a person approaching the sliding glass door from inside is a cue to sit and wait to be invited in. Sitting and waiting can also be the desired response to the cue of the dog's meal being prepared. Teaching a dog that the doorbell is her cue to go find and carry her toy (e.g., a Kong) is a great way to approach the problem of a dog who barks when visitors arrive. Tricks can be incorporated as well; the dog who sits and waves at arriving visitors is not only adorable, but is also not barking or jumping on them.

The more tools in a trainer's "toolbox" the better. So in addition to solving in-home issues in the usual ways, consider creative ways to incorporate environmental cues as well. ❖

Retreat 'n Treat

Ian Dunbar, Edited by Terry Long, September/October 2006

I believe the term "Retreat 'n Treat" was first coined by Suzanne Clothier after she heard me talk about a method I used to address fear aggression. I initially called the technique "Retreat With Honor" after getting into a dodgy situation with an Akita. Basically, the Akita and I were much too close to each other, and the situation was beginning to escalate … the Akita growled and I reprimanded. Both of us desperately wanted to normalize the interaction without losing face.

The Akita had bitten four men, each with hard Level II bites (considerable bruising, but no skin puncture), so I had instructed the owners to muzzle him before I arrived. As I introduced myself in the usual fashion, "Hi Mr. Akita, I'm your trainer and here's some food treats," he stoically lifted one front leg and flipped off his muzzle. I quickly tossed some kibble over his head and delicately back-pedaled, dropping several pieces of freeze-dried liver as I retreated. The Akita turned to truffle up the kibble—and then turned again—and approached—agonizingly slowly—eating each piece of liver as he came closer. I was trapped at the end of the hallway, so I threw some more kibble over his head and then some more liver behind him as he retreated. This time his approach was a little quicker and a little less stiff, and so I repeated the procedure. After cautiously sniffing each piece of liver, he would look up at me—the anthropomorphic among us might say, suspiciously—before eating the treat. But after half a dozen or so repetitions, his approach became much more relaxed, and so I offered him three pieces of liver from my hand. His body language seemed to say that everything was cool and so I retreated and lured him to come and sit and lie down. We repeated this over and over and then embarked upon some routine handling exercises. The entire session took about one hour, in which time the Akita learned that there was at least one male human that he could begin to trust.

Obviously, I made several pretty dumb mistakes working with this dog. However, in my own defense, I should mention that this was way back in 1982 and that I haven't made the same mistakes since. In that sense, I learned a lot: 1) always remember to instruct owners to tie the muzzle to the back of the collar; 2) never work with biting dogs in confined spaces; and 3) always wear protective clothing and Kevlar gloves when working with biting dogs. Much more important though, I learned that even when interactions are headed in the wrong direction, just a few liver treats can quickly turn them back to gold.

At that time, the dog training climate was a bit different from today. The standard approach for biting—and even growly—dogs was, "Show them who's boss!" Even back then, this approach didn't make much sense (and it makes even less sense to me now). Presumably, dogs have darn good reasons for growling and biting, and to respond physically would only give them yet another reason to growl and bite. However, when I lectured about my techniques, the usual response was, "You gave a treat to a biting dog!?!" It's indeed refreshing to think that nowadays—a little over twenty years later on, classical conditioning and lure-reward training are techniques of choice for dealing with fearful and/or biting dogs.

In a nutshell, Retreat 'n Treat comprises lure-reward training a fearful dog to retreat—a nice alternative behavior to lunging at someone—but super-luring and mega-rewarding him for approaching. Once the dog approaches quickly and loosely and takes a food treat (both of which are extremely powerful and revealing temperament tests), you have him. As a trainer, you now own his brain, his feelings, and his actions. It's now easy to establish control and teach the dog to sit- and down-stay. And whether he wants to or not, the dog will begin to like you.

When working with fearful dogs (and most biting dogs are fearful), a common pitfall is to work too fast and too close, thus making the dog more fearful. The dog will approach only so close and will always remain within his safety zone (flight distance)—a highly specific distance for each individual dog. If you approach, or reach forward, you will stress the dog, who will likely retreat. A common mistake is to reach forward with a food treat to try to lure the dog to approach. The dog may tolerate your hand penetrating his flight-distance and take the food treat, but then he'll quickly retreat or snap and lunge (to prompt you to retreat). There is a big difference between a hand with food treats penetrating the flight distance and an empty hand that is already too close. Always remember to have a bunch of treats in your hand, so that as the dog eats one treat, you can immediately show him that you have more.

Retreat 'n Treat is yet another example of Murphy's Law in Dog Training—whatever you really want the dog to do, ask him (or lure him) to do the opposite. In this case, if you would like the dog to come closer, try to teach him to go away.

In terms of animal behavior (and underlying emotions), proximity pretty much reveals everything, and the manner of approach or retreat tells the rest of the story. In our research of social hierarchies at UC Berkeley, we found that "buddies spend time with each other" and that dogs approach friends very differently than other dogs. These are hardly world-shattering findings for anyone who lives with a dog, but the raw data on proximity and approach were blindingly striking. With fearful dogs then, a major goal is to build their confidence so that they approach quickly and loosely and then stick around (sit- and down-stay).

This, of course, raises the popular psychology question: Do animals become more confident when taught to model confident behavior? Most likely, yes. Teaching the dog to come and sit and lie down on cue encourages and reinforces prosocial behavior. Also, it teaches the dog how to act. Not knowing how to act when stressed can cause an animal to display an entire repertoire of hyperactive tics and stereotypies. Simply teaching a dog to sit-stay decreases activity and induces calmness. In a sense, the sit-stay acts as a "behavioral pacifier." This technique is much the same as teaching scared public speakers to stand with their feet one foot apart and to hold their hands behind their back.

Equally important—especially with biting dogs—by teaching the dog to come and sit and lie down the trainer is establishing control and the dog is demonstrating compliance. Certainly the dog responds happily and willingly, but of course in pet dog training, happy and willing compliance is the only way to go.

In my brief encounter with the Akita, I was very lucky because the dog loved food treats. Indeed, whether or not a dog takes a food treat can be very revealing: 1) if the dog takes a treat from the trainer, usually the dog's training will proceed smoothly and quickly; 2) if a dog refuses to take treats from both the trainer and the owner, most likely the dog feels stressed by the situation, and so proceed slowly; and 3) if the dog refuses to take treats from the trainer but readily does so from the owner, most likely the dog feels stressed by the trainer (i.e., you!), and so proceed very slowly.

The major prerequisite for classical conditioning and progressive desensitization is that the dog will readily accept a primary reinforcer. The two reinforcers (hugs and praise) that we would most like to use with shy and fearful dogs often make fearful dogs more fearful. That's why we use food. If the dog accepts treats, you have a great shot at quickly changing his behavior and temperament. However, if a dog refuses treats, both classical and operant conditioning will take a very (VERY) long time. To facilitate success, the most useful advice is to instruct the owner that family members and friends should hand-feed the dog for at least one week prior to your first session.

❖

Rally Junkies Unite!

Laurie Williams, January/February 2007

In my neck of the woods I'm known as "the Rally dealer." I have aptly earned that moniker by systematically getting people addicted to the sport of Rally obedience. My friends chide my new students and acquaintances by saying, "stay away from her or she'll turn you into a Rally junkie by next week," which is a complete exaggeration. I usually give people at least two weeks before I start to woo them. Few, if any, have been dragged kicking and screaming into this world. I haven't had to stand on street corners, lurk in bushes, or get carted away by the police. Though, on occasion, my husband has come looking for me on Rally class nights that run long, but so far he hasn't had to bail me out of jail…yet. Most importantly, I don't at all feel guilty about what I do. The way I see it, I'm turning people on to one of the best relationship building activities they could share with their dogs. That's why I'm happy to be writing this Rally column for *The APDT Chronicle of the Dog*. This column will appear regularly and will help spread the word about this exciting sport, introduce you to some awesome Rally teams, and offer performance tips.

I had the opportunity to attend my first APDT annual conference last September. Meeting and networking with other instructors and canine education professionals from all over the world was incredible. However, I was surprised at the number of attendees who weren't familiar with APDT Rally. I wasn't expecting it to be one giant "Rally Anonymous" meeting, but I did think I'd encounter a lot more people who shared this passion. Frankly, I met more people who'd never even seen Rally than people who had. That was not what a "Rally dealer" wants to hear.

During the Q&A session of the general meeting held at the conference, an attendee asked, "How is the APDT working to offer more Rally trials throughout the country?" As expected, the answer was clear. It's not the APDT's responsibility to offer Rally trials—it's ours, the enthusiasts. APDT has provided the sport, the rules and regulations, and the opportunity. It's up to us to take the ball and run with it.

Steps To Hosting A Rally Trial

One of the biggest misconceptions I've found is that people believe it takes a club to offer an APDT-sanctioned Rally trial. While this is the case with AKC, UKC, and most other dog event sanctioning organizations, thankfully it's not so with the APDT. An APDT-sanctioned Rally trial can virtually be hosted by anyone, an individual or a group, and they don't even have to be a member of the APDT.

1. Become a Rally dealer. As I stated above, anyone can apply to host an APDT Rally trial, but you really do have to be passionate about it and willing to work hard.

2. Get your PhD in APDT Rally. Study the sport, exercises, rules, and regulations just like you studied for your SATs! If no one else is offering APDT Rally in your area, you will become the designated rally expert. That means you'll be looked to

for answers to those burning questions like, "if my dog sits when we are doing exercise #19, how many points off will we get?" "What is an ARCH?" "What height does my Beagle have to jump?" You will undoubtedly encounter people who are familiar with AKC Rally, so it will be even more important that you can articulate the similarities as well as the differences between the two.

3. Construct a Rally kit. Basic necessities:

   • Signs for all levels: These can be downloaded from the Rally section of the APDT web site. The signs can be printed on cardstock and laminated or placed in page protectors.

   • Sign holders: I've seen sign holders constructed from dollar store plate holders, plant/wreath holders, flower pots, and even hockey pucks! See the various Yahoo Rally groups for all kinds of creative ideas.

   • Exercise/station numbers: The least expensive way to make these is to print the 4" numbers on cardstock, laminate them, and tape them directly to the signs. Again, see the Yahoo Rally groups for more creative ideas.

   • Four food bowls with covers: These can be made from stainless steel food bowls and plastic or wire screens that can be secured in place.

   • Seven traffic cones: These should be at least 12" high (taller than agility cones) and can be purchased online for as low as $3.00 per cone. One great source: www.schoolmasters.com.

4. Teach/offer Rally classes. When you've become proficient with the rules and exercises, it's time to share the wealth! Out of all dog sports, APDT Rally is arguably one of the most user-friendly. Because ongoing dog/handler communication is encouraged throughout the course, handlers can use both hand and verbal signals simultaneously and may repeat most exercises; it's so much fun, the majority of people introduced to the sport will view achieving a title as a realistic goal. The more classes you offer and the more comfortable, knowledgeable and better your students and their dogs become, the more competitors you'll have at future trials. Special note: Make sure you distribute APDT Rally dog registration forms to your students! All dogs that compete in APDT Rally must first be registered. I give registration forms out with my Class 1 handout!

5. Attend an APDT Rally trial. If you live in a part of the country where there are no trials, this can be difficult, but in order to host an APDT trial you really should attend one first. Unfortunately, attending an AKC Rally trial will not give you the same insight. As anyone who has attended both will tell you, it's like comparing apples to oranges. So out of all the initial required financial investment, this might be your greatest expense if you have to travel far, but it will be well worth it in the long run.

6. Become an APDT Rally official. When you do eventually host your trial you will need officials. You'll need a Rally representative and judges for the levels you plan

to offer. Assuming there are no local representatives and judges in your area, you will have to not only pay your officials to work at your trial, but you'll have to pay for their travel and lodging expenses as well. There's no cheaper way to do this than to act as an official at your own trial, assuming you wouldn't charge yourself a fee! There are certain criteria for becoming an approved official, but it may not be as difficult as you think. The representative and judge requirements and applications are located on the APDT web site.

7. Find a trial location. APDT Rally courses are typically run on a 50x80 ring. However, if your ring size is somewhat irregular or smaller, if you include a diagram with the trial application, the APDT Rally Coordinator will consider the request. Your potential location will have to provide not only space for the ring, but space for the exhibitors, their dogs, crates, judge's table, and spectators. More than likely, finding an outdoor space with these accommodations will be the most economical. Moreover, indoor trials require rubber matting on the floor to ensure safe footing.

8. Locate prospective officials/judges. Even if you do become a representative and Level 1 judge, you'll still need at least one other trial official because you cannot be both judge and representative during the same course run. However, you could act as the representative during any course you're not judging. Approved APDT Rally judges and representatives can be found in the Trial Officials section of the APDT web site. They are listed by state. Current Rally judges and representatives want to see the sport grow, so you will undoubtedly find officials more than willing to assist you.

9. Submit a trial host application, which you can find on the APDT web site. First you have to determine the levels you wish to offer. This is usually quite simple—for your first trial, offer only Level 1. Why? If there haven't been any trials in your area, the likelihood of having enough Level 2 and 3 entries to make it economically feasible is low. Next, you need to determine the number of trials you wish to hold. Many hosts offer four trials in one weekend, two per day, so that exhibitors can earn a title within the weekend. However this may not be necessary for your first trial. Limiting your trial to two trials on one day will keep expenses low while still giving your exhibitors a chance to earn two legs toward their title! That means you'll be setting your next trial up for success when they have to come back for that final leg! Remember, the host application must be submitted four months in advance of your trial date(s), so plan accordingly.

10. Publicize, Publicize, Publicize! As soon as your trial application has been accepted, you've locked in a location, and your officials are in place, you should create your premium list (entry form) and start distributing it to all the area dog clubs and classes. A downloadable generic premium is located on the APDT web site. Post your trial information on every dog event e-mail list that will let you. Put up flyers

everywhere you can. If you build it, they will come, but you have to let them know where the building is!

11. Surround yourself with volunteers! Feed them, make them comfortable, return favors, even sign over your first born if you have to. Do whatever you need to do to get volunteers to help you. Your students will be a great resource. It's really amazing what people will do if you just ask, so ask! Chances are there are many others who want to see APDT trials held in your area just as much as you do. Seek them out and let them help you make it happen.

12. Other important details: Make sure you order your ribbons and rosettes at least four to six weeks before your trial. And make sure you order enough! You will need qualifying ribbons for every qualifying team in each level offered in each trial offered. You will also need 1st through 5th placement rosettes for the A Class in each level offered in each trial offered. Make sure you have enough equipment. Do you have enough of each sign? Do you have enough holders? Enough numbers? Enough cones? If you're running more than one ring at a time you'll need enough of everything for two full courses.

13. Halt, Breathe, Smile! And lastly, even though all this may seem overwhelming, remember the Rally motto! While the trial is going on, take a moment to pause and look at what you've helped create. Some of the proudest, brightest smiles you will ever see are on the faces of Rally teams who've just completed their title. And yes, I believe the dog is smiling too.

States with APDT Rally Trials

- Alaska
- Arizona
- California
- Illinois
- Indiana
- Maryland
- Massachusetts
- Michigan
- Minnesota

- New Jersey
- New York
- North Carolina
- Ohio
- Oregon
- Pennsylvania
- Virginia
- Wisconsin
- Canada

The Rally Relationship

Laurie Williams, May/June 2007

When you really think about it, and personally I hate to, our dogs are only with us for a short period of time. If we're lucky, we have them for 10-15 years, sometimes a little longer, sometimes a little less, and yet they leave such profound paw prints on our hearts. Their passage from puppydom to adulthood happens so quickly and one day we wake up to find a senior dog staring back at us. But there is so much we can and should do with them in between.

I look at Rally as a full circle dog sport. It's an activity that can be implemented in the beginning when first establishing a positive, healthy relationship, and teamwork with your dog; one that can be practiced throughout your training to reinforce the relationship, build trust, and confidence; and finally as an opportunity to rekindle that special spark between a handler and a seasoned dog. All one needs to do is look at the diverse group of APDT Rally teams making magic together.

At first glance, most would describe Fluke as your typical young Labrador Retriever: exuberant, happy-go-lucky, and ready to burst at the seams any minute! But it's likely they've never seen him in the Rally ring. Fluke's teammate, Tara Mickelson of Fredericksburg, VA, started the young dog in Rally training right after he graduated from puppy class. "I knew he was a dog I had to keep busy," says Tara. She enrolled him in a beginner's Rally class when he was just under six months of age and was pleased with the attention and focus he displayed. With a local Rally APDT sanctioned trial only a few months away, she decided to go for it. "I'd competed with my horses in equestrian events, so I thought Rally might be fun," says Tara. Fluke was a quick study, but just like many sharp puppies, he became bored just as quickly. Rally enabled Tara to give him feedback when he needed it the most. When he became distracted, rather than give him a correction, she made it fun for him to look back at her. "I really think this boosted his confidence and helped him learn that looking at me is better than looking anywhere else... well almost," she laughs. Fluke earned his Rally Level 1 title at 11 months of age and is currently finishing up his Level 1 championship. Tara adds, "We've definitely gotten the Rally bug."

Jenny is the first dog Ann Ford of Frederick, MD ever trained. Knowing what a challenge a Border Collie can be, Ann enrolled Jenny in an obedience class in 2001. Unfortunately the team didn't get off to a good start. The training class utilized aversive methods. "I did not want this for her or for us," says Ann. The training was very militaristic and both Ann and Jenny were frustrated and unhappy. "Jenny literally dragged me around the ring at class and there was no incentive, desire, or reason for her to want to be with me in that environment," Ann continues. For three years they labored with these methods until finally Ann found a trainer who used only dog-friendly methods and introduced her to positive reinforcement and clicker training. Shortly thereafter Ann attended an APDT Rally workshop conducted by Pam

Dennison and she immediately realized that she and Jenny had found their niche. The challenge and excitement of Rally helped her reactive dog remain focused. "It's amazing. Sometimes she misses a jump because she is so focused on me," Ann beams. Since beginning Rally in January 2005, the team has titled in all three levels and has earned their ARCHX. The teamwork and camaraderie they've built through their Rally experience has opened the door to other dog sports and activities such as traditional obedience, herding and musical freestyle. For Ann, their Rally experience can be summed up in one sentence: "I finally feel like Jenny and I are speaking the same language."

Terri Greer and her 12-year-old Shih Tzu Tara discovered Rally late in their training. Together the two had already earned both the AKC and UKC CD titles, were dabbling in Agility, but concerned about Tara's luxating patella, Terri decided it was time to retire. "I just didn't think the jump heights were safe for my little Tzu," Terri explains. She first became familiar with the sport of Rally at exhibitions conducted during AKC obedience trials. Then they discovered APDT Rally. "It was obvious that APDT really cares about the relationship between the dog and handler and the safety of the dog," says Terri. Knowing that she could lower Tara's jumps to protect her patella sealed the deal.

The team competed in their first APDT Rally trials in January 2005 and has never looked back. "Here was something fun, where I could talk to and encourage Tara, show her off, and wow, did she ever shine!" For Terri, Rally has been the perfect combination of Agility and Obedience, all the challenge and fun minus the safety issues. She adds, "Our Rally experience has bonded us even more than we were before. There's been no better way for us to spend time together doing something we both obviously love." As a result, Tara is the first Shih Tzu to attain both the ARCH and ARCHX titles and is the highest nationally ranked Shih Tzu in APDT Rally. When asked what the two would be doing if it weren't for Rally, her answer is clear. "We'd both be bored to tears!"

Another team dispelling the myth that you can't teach old dogs new tricks is Amy Grimm and her Pug, Dutch, of Berryville, VA. The two had competed in both Agility and Competitive Obedience for many years. "As Dutch got older I could see him shutting down in the obedience ring," says Amy. He earned one leg toward his CDX, but she could tell it was time to either retire or try something new. She decided to try Rally merely as a fun retirement activity and was delighted to see Dutch perk up again! "He seems to love coming to trials now and is so proud of himself in the ring," Amy adds. The allowance of food rewards in the ring excited both Amy and her food motivated dog. "That's really the icing on the cake," she adds.

The challenge of learning new APDT Rally exercises continues to strengthen their training bond. Like many households, the Grimms are a multi-dog family. Dutch's favorite thing in the world is going with Amy to train and leaving all the other dogs behind. "He just beams as if he's saying to the younger ones, 'ha, ha, I get mom all to myself,'" she laughs.

While discussing Rally relationships, there's another important one we can't leave out: the relationship between handlers and exhibitors. While APDT Rally is, by design, a competitive dog sport, many comment on a different feel than other dog sport venues. There is a camaraderie and overall team spirit in the air that can't be denied. "Everyone is so supportive, friendly, and kind ... exhibitors and judges alike," adds Terri. "Every trial we've been to is like going to a big family party."

Rally and party on! ❖

Pursuit of the Perfect ~~200~~ 210

Laurie Williams, September/October 2007

Okay, let's all just agree that the greatest thing about APDT Rally is that it's something fun to do with our dogs. But we should also agree that it's a competitive dog sport with rules, regulations and standards for performance by which you and your dog will be judged. You might still find some long time traditional obedience and/or agility competitors out there who look down on Rally as somewhat of a lesser sport. Some believe you can take a dog with relatively basic obedience skills and achieve a Rally title. While this may or may not be true, focusing on the minimum requirements is missing the point. All one needs to do is watch a beautifully in sync dog and handler team running a Rally course and the point becomes crystal clear. It is a beautiful display of sheer poetry in motion and something that takes training and preparedness. So while there's absolutely nothing wrong with entering a Rally trial simply to have a good time, striving to put your best foot and your dog's best paw forward shows a respect for the sport and all the hard work necessary to perform it well.

When a Rally team steps foot in the ring they start out with a score of 200. Based on their performance, the score can decrease when deductions are taken for incorrectly performed exercises. Maintaining that 200 score is not easy, but the most common deductions are avoidable.

Tight leads. Tight leads are the most common Rally deduction in Level 1. While perfect heeling is not essential, your dog's ability to walk on a loose lead alongside you is a key skill in this sport. Every time the leash gets tight you will receive a one point deduction. If it happens only infrequently, it's possible to qualify, however a consistently tight lead throughout a Rally course will earn a non-qualifying (NQ) score. One of the exercises I do in my beginning Rally courses is to have the team walk a course without any stationary exercises. As a class we count the number of times the lead gets tight. Hearing your classmates call out "One, two, three, four ..." and so on can be very eye opening.

Heeling faults. Depending on the length of and how you hold your leash, a good handler can manipulate it so it never becomes tight. But if your dog excessively lags, veers wide, forges ahead of you, bumps into you, or stops to sniff, you are susceptible to a one point heeling fault deduction. Again, although perfect heeling is not essential in Rally, it is a team sport of dog and handler working together. Therefore the dog should maintain an awareness of where the handler is and should always give the appearance of moving along with him or her on moving exercises.

Crooked/Poor sits. In addition to loose leash walking, straight sits are another key skill that greatly aids a team's performance in Rally. Crooked or poor sits that are substantially out of position can result in a one+ point deduction, depending on the severity. On any given Rally course, a team could be required to perform up to ten or more sits, so point deductions can add up quickly if not performed correctly.

While all the above offenses have solely to do with a dog's training, or lack thereof, there are many common deductions that can be attributed to errors made by the handler. Often, these errors are nothing more than honest mistakes that can happen to anyone, especially when nervous. Missing an exercise sign, misreading a sign and losing your way on a course are all pretty common, particularly with newer handlers. However, some errors can be attributed to a lack of preparedness, understanding, grasp, and knowledge of the rules and regulations.

There are two errors that clearly display a participant's lack of knowledge or complete disregard for the rules: physical or harsh verbal corrections and luring. APDT Rally is a dog-friendly sport, therefore aversive behavior is not tolerated. And luring, categorized as using food to guide or lead the dog into position, or pretending to have food in the hand in order to guide or lead the dog into position is also not allowed. Because these offenses are so clearly pointed out in the rules, there is absolutely no excuse for a handler to make these errors.

Failure to perform all the elements of an exercise properly, particularly when it is a key element of the exercise, can display a handler's lack of knowledge and preparedness. During the walk thru at a trial is not the time or place to learn how to perform an exercise. If there are exercise signs on a course that you've never seen before, it should be a red flag that you need more training. This happens often during move ups from one level to the next after you've achieved a title. Just because you can move up a level at a multi-trial event doesn't necessarily mean you should.

The ability to think quickly on one's feet is an essential handler attribute. Sometimes while on a course a handler has to quickly determine whether or not it would be beneficial to repeat an exercise that has received deductions or to leave things well enough alone.

Scenario #1

When performing Exercise #17—Call Front, Finish Right, the dog sits at a 90 degree angle on both the front and the finish. The handler repeats the exercise, and the dog has a perfect front and finish this time around. Was repeating the exercise a good handler decision?

The two poor sits would each result in a one point deduction for a total of two points off, but repeating the station results in a three point deduction. In this particular case, the handler's decision cost the team an additional point deduction.

Scenario #2

When performing Exercise #27—Halt, One, Two, Three Steps Forward, the dog sits immediately at the first halt, but the handler must give an additional cue for the dog to sit at each of the following three halts. The handler finishes the exercise and proceeds to the next one. Was this a good choice?

This one is tricky and ends up being a bit of a gamble. Each additional cue results in a three point deduction for a total of nine points off. On the one hand, if the handler had decided to repeat the exercise, the nine previous points off would be cleared, and the team would receive a three point deduction for the repeat. Provided the dog performed the exercise perfectly this time around, the handler could have saved her team six points. However, if after repeating the exercise the dog still needs additional cues, sits crookedly, gets out of position, etc., the team is at risk for non-qualifying. Deductions totaling ten points or more on any single exercise sign require the judge to score the entire performance as non-qualifying.

These are decisions that have to be made in an instant, but the more Rally ring experience a handler gains, the better equipped he becomes.

Ways to Improve Your Rally Ring Performance

Train and prepare your dog. Make sure you have properly trained him in the behaviors and exercises he will be required to perform. He is your teammate and is counting on you to set him up to succeed, not fail.

Become the best handler you can be. Practice, practice, practice. If you have access to a Rally class in your area, enroll! If there are no Rally classes, print out the signs and practice on your own. If you have access to the internet, join the Rally-O list on Yahoo. Learning from others' experiences in the ring can be just as helpful as learning from your own.

Know the rules and regulations. This is a non-negotiable. The APDT General Competition Rules consist of two to three pages. Learn those rules and know them like the back of your hand. Print them out and take them with you to each Rally trial and read through them again before you run.

And lastly, master the Bonus Exercises! At present, each level has three different optional bonus exercises that, when performed correctly, can add up to 10 points to a team's score. Provided the team does not commit an offense that results in an immediate excusal from the ring or a non-qualifying score (displaying aggression, eliminating, becoming ill, leaving the ring), attempting the bonus can only stand to improve their score. In other words, if you blow it, you gain nothing, but you also lose nothing. Simply put, mastering the bonus exercises is the easiest way to significantly bump up your team's score.

Earning a score of 170 or better will get you a Q. But show me a team with a 170 and I'll show you a team with a handler who knows he or she could have done better and vows to do so next time.

Happy Rallying! ❖

Frequently Asked Questions in APDT Rally

Laurie Williams, July/August 2007

When you're a new competitor, maneuvering around an APDT Rally course can be confusing, but working your way around the rules, regulations and particulars of the sport can be equally challenging. To address some of these issues, I've compiled a list of some of the most "frequently asked questions" I've encountered from many new (and even seasoned) competitors.

Double talk—What constitutes an "additional cue?"

This can best be described by viewing a few different scenarios.

Scenario one: You approach a station with Exercise #1—Halt Sit. You say "sit" to Sparky and he looks at you like he's never heard that word before and just stands there. You tell Sparky to "sit" again, and he finally does and you continue to the next station. That would be considered an additional cue and you would receive a three point deduction from your score.

Scenario two: You approach Exercise #1—Halt Sit. You say "sit" to Sparky and again, he just stands there. You then give Sparky a hand signal and he finally sits. That would also be considered an additional cue and you would receive the three point deduction.

Scenario three: At Exercise #1—Halt Sit, you say "sit" to Sparky, he doesn't, and then you look at him and say "ahem" or clear your throat loud enough for him to hear you. He finally sits. You would receive a three point deduction for an additional cue.

All three scenarios have one thing in common—the dog didn't comply with the first cue. If you cue your dog to perform an exercise or part of an exercise and he fails to do so, an additional cue is anything you say or do subsequently to get your dog to perform the behavior. Rally is the sport of communication so handlers should never be afraid to talk to and encourage their dogs. The additional cue rule is not an attempt to limit your communication, but rather is a valid gauge of your dog's attention, grasp of and willingness to perform an exercise.

To treat or not to treat—That is the question

The allowance of food rewards in APDT Rally distinguishes it from many other dog sports, but there are clear cut rules governing when and how the rewards can be delivered. Firstly, a food reward may only be given at the completion of a stationary exercise and before moving on to the next exercise station. (The same goes for touch rewards as well.) Further, food must be completely concealed in a pocket at all times. If the food is inside a baggy in your pocket, the baggy has to be completely tucked in. You cannot hold food in your hand at any time along the course or even give the appearance of holding it in your hand. This would be considered luring and will result in an NQ (non-qualifying score). You cannot have food in your mouth, and you will receive a three point deduction if it is dropped on the floor at any time. Most importantly, the food rewards are meant to enhance team performance, not impede it. Delivery should be smooth and not interrupt the flow of the course.

What's the difference between "A" and "B" Class?

The class you enter is determined by the dog in the team. The "A" classes are for dogs that have not yet earned a title in that particular level. Even if the handler has achieved that level title with a different dog, he/she would still enter the "A" class if the dog in question has not yet achieved that title. A team must achieve a qualifying score (170 and higher) three times under two different judges in order to receive a title in any level. Once the team earns a title, they may continue to compete in that level, but must move up to the "B" or "Championship" class. For example, a new Rally participant would start in Level 1-A. Once the dog qualifies for a Level 1 title, they can continue to compete in Level 1, but would move to the Level 1-B class, so that you would only be competing against other dogs with the Level 1 title.

What exercises can I repeat?

All exercises can be repeated, but there are a few elements of exercises that, if performed incorrectly, will result in an immediate NQ. Once you NQ, it cannot be erased or taken back no matter how many times you repeat the exercise. Following are some of the situations that require the judge to score an immediate NQ:

Jumps. Once a dog refuses, goes around, stops at, knocks off a bar, or uses the jump as an aid in going over, it results in an immediate NQ.

Stays. Once a dog breaks the stay in any of the walk around exercises or breaks the stay and advances toward you in any of the "Leave Dog" exercises, it results in an immediate NQ.

Cone Exercises. Once a dog and handler pass on opposite sides of a cone, it results in an immediate NQ.

Left About Turn (Level 2). Once a dog aborts the turn it results in an immediate NQ.

What kind of collar can my dog wear?

Prong and/or choke collars, "no-pull" harnesses, or head halters of any kind may not be used in APDT Rally. Flat buckle or snap collars, properly fitted limited slip or martingale style collars and standard body harnesses may be used. Tags can remain on the collar, but they must not interfere with the dog's motion. If your dog has a fancy collar with braiding, beading, bling or studs, or anything dangling, again, nothing must interfere with the dog's motion. To be safe, check with the trial rep or your judge before you enter the ring to make sure the collar is appropriate.

How to Perform "Married Signs"—Exercises that share a Halt

Sometimes judges will connect or "marry" exercises on a course that follow each other when the previous one ends in a stationary element and the next one begins with a stationary element. Judges marry signs solely for the team's benefit, not to trip you up. Each exercise may still be performed as a separate entity, and if you'd like to give a food reward, you can do so after you've completed the first exercise in a married set before going on to the next one.

What do I need to bring to a Rally trial?

Rally Trial Checklist:

- **Food/Treats (for your dog)**. Even if you don't intend to use food rewards on the course, make sure you bring some nourishment for your dog in between trials and runs.

- **Food/Treats (for you)**. Sometimes we forget about ourselves. Most trials run for at least three to four hours, so you need to keep your energy up in order to keep your dog motivated.

- **Water and Water Dish**. Even though there should be, don't depend on there being a readily available water source at the trial. You don't want to have to go hunting for the fountain.

- **Crate**. Remember your dog cannot accompany you on the walk through and cannot be left unattended, so you need somewhere safe to secure him. If you don't crate your dog, make sure you have someone available to hold onto him while you walk.

- **Extra Collar/Lead**. Always have a spare lead and collar "just in case" you misplace one or find out the collar/lead is inappropriate.

- **Comfortable Chair**. Even if the trial host provides seating, it tends to go quickly. Having a comfortable place to rest and regroup in between runs can be a great benefit.

- **Appropriate trial clothing**. This may seem like a no-brainer, but that cute outfit you have picked out for the trial may be missing an essential element if you intend to use food rewards along the course. Moreover, make sure the pockets are still intact! If you have dogs like mine who like to dig your pants out of the hamper and chew on the treat residue, you could find yourself doing a Hansel and Gretel along the course if your pockets have holes in them!

- **A Positive Attitude**. Inarguably this is the most important thing to bring with you to an APDT Rally trial. Sure, it is a competition and we do want to achieve good scores, but in the process we all need to remember why the sport was created in the first place: to promote a positive, dog-handler friendly experience for all participants.

Happy Rallying! ❖

Nature and Nurture of the Sheep Herding Dog

Eve Marschark, May/June 2005

What goes into training a skilled stockdog? Training a herding dog to work livestock may be a little different from what most people imagine. There are a number of myths regarding the education of a useful stock dog, ranging from the old-school philosophy of "let the older dog teach him" to incorporating our current technology to use "a clicker and train him the same way we do for everything else." This article will examine elements that go into developing a capable stockdog, including the ethological underpinnings, how training is begun, what reinforcers are used, basic target skills, and where to get help.

Herding breeds can be categorized according to how they handle livestock. Corgis and other "heelers" have a natural tendency to nip at heels to drive sheep away (thus making them good for cattle as most people don't like to be run over by a herd of half-ton animals). The German Shepherd Dog is an example of a tending breed used to keep large flocks of market-bound sheep off of roadways by running up and down a perimeter boundary. The present discussion is geared toward gathering types such as the Border Collie since it is the breed with which I am most familiar. But many of the basic points can be applied to other types of herding.

Fundamental Principles of Herding

Training of the herding dog involves modifying the *distance, placement, and speed* of the dog as he performs specific "instinctive" predatory motor patterns. Coppinger[1] lists this sequence of canine predatory motor patterns: "orient/eye/stalk/chase /grab-bite/kill/dissect/consume." The main behaviors we are modifying are the stalk and chase, with the grab-bite only performed when appropriate or when requested.

The herding paradigm offers us a unique opportunity to see where nature and nurture interface. Dogs bring a biological predisposition to display what we think of as "instinctive" behaviors, which we can influence through operant conditioning. "Instinctive" behaviors in the Border Collie include balance (the ability of a dog to place himself, relative to the sheep, such that the flock stays together and moving toward the handler), power (the ability of a dog to move livestock without biting as a first measure), eye (the intense stalk and stare), and biddability (a willingness to work with his handler). Our operant techniques allow us to develop tools (i.e., verbal and/or whistle cues) that modify, override, and re-direct these "instinctive" responses.

People train somewhere along the instinctive-operant continuum producing a dog that can either work independently or one that must have direction. Where exactly along the continuum each individual dog needs to be depends on a number of factors such as the natural ability levels of the dog or handler and the purpose or goal of the training program. The less-talented dog[3] and the more assertive dog both need more control.

If an owner wants to accomplish just a few simple, basic competition courses, then drilling for complete control may be the most efficient means of achieving this goal. A hill shepherd that must send his dog out of sight will need a dog that is proficient at making his own decisions if he is to succeed at bringing all of the sheep down from behind rocks and hilltops.

Training starts with the physical relations between dog, sheep, and human: Where a person stands will "elicit" predictable movement from the dog. (I use the term "elicit" because this is an "instinctive" response.) How a dog will move is based on what I call the centerline concept (see diagram), which is used to explain balance training.[2, 4, 5, 6 & 7]

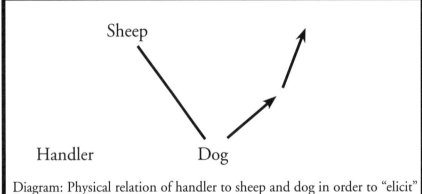

Diagram: Physical relation of handler to sheep and dog in order to "elicit" counter-clockwise movement in the dog to go around the sheep. Centerline is the solid line between the dog and sheep.

Imagine an invisible line that runs from the dog to the sheep and extends beyond. As these two points (sheep and dog) move, so does the centerline. If the handler stands to the dog's left shoulder (to the left of the centerline), this will "elicit" the dog to move away from the handler toward the right (counter-clockwise) around the sheep. We have set up this scenario so the dog moves away-to-me. Conversely, if we stand on the dog's right shoulder (off to the right of centerline), the dog will move in a clockwise direction around the sheep (come-bye). We do not use any command at this point, only our tone inflections are used to influence the dog's attitude. Cheerful, reassuring tones encourage contact with the sheep and low-growls discourage rough, close work as we walk about the field, changing directions and allowing the dog to practice his skills.

Access to sheep is the reinforcer. Research has demonstrated that access to sheep serves as a reinforcer to get a dog to stay a distance away from sheep, even when close-and-fast is what his passion tells him.[7] The same study showed that blocking a dog's access to sheep serves as a punisher for coming in too close. [Note: "blocking" is defined here as removing the dog's access to sheep and is not the learning theory definition.] Punishment or blocking is achieved by standing on the centerline, thereby "eliciting" a hesitation in the dog. At that very moment when we are on the centerline, the dog hesitates because he is in the process of deciding whether to go clockwise or counter-clockwise. This gives us a split-second to tell the dog we wish him to lie down or to get back away from the sheep. As you can imagine, this sounds pretty straight-forward on paper, but is sometimes difficult to execute with an eager pup! When the dog or sheep move just one hoof or paw, the centerline shifts and we are no longer in a position to stop the dog! What fun! But by carefully and consistently manipulating the environment so that the dog performs the task correctly we can reinforce and develop the desired behavior.

Many things can serve as primary reinforcers (i.e., food, play, contact with prey) and many things (i.e., clickers, voice markers) can function to help maintain behaviors. In traditional herding, the flanking command (come-bye) can serve as both a cue to perform the behavior and at the same time act as a reinforcer to maintain the behavior that came immediately before it. A good example is one that occurs frequently in herding training.

Dogs are often unwilling to stop for fear of losing their sheep. And, when one gives us a solid lie down, we run the risk of losing that terrific response if we do not reinforce the behavior. By sending him immediately back to make contact with the sheep again, we have reinforced that wonderful lie down.

Because events change so rapidly during herding, the "teachable moment" is extremely precise. Since the likelihood is that only one auditory stimulus can be perceived in such a moment3 (as the desired behavior is performed) I would rather mark it with a highly relevant and powerful secondary reinforcer (flank) than a less relevant stimulus such as a verbal "yes" or click. It is more likely that such a stimulus will be perceived and produce the desired effect (for a discussion of biological preparedness see Seligman, 1970 and Schwartz, 1974)[8, 9].

A flanking command can be a discriminative stimulus that signals the "opportunity for a reinforcer" is available if and when the correct flanking behavior is performed. It can also serve as the secondary reinforcer for the previously requested behavior (as when the dog is staying a good distance away from the sheep while moving in the requested direction). A repetition of the flank puts the dog in immediate contact with sheep, therefore I feel that this serves as a more appropriate and potent secondary reinforcer than other markers.

Basic Target Skills

Beginning target behaviors are: going around the sheep both clockwise (come-bye) and counter-clockwise (away-to-me), stopping (lie down), walking directly in to the sheep (walk-up), moving more slowly (take time, or time, or steady, or easy), and coming off of the sheep (that'll do).

Beginning target "instinctive" behaviors are: going in both directions and balancing properly, keeping a comfortable distance off of the sheep so as not to disturb them, and developing enough command or confidence (power) to move sheep in a controlled and calm manner. These should ultimately be performed without commands.

A key element to proper herding training is the dog's work ethic. I like a dog that is a thoughtful team player, not a loose cannon ready to explode. This is accomplished over many training sessions during which time he has become habituated to sheep and has developed a calm attitude for learning.

A dog must develop his own ability to "read" sheep and his education is a product of a number of factors. First, the more skilled his trainer, the more quickly he will move along in his training and he will make fewer mistakes. The more frequently he is able to work sheep, the sooner he can develop calmness.

He is a product of the sheep he works. Fast, flighty sheep do not allow a dog to learn in a calm, thought-enhancing environment. Heavy sheep that move too slowly or may turn to fight a dog do not allow him to gain confidence or develop balance. If a sheep butts him, his herding career may be ended forever.

Sheep that are used for training young dogs often become conditioned to always run directly to the person standing in the field. This type of sheep does not allow a dog to develop his balance or sheep sense and can ruin a talented dog's ability to "read" sheep, setting him up for a pattern of responding that has nothing to do with the management of a real farm flock (much to the surprise of the novice handler/owner).

Finally, he is a product of the other things he does in his life. If we want a dog to act calmly and thoughtfully on sheep, then we must teach him to conduct himself that way off of sheep. Dogs who participate in highly charged, "high-drive" activities like flyball often have difficulty transitioning to shepherding.

Summary

In this overview, we have taken a peek at the fundamentals of stockdog training. For specific techniques some suggested reading is listed. Even after reading all of the books and watching all of the videos, the best way to progress with your dog is to get out there and get your feet wet! The most efficient method is to work with an experienced and qualified trainer.

Finding someone who has trained their own dogs to a level that enables them to compete successfully in sheep dog trials is a good start. Auditing a stockdog clinic or friend's herding lesson will allow you to observe the trainer's techniques and philosophy. As with any training, you will want to make sure that the techniques used match your own goals and philosophy.

Regional and national herding organizations are good resources. The national organization that sanctions traditional sheep dog trials for the working Border Collie is the United States Border Collie Handlers Association, (www.usbcha.com). A regional organization near you should be listed on this Web site. The AKC also hosts herding venues that can be found through the AKC site (www.akc.org).

I wish you the best of luck as you learn how to ride sheep backwards and rise gracefully out of the mud with a smile on your face! Training a herding dog can be a delightful learning experience, but be careful. You may not be able to stop with just one dog! ❖

References and Suggested Reading

[1] Coppinger, R. & Coppinger, L. *Dogs: A New Understanding of Canine Origin, Behavior and Evolution.* New York: Scribner, 2001.

[2] Fogt, B. *Lessons from a Stock Dog.* Sidney, Ohio: The Working Border Collie, Inc., 1996.

[3] Goldstein, E.B. *Sensation and Perception.* Pacific Grove, CA: Brooks/Cole Publishing, 1999.

[4] Holland, V.S. *Herding Dogs: Progressive Training.* New York: Macmillan, 1994.

[5] Jones, H.G. & Collins, B.C. *A Way of Life: Sheepdog Training, Handling and Trialing.* Frome, Somerset; Butler & Tanner Ltd., 1987.

[6] Larson, J. E. *The Versatile Border Collie.* Loveland, CO: Alpine Blue Ribbon Books, 1999.

[7] Marschark, E.D. & Baenninger, R. "Modification of instinctive herding dog behavior using reinforcement and punishment." *Anthrozoos,* 15(1), 51-68, 2002.

[8] Schwartz, B. "On going back to nurture: A review of Seligman & Hager's biological boundaries of learning." *J Exp Anal Behav,* 21, 183-198, 1974.

[9] Seligman, M.E.P. "On the generality of the laws of learning." *Psychol Rev,* 77, 406-418, 1970.

Field Sports for Family Dogs:
They're Not Just for Hunters Anymore!

Jim Barry, September/October 2007

Among the American Kennel Club (AKC) breed groups, the Sporting Group is by far the most popular. In 2005, nearly a quarter of a million sporting breed dogs were registered, and this does not count the untold thousands of dogs not registered by their owners. In our training programs in southern New England, 30 percent of the dogs that participate are sporting breeds or sporting breed mixes; Labrador Retrievers and Lab mixes alone constitute more than 20 percent of the dogs in our classes.

These dogs are bred to hunt. They have been selected for generations to emphasize the ability to find, point, flush, and retrieve game. Even sporting dogs from show lines are likely to display these behaviors to a high degree; those from field lines can be completely consumed by them! At the same time as sporting dogs have been increasing in popularity, the number of people who hunt has been declining. Between 1991 and 2001 (the last year for which comprehensive figures are available) the number of hunters in the United States declined by nearly 10 percent.[1] And most hunters pursue big game, an activity in which dogs are rarely used. So the vast majority of sporting breed dogs will never have a chance to participate in the activity for which they were specifically bred.

Pleasures and Problems of Sporting Breeds

The popularity of sporting breeds is not surprising. They are companionable, enthusiastic, and highly trainable. They appeal to people who want an affectionate family pet, and have a reputation for being good with children. Because they were bred to work closely with their handlers, they are perceived as "loyal." The retrieving breeds in particular exhibit a propensity for tasks that involve working closely with a person, including service and guide work, drug and explosives detection, and search and rescue. They also excel at many canine sports, including agility, flyball, and competitive and Rally obedience.

On the other hand, behavior problems are common in these breeds. Most are large dogs, so that problems are magnified, especially in families with children. Perhaps the most frequent problem that we see as canine behavior consultants is a variation of what I call GLS or "Goofy Lab Syndrome." The symptoms of GLS are excessive exuberance, impolite greeting behavior, attention-seeking, and sock-stealing. Among the pointing and flushing breeds obsessive hunting, chasing, and excessive activity levels are typical problems. These are not necessarily dangerous behaviors, but they are annoying and can potentially lead to owner disappointment and sometimes to rehoming or even euthanasia.

Treating GLS and Other Challenges

When consulted about this array of problems, one of the things that we most often recommend is increased exercise. Regardless of the other management, training, or behavior modification suggestions we may make, greatly increasing physical and mental activity often has a profound effect on the dog's behavior. It also can give the family more pleasure as well. And what better way to increase the dog's activity level than through the task that it was bred to do—working in the field!

Admittedly, field sports are not an automatic fit for many families with sporting breeds. There are several reasons for this, but two stand out. First, most trainers who specialize in field work use methods that involve physical force and aversives.[2] Many families are uncomfortable using these techniques on their beloved pets. Second, most people equate field sports with hunting, and many do not hunt, nor wish to see animals killed just to give their dogs more exercise.

Fortunately, two recent developments are easing these concerns and providing more options for people to train their sporting dogs in a humane and enjoyable manner. In the past year, two new books have been published that advocate positive methods for field training. British trainer and author Helen Philips' book, *Clicker Gundog*, focuses on basic training with an emphasis on pointing and flushing breeds; Susan Smith, Mary Emmen, and I have recently published *Positive Gun Dogs: Clicker Training for Sporting Breeds*, which includes comprehensive sections on learning theory, obedience tasks, record keeping, retrieving, and upland hunting. Both books are available from Karen Pryor's Sunshine Books (www.clickertraining.com). There are also online discussion groups based on both books available through Yahoogroups: the "clicker_gundog," and "PositiveGunDogs" groups.

In addition, a new gundog club has recently formed in the United Kingdom that gives handlers an opportunity to earn awards for field work by using retrieving dummies rather than actual game. So families can now have the satisfaction of getting tangible recognition for their efforts, without actually having to hunt or experience shooting. Hopefully, these new options will motivate more owners to participate in field sports.

The Field Sports Spectrum

Field sports involve training dogs to perform actual or simulated hunting tasks, and then evaluating them against each other or against a prescribed standard. Gun dog tasks fall into roughly three sub-groups, depending on the breed's particular work in the field. Flushing dogs like spaniels search for birds within gunshot range from the hunter. When they locate a bird, they flush it into the air and then retrieve it when shot. Pointing breeds, including those with "pointer" in their name as well as setters and several other breeds, hunt and point game. In the United States, the practice is that the game is then flushed by the hunter; in other countries the dogs may flush on command. They must then retrieve on both land and water.

Retrievers, of course, retrieve! They are used mainly in hunting waterfowl and must bring back birds from long distances, over land and water, in icy conditions, and in difficult terrain. Many retrievers also are good upland hunters.

Some gun dogs are "versatile hunting breeds," defined by the North American Versatile Hunting Dog Association (NAVHDA) as "the dog that is bred and trained to dependably hunt and track game, to retrieve on both land and water, and to track wounded game on both land and water." They include the pointing breeds and the Weimaraner, Viszla, Brittany Spaniel, and Spinone. The three setter breeds—Gordon, English, and Irish—are also quite versatile, although not included in the NAVHDA registry.

The organized field sports reflect these groupings. At the top of the hierarchy are field trials under the auspices of the AKC. These are competitive affairs, with dog/handler teams surmounting increasingly difficult tasks until one is named the winner. A dog that achieves a series of victories is deemed a "Field Trial Champion." Field trial champions are highly desired for breeding programs and may command very large stud fees. Field trials tend to be dominated by a relatively small number of professional and dedicated amateur trainers. Some of these individuals have developed their own training programs, organized around field trial requirements. Most involve using electronic collars and other forceful tools to develop highly reliable performance under very demanding conditions. "Campaigning" a field trial dog is costly and involves much travel.

Another category of field sports is hunt tests. In hunt tests, the dogs are judged not against one another, but against a performance standard. Hunt tests are sponsored by the AKC as well as other organizations including the United Kennel Club, the North American Hunting Retriever Association, and NAVHDA. Most of these organizations award titles at three or four levels. In the AKC system, for example, the titles are Junior Hunter (JH), Senior Hunter (SH), and Master Hunter (MH). The standards increase in difficulty as the dog progresses. A JH retriever test involves two retrieves on land and two in the water at distances up to 100 yards, with distractions typical of an average hunting day. At the MH level, dogs may have to retrieve multiple birds, at distances of hundreds of yards, and in very difficult terrain. They also must find "blind retrieves," locating birds that they have not seen fall, following the directions of the handler. The progression of difficulty is similar for flushing, pointing, and versatile breed hunt tests.

Most of the national breed clubs for sporting dogs also award working certificates. These tests indicate that the dog has reached at least a minimal level of hunting ability. For example, the working certificate for a Golden Retriever requires the dog to make two "double retrieves' (picking up two birds in the order indicated by the handler) at distances of about 50 yards on land and in the water.

No Birds are Harmed in These Programs!

A common characteristic of field trials, hunt tests, and working certificates is that the dog is required to work with live, or "formerly live" birds. In most of these activities, birds are shot during the tests. This is a turn-off for many dog owners, and undoubtedly limits the participation of family dogs in these sports. There are, however, two programs that families can pursue that involve gun dog tasks, but without the guns.

We mentioned above the Gundog Club that has recently been organized in the UK. One of the objectives of the founder, Pippa Mattinson, was to provide options for non-hunters to participate in field activities. As she puts it, the club mission includes as a goal:

> To raise standards of skill and behaviour amongst working and pet gundogs. For every gundog fulfilling his potential in the field there are many who fail to do so. Every dog in the field deserves the chance to be a capable member of the team: every pet dog deserves the chance to experience the joys of field-work.[3]

Teamwork is the key to success in the field, and also to good behavior in the home. A teamwork approach is highly preferable to the adversarial relationship between dog and humans that too often accompanies behavioral challenges. Gun dog trainers use a collaborative strategy with their dogs, requiring them to perform tasks in order to earn real life rewards, including meals, affection, and continuing the hunt or retrieve. This Nothing in Life is Free (NILIF) approach is also very effective in behavior modification programs for family dogs. Moreover, the very behaviors that most owners want in their pets—calmness in distracting situations, walking politely alongside, and returning reliably when called—are the foundation of training for field dogs. To see good examples of teamwork in action, you and your clients can watch some of the hunting programs on outdoor TV networks, especially Dez Young's *Hunting with Hank and Dash* in the Uplands series. (Dez is notable for his ironic maxim, "Never spoil your bird dog!" Of course he treats and praises his dogs all the time.) Another interesting show is *Ducks Unlimited Waterdog*; although the training suggestions are not always positive, the relationship between Justin and Yella is a model of teamwork.

In pursuit of the goal of promoting teamwork, the Gundog Club has developed a six-level award system, with categories for retrievers, spaniels, and versatile dogs (which the British call HPRs, for hunter-pointer-retriever). The first three award levels can be achieved by working with retrieving dummies, rather than actual game. Another advantage of this system is that it begins with relatively simple tasks, and increases in small steps that most handlers can manage with due diligence. This makes the awards more accessible than in the AKC and other hunt tests, in which the "criteria jumps" are much greater. For example, in the Gundog Club program, a Beginner Retriever must:

- Heel on lead for 20 yards
- Sit on a single command
- Stay in position for two minutes with the handler 20 yards away
- Recall on command

- Retrieve two dummies at 25-30 yards

A Junior Retriever must:

- Work off lead during the test

- Heel for 30 yards and stay for three minutes

- Retrieve two dummies at 50 yards

- Find a dummy dropped surreptitiously by the handler at a short distance

- Recall and sit on a whistle command

This step up is much more manageable than the AKC retriever programs, where the increment between Junior and Senior levels requires the dog to master longer distances, blind retrieves, directional control from the handler, and steadiness throughout the test. Thus, the Gundog Club program is well suited for clicker training and other positive methods.. We have begun to organize weekend training programs that culminated in the beginner, junior, and intermediate tests, so the owners can proudly display their ribbons and certificates to mark their accomplishments.

Another way to work with a dog in the field is an individual activity that I dub "non-hunting." This can range from a very simple to a very elaborate sport. It essentially involves training a dog for, and then carrying out, hunting tasks without actually shooting anything. Sporting dogs can be trained to find, point, and retrieve dummies in the back yard. By investing in some equipment, such as dummy launchers or remote bird releasers, the handler can extend the distance and incorporate other tasks such as flushing and steadiness under simulated field conditions. The pinnacle of non-hunting is to don camouflage or upland hunting garb and take a dog into an area where it would be likely to encounter game. The handler can then encourage the dog to perform all of the tasks appropriate to its breed and the conditions, but using reinforcers other than actual prey. Pointers can hunt bird fields for pheasants, hold steady on point, and be rewarded with a treat or a retrieving dummy. Spaniels can flush a bird and chase a "happy bumper." Retrievers can hold their position in the blind, and then find a hidden dummy for a treat or toy. The handler can carry a gun or not, as best suits his or her style and values, and can load one with blanks, or "poppers" rather than shot. It may seem silly to hunters, but the experience of taking a sporting dog into the field or marsh at sunrise, and collaborating on a challenging task, is not to be missed. And the dog is very likely to be happier and better behaved as a result.

Getting Started

Helping owners to get started with field sports is much easier now that there are positive alternatives for training. The first steps are to work on basic obedience, especially heeling, stay with distractions, and recalls. Next, there are some specific gun dog skills that can easily be taught with a clicker or reward marker, by capturing, shaping, and luring.

Retrieving: It's easy to free-shape a retrieve by successive approximation, starting with looking at a dummy and proceeding in steps through targeting, touching with teeth, taking in the mouth, holding, moving forward, and bringing back. There are good methods in both of the books mentioned above, as well as in Morgan Spector's *Clicker Training for Obedience*, also available from Sunshine Books and on Shirley Chong's Web site, www.shirleychong.com.

Quartering (systematic hunting): Pointing and flushing dogs hunt in a zigzag pattern, and dogs can be trained to do this starting when they are quite young. The handler simply walks with the dog and changes direction, marking and rewarding the dog when it turns to follow. A whistle cue can then be added. After the dog learns the pattern, the handler can hide dummies, or even cheese, at the points where the dog should turn and it soon learns that moving in a zigzag is a rewarding activity.

Scent Games: Sporting dogs naturally hunt by ground or air scent, but this instinct can be sharpened and put on cue by training three tasks: scent matching, scent tracking, and scent discrimination. To start, impregnate an object like a napkin or a retrieving dummy with an intense scent. Bottled bird scents are available from gun dog supply shops. Let the dog sniff the original scent source and then coax it toward the impregnated object, rewarding a successful match. Then gradually increase the distance to the object and hide it in other areas, encouraging the dog to "hunt it up." You can then make a scent trail for the dog to follow, and place other scented items nearby, rewarding the dog when it finds the right one.

Pleasures Enhanced and Problems Resolved

Why bother with all of this training? There are two simple reasons. It's fun, and the teamwork that field sports require deepens the bond between dog and handler. And it's a great way to help resolve those knotty behavior problems that result from lack of exercise, boredom, and inappropriate attention. Try it—your clients, and especially their dogs, will love it!

Training Resources

Here are some suggested resources that can help you and your clients to get started in field sports:

Books. There are dozens of books on training gun dogs, but most are not oriented toward family dogs. The traditional books also recommend forceful methods that may not be comfortable for many pet owners. Two recent books, however, provide information on positive training alternatives. They are:

- Jim Barry, Mary Emmen and Susan Smith, *Positive Gun Dogs: Clicker Training for Sporting Breeds* (Sunshine Books: Waltham, PA, 2007)

- Helen Philips, *Clicker Gundogs* (E-book, Sunshine Books)

Both are available from Sunshine Books at www.clickertraining.com

Equipment. All you need to get started is a couple of training dummies and a whistle, available from many local sporting goods stores. For a more extensive (and expensive!) array of training supplies, try two excellent online suppliers:

- Gun Dog Supply: www.gundogsupply.com
- Dogs Afield: www.dogsafield.com

Tests and Trials: Information on American Kennel Club hunt tests and field trials is available at www.akc.org/events/index.cfm?nav_area=events. Other organizations also provide information on tests online:

- North American Hunting Retriever Association: www.nahranews.org/
- North American Versatile Hunting Dog Association: www.navhda.org/
- National Breed Clubs: www.akc.org/clubs/index.cfm?nav_area=clubs

Online Discussion Groups. Two traditional US discussion groups are:

- Retriever Training Forum: www.retrievertraining.net
- The Refuge: www.duckhunter.net/gundoglinks.html

Many forum members have extensive hunting, trial, and test experience. The methods discussed are primarily traditional, including force fetch and e-collar use. Two British discussion groups are more inclusive in their discussions, with many members open to using positive methods. They are:

- Gun Dog and Bird Dog Forum: www.less-stress.com/discuss2
- The Gundog Club Forum: www.thegundogclub.co.uk

There are two groups that focus on positive training for field sports. To join, go to http://www.yahoogroups.com, establish an account and follow the instructions to join a group. The groups are:

- Positive Gun Dogs: positivegundogs@yahoogroups.com
- Clicker Gundogs: clicker_gundogs@yahoogroups.com ❖

References

[1] United States Fish and Wildlife Service, 2001 *National Survey on Fishing, Hunting and Wildlife-Associated Recreation*, October 2002.

[2] Jim Barry, "Training the Hunter/Retriever: An Emerging Challenge for Positive Trainers," *The APDT Chronicle of the Dog*, September/October, 2004.

[3] http://thegundogclub.co.uk/missionstatement.htm

Breaking the Sound Barrier:
Training the Deaf Dog

Elisabeth Catalano, March/April 2007

When I tell people that the sweet little white dog they have been playing with is deaf, I always get the same response; a sad, troubled look and an "Oh, that's too bad." I always reply with a big grin, "It's OK, he doesn't know it!" And, he doesn't. Never having heard anything, as far as I know, he doesn't know what he's missing. His world is perfectly normal to him. Announcement of his deafness is often followed by astonishment, usually because he is so friendly and well behaved. "Is it hard to train him?" My answer is always an unqualified, "No!"

With some limitations, it is very possible to train a deaf dog. Trainers often fail to see the potential in these dogs—not to mention the benefit of skill development for themselves. The deaf dog can increase awareness of our own non-verbal communication. As trainers, and more importantly humans, we rely heavily on sound, so the deaf dog will force you to be more creative. Communication for dogs has always been far beyond sound; the deaf dog causes us to embrace that fact. There are some advantages in working with deaf dogs, too: no fear of loud noises, no getting distracted by barking, and no hearing the rustling of the food pouch!

Deaf dogs can and should be encouraged to attend regular obedience classes which use positive training lure/reward methods, because the hand signals used are largely the same. They can and do compete in the sports of obedience, Rally, and agility (with the exception of AKC events), and many are therapy dogs.

Studies on the prevalence of deafness in dogs are limited, but it is estimated that thousands of dogs are born deaf each year. Eighty different breeds are affected by deafness and that number is increasing. Additionally, dogs can and do lose their hearing as a result of illness, infection, trauma, or old age. Unfortunately, many deaf dogs are euthanized due to irrational myths and a lack of understanding. The Dalmatian Club of America has an official position calling for the euthanasia of deaf puppies.

Dogs that lose their hearing later on in their lives may have an adjustment period, but adapt well. All deaf dogs can lead normal, happy, and full lives that differ little from their hearing counterparts. They only require a little patience and a creative trainer willing to think outside the box.

The two most pervasive myths regarding deaf dogs are that they are brain damaged or are more prone to aggression. In the case of deaf Dalmatians, it was shown that the portion of the brain (the auditory cortex) that deals with auditory impulses was greatly reduced in size (Tindall, 1996). George M. Strain, PhD, however, writes in the same article: "The brain responds to the loss of a sensory modality by various forms of plasticity, whereby CNS structures that would have received input from that sensory modality constrict and adjacent structures expand to take advantage of the available space." According to Dr. Strain, "The findings in the Dalmatian are undoubtedly a reflection of the same pathology." He further summarized that "… these animals do not have diminished mental capacities, any more than the average deaf or blind human has diminished mental capacity." (Tindall, 1996)

There are simply no studies quantifying the prevalence of aggression in deaf dogs or demonstrating that aggression has a higher incidence than is generally observed in the canine population as a whole. There are however, numerous anecdotes to support both sides of the argument. As trainers, we acknowledge and accept the potential for "aggression" in the canine population as a whole. Therefore we can expect that deaf dogs will be no exception. It is unrealistic to expect that we would not encounter an aggressive deaf dog. However, claims that deaf dogs are more likely to be aggressive are unsupported.

The chief concern expressed by those who claim a higher incidence of aggression is that the deaf dog will startle easily and bite. Realistically, any startled dog can bite. While it may be easier to startle a deaf dog, good preventative training can minimize problems. Wake the deaf dog gently by blowing a gentle puff of air across his fur or lightly touching him. When he wakes, smile and call him to do something fun. Using high-value food will also make the transition to waking more pleasant, especially for dogs whose history is unknown. Traditional classical conditioning/desensitization exercises for touch can take the edge off the startle effect and even make it a welcome event.

Counseling

While training a deaf dog can be challenging and rewarding, you should be prepared to do a little work up front before you offer your services or welcome them into an obedience or puppy class. You may be counseling owners that have unexpectedly found they are living with a deaf dog and have no idea what to do.

Owners that have just discovered that the cute little puppy they are in love with is deaf are often disappointed and worried. They may feel overwhelmed by the prospect and the responsibility of training a deaf dog. Owners whose dogs have lost or are losing their hearing are sad and may worry about quality of life. You may be the deaf dog owners first, only, or last resource. The information you give them will determine that particular dogs' outcome. It is important that you provide them with accurate, effective information and lots of hope.

I remember how I felt the first time I realized that I would never see my puppy "light up" when I called his name. It is something that I had always enjoyed, but had taken for granted with my other dogs. Knowing I would never have that made me sad. One day, not long after Nevar joined us, I found him playing with the other dogs. I waved my arms high over my head to catch his attention, and there it was! The bright look, the perked ears! No hearing, but pure joy just the same. That is how it is with the deaf dog: the same, but different.

Things to Consider

Owning a deaf dog is not to be taken lightly. There are serious training and safety considerations that make it a huge commitment of time, energy, and patience. While some breeds come equipped with traits that make them easy to work with, other breeds possess traits that make them more independent and aloof. Deafness in these dogs can exacerbate training problems.

Many ordinary scenarios can pose a risk to the deaf dog. Enter my backyard on any given day when the dogs are out and I promise, they will know you are there long before you reach the gate. The deaf dog however, may be unaware of a visitor's arrival and be overlooked. Gates may be left open simply because no one knew the dog was even there. Signs advising visitors that "a deaf dog is in residence" and to "close all gates," are a must, as well as spring-closed gates, if possible.

Initially, the responsibility of keeping my puppy safe was overwhelming. If a leash came undone, or a car came too close, there was no way to call him out of harm's way. What if my attention was diverted? He could not hear approaching danger and react. Having a deaf dog means being diligently aware of what is going on around you and being prepared for possible dangers.

Supervision plays a key role in any early training, but it is particularly demanding with the deaf dog. You must be close to get his attention. Eh-eh won't work! You will have to go to him in order to redirect him to something else. After getting my pup's attention, I used a wag of my finger, a traditional "no-no" sign when I stopped the behavior and then moved him on to something else.

The need for early socialization cannot be overemphasized, especially for the deaf puppy. Initial interactions with other dogs must be supervised because growls, yelps, and other auditory warnings cannot be heard. Well-socialized and patient adult dogs can teach puppies to recognize the subtle visual cues (lip lift, hard stare, freezing) that occur prior to a correction. This experience will lay a good foundation for canine relationships later on.

Training

Being an avid clicker trainer, I worried (needlessly as it turned out) about not being able to use my favorite training tool. Thankfully, markers come in all shapes and sizes. I chose a "thumbs up" sign as a marker. For more rapid training, when a hand signal was too slow or cumbersome, I used a small "squeeze" flashlight on a key chain. Some sources suggest the use of lasers as markers. Due to the potential for retinal damage when looking directly at a laser, however, they are not recommended.

It is important to be thorough when establishing a secondary reinforcer or conditioned stimulus. Unlike the clicker, which is a distinct sound that is easily noticed, the dog needs to have a visual marker in his peripheral sight to detect it.

Teaching attention and rewarding check-ins is a pre-requisite for training. There are several ways to establish attention early on. A light tap-tap on the shoulder or flank should prompt the dog to turn; the behavior can then be marked and rewarded.

A tap-tap is preferred over a single touch because it is more intentional and won't be confused with an unintentional passing bump. This attention exercise serves a dual purpose—touch is good! At a distance, floor stomping, arm waving, or a shake of the leash will also work.

Non-Verbal Communication

Be creative, but practical when using visual cues and hand signals. Signs that can be made with one hand are faster and require less effort. Slightly exaggerated signals should be used for clarity so that they are obvious in the peripheral vision. Signals that use movement are easily distinguished. Of course, as training advances, the signals may be faded to a more refined system of communication. Because I planned to do agility, I taught Nevar hand targeting early in his training. I found it to be an indispensable way of communicating, whether it was moving him to a desired location or directing his attention to an approaching visitor.

Teaching bite inhibition to puppies can be a bit tricky since a yelp from another puppy or an "ouch!" from a human will do no good. I allowed Nevar to mouth me initially, but when the biting became uncomfortable I would abruptly withdraw all interaction and walk away. Consistency is the key for bite inhibition as well as all unwanted behavior! All the same training rules that apply to hearing dogs apply to deaf dogs as well.

Remote Communication

For working with the deaf dog at a distance, the best, and probably most elusive, training tool is a vibrating collar (V-collar). The collar vibrates when the handler presses the button on a remote. Traditionally used as a warning for the shock collar, the vibration offers a unique paging system that lets your dog know you are trying to get his attention.

It can be difficult to find a collar that has a vibration strong enough to catch the attention of a distracted dog and cover a practical working range. There are a few electronic shock collars available that offer a vibrating feature and cover ½ mile radius or more. Deactivating the shock to avoid accidents or mistakes is easy enough. Remove the contacts and expose the screws. The screws can then be covered with the rubber tips used for prong collars.

There are some limitations to the equipment though. Because of the size of the unit and the need to have it on tightly, it is not practical or comfortable to have it on for long periods. Smaller and lighter units, to accommodate smaller dogs, can be made using common items. Furry dogs may find it more difficult to detect the vibration and, if more than one handler is present, the dog may become confused as to who is "paging" him.

Some resources suggest using the V-collar as a marker, but I selected it for attention at a distance. I purchased a strong unit that would reach a ½-mile radius. I began Nevar's training by creating a very strong conditioned emotional response (CER) to the vibration. I paired the stimulation with fresh liver and steak that I had cooked with garlic. After a few training sessions, Nevar's ear would flick every time I pressed the button. Shortly after, his eyes began to drift toward my food pouch whenever I paged him!

I immediately began "calling" him (via page), when he wasn't looking and then gradually added mild distractions. We rapidly progressed to outdoor work and then eventually to out-of-sight recalls. His happy expression and his quick response were proof that the training worked properly.

Rule of thumb for most experts is deaf dogs should never be allowed off-leash. I believe that depends on the individual dog and the quality of training. There are many hearing dogs that never make it to off-leash status simply because they are unreliable. Again, deaf dogs are no different.

Conclusion

Recently I found the following quote, which has become one of my favorites:

For perhaps, if the truth were known, we are all a little blind, a little deaf, a little handicapped, a little lonely, a little less than perfect. And if we can learn to appreciate and utilize the dog's full potential, we will, together, make it in this life on earth. (author unknown)

Working with a deaf dog will stretch your skills as a trainer and test your flexibility and creativity. There is a unique bond to be enjoyed with these gentle creatures that wait to share their quiet world. Don't be afraid to move beyond the familiar—you will all be better because of it. ❖

Resources

- Deaf Dog Education Action Fund - www.deafdogs.org
- Deaf Puppies, Deaf Dogs - www.critterchat.net/deafpuppies1.htm
- Deafness in Cats and Dogs - www.lsu.edu/deafness/deaf.htm

References

Becker, S.C. *Living With a Deaf Dog.* Cincinnati, OH: S.C. Becker, www.deafdogs. org, 1997.

Lindsay, S.R. *Handbook of Applied Dog Behavior and Training, Volume One: Adaptation and Learning.* Ames, IA: Iowa State University Press, 2000.

Strain, G.M. "Deafness prevalence and pigmentation and gender associations in dog breeds at risk." *The Veterinary Journal,* 167, 23-32, 2004.

Tindall, B. "Aetiology, prevalence and diagnosis of deafness in dogs and cats." *British Veterinary Journal,* 152, 17-36, 1996.

Living with a Special Needs Dog
Merope Pavlides, May/June 2007

One of the most difficult moments in parenting is learning that one's child has a disability. For some parents, this knowledge comes in an instant—in a hospital or obstetrician's office. For others, it comes over time. Mom may start to notice small differences between her son and his playmates or dad may start to question why his little girl doesn't seem to be on the same developmental trajectory as her big sister. However the diagnosis comes, processing its meaning is a life-long endeavor.

For dog owners with special needs dogs—dogs with health and/or behavioral issues—a similar process may occur. There was a time when a dog that required special care or management would simply be euthanized. But the role of the dog in our society has changed. Many owners now view themselves as "pet parents," experiencing intense emotional responses to the events in the life of their canine companions. And because trainers and behavior consultants are often not called in until issues arise, it is prudent to understand and work with these emotions to best help both the client and the dog.

We've all heard of the five stages of grief articulated in 1969 by psychiatrist Elizabeth Kubler-Ross in her book, *On Death and Dying*: denial, anger, bargaining, depression, and acceptance. To a certain extent, parents of children with disabilities go through these same steps (Boushey, 2004). Similar emotions—on a lesser scale, but nevertheless meaningful—can be experienced by dog owners with special needs dogs. Although no literal death may occur, a perceptual death does. There is a death of the image of the typical child. The child who will play freely with friends, who will go out for sports, who will appear in the school play, and will one day jauntily set out toward independence. For dog owners, the loss is of the image of the dog who will joyfully accompany his people to the park, on vacations, or to soccer games; who will sleep blissfully in the family room, cuddled next to the kids; and who will welcome guests happily into the home. Increasingly, dog owners want their dogs to be integral participants in family activities. When this is not possible, there is indeed an emotional loss, and trainers would do well to recognize this as such.

Not only do parents of special needs children experience grief, they pass through numerous other emotions as well. Life with a special needs child is fraught with challenges and uncertainties. Parents may feel fear, guilt, confusion, powerlessness, and rejection (Smith, 2003). They may emotionally withdraw from or reject the child (Ziolko, 1991). For dog owners, this period of withdrawal may be the time when owners decide to euthanize or rehome their pet. As trainers, we need to acknowledge that rarely do clients make these choices lightly, and be wary of personalizing our responses. Conversely, should owners decide to seek treatment for their dog's challenges, we must understand the level of emotional commitment they are making to their pet, and guide them toward appropriate options. It is never helpful to curtly recommend euthanasia, even in the face of a dismal treatment outcome. Yet trainers and behavior consultants who work with reactive and aggressive dogs all too often hear that pet owners have been told to "just put the dog down!" If such a choice becomes the only safe and humane option, we serve clients best by acknowledging how difficult such a decision is, being supportive through the grieving process, and making abundantly clear that our role is not to pass judgment.

Fear

The type of fear experienced by parents of a child with special needs will depend on the specifics of the illness or disability. Parents may worry about the progression of the child's condition, possible complications, or potential accidents. For dog owners, the experience of fear may be two-pronged. On the one hand, they may be concerned that the dog's issues will worsen, possibly resulting in natural or assisted death. They may fear that their beloved companion will experience pain or stress that may be difficult to manage. On the other hand, dog owners may fear that their special needs dog will hurt someone else. Because dogs with illness, disability, or behavioral disorders can be so unpredictable, owners often feel as if they are constantly on guard when their dog is around anyone else.

Guilt

Although friends and family members don't always understand why a parent of a special needs child undergoes feelings of guilt, this emotion can be overwhelming and devastating. A mother may wonder if something she did during her pregnancy caused her child's illness or disability. Evidence may point to a genetic component, which in turn, fosters guilt. Or parents may blame themselves for choices they have made, either in health care or nurturing. Unless they are also the breeder, dog owners rarely feel responsible for congenital challenges. They may, however, experience guilt regarding their choice of breed or dog. Many certainly wonder if the dog's early experiences in the home created troubling consequences. Were injuries sustained through extreme activities? Were illnesses caused by diet or accidental ingestion of non-edibles? Were early social experiences with humans and other dogs either too limited, or detrimental?

In truth, it is possible that choices made on the part of dog owners have affected their dog's health or behavioral well being. However, for many special needs dogs—as for many special needs children—the origin of the condition is unknown or extremely complicated. Feelings of self-blame can hamper progress, and professionals must do their best to assuage these emotions, at the same time they help owners make whatever environmental changes will be most beneficial to their animal.

Confusion

Some illnesses and disabilities are immediately apparent, while others require lengthy diagnostic procedures. Parents are often confused about how to procure an accurate diagnosis, and sometimes, which diagnosis to believe. Once the nature of the illness or disability is ascertained, parents struggle with deciding how to proceed with intervention. Likewise, dog owners face a plethora of protocols for treatment. It is crucial to locate trustworthy professionals, doctors, consultants, or teachers who are able to offer advice based on best practices and an understanding of family dynamics. Advising clients through these times of confusion means putting aside ego, in favor of acknowledgement of treatment alternatives. Indeed, it may mean referring a client to another trainer or behavior consultant, veterinarian, or veterinary behaviorist. It certainly means helping dog owners locate and understand reliable information regarding their dog's condition. It may mean helping them understand data validity. It is crucial to provide information in a supportive manner, making sure to acknowledge the value of their questions and ideas.

Powerlessness

The underlying assumption of parenting is possession of a certain kind of power. Power to keep a child safe. Power to provide not only the essentials for survival, but emotional well being. Power to guide a child through moral choices. Illness or disability often strips parents of their sense of having control over their child's health, comfort, and future happiness. In the face of developmental or behavioral disorders, parents may feel especially helpless. Parents often think that no matter what choices they make, the child's condition does not seem to improve. Special needs dogs, especially those with reactivity or aggression issues, may exhibit symptoms or behaviors that seem to render their owners equally powerless. In spite of careful management and training, a dog may deliver a bite, continue to struggle with appropriate potty behavior, or quake in fear around strangers. Some dog owners seem to need permission from the trainer to develop leadership skills with their dogs, especially if they perceive the dog as physiologically or behaviorally challenged. Empowering owners means developing training protocols for special needs dogs with—not for—them. Being involved with the intervention plan will more likely motivate owners to carry through effectively.

Rejection

The families of children with illness and disability frequently note that one of the most emotionally difficult aspects of their journey is the stigma that surrounds the condition (Dudley, 2000). Not only do they feel rejected by "normal" society, but the child's abilities may be dramatically underestimated based on a diagnostic label as well. When a dog's social movements must be restricted, dog owners may experience rejection. They may not be welcome at dog parks, doggie daycares, or traditional training classes. Neighbors may cross the street when passing the special needs dog. While precautions are often mandatory for the safety of others or the dog, trainers must acknowledge that this sense of stigma may impact both the owners' relationship to the dog, and their willingness to seek help. They may, for instance, choose to avoid social situations, rather than habituating the dog to triggers. They may limit their own social interactions and thus develop resentment toward the dog. Validating these feelings and helping owners find successful venues in which to work can contribute greatly to owner and dog confidence.

As much as we adore our furry friends, they are not children. Parenting a special needs child can present an overwhelming challenge, one that is often met with the philosophy that progress is made "one day at a time." Owning a dog with health or behavioral issues does not compare in intensity to this experience. But it does present enough emotional similarities to extrapolate techniques from human service best practices, helping us provide clients with a truly supportive training experience. ❖

References

Dudley, J.R. "Confronting stigma within the services system." *Social Work*, 45(15), 2002.

Kubler-Ross, E. *On Death and Dying*. New York: Macmillian, 1969.

Smith, P.M. *You Are Not Alone: For Parents When They Learn Their Child has a Disability*. National Information Center for Children with Youth and Disabilities News Digest, 20(3), 2003. Online at www.nichcy.org.

Ziolko, M.E. "Counseling parents of children with disabilities: A review of the literature and implications for practice." *Jrnl Rehab*, 57(2), 2004.

Supporting the Peaceable Kingdom

Janet Velenovsky, September/October 2007

The APPMA (American Pet Products Manufacturers Association) reports there are 74 million pet dogs in American households. That's a lot of canine best friends! Guess what? The same source reports there are 90 million pet cats in America. Wow! Why is this important to dog trainers? Why are cats being discussed in *The APDT Chronicle of the Dog*?

Think about it this way. There are a lot of households where dogs and cats need to exist peaceably together. Those owners often have questions about avoiding conflict while meeting the needs of each pet. Therefore, it pays for each of us family dog trainers to know at least a little bit about dealing with "man's other best friend." If you are called upon to help with family pet training, ignoring this other population of pets would be similar to trying to deal with the dynamics of the family while ignoring the children or the spouse.

How many times have you been asked by a new puppy owner, "So, how do I keep him from chasing the cat?" or "How do I keep my puppy out of the cat's litter box?"

On the surface, both questions sound like dog management issues. True, each has a management component, but giving really good advice for the first question should include a healthy dose of information on getting the cat accustomed to the puppy's presence. After all, a cat that doesn't immediately run from the puppy is less likely to invite chasing. Keep in mind too that, if the chasing "harassment" is not controlled, there is a strong possibility that the stress on the cat could result in physical or behavioral problems.

Regarding the second question, positioning the litter box to keep the dog away, must not result in making it inhospitable to the cat or inappropriate elimination may occur. The dog trainer with some understanding of cat behavior is going to provide more complete solutions for their clients.

Introductions

As with so many things in life, planning ahead and getting started on the right foot can greatly reduce future problems. If you have the chance to help the owners make a good choice in pet selection—great! Then, help them prepare for the introduction by instilling impulse control exercises and basic obedience behaviors in the dog, followed by a structured, slow, careful introduction of the pets, relying heavily on classical conditioning through yummy treats and fun activities. Dog Appeasing Pheromone (DAP)™ and Feliway™ may be helpful through this process.

Many owners want to rush the introduction process. Spending a week or two to desensitize and counter-condition cat/dog interactions can seem to them like a slow process, but it is well worth the investment of time. In fact, it can take up to six months to normalize the relationships. Many owners expect that if the pets aren't "friends" in the first week that it will never happen. We can help by managing their expectations and normalizing a lot of the behavior of each species throughout the process.

If, as most often happens, you are called in to "fix" an introduction gone wrong, your job may be a bit harder. Imagine yourself in a situation where someone you don't know and didn't agree to share space with suddenly moves into your house. What might have had some chance of success under diplomatic and careful negotiation would be fraught with anger, anxiety, and fear.

Cat Behavior: The Basics

What basic cat behavior information should you know? The most often reported cat behavior problems include litter box issues, fear or territorial aggression directed toward other pets, redirected aggression toward humans, and destruction of property by marking or clawing. Many of these might be initiated or exacerbated by the introduction of new dogs or other pets into the household.

Cats are very territorial animals (Case, 2002; Beaver, 2003; Overall, 1997; Landsberg, Hunthausen, and Ackerman, 2003). They use scent to leave their messages around their living spaces to mark them as "owned." This might include facial rubbing and scratching, or may escalate to urine spraying and leaving feces as "markers," especially during the introduction of new pets. Obviously, spraying and feces on the floor are likely to be upsetting to the owners. Urination outside the litter box can result when a cat isn't comfortable getting to his "bathroom." It could also be part of generalized anxiety or might indicate a medical problem.

The rule of thumb is to always provide at least one litter box per cat, plus one. Because of a cat's territoriality, you do not want the boxes to be a scarce resource. The boxes should be easily accessible and convenient for the cat to use. It is important that cats feel they can comfortably enter and leave the litter area without danger of confrontation or attack (from dogs, other cats, or even kids!). Noisy or high-traffic areas may also be unsuitable for shy or timid cats, resulting in the cats finding more hospitable places to relieve themselves.

Studies by veterinary behaviorists have shown cats have a general preference for roomy litter boxes with one to three inches of a soft sandy or pebble type litter, with no lid to the box and no heavy perfumes to the litter (Nielson, 2001). Frequent, regular cleaning is essential. These studies recommend owners refrain from buying "whatever's on sale," as changing litter too often can result in avoidance of the litter box. Of course, "your mileage may vary," as not all cats have the same tastes. These are only guidelines; chronic litter box problems may require a consult with a veterinarian to rule out medical issues.

For multiple cat households, it may be wise to provide multiple feeding places, too. This helps timid cats who might not feel comfortable sidling up next to a more confident cat at one bowl at dinnertime.

Don't forget that the owners are an important resource to all the household pets too. While many of us love opening our homes to multiple pets, we need to be sure we can provide adequate attention for each animal.

Cats often "time-share" their favorite people and places. A cat that likes to languish in the morning sun in the kitchen may readily relinquish the spot to other cats or dogs later in the day. Though cats are not dependent upon social interaction generally for their survival, domestic cats often develop a social hierarchy (Beaver, 2003; Overall, 1997) with other cats or with dogs, though the relationships tend to be flexible depending upon context.

Cats are fond of using vertical space for retreating from stressful situations, surveying their worlds, and safe napping. Offering cats perches on bookshelves, window sills, balconies, tops of stairs with baby gates at the bottom, or "cat trees" (carpeted structures with multiple levels) can make use of normally unused space that will provide safe places for avoiding that pesky puppy until he can be trained not to chase.

If you have ever had the pleasure of taking the average housecat to a veterinary visit, you may be aware that cats can escalate from calm to terrified in no time. Once highly aroused, it can take hours for some cats to return to a calm state. This kind of arousal can also occur when an indoor cat observes an unfamiliar cat out a window, or is startled by loud or unusual noises. Redirected aggression toward humans or other animals often happens in this kind of situation. When the owner or another animal comes into contact with the aroused cat, it may lash out.

When a cat is overly aroused, it is best to give it time by itself to recover. As long as it is safe, it is best to allow the cat to hide under the bed or behind the furniture as it wishes. After some quiet time—if the initial stressor is gone or reduced—most cats will emerge. This might be a good time for some wand or "fishing pole" or string play. Play can be a great reliever of stress, but be sure to use something that keeps space between your skin and the cat's claws and teeth until you are sure the cat has calmed down.

Cat behavior specialists agree that most indoor housecats are under-socialized and could benefit greatly from enrichment opportunities in their environment (AAFP). In addition to lots of catnip, strings, and other available toys, they recommend finding ways to encourage kitties to work for their food, to train cats to target and do tricks, and even try clicker training for helping kitty accept handling, grooming, and other challenging interactions.

You may have heard about a movement to offer kitten socialization classes to take advantage of a cat's early learning period, which—at three to eight weeks—occurs much earlier than that for our canine companions. Kittens do continue learning social skills through 16 weeks, but much of their socialization to people may happen long before the owner adopts!

Kitten Kindy™ is a very successful early socialization class concept created by veterinary behaviorist Kirstie Seksel in Australia (www.fecava.org/files/ejcap/159.pdf). Many shelters, trainers and veterinarians here in the US are beginning to offer similar educational opportunities. Introducing cats to more novel experiences and a variety of situations early in life makes veterinary office visits, new pets, children, and other exhilarating experiences easier for the cat as an adult, just as it does for dogs.

Learning Resources

Learning about cat behavior can be just as interesting—and time-consuming—as dog behavior. One of my favorite books for understanding cats is *Roger Tabor's Cat Behavior: A Complete Guide to Understanding How Your Cat Works* (1998). Tabor takes time to not only discuss cat behavior, but details feline anatomy and describes how that affects or enhances the behavior.

Pamela Bennett-Johnson has written several wonderful books that not only help you understand cat behavior, but make for enjoyable reading, as well. Dr. Nicholas Dodman's book, *The Cat Who Cried for Help* (1997) is also a very entertaining and enlightening book.

You can find excellent references online, such as the Denver Dumb Friends League (www.ddfl.org), Pets For Life (www.petsforlife.org), the San Francisco SPCA (www.sfspca.org), and Animal Behavior Associates (www.animalbehaviorassociate.com.)

The American Association of Feline Practitioners (AAFP) offers a downloadable PDF document called Feline Behavior Guidelines on their Web site (www.aafponline.org). While directed toward the veterinary community, it contains valuable information in a clear and easy-to-read format. Including area chart of feline developmental periods, illustrations of body language, and a set of handouts you can share with clients.

The International Association of Animal Behavior Consultants (www.iaabc.org) has a division for cat behavior, and offers high-value educational opportunities with membership.

The Indoor Cat Initiative, www.vet.ohio-state.edu/indoorcat.htm, has some great information found about enrichment and cat behavior problems.

Kitten Kindy comes from Dr. Kersti Seksel's book Training Your Cat. An online source for information is www.fecava.org/files/ejcap/159.pdf.

Think about learning a new "language" to broaden your knowledge and become more valuable to your client owners. Studying cats and their interactions with canines offers great challenges and rewards. ❖

References

Case, L.P. *The Cat: It's Behavior, Nutrition and Health*. Ames, IA: Iowa State Press, 2002.

Beaver, B. *Feline Behavior, 2nd edition*. Philadelphia, PA: W.B. Saunders Company, 2003.

Overall, K.L. *Clinical Behavioral Medicine for Small Animals*. St. Louis, MO: Mosby, Inc., 1997.

Landsberg G., Hunthausen W., Ackerman L. *Handbook of Behavior Problems of the Dog and Cat, 2nd edition*. Philadelphia, PA: W.B. Saunders Company, 2003.

Neilson JC. "Pearl vs. clumping: litter preference in a population of shelter cats." *Abstracts from the American Veterinary Society of Animal Behavior*. Boston, 2001.

The Cat's Meow

Pat Miller, January/February 2006

Barney and Viva come running when we call. Ask Viva to "Sit up!" and she perches neatly on her haunches. Barney politely asks permission before jumping onto my lap, then lies down on cue. Toss a toy across the living room floor, and Viva eagerly fetches, and drops it at my feet.

Sounds like a pair of well-trained dogs, but in fact, Viva and Barney are our cats. Long maligned as "impossible to train," cats are easy to teach to offer behaviors on cue. They don't respond well to verbal or physical punishment, but along with the increased interest in positive training methods has come an increased awareness in training possibilities for cats.

This is no small thing. Ours is a profession whose members sometimes must get creative to find revenue to make ends meet. If you can claim a body of knowledge and experience with cats, you could add "Cat Trainer/Behavior Consultant" to your business card.

Cats respond to principles of behavior and learning, as do all animals. Common cat behavior problems include inappropriate urination and defecation, scratching, and biting/attacking. Most of your cat-owning clients will be more interested in behavior modification than training discrete behaviors, but if you can resolve cat behavior problems for owners and also get them interested in putting behaviors on cue, there's often no holding them back.

Litter Box Problems

A medical check-up is the first order of business. Urinary blockages and kidney disease are likely medical causes of litter box failure. The most common cause, however, is poor sanitation. Boxes should be cleaned a minimum of once daily, and owners should provide at least one more box than the number of cats. For a fastidious cat, boxes may also need to be washed when they are cleaned. Suggest the owner keep a couple of clean, filled boxes in a closet, so she can do a quick switch if she's in a hurry.

Proper substrate is also key to litter box success. Cats don't always like the tidy, perfumed, clumping litters that appeal to humans. Have the owner set out six different boxes with six different litters and see which one the cat prefers. Then switch to that kind of litter.

Litter box trauma is another frequent cause of feline house soiling. This could be a one-time incident, such as a pile of laundry falling on Felix while in excremento, or ongoing disturbances, such as another cat bullying him out of the box. Be sure the box is in a safe, disturbance-free, easily accessible location—and never punish a cat for an accident by tossing him in his box. Cats may need to be kept in separate parts of the house if one is tormenting another at the box.

Spraying is a separate challenge. Most often a territorial statement, spraying can occur if a new cat moves into the house, or even into the neighborhood. Neutering (of course!) can help, but not always solve, a spraying problem. Separating cats, blocking visual access to outdoor intruders, and hormone therapy (per a veterinarian), can be effective for sprayers. Sadly, rehoming the last-added cat often fails to un-pull the trigger; the sprayer may well continue to spray.

As with puppy housetraining accidents, diligent cleanup of soiled areas is mandatory.

Scratching

I find declawing abhorrent, especially done as a preventative, rather than a last resort for a dedicated clawer. There are many options for redirecting scratching—a natural cat behavior—to appropriate outlets. Try different types of scratching posts. Our cats' favorite is a redwood log scavenged from a Sonoma County beach almost 20 years ago. Woods, sisal, carpet, and cardboard are all inviting scratch surfaces; you can buy them—or make them. Some cats like vertical scratchers, some prefer horizontal, some like them on an angle. Set up several, sprinkle them with catnip to entice the wayward feline, and prevent access to previously-used inappropriate scratch surfaces until new scratching habits have formed. Pointy-side-out pieces of plastic carpet protector, or even double-sided tape, attached to sofa corners, can discourage cats from using that popular scratching spot.

Biting

Aggression in cats can be as varied as aggression in dogs, and too complex to address here. Suffice it to say that aggressing in response is rarely effective. As with dogs, violence can increase aggression in the receiver. Removing stressors, using counter-conditioning and desensitization, negative punishment, and redirecting aggressive play are good strategies for addressing feline aggression.

Teaching Behaviors

Cats can learn behaviors that are useful as well as behaviors that are just darn cute. They respond well to a clicker, or other reward marker, to enhance training. Even more than dogs, it's helpful to keep cat training sessions short; no more than five to ten minutes at a time, and you must use tiny bits of very high value rewards. In the useful category, try:

- **Kennel Up!** Use lots of positive classical association (good stuff in the kennel!) to overcome Felix's natural suspicion of this box trap. Then use treats and your clicker to teach the cat to "Kennel Up" on cue. Cat owners can understand the value of being able to corral their cats for trips to the vet, or in a disaster such as an earthquake or fire.

- **Walk on Leash**. You probably won't actually teach Felix to heel—rather he'll learn to accept a harness with you on the other end of the leash. A huge boon for owners of indoor cats who want to safely give kitty some fresh air and sunshine.

- **Come!** Useful, not just at dinnertime, but also during disasters, or if Felix goes missing. Simply pair the word with a click and an out-of-this-world yummy, and you'll get a reliable recall in no time.

Fun stuff

- **Sit Up**. Cats have such great balance; this one's a piece of cake. Lure, click, treat, and you've got it. Gradually fade the lure.

- **Touch**. Cats explore more with their paws than their mouths, so I teach feline "Touch" with a paw instead of a nose. Elicit a curious paw-pat to the tip of a wiggling pencil (i.e.: target stick), click, treat, and you're on your way. Get this one solid and you can use it for lots of other behaviors. Service cat, anyone?

- **Cat Agility**. Cue up the last clip on Karen Pryor's classic video, *Clicker Magic*. As you watch a talented cat negotiate the obstacles on a kitty-sized agility course, any lingering doubts you may have about training cats will be forever laid to rest.

Time to grab a cat, your clicker and treats, edit your business cards, and get practicing. Who knows—perhaps an APCT is next? ❖

ASSOCIATION of PET DOG TRAINERS

Working with Problem Behaviors

Unfortunately many owners do not seek out the services of a pet dog trainer until their dogs begin to exhibit problem behaviors. Sometimes basic good manners training will solve the problem, but in order to be consistently successful the trainer will need to be skilled in dealing with such issues as housetraining, aggression, resource guarding, separation anxiety, even "sibling" rivalry within multi-dog households. The demand to solve such problems is such that some trainers even specialize in solving one or more of these problem behaviors. Learn how trainers who focus on these issues deal with these problems in the following articles including several case studies.

Shape for Confidence

Terry Long, March/April 2006

This is the story of Kippy, a female Coton de Tulear, and her journey from wall-flower to center-stage trickster. It is also the story of how clicker-based shaping can be used to help dogs overcome their fears and why this hands-off training technique is especially suited for working with extremely shy dogs.

A frequent criticism from some people is that clicker trainers never touch their dogs. It is not my intent here to dispute that myth; rather, by sharing my experience with Kippy, I hope to demonstrate how a hands-off training technique that relies upon shaping can be very apropos in cases where touching the dog would be aversive and, as a result, delay training progress.

In Kippy's case, my training partner, Nikki Myers, CPDT, and I chose not to spend time desensitizing and counter-conditioning Kippy to a trainer's proximity and touch before beginning training. Instead, we used shaping to begin training immediately. We knew Kippy would benefit from classical conditioning taking place during the normal course of our training sessions simply by the pairing of treats with the presence of the trainers.

History

When we first met her, Kippy was 18 months of age. She attended doggy daycare several days a week along with her eight-month-old Coton housemate Kosmo. We met at the Long Beach-based doggy daycare, The Pet Set, where Nikki and I were invited by the owners of the facility to run a doggy day school program. The program is designed to teach basic manners to enrollees while their owners are at work. Kippy's owner, Lynne Craig, ran a busy catering business and wanted to enroll both dogs in the day school program.

During my interview with Lynne, I found that she had purchased Kippy from a rural East Coast breeder and had her shipped cross-country to her new home in megalopolis Southern California at the age of 12 weeks. Kippy had a history from the beginning of being shy with new people, places, and things. Kosmo had been purchased locally and brought home at ten weeks of age and had always been outgoing and feisty.

Lynne's goals for Kippy and Kosmo were walking on a leash (they had never been leash trained), and tricks. "Yes, tricks," she said, "I want them to have fun." Only my professionalism kept me from leaping out of my chair, kissing my new client and dancing her across the daycare lobby using clickers as my castanets. After many years of clients telling me "I don't want any silly tricks, I just want my dog to behave," I was ecstatic. I am a firm believer that teaching tricks is one of the best ways for dogs to learn to offer behaviors from which the trainer can select.

When the daycare staff brought Kippy and Kosmo to the lobby after the interview, Lynne grabbed Kippy into her arms for hugs and smooches while Kosmo danced around the lobby, running up to everyone there, outgoing and quite the social butterfly. Both dogs were absolutely irresistible and would soon have a variety of nicknames, including "the white fluff balls," "K&K," and "the Daring Duo." I couldn't wait to get started with the training.

Benched

Lynne had chosen 30-minute training sessions three times a week. We would split the half-hour between the two dogs. When I arrived for the first training session, I retrieved the container of pre-cut Dick Van Patten Natural Balance™, as well as the dogs' harnesses and leashes that Lynne had left per my instructions, while the daycare staff brought Kosmo to the lobby. He took to the training like a fish to water, quickly learning that his behavior is what elicited the click and then the treat.

Kippy, on the other hand, ran away from me if I didn't have her on a leash and submissively urinated when I picked her up. The problem was that since she had never really been on a leash before, a leash was aversive to her and made her panic. I decided to let Kippy sit nearby on a large high-backed bench while I worked with Kosmo. Several times during each training session with Kosmo, I would briefly go over to Kippy and give her treats, which she loved. After one or two sessions of eating treats, I sat on the edge of the bench and offered my finger for inspection. She tentatively leaned forward, and I verbally marked ("Yes!") and rewarded. (We don't use a clicker in the early stages of training fearful dogs. We have found many of them have a heightened startle response and are afraid of the clicker, possibly transferring their fear of the new person to this novel sound, as well.)

After two weeks, Kippy was still on the bench. Although she was comfortable with finger targeting, she was still avoiding me if I leaned toward her, and she still urinated when I picked her up. Meanwhile, Kosmo had learned to sit, down, walk nicely on a leash, and spin on cue. He was his momma's shining star. Lynne had adjusted her expectations of Kippy, assuming we would be lucky to get Kippy acclimated to a leash, if anything.

Floored

One day, I set Kippy on the floor next to Kosmo, hoping that she would now be comfortable enough with me not to run away, and that I would get some benefit from social facilitation. That is, if her housemate was getting all those treats, how was he doing it?

It worked! She was able to finger target on the floor even though she would still avoid any movement initiated toward her. I decided to simply click anything that she did. This included backing away from me, looking up at me, jumping on her hind legs to try and grab Kosmo's cookie, and barking. She soon knew that she could do just about anything to get clicked. She soon became very creative in her efforts to get clicked.

Each session now started with both dogs working together, and then I would put Kippy back on her bench so that I could concentrate on Kosmo. One day, after putting Kippy on her bench, I returned to work with Kosmo only to find that Kippy had jumped off the bench to join in the fun, pushing her way in front of Kosmo for the treats. This was a huge milestone!!!! From that day, Kippy would not be left out of the training game. If you put her on the bench, quick as a bunny she'd hop down and prance around, vying for attention.

After that, we were able to split the half-hour training session between the two dogs, Kippy now perfectly happy to work one on one without Kosmo there. I also had Nikki start working with both dogs. Kippy quickly learned that she could "operate" Nikki as well.

Shaping for Bravery

Kippy was a veritable gold mine of behaviors. She was a clicker trainer's dream: lots of behaviors, one after the other, just waiting to be split apart, chained, and put on cue. She would jump, hop, toss her head, spin, bark, and bow—all within a second or two. Although we couldn't resist shaping a variety of tricks (see "Kippy's Repertoire" below), there were three behaviors that helped Kippy the most: 1) back up; 2) relaxed down; and 3) check it.

Back up. Kippy frequently backed away from people since she was not comfortable being closer than about three feet. We decided to change that from a learned avoidance behavior to one positively reinforced and put on cue. We simply clicked as soon as she twitched a muscle backing up. When she realized that backing up was a bankable behavior, her backup soon came with a gleam in the eye instead of her previous wary look. Along the way, we captured a very cute head toss. Now, instead of trying to shrink into the background, Kippy seemed to be saying, "Hey, look at me do this!" It became one of her most frequently offered behaviors that delighted the people she would be entertaining in the future.

Relaxed down. Kippy appeared happy offering behaviors, but if we stopped training to make notes or talk to someone, she became nervous and didn't know what to do. She would stand or warily wander around, still staying out of reach. We needed to teach her an incompatible behavior, and one that would help her relax. Down was the obvious choice, but she never offered a down, and she was still nervous about someone getting too close to her, so luring wasn't an option. Nikki successfully elicited this behavior one day by sitting on the floor, her back against a wall, with legs straight out in front of her. She took slow, deep breaths, exhaling fully and slowly, relaxing all of her own muscles. After a few minutes, Kippy lay down. Click, treat! An interesting side effect of this method of capturing a down was that Kippy would down only if you sat on the floor and exhaled. We joked that the cue would be exhalation alone once we desensitized her to our body position. (Later, we did successfully add both a verbal and a hand signal.)

Check it. One of the most helpful cues we taught Kippy was "Check it!," a cue I teach dogs who are fearful of new objects in the environment. It is taught using basic target training, i.e., touching a nose to something. We introduced a target stick, holding it in our hand. Not surprisingly, she was afraid of it. We placed it on the floor, and gradually shaped the behavior, first clicking for anything other than looking away from it, until she would glance at it, look at it, sniff toward it, take a step closer, etc., until she was touching her nose to it. We then added the cue ("Check it!"). Next, we introduced new objects such as picture frames on the floor (what's that doing there?!?), trashcans, grooming tools, hoola hoops, etc. Later, when we noticed that she was afraid of something, we simply cued "Check it!" and she immediately would try and overcome her fear of the item, stepping closer and closer to it, eventually investigating it. The combination of classical and operant conditioning used in the training process transferred nicely to new scary things with this cue.

Moving Challenges

The most difficult behaviors for Kippy were those that involved moving objects. One of the daycare staff's favorite tricks was "Let us pray!" performed by my dog, Kiwi. It involves teaching the dog to put his paws up on an object and then tucking his chin between his paws. I really wanted to teach it to Kippy and Kosmo since I knew it would be so cute if they could do it together. Kosmo learned it quickly, while Kippy was always concerned that the little stool we used would move. Any inadvertent movement could set us back days in training time. Our "Check It" cue helped accelerate past some of these bumps in the training plan, but extra care was always given to making sure the stool didn't move when she got brave enough to place a paw on it.

And in some cases, the environment itself was a challenge. For example, if she was just getting bold enough to touch her nose to a new object, and someone slammed a door, she would startle and jump away as if the object burned her. However, improved bounce-back was part of our goal with Kippy. That is, could we, over time, give her enough practice in overcoming these fears and setbacks that her ability to "bounce back" from startling events became better and better. In some cases, this worked and in others, it didn't. If she had a longer history of interaction with an object before that door slammed, she would bounce back more quickly. If not, it could take several additional training sessions to get back to where we had started when the startling event occurred. Overall, we were pleased with her steady progress in this area. In those early wallflower days, she would "shut down," and we would have to end her training session for the day. That rarely happened as we progressed with her training.

A Star is Shaped

Several weeks after Kippy gave up her wallflower status on the bench, we had to move our training to a small area away from the lobby … we simply were drawing too much attention. We couldn't go more than a few minutes without someone coming over to ask how we were doing what we were doing or simply exclaiming about the Daring Duo's feats.

Lynne was thrilled with both her dogs' progress, but Nikki and I have always been most pleased with Kippy's transformation. We know how difficult it is for dogs to overcome fears and what a rare opportunity we were given to play a role in helping Kippy become more confident and outgoing.

After about six months of training, Kippy and Kosmo were coming along quite well. Kippy's overall confidence level with new people had improved, and her owner was delighted.

Kippy's performance debut came at the Daring Duo's joint birthday party where Kippy—in a lobby jammed with daycare staff and Lynne's friends and family—executed synchronized spins with her brother. Her hip-hop back up—complete with her trademark sassy head toss and gleam in her eye—said it all. Wallflower no more. Center Stage for Miss Kippy. ❖

Kippy's Repertoire

- Sit

- Down

- Close (walk on a leash)

- Check it

- Say Please (bark on cue)

- Chin (place chin on the floor)

- Hoop (jump through the hoola-hoop)

- Come

- Here (touch nose to hand)

- Scoot (scoot backwards, butt in air)

- Let Us Pray

- Settle (on a mat)

- Score! (fling a foam ball through the air, up and over her shoulder)

- Hip Hop (back up)

- Wait

Winner, 2006 Dog Writers Association of America Writing Competition: Best Feature in Canine Newspaper or Newsletter: Other Topics

Aggression: The First Act

Pamela S. Dennison, March/April 2006

In the July/August 2005 issue of *The APDT Chronicle of the Dog*, I talked about the core behaviors needed before setting up systematic desensitization sessions. I am a big proponent of teaching a dog what to do instead—in this case, instead of aggressing. If your dog is busy doing fun stuff and interacting with you, they will be less likely to aggress at their provoking stimuli (a.k.a., the scary bad thing).

Once you have defined each and every one of your dog's triggers, you are ready to start designing your sessions. I know this is a very hard thing to learn how to do, since very often one must go by "feel." I define "feel" as learning to read your dog's body language instantly and accurately (or as much as we humans can accurately read a language to which there is no perfect interpreter), knowing how to break each issue down into the smallest of approximations imaginable, and how to see progress in each one of those steps. "Feel" is further classified as knowing when to start a session, end a session, how many minutes each session should be, as well as what each session should encompass.

This article is a case study of one of the more difficult cases (as in a dog with many issues) I have worked with. You will be able to see how we defined each of the dog's problem areas, taught the behaviors needed to work with her, and how we planned sessions to go with her issues. I have listed the steps we have taken so far and then added my commentary where I felt an explanation was in order.

Name: Moni

Breed: Beagle

Sex: Spayed bitch

Age: Approximately four years old, rescued at about two years of age from a shelter.

Owners: Kathy and Ellen

History: Moni had a history of attacking Ellen on a continuing basis. Just her presence alone would cause Moni to attack Ellen. She could not interact with Moni at all—she couldn't put her leash on or take it off, touch her, walk by her crate, or be in the same room with her. Moni would go out of her way to attack Ellen and on one occasion "treed" Ellen on the kitchen counter and wouldn't let her down. Moni had attacked Ellen numerous times, drawing blood from puncture wounds (biting and re-biting numerous times), leaving quite a few scars but no wounds requiring stitches. Moni also sporadically attacked their other four dogs and seven household cats plus a varying number of foster cats. She had a tendency to guard objects—bones and food. If any one of the other animals walked by anything that Moni perceived was hers, she would go into an aggressive display. All of the other animals in the household are very dog savvy and she never did any damage to them. Moni was particularly sensitive to feet and hands—moving or not moving. She would also give no warning growl that she was going to attack. Strangers also got the same response from Moni. She would attack anyone other than Kathy. They lived like this for a year before coming to me for help.

How We Started:

Setting everyone up to succeed. The first thing we needed to do was to have Ellen be able to safely interact with Moni. Kathy and Ellen drove to my place in separate cars to avoid having Moni attack Ellen in the car. For the first few sessions, Kathy would bring Moni in the building with Ellen following at a safe distance.

To start the training sessions, we had Moni tethered to the wall so Ellen (and I) could stay out of leash range and remain safe and calm. The one real benefit we had to start the process was that Moni is a real chow-hound (pig would be more accurate). We moved very slowly, always within Moni's and Ellen's threshold, for at this point, Ellen was terrified of Moni.

Beginning to teach basic core behaviors (bridge response, name response, come, sit). In the first session, we taught Moni what the clicker meant, eye contact, name, come (all stationary behaviors—I train the recall as a non-moving exercise to start), and sit. Ellen was too afraid to try the down since that entailed leaning over. Ellen practiced these behaviors at home, along with more stringent management, making sure that Moni had no chance to attack her anymore. Kathy crated Moni when she left for work, so if Ellen came home before Kathy did, she didn't have to worry about being bit. By the second session, Ellen felt somewhat more hopeful. Kathy and Ellen still drove in separate cars for an added safety measure. We reviewed the lessons learned and added in some new ones.

Continue training basic core behaviors. Ellen felt confident enough (she actually admitted later that she was scared to death) to sit in a chair and work on eye contact and name recognition, dropping the food on the ground at her feet for Moni. She was very careful to keep them still, so as not to incite Moni to aggress at her. After a minute or two of the "closeness," both Moni and Ellen started to get nervous, (Ellen told me she was nervous and I could tell she had stopped breathing and Moni's body stiffened slightly) so I had Ellen throw the food away from her instead of at her feet. This way, Moni would be moving away from her and they both could get some breathing room. In addition, I had Ellen sing. (If you are singing, you are breathing.) I was very cognizant of both Ellen's and Moni's comfort level, changing the context slightly before Moni reacted.

We also worked on the recall; Ellen threw a treat across the room and Moni raced to get it. As Moni ran back to her, Ellen said "come" and dropped some treats on the ground for her. They repeated this numerous times and about 30 minutes into the session, I decided that a nice walk in the field next door was in order. Kathy held the leash while we walked next to her (Ellen and I stayed out of leash range). Being a Beagle, the smells were heaven on earth for her and gave everyone a chance to relax. We worked on the more active recall, to not only teach Moni what "come" meant, but also to pair food with going right up to Ellen. Ellen also gained some confidence here as well—Moni was coming to her and waiting patiently for treats, rather than trying to take a hunk out of her leg. Even though Moni was doing great, I was sensing some anxiety on Ellen's part. Ellen had a long history of being terrorized by this dog. Rather than prolong the session, possibly having Ellen's fear create an aggressive response from Moni (setting them both up to fail), I decided to take a break from the "formal" training session to relieve some of the tension buildup.

I continued in this vein for a few weeks—reviewing what Moni already learned in the previous week and slowly, carefully adding in new behaviors. We were eventually able to have Ellen wiggle her feet while feeding Moni, with no reaction—remember, one of Moni's issues was moving feet. I never pushed Ellen or Moni at any time. We found that Moni is completely and utterly brilliant and learns new behaviors very quickly. She was starting to pair all of this fun stuff with Ellen's presence and started to display a softer body posture and was very attentive. Dare I say "happy?" We continued to work on hand feeding, sit, down, come and stay, with lots of calming walks in between. I saw that Moni made more progress when we took breaks for walking and sniffing. (Thank you Turid Rugaas!)

I continue to learn something new from each dog I work with and now add these little breaks into every training session—even if the dog doesn't have any issues. When I first meet a new human aggressive dog, we don't start out by "training." We start by taking a nice long walk together, pairing me with tons of good smells, in a wide open space. This then sets the stage—the dog is comfortable with me and I can safely judge his or her threshold. I always err on the side of caution and try to stay within the dog's comfort level, continually watching for signs of stress. Once we are relaxed with each other, then we go inside my building and start training the core behaviors. Starting a new student like this has the added benefit of relaxing the owner as well, so everyone is practicing calm behaviors from the very beginning.

Around the six-week mark, Kathy and Ellen started coming in the same car with only a few growls from Moni. (This is good—in the past, Moni would just bite without the warning. Now she was warning with no biting.) There were still a few sporadic posturings toward Ellen, but the intensity and duration were greatly reduced and no more blood was shed. Ellen was now feeling more comfortable and started touching Moni very lightly for a few seconds, while she was feeding. We also taught her to "go to your bed," "directionals," (moving in the direction that Ellen was pointing) and a drop on recall. We added these advanced behaviors as an added safety measure—this way, if Moni was charging Ellen, Ellen would be able to literally redirect Moni to either her bed, another part of the room or drop her instantly. A week or so later,

Ellen was able to utilize these behaviors for the first time in a real life setting and Moni complied instantly.

From Ellen's diary:

Kathy had to go away for the weekend for a family obligation and I needed to care for Moni on my own. This included feeding and being able to take the leash on and off to let her outside and I was really scared. At this point I was still really nervous and one time Moni charged me from across the room and pinned me on top of the counter. I tried to remain calm and luckily had been working with her and had some hot dogs on the counter. You taught me to visually get her in her bed. Look at the bed meant go to the bed and lie down. I was able to do this—even though the bed was 15 feet away. (At that point Moni did not know the verbal cue.) I gave her a jack-pot and told her how good she was and got down off the counter and she was fine. I did have some challenges with putting her leash on and I tried several times and she would growl and I walked away. At about 12 AM she was crying so bad I had a talk with her and told her that she had to trust me to put her leash on. I sang and I was able to let her out and in. Miracle!!!!!

I have subsequently added the drop on recall (which can also become a "drop if you are charging someone") and directionals into my basic core behaviors.

At this point we all agreed that Moni needed more than the required minimum of six privates before moving onto the aggressive dog class. While Moni had mastered eye contact, name and come response, sit, down, stay, door etiquette, drop on recall, directionals and "go to your bed," Ellen still wasn't completely comfortable working with Moni.

During the next set of lessons, Ellen was confident enough to bring Moni to her appointment without Kathy. She had to gear herself up for this—for driving alone with "Ms. Cujo," as well as for picking up the leash. We always worked Moni with the leash dragging so Ellen wouldn't have to put it on her. She did however, have to pick it up off the floor and for this we ended up using a lot of food thrown on the ground and picking up the leash as Moni was eating. This didn't completely negate any aggressive response from Moni—especially if Ellen stopped breathing, but it did lessen the intensity of any response Moni had.

Adding free shaping and play. We added in some play in the form of free shaping and jumping a sequence of very low jumps. At no time did Moni react poorly to our hand movements in directing her over the jumps. We started teaching Moni to "wipe her feet" on a towel (she won't allow handling of her feet). She had missed one treat and rather then bend over to point to it, I tapped my toe on the ground to show her where it was. Moni bit my foot (multiple bites) with no warning. I didn't react; no verbal reprimand and I didn't move my foot away and after about six or seven bites, she looked at me, saw I wasn't reacting and walked away, grumbling. (This was easy for me to do—Moni is very small. Had she been a 70 pound dog, well, that would have been a different story. I was much more careful with my feet after that incident.)

In addition, we started to teach her to play with toys, so we would have another way to reinforce her other than always using food. At this point we couldn't use petting as a reward.

Working on triggers. Ellen asked me if we could also work on Moni's crate behaviors—she was still, at times, not letting Ellen near her crate without aggressing and she didn't want a repeat of what happened when Kathy had to go away for the weekend. We worked it in this manner: we put Moni in the crate with some food. We left her and walked up to the crate while flinging food at her. She did not aggress. We stood there and continued to feed her if she didn't react. If she got nervous and had, what Ellen calls a "tantrum," we stood passively until she was able to collect herself, then waited a few seconds and resumed feeding. After a few successful sessions of this, we also started moving our feet. Quiet behaviors were rewarded with food, aggressing was ignored and not rewarded. Once she was doing well with this at my building and at home, we added in two new elements; our hands and leaning over.

Over the next few weeks, we went to the local ball field that had a batting cage (protected contact). We put Moni in the cage and we stayed outside of it. We started out with parallel walking, threw her food, we walked straight up to her, threw her food, stomped our feet, threw her food and leaned over and reached out our hands as if to pet her and threw her food. If at any time, she aggressed, we continued to do whatever it was we were doing at the time—stomping our feet, reaching over and once she was calm for at least ten seconds, resumed feeding. At no time did we go out of our way to make Moni feel uncomfortable (in this context or any other contexts)—we did this slowly and carefully, always watching her for signs of stress and in fact, she only aggressed a few times. Both Ellen and Moni became quite calm and Moni had learned that not reacting yielded her more benefits.

From Ellen's diary:

> You also had me keep a journal of the timing of her tantrums. Over a two month period they went from one minute down to 5 seconds. The journal gave me confidence because over two months it is easy to overlook progress and I was able to see it in the numbers. There was also a session where Moni had just bitten me that morning and you just had us walk around. I can't remember the particulars but the walk was good for both of us. Just having fun together and not stressing.

We continued to do more prep work for eventually joining the group class, and started to really get serious about loose leash walking with attention outside. Not a piece of cake with a Beagle, however, we had fun doing it anyway. She is now very good at giving Ellen attention outside, and does a great imitation of competition style heeling, wagging her tail the entire time.

Dealing with regression. There have been times when regression reared its head. At one point, after being so good for so long (over a year), Moni started aggressing more and more toward Ellen and the cats. We made the sessions easier for Moni, however, the behavior did not stop. I asked Ellen if there was anything different going on at home. It seems that Kathy was getting "fed up" with Moni's behaviors and was acting out—not anything physical, but definitely yelling at her. We told Kathy that she had to stop yelling because it was causing Moni to redirect back to the cats and Ellen. The instant Kathy was able to control her anger and frustration toward Moni, Moni stopped aggressing at Ellen. (Interesting isn't it? It is fun playing detective, especially when we find the solution.) I wasn't positive that Kathy's yelling was creating the problem and I was lucky that I guessed correctly. At this point, Moni doesn't aggress at any of the dogs anymore.

Conclusion

Moni and Ellen have been with me about 18 months now. They are in the group class and almost every week Ellen has a brag to tell us all about how Moni didn't bite her. Moni can work in the building with all of us standing by. We stomp our feet, reach toward her with our hands and she ignores us. She is still a "work in progress" however, because she still does have some issues that crop up as we go along. For instance, Ellen was feeding her and Kathy was petting and Moni got very upset (actually growled at Kathy—no biting) and didn't want to be bothered by the petting. We addressed that instantly and are continuing to work on her proficiency of old behaviors, constantly to add new ones, all the while building up Ellen's relationship with Moni.

From Ellen's diary:

I can pet her when she jumps up on me with joy, we can ride in the car, take her leash on and off. I actually really enjoy her now and she me. Every once in a while now the cats will annoy her, but she growls and they know to stay clear. Growling is great; who would have ever thought? ❖

Aggression: Before the Games Begin

Pamela S. Dennison, July/August 2005

Whether we accidentally adopted one, or inadvertently created one, no one in their right mind ever wants to own an aggressive dog. The good news is that many more people are now willing to work with their dogs rather than deciding on euthanasia. The bad news is that there seems to be a mindset of, "I just want my dog to stop aggressing," and to that end, "quasi-desensitization" sessions are attempted. I say "quasi" because it appears that the desensitization process is often misunderstood or misapplied. Essentially, systematic desensitization is all about defining your dog's triggers, which begins with writing a list and breaking down each fearful event into its smallest components. Once those triggers are understood, beginning at the bottom or least scary step, associate the tiny steps with relaxation and alternate behaviors. If at any time, there is an aggressive response from the dog, the step was too large. "Oops! We goofed." Back up, review what happened, and try again later.

Taking the time to slowly and carefully teach the dog other behaviors is often neglected, because, "I just want my dog to stop aggressing (now!)." Without a concrete plan of action, the naive handler then continues to expose her dog to situations he can't handle, with no alternate or incompatible behaviors in place. Also absent is a long history of calmness during sessions before moving onto the next carefully orchestrated session.

No matter what the dog's issues/triggers are, I start with teaching the same set of core alternate and incompatible behaviors before starting the systematic desensitization process. Why before? Most of the dogs I come in contact with possess little or no basic training. They may have learned that sit, stay, come, and walk on a loose leash are optional behaviors. They may have been traumatized, perhaps through harsh punishment methods. Often trust needs to be re-established or they (dog and handler) must learn what the rules of the game are.

For the aggressive dogs I work with, it is a prerequisite that all of them know certain behaviors and know them to a certain degree of fluency before being allowed to join my group class. I am a big stickler about this because it isn't safe to have untrained dogs in the class. It is also important to teach the human halves of the team the proper response if their dog does react (this would be "nothing, just hang on tight and whatever you do, don't drop the leash!"). During those first six weeks (minimum) of private lessons (one hour per week), we work on some basic and some not-so-basic behaviors—for the dogs and the people. We discuss the pitfalls of using punishment (many of them experience an "aha!" moment once they understand that their behavior affects their dog's behavior), how to properly read signs of stress, how dogs learn (a tiny crash course on classical and operant conditioning), and how to reclaim a better relationship with their dog.

The basics include:

- Eye contact (my definition of eye contact is a calm willingness to look at the owner, without the constant nagging "watch me, watch me, watch me" ad nauseum).

- Instant name response and instant recall (if your dog happens to look away at the scary bad thing and you don't have constant attention or instant name response, it will be harder to get his focus back on you and stop him before he reacts).

- Attention heeling on a loose leash (at the very least, to get from point A to point B without a reaction).

- Door etiquette (you can't start a session properly if the dog charges out of the gate with teeth bared).

- Sit, down, and stay (good for more advanced training or at the very least to do the puppy push-up game).

- Nose targeting the hand (my version of getting the dog to look away rather than using a head halter).

- A few APDT Rally moves, such as the come front ("Oops! I didn't see that person/dog coming around the corner!"), moving down ("Oops! I didn't see that person/dog coming around the corner and there is no place for me to get away!"), and the 180-degree pivot (and run like heck).

In addition, depending on the dog's issues, I teach them the drop on recall, "go to your bed" (two great behaviors if the person the dog is charging at is you), drop while running away (a "must have" if the dog gets loose or the leash breaks and you need to stop them now!), and directionals—move away in the direction I am pointing (a wonderful way to make it fun for the dog to move further away from their provoking stimuli).

Once the basic core behaviors are learned (and are pretty reliable inside my building as well as outside in the "real" world), I often add in free shaping for confidence (for both dog and handler), problem solving, and just for some enjoyment. When working with aggressive dogs, it is important to add that fun element—otherwise the entire process becomes too stressful. I teach shake paw ("nice to meet you"), doing a figure eight around two cones, balancing on a Buja board, riding a skateboard, jumping through a hoop or over a low jump, "wipe your feet," and any number of silly things I can think up.

This may seem like a huge amount of behaviors to teach the dog in only six weeks, but most of the dogs actually learn them quite well. Their owners practice and are quite motivated to get into the group class. Sometimes I run into a dog that needs more training than the six lessons—their owners haven't practiced enough or they can't pay attention outside. Most of the aggressive dog classes are held in local parks or on trails, so if the dog can't focus outside, they are not allowed to join the group.

For the primate half of the team, we work on breathing techniques, positive mental imagery, and actually practicing certain scenarios that may happen in the real world. In addition, we work on building up the confidence, timing, and "muscle memory" of certain behaviors, so when presented with an "Oops!" moment, they will know what to do so they don't panic. For instance, I am working with two dogs right now that have a hard time passing people and holy-moley if that stranger says, "Hello!" So, we work on just those types of situations, while still working in privates. That way, the dog is comfortable with me doing potentially scary things and the owner relaxes as well. Once they are allowed into the group, dog and handler are both more at ease with the contexts we design in class.

Some students are just too nice and have a hard time making sure that people or people with dogs stay beyond their dog's threshold. I have one such student now. She is quite timid and was continuing to allow people to approach her human aggressive dog, which of course, was not doing anyone a bit of good. I taught her to be more forceful and gave her some key phrases to practice with. At the same time that she was screaming at the pretend person (actually the television), she was shoveling food to her dog so he would not become afraid if she started screaming at someone to stay away!

The dogs that make the most progress are the dogs that have a large repertoire of alternate or incompatible behaviors to fall back on. Their owners practice them diligently using positive methods, and make these behaviors fun to do. I have found that most of my students become completely enamored with how easily their dogs learn new things and it seems to take away some of the angst they may be feeling about their dog's aggression. I always encourage them to come and watch my group class at least once (before signing up or during training). They see how supportive and calm everyone is and how rare it is that any aggression occurs. The people in the group love showing off for guests and relating their stories and successes.

When new people see how the core and other behaviors are utilized within the class, this oftentimes rejuvenates their dedication to help their dog. Those skills, coupled with the new bond between them, will create a climate where a huge amount of the anxiety, fear, and aggression will dissipate. Once that is accomplished, then the process of desensitization can begin.

Initial Interview Tips for Aggressive Dog Owners

When I interview a client on the phone to assess whether or not they should come for training, I take a history on the dog, including any incidents that have happened. These include exact details of not only the dog's reactions, but the person's reactions to the aggressive incident(s) as well. I also ask how long these types of behaviors have been going on, if they have used other trainers to rectify the problem, and if they have had a health check recently. In my opinion, the most important aspect is not necessarily the dog, but how committed the owner is to dealing with their dog's issues. I try to make it very clear that there is no quick fix—it will take as long as it takes. I also encourage them to come and watch the group class before signing up. If they aren't dedicated (don't have the time, money, or real desire to see this through the long haul), I will not take them as students. ❖

Dominance: The "Dirty" Word

Lore I. Haug, Edited by Terry Long, May/June 2005

The concept of and, certainly, the word "dominance" has become a fire bed of controversy and emotional turmoil in recent years. When discussing dog behavior, some use the term pervasively while others avoid it entirely or develop various substitutive names. Opinions vary about the importance of dominance in the canine world, particularly its relevance to behavior modification. Before formulating an opinion, it helps to understand how we got to this point and what factors contributed to the current controversy. Also, this article shall consider the general theory, the relationship between dominance and aggression, the significance of dominance relationships in dogs, and what role, if any, this may play in human-dog interaction.

Different Things to Different People

The term dominance means different things to different people. Ethologists often use the term differently than clinical behaviorists, and the non-professional public has its own, often completely distorted, interpretation of what constitutes dominance. Admittedly, we, "the professionals," are to blame for much of that misrepresentation. Because wolves are known to be the genetic ancestors of domestic dogs (Clutton-Brock, 1995), many people have translated wolf behavior in a literal fashion to dogs. There may be usefulness to this, but it is generally an erroneous approach, as this article will discuss later.

Dominance should not be used to indicate a temperamental attribute, motivation, territoriality, or aggressive act (even offensive). A dog who shows aggression toward a territorial intruder is not "dominant." The dog is driving off a perceived threat and the dog happens to have a home field advantage, which means the dog will show more confidence because it stands a better chance of being successful.

Dominance describes a relationship between two individuals based on the outcome of an agonistic encounter (Lindsay, 2001; Shepherd, 2002). Dominant-subordinate relationships permitted the evolution of social hierarchies to allow for more harmonious group living. Hierarchies allow animals to live in close contact in competitive situations without constant conflict and injurious, and potentially fatal, fighting. Social living has biological advantages, but social behavior did not evolve around social hierarchies. Some social species, such as Bonobo chimps, do not even develop hierarchies (Hohman et al, 1999). So dominance also is not synonymous with social behavior or group living.

Dominance is a "predictive inference based on a pattern of win-lose contests between two or more animals" (Lindsay, 2001). A single interaction cannot accurately reflect the nature of the animals' relationship with each other. Dominance and subordinance are based on which animal wins the encounter the majority of the time. If animal A is dominant to animal B, we can infer that animal A will win an agonistic encounter between the two most or all of the time. Dominance is not absolute. Every individual assumes the subordinate role at some point with, some individual, in some context unless the individual is pathological.

Dominant-subordinate relationships are not established in every encounter an animal has with a conspecific. Imagine how odd it would look if a human squared off or postured to the bank teller, the gas station attendant, or the nurse at the doctor's office. These are casual interactions. Similarly, when a dog first meets a particular human, the dog is not immediately attempting to test or establish dominance.

Studies testing dominance hierarchies indicate that social rank is distinct from the feeding rank. Social dominance is related to the level of the individual's freedom in relation to others (Zimen 1981), but feeding rank is related more to the actual resource-holding potential. This is supported by the observation that dogs can have food/possessive aggression that is unrelated to conflict over social rank and vice versa.

Dogs or Wolves?

As previously mentioned, most of our interpretations of dominance and hierarchy behavior in dogs has been extrapolated from wolf behavior. Numerous errors have occurred in this translation even if we assume that dogs are identical to wolves. Even in wolves, the alpha does not have absolute control over the will of the group as a whole (Zimen, 1981). Additionally, the dominance relationship is maintained by voluntary deferential behavior from the subordinate. A high-ranking animal does not casually intrude upon individual privileges of subordinates, nor does the animal show gratuitous displays of rank or aggression. High-ranking animals are more concerned with macro-management, rather than micro-management, of the other members' behavior. This factor alone illustrates the absurdity of blaming sub par obedience performances and behavior problems such as digging and chewing on dominance issues.

In most higher social species, rank structure can be complex, fluid, or context specific. Alliances and triangular relationships complicate the picture. Using food tests to determine hierarchies is flawed if feeding hierarchies are different from social rank. It is often difficult to accurately assess rank order or, at times, whether a social rank even exists.

We know that dogs show social behavior, but do dogs have social hierarchies? Dogs are not wolves, and their behavior is not identical. Most authorities agree that domestication produced some degree of neoteny in dogs, both in their physical appearance and their behavior. Wolves do not show strong ranking (status climbing) behavior until social maturity. Dogs would be more similar to juvenile wolves than adult wolves. Dogs and wolves are essentially genetically identical and interbreeding could easily occur. However, in areas where the ranges of wolf packs and dog groups overlap, little interbreeding occurs primarily due to behavioral segregation (Boitani et al, 1995). Dogs prefer to associate with dogs (or humans) and wolves prefer to associate with wolves. Furthermore, if wolves and dogs showed identical packing behavior, we should be able to live as successfully with wolves as we do with dogs. See "What is a Pack?" below.

During the process of domestication and selective breeding to produce dogs for different functions, humans have manipulated a variety of physical and behavioral characteristics. It would be impossible to develop the physical alterations responsible for breed diversity without also affecting social behavior. Considering that pack behavior and hierarchy formation was not the primary goal in the development of most breeds, the resulting effects on social behavior would be haphazard at best. Dogs demonstrate a greater degree of behavioral plasticity than wolves and can combine behavioral patterns in novel ways (Coppinger et al, 1995). Additionally, studies on feral dogs observe that dogs live in small, loosely organized groups. Feral dogs studied in central Italy did not show social bonds that followed the rules of pack living, and there was no reproductive suppression among subordinate females as is seen in wolf packs (Hohman et al, 1995). Coppinger's observations of free-ranging village dogs illustrate that these dogs also do not show pack structure, but live semi-solitarily (Coppinger, 2001). Other studies of free-ranging dogs support the idea that dogs generally live in pairs or solitarily.

Dogs obviously show dominant and subordinate postures to each other; some dogs more so than others. However, many "submissive" signals are similar or identical to appeasement or cut-off signals. These are designed to avoid or abort impending aggression, but not necessarily in the context of a hierarchical system. Since dogs are descended from wolves, we can expect that some of the social behavior of wolves is retained in dogs. However, there appears to be a wide variation between breeds and individuals in the amount of hierarchical and agonistic behavior demonstrated by dogs. In general, when dogs do develop hierarchies, they may be comparatively unstable. Hierarchies in dogs might also be so complex and fluid, and affected by so many different factors in any given situation, that it is pointless to try to define them.

Relationships with Humans

How does all this relate to dogs' relationships with humans and the development of "dominance aggression?" Since dog-dog aggression is not correlated with dog-human aggression, we know that dogs know humans are not dogs. Dogs also are able to adapt their behavior when interacting with other species; they don't treat cats exactly like dogs or horses exactly like dogs, so they won't treat humans exactly like dogs. This does not mean that some communication signals cannot be recognized across species. It does mean that we must acknowledge that dogs will behave differently toward people than toward other dogs.

There has been a long-standing misconception that all dogs are vying for the "alpha dog" position in relation to both other dogs and humans, and that most or all aggression is related to status. This has resulted in a variety of "dominance exercises," ostensibly based on wolf behavior, designed to prevent or treat status-related aggression. These approaches presume that all dogs are behaviorally normal and can be cured by asserting the "appropriate" amount of dominance over them. Pinning a dog on its back or side, staring at the dog until it looks or turns away, and other interactions designed to force the dog to show "submission" can be interpreted as random, non-contingent threats or acts of aggression by dogs, especially if dogs don't understand "alpha wolf" behavior by humans anyway. Non-contingent punishment (including threats) is a definitive way to induce a variety of neurotic behaviors.

Dominance is not synonymous with aggression. Although aggression at times is used to establish dominance, agonistic encounters, particularly between familiar individuals, are normally resolved with non-injurious ritualistic behavior. Injurious or escalating aggression is atypical and counterproductive to group cohesion. In fact, in many social species, the level of aggression shown by a particular individual is inversely correlated with the animal's ability to attain high social ranking. Studies in humans and several primate species show that escalating levels of aggression are correlated with impulse control disorders and are inversely correlated with social status and brain serotonin levels (reviewed in Haug, 2003). In humans, boys with high levels of aggression are more likely to be interpreted by their peers as bullies rather than leaders. Thus, it is not appropriate to discuss dominance relationships and hierarchies in terms of aggression, particularly when referring to stable groups.

Aggression is ultimately about control, i.e., one individual trying to influence the immediate behavior of another (Lindsay, 2001). (This refers to non-predatory aggression; however, one could argue that even predatory aggression is control related, but for a different motivational purpose.) There is a significant link between anxiety, control, and predictability. In a situation where an individual feels as though he or she has some control over the outcome, anxiety levels remain low. A feeling of control injects a sense of predictability into the environment. Control and predictability reduce anxiety; a feeling of a lack of control and predictability is a recipe for anxiety, depression, and learned helplessness. For example, one major reason that some people are optimists is that they overestimate how much control they actually have over a situation; their anxiety levels are correspondingly low. Pessimists have a more realistic picture of how much control they have in any particular situation.

Aggression is usually about regaining control of a situation, not an individual. There are a number of factors that support the theory that most aggression (including owner-directed aggression) in dogs is about situational control rather than status. First, many dogs begin showing aggression when very young, sometimes as early as five to six weeks of age. There is no natural correlate for a young canid mounting a true dominance challenge against an adult conspecific. Second, most dogs show some degree of preliminary and/or concurrent anxiety before or during an attack. The dog also may withdraw from the owner or run and hide immediately after the attack. Individuals who feel they are in charge do not mount an attack (or challenge) and then run away—running away is a behavior demonstrated by the loser or "subordinate."

In addition, if "dominance aggression" was about status, then severe punishment by the owner should suppress the problem. Individuals who feel that humans can adequately mimic dominance behavior (and that dogs are motivated by it), overlook the fact that those very actions toward the dog either: 1) trigger increased aggression; or 2) do not ultimately resolve the problem. This implies that humans cannot deliver these messages in a meaningful way and/or dogs cannot read them.

Furthermore, many dogs show aggression highly out of proportion to the actual threat or challenge presented during the interaction. Owner-directed attacks often escalate rapidly and include actual injuries; often there is little ritualism about them. Severe explosive biting is characteristic of a defensive attack.

Finally, dogs with "dominance aggression" often show significant levels of solicitous and attention-seeking behaviors toward their owners. In a wolf pack, attention is directed toward the leader animal—up the hierarchy—not down. Excessive attention-seeking behavior is not characteristic of a typical aloof, confident leader, but it is well within expectations for a subordinate.

(Note: There is a small population of dogs that appear to show true dominance aggression. Among other things, these dogs are very confident, show considerable warning before biting, and do not retreat afterward. The aggression is usually very predictable in context and intensity. See "Erroneous Use of Dominance.")

Avoidance-Motivated Aggression

So if owner-directed dominance aggression is not about status, what is the problem? This behavioral pattern may arise in several ways, but almost all of them are forms of avoidance-motivated aggression (Luescher, 2004). As mentioned, habitual use of "dominance" exercises can be interpreted as random attacks on the dog, leading to defensive behavior. Similarly, punishing a dog that is already fearful will exacerbate the fearfulness. If done in consistent interactions, the dog will develop an expectation for conflict in those situations. The dog then may show preemptive defensive behavior in an attempt to avoid or abort the interaction.

Some dogs may use aggression to terminate an ongoing interaction that they find frustrating or irritating. Humans routinely project their own thoughts and feelings on dogs, and thus misinterpret the dogs' intentions and desires. For example, most dog owners would indicate that a dog wants its belly rubbed when it rolls onto its back, even if they recognize this as a submissive posture. They fail to understand the reaction that the dog (at least originally) expects in return: a brief interaction equivalent to another dog sniffing, and then the signal receiver walking away. Similarly, when dogs approach people, people assume the dog wants to be petted. When a dog desires proximity to the owner, it does not automatically follow that the dog wants to be petted, hugged, and/or kissed. These latter two interactions are, to some degree, innately hostile and threatening to dogs. Again, the dog may use aggression to avoid or abort the interaction. In any of these scenarios, when the dog learns to use aggression to regain control of the situation by terminating the encounter, the dog will receive significant reinforcement. The more control the dog feels it has in any given situation, the more confident the dog will be. The dog's posturing will look more offensive, making the dog appear to be acting "dominant." This does not mean the dog has increased its social rank.

Normal vs. Abnormal

Some dogs "are simply obnoxious subordinates who have not been properly trained to respect appropriate social boundaries" (Lindsay 2001). But another population of dogs is probably truly abnormal. Behavior is dynamic on an individual and a population basis. We cannot expect to manipulate breed genetics and produce all normal animals; some individuals will fall outside the bell curve. Dogs' brains are similar enough to humans that we can infer that they may suffer from mental and neurological disorders similar to some of our own. Presuming that all dominant-aggressive dogs are just normal, obnoxious animals that need a dose of "leadership" is unfair to the animals and dangerous to the humans around them.

Although we are learning more and more about canine behavior, there is still a paucity of research on social behavior in dogs. The more we analyze canine behavior, the more we realize how complex it can be. What business do we have trying to translate and mimic a language that we do not even understand? Focusing on dominance and hierarchies in therapy grossly oversimplifies the concept and can divert attention from more productive therapeutic approaches. That is a recipe for disaster and our dogs have been trying to tell us this for some time.

What is a "Pack?"

True "pack" behavior involves cooperative behavior between the adult individuals with a clear leader. True packs are unreceptive to outside individuals and typically attack intruders on sight. Humans expect dogs to allow the approach and integration of other dogs at random, and, indeed, most dogs do allow this. There is little evidence that dogs form true packs, but much more that they tend to form aggregations and loose social groups with open to semi-open memberships. Individuals can come and go with relative ease. Although groups of dogs may engage in the same activity, one has to differentiate cooperative behavior from social facilitation and local enhancement, of which the latter two are much more common in dogs.

Erroneous Use of "Dominance"

Behaviors erroneously attributed to, or labeled as, "dominance:"

- pulling on leash
- getting on furniture
- disobedience
- running away
- jumping up
- aggression and fighting
- rushing through doorways
- digging and other destructive behaviors

- puppy mouthing and nipping
- aggression during veterinary exams
- intolerance of handling
- pawing people

Appropriate Use of "Dominance"

The term "dominance" can be appropriately used to describe the individual in a dyad who wins an agonistic encounter the majority of the time and/or who is able to persistently control access to a resource or behavioral freedom in that specific context. I restrict the term to describing those individuals who have a close social relationship or repeated contact with each other. Using the term during a casual encounter could result in false presumptions about the animals' relationship. Aggression may be used to establish or solidify the relationship, but is not a typical aspect of a stable dyad.

Terms often used to describe owner-directed aggression:

- Dominance aggression
- Dominance-related aggression
- Status-related aggression
- Conflict aggression
- Avoidance-motivated aggression

The term "conflict aggression" may be the most descriptive of the true etiology of most owner-directed aggression cases. ❖

References

Boitani, L., Francisci, F., Ciucci, P., Andreoli, G. "Population biology and ecology of feral dogs in central Italy." In J. Serpell (Ed.), *The Domestic Dog: Its Evolution, Behaviour and Interactions With People* (pp. 218-244). Cambridge: Cambridge University Press, 1995.

Coppinger, R. & Coppinger, L. *Dogs.* New York: Scribner, 2001.

Coppinger, R. & Schneider, R. "Evolution of working dogs." In J. Serpell (Ed.), *The Domestic Dog: Its Evolution, Behaviour and Interactions With People* (pp. 21-47). Cambridge: Cambridge University Press, 1995.

Haug, L.I. "Blood androgens and 5-HIAA in dogs with inappropriate intra-specific aggression." Master's thesis, College Station, Texas A&M University Press, 2003.

Hohman, G., Gerloff, U., Tauty, D., Fruth, B. "Social bonds and genetic ties: Kinship, association and affiliation in a community of bonobos" (Pan paniscus). *Behavior* (136), 1219-1235, 1999.

Lindsay, S. R. *Applied Dog Behavior and Training, vol. 2.* Ames: Iowa State University Press, 2001.

Luescher, A. "Dominance and conflict-related aggression in dogs." *Proc WVC*, Las Vegas, NV, 2004.

Shepherd, K. "Development of behaviour, social behaviour, and communication in dogs." In D. Horwitz, D. Mills & S. Heath (Eds.). *BSAVA Manual of Canine and Feline Behavioural Medicine.* (pp. 8-20). BSAVA, Gloucester, 2002.

Zimen, E. *The Wolf: A Species in Danger.* New York: Delacorte Press, 1981.

Fear Factor—Frightened Fidos

Pia Silvani, January/February 2007

Afraid? Everyone knows what it feels like. We have all been there at one point in our lives— whether it's dropping 100 feet in the air after hitting a pocket of turbulence, standing up on stage speaking to 500 people, or stepping into a snake pit. Research on anxiety disorders in people suggests that the intensity of the feeling and the ultimate success of treatment are related to the individual's level of physiological arousal. A person cannot get over a fear during behavior modification unless this is accompanied by mental and physical relaxation.

We assume that animals, in particular dogs, have similar feelings based on behavior research. Degrees of fear range from mild anxiety to extreme phobias. Fear is an emotional reaction to a particular object or situation that the dog perceives as being threatening. Fearful responses are useful and help to protect the individual from harm. However, when the fear becomes chronic in the absence of any threat, it results in anxiety. Anxiety can be associated with an easily identifiable trigger, or a trigger that is known only to the dog. Anxiety is a problem when it disrupts normal functioning of the individual. Overall, anxiety that motivates an appropriate response is adaptive; anxiety that disrupts normal functioning of the individual with inappropriate responses is maladaptive.

Fear related problems can often be treated with great success. Vital to the process is that the events which trigger the behavior must be identified and the dog must eventually be able to relax in the presence of those triggers. If you attempt a "tough" method with an "oh, get over it" treatment plan, the problem can be exacerbated. An easily identifiable trigger could be a truck backfire encountered during a daily walk. The event might elicit a fearful response from the dog, an appropriate reaction to a loud noise. However, if the dog begins to exhibit threatening or aggressive behaviors toward all vehicles, the fear has generalized to non-threatening situations. Any behavior modification program should be tailored to counter-condition an emotional response to vehicles. However, if the dog begins to exhibit a generalized fear when on walks, and the owner cannot identify what originally triggered the anxiety, the condition becomes much more difficult to treat than in one where a specific trigger was identified.

Phobia disorders are similar to anxiety disorders in that they are triggered by exposure to particular objects or situations. As with general anxiety, the fearful reaction is triggered by exposure to a person, child, dog, object, or a situation such as thunder, loud noises, or the owner leaving. However, with phobias, the fear reactions are extreme and largely out of proportion to the trigger.

When dogs are fearful (not phobic) of something (a person, an object, another dog, children, etc.), they can avoid the situation by running away or, when escape is not possible, bark and lunge in an attempt to keep what has frightened them at bay. With a phobia disorder, the dog's reaction becomes one of panic and attempts to escape the situation may result in harm to the dog or the surroundings. Dogs may claw at or chew out of a crate, or scratch or bite at door moldings or walls in an attempt to escape.

Phobic dogs may self-mutilate if unable to escape a situation. I have counseled many cases where anxious dogs compulsively licked their paws to the point of discoloration, bitten their nails to the point of bleeding, and gnawed and licked at themselves causing granulomas and even worse.

Correcting Misperceptions

Owners rarely accurately understand the behavior of the fearful dog and misconceptions about this condition can make the situation worse and erode the human-animal bond. The following are some common statements made by owners with dogs that exhibit fear and anxiety. Our job is to educate them about the misconceptions.

- **"He'll grow out of it."** As we know, dogs do not grow out of their fears as they age. They sometimes can habituate to the frightening objects or situations (stop responding since after repeated exposure, it no longer has any effect on them). This can occur with mild fears. However, fears can also worsen with age and become more difficult to modify. "Fears that have a specific link with an event in a dog's near past appear to be more responsive to simple counter-conditioning efforts than fears developing over years of exposure." (Lindsay, 2000, p.106)

- **"He must have been mistreated."** While this might be true, it typically is not. Dogs that have not been well socialized can exhibit behaviors like cowering, ducking or backing away when someone attempts to pet him. On the surface, this appears as if the dog was mistreated. However, he may not have been socialized properly. Defining socialization to pet owners is critical. Pet owners feel socialization is about "exposing the dog to new situations and people." While this is partially correct, the true definition is "exposure to a variety of situations, people and animals, ensuring that each experience is positive and pleasant and the dog's reaction is non-fearful!" This is a particularly important point to make with new puppy owners. Continued socialization should also be stressed to owners of adolescent dogs to ensure that their early positive experiences are retained.

- **"It must be a result of trauma."** When a dog will not jump up into a car, for instance, people assume that the dog had a traumatic experience associated with cars. Again, this may be true. Rather than speculating on an unknown past, training the dog so he learns that jumping up into the car can be fun will help to build confidence. Additionally, a veterinary check-up should be recommended prior to training to rule out a medical condition, which may have inhibited him from jumping.

- **"Punish him so he stops this silly behavior."** Punishing a fearful dog for behaviors you find inappropriate (i.e., growling or lunging at people) will not help. If anything, it does more harm than good. If you punish the dog for growling because he is afraid, he will probably stop growling, but it is very unlikely to change his emotional state.

- **"He's mad at us for leaving him alone all day."** If a dog is destroying the house as a result of being left alone, is the dog simply having separation "fun" with little or no anxiety related to the owners' leaving, or is the dog truly anxious and perhaps exhibiting separation anxiety?

- **"Don't pet him when he is afraid or you will reinforce his fears."** With all due respect, this does not make a bit of sense. A fearful dog that is being consoled is not going to become more fearful as a result. The philosopher Spinoza described counter-conditioning in his Ethics: "An emotion can only be controlled or destroyed by another emotion contrary thereto, and with more power for controlling emotion." (Lindsay, 2000, p. 225).

Behavioral Modification

The treatment of fear does not necessarily require knowledge of how or why the fear developed in the first place. This may help your clients feel better if they have been concerned about not knowing their dog's past history.

When you attempt to alter behavior, the use of classical and operant counter-conditioning and desensitization is critical. If you are unfamiliar with these terms, I recommend mentoring under an educated, skilled, experienced behaviorist or trainer, rather than taking on a case that may be above and beyond your level of expertise.

Provided you do have adequate experience, can you take a detailed behavioral history, knowing what questions to ask and how to extrapolate as much information as possible? When dealing with fears and anxieties in dogs, you will need to learn as much as you can about the behaviors of the dog and all triggers.

For example, if an owner calls you concerned that the dog is fearful of children, my first question is: What does that mean? Have the owner describe the behavior of the dog, not what they think the dog thinks. The words "children" and "fearful" encompass many things in my mind. Have the owner describe the exact triggers that encompass the word children (i.e., age, gender, size, movement, personality, behavior, etc.).

First, perhaps the dog tolerates some children, enjoys the company of others (e.g. 12+ years), yet exhibits fear of some (under the age of 10).

Second, how does the dog react when exposed to children? What is the dog doing? What is the child doing? Is it all children or only certain children? Is it groups of children and if so what are the children doing? Touching? Sitting still? Running?

There are many types of fearful behaviors in dogs where they might exhibit aggressive behavior. Using operant conditioning can influence behaviors that are linked to emotional states. However, you should be aware that operant conditioning might change the behavior of the dog and not the emotional state. For example, if a dog lunges at cyclists going by and the trainer teaches the dog to sit and stay, the dog may do very well with a sit stay, yet his emotional state may not necessarily change as a result and the dog may continue to exhibit aggressive/dangerous behaviors.

There is no cookbook recipe when dealing with behavioral problems, especially when fear and anxiety are the culprits!

There are some important questions to keep in mind when working with a fearful dog:

1. Can the environment be managed so the dog's exposure to the fear induced-stimulus is reduced? For example, if a dog is fearful of a relative that has come to stay, can you manage the dog to help prevent him from being afraid? Can the exposure to the relative be limited so the dog has time to get to know the person?

2. Can the owners identify what triggers the dog to become fearful or anxious? For example, saying that the dog is afraid of people does not give me enough information. Is it all people? Are they able to identify them by ranking them? On the other hand, you have heard people say, "It's unpredictable. I just don't know."

3. Is the dog injuring himself because of his anxiety or fear? For example, an owner comes to you with a thunder phobic dog that has jumped through a window so they are crating the dog as a result. The dog is no longer jumping through windows, but is injuring himself due to the confinement. Know when to refer the case!

4. If the dog has bitten because of his fear or anxiety, how bad were the bites and how long has the dog been biting? Is this a new behavior or a behavior that has been going on for 10 years and suddenly it has become a problem?

5. Is there a dog wreaking havoc in the household, causing another family dog to become anxious and fearful, not wanting to make a move in fear that he will be attacked? Can this be managed? Even if the owners can manage the situation, is the anxious dog's quality of life poor as a result?

Conclusions

As stated above, there is no recipe to follow. The use of classical and operant counter- conditioning and desensitization are necessary to achieve success. Dr. Suzanne Hetts, in her book *Pet Behavior Protocols*, has a wonderful guideline (p. 163) to follow when implementing counter-conditioning and desensitization procedures.

However, there are times when using counter-conditioning and desensitization may not be practical. For instance, if a dog is afraid of cars and lives in New York City, desensitization can be extremely difficult, if not impossible, to implement.

Flooding (continuous exposure to particular stimuli until the dog's fear response is no longer elicited) is another option when dealing with behavior problems. Recent research (Williams et al, 2003; Williams & Borchelt, 2003) investigated the flooding technique using dogs and verified the efficacy and safety of flooding when properly conducted. An inappropriate use of flooding can result in stress for the dog and other problems. If a flooding technique is selected, it can be very effective under the supervision of a qualified professional. Our extremely successful Feisty Fidos™ classes incorporate some form of flooding. Years of experience allow us to recognize when to incorporate flooding, or not.

So, can dogs get over their fears? If treated correctly, yes. Yet, there is no short cut or easy solution. Time and owner buy-in is what will help the dog become more relaxed in his environment.

I would like to give special thanks to two people who helped me edit the article, as well as helped with some research. I feel a thank you is so important because we need to talk to our peers more often than we do to be more effective. Sadly, we tend to focus on criticizing instead of using critical thinking and following the guidelines of what Dr. Ian Dunbar wanted from this organization—to help each other to become more educated and better trainers! The two people are Nancy Williams, MA, RVT, CAAB (associate) and Elisabeth Catalano, CPDT. ❖

References and Resources

Dawkins, R. *The Selfish Gene. 30th edition*. New York: Oxford University Press, 2006.

Dawkins, R. *The Blind Watchmaker: Why the Evidence of Evolution Reveals a Universe Without Design*. New York: W.W. Norton & Company, 1996.

Delta Society. *Professional Standards for Dog Trainers: Effective, Humane Principles, 2001*. www.deltasociety.org.

Hetts, S. *Pet Behavior Protocols: What to Say, What to do, When to Refer*. Lakewood, CO: AAHA Press, 1999.

King, T., Hemsworth, P.H., Coleman, G.J. "Fear of novel and startling stimuli in domestic dogs." *Appl Anim Behav Sci*, 82(1), 45-64, 2003.

Lindsay, S.R. *Handbook of Applied Dog Behavior and Training: Volume one: Adaptation and Learning*. Iowa State University Press, Ames, IA, 2000.

McConnell, P. *For the Love of a Dog: Understanding Emotion in You and Your Best Friend*. New York: Ballantine Books, 2006.

Overall, K.L. *Clinical Behavioral Medicine for Small Animals*. St. Louis, MO: Mosby, Inc., 1997.

Pinel, J.P.J. ed. *Biopsychology, 4th edition*. University Of British Columbia, 2000.

Schwartz, B. & Reisberg, D. eds., *Learning and Memory*. New York: WW Norton & Company, 1991.

Voith, V.L. & Borchelt, P.L. "Fears and phobias in companion animals. In V.L. Voth & P.L. Borchelt." (Eds.), *Readings in Companion Animal Behavior*. (pp 140-51). Trenton, NJ: Veterinary Learning Systems, 1996.

Wilde, N. *Help for Your Fearful Dog*. Santa Clarita, CA: Phantom Publishing, 2006.

Williams, N.G. & Borchelt, P.J. "Full body restraint and rapid stimulus exposure as a treatment for dogs with defensive aggressive behavior: Three case studies." *Intl J Comp Psych*, 16, 226-236, 2003.

Williams, N.G., Borchelt, P.J., Sollers III, J.J., Gasper, P., & Thayer, J.F. "Ambulatory monitoring of cardiovascular responses during behavioral modification of an aggressive dog." *Biomed Sci Instrument*, 39, 214-219, 2003.

Sibling Rivalry: The Intra-Dog/Intra-House Problems

Daphne Robert-Hamilton with Terry Long, Published in Two Parts, January/April 2006

PART I

When two or more dogs in the same household fight, with either intermittent bouts or high-frequency fur flying, it is referred to as "sibling rivalry" or "intra-household dog-dog aggression." These are some of the most challenging cases for trainers and are extremely stressful for the family. A case of sibling rivalry often involves two or more dogs of different breeds, sizes, and ages. It's reported that fights are more frequent between same-sex dogs, and that the most severe cases are between female dogs that are usually not related in any way.[1]

Part I of this article will explore the biological role of sibling rivalry and strategies for prevention, and Part II will delve into management and behavior modification options.

The Biological Role of Rivalry

There aren't enough good scientific studies on the social systems of companion dogs to make major conclusions about their social structures. We do know that domestic dogs are more fluid and contextual in their behaviors than, for example, a wolf pack.

Darwin, Wallace, and Malthus held a common belief that organisms compete for critical resources.[2] Aggression can be a highly beneficial behavior for survival. The "selfish gene" is about doing what is required to survive and pass on one's DNA.

The competition for passing on DNA has caused certain species to develop early onset of aggressive behaviors and even siblicide, the killing of an animal by its sibling. Some species, such as pigs and hyenas, are born with fully erupted incisors and canines, and demonstrate a "bite-shake" killing behavior within 40 minutes of birth. Arctic and red fox pups are known to practice siblicide. Serious injuries and fatal fights between fox siblings occur around three to six weeks of age.

Mammalian sibling rivalry can begin in the embryonic stage and continue well into adulthood. Competition over resources that may cause sibling rivalry include:

- Uterine space and nutrients

- Milk supply

- Post-weaning food acquisition

- Reproductive opportunity

In contrast to the "selfish gene" are altruistic traits found in some groupings of animals. Hamilton (1964) found some animals perform certain behaviors that benefit other individuals. Dr. Hamilton3 came up with a theory of "inclusive fitness" also known as Hamilton's Rule, which "neatly specifies the conditions, in terms of gains and losses … under which an individual should behave unselfishly on behalf of a genetic relative.3" That is, altruistic behavior can enhance survival of a group of related individuals, which supports the survival of a specific gene pool.

Sibling rivalry sits on an evolutionary fulcrum between selfishness and kin-selected altruism. Sibling rivalry correlates with ecological conditions and its evolutionary history: whether an animal chooses competitive or altruistic behavior in any given circumstance depends partly on the nature of critical, limited resources, and partly on the competitor's own behavior. The most common contributing factors are limited space and resources.

Individuals and Social Groupings

If you want to fill up a day or newsletter all you have to mutter is the word dominance. Rather than getting mired in defining dominance, rank, or status, look at the individual animal and what happens when you get a grouping of domestic dogs together in a household situation. The social behavior of unrelated dogs in a given household does not apply to a grouping of dogs at a dog park or doggy daycare, but similar behavioral interactions can occur in those settings. The big difference is that "sibling rivalry" deals with dogs living together 24/7 for a large part of their lives.

To adapt to a changing environment a dog needs to assess its opponent's "resource-holding" potential and the value of the available resources, and then learn which behaviors have the most favorable outcome. Normal social communication is a constant "dance" involving deferential behaviors that help lay out "social maps" that govern social attraction, social codes, and fair play in order to avoid aggression. However, dogs in a multi-dog household who live together 24/7 form a unique group dynamic that fluctuates depending on the interactions between given individuals, resources present, health conditions, etc. Living together in such a "forced group" interaction will have a marked effect on each individual. Each group will develop specific social interactions that impact each individual dog's ability to cope and form strategies for their own benefit. Also contributing to the dynamics are socially facilitated behaviors and innate species-specific behaviors. Social structures are complex and depend on cooperation, and each group is unique in the ability to form friendships, allegiances and the ability to share resources.

It is easy to see, too, why some groups could have a "cocktail mix" of individuals that poison the social interactions of the entire group. Imagine a group with any number of the following individuals and/or behaviors: resource guarding, proximity-sensitive individuals, individuals that react inappropriately to environmental cues (which may elicit aggression from housemate(s)), redirected aggression, impaired communication skills, etc. The resultant stress and tension would be non-stop due to the fact that the individuals are in an enclosed (usually very limited) spatial environment.

Some animals become flooded and sensitized to just being in the same area as the "threat." They may, in fact, initiate aggression in a pre-emptive strategy best described as "the best defense is a good offense." Another individual might choose a lot of appeasement gestures, another might avoid that particular individual all together, while others get anxious. Such tensions can lead to aggression whether overtly provoked or not. Depending upon the resultant reaction of others in the group to these dynamics, aggression could become more and more impulsive and explosive.

Dogs Assessing Dogs

When individuals in a group are put together, either for the first time or in daily routines, they are constantly assessing each other and the environment, e.g., is this safe for me, what's in this for me? It is to each animal's advantage to resolve competition through such assessment. Dogs assess and communicate with each other in several different ways.

- Play behaviors (e.g., investigation, play skill, bite inhibition, communication style, assessment of strength)

- Values placed on resources (e.g., space, toys, unique objects, food, multiple objects) in the environment and the resource-holding capabilities of the various individuals

- Appeasement behaviors used to diffuse conflict, signaling that the potential for damage costs more than gaining the resource

- Aggression as a strategy in keeping a critical distance between the "threat" and/or the valued resource

Dogs adopt behavioral strategies as a result of their assessment of each other. The chosen strategies will depend, in some part, upon how those strategies have been reinforced. That is, the chosen strategy is a product of prior learning. For example, if appeasement behaviors have worked to avoid conflict, that particular individual will be more inclined to offer appeasement behaviors in future conflicts. That strategy becomes a learned behavior for that individual. Conversely, an animal that has had aggression reinforced will be more likely to try that strategy in the future.

The Human Factor

Although sibling rivalry can occur even in households whose owners understand canine behavior and have trained their dogs in basic obedience, it is more common to find cases of sibling rivalry in households in which owners have little influence with their dogs, and/or have inadvertently contributed to rivalry between them. This can result from lack of impulse-control training or inadvertent reinforcement of inappropriate behaviors, e.g., pushiness, possessiveness. And, of course, the human himself can be a valuable resource over which conflicts erupt, e.g., the owner whose dog is sitting next to him who snarls at another dog who approaches.

In addition, resolution of sibling rivalry is often complicated by many pet owners' sources of information. Trainers, veterinarians, friends, family members, and the Internet, etc., confound owners when they attempt to implement methods that are often inappropriate—and dangerous—in dealing with aggression. Pet owners have misconceptions about behavior in general and even more so with aggression, often believing that much of canine behavior has a direct relation to the "alpha" status of an animal. This sometimes pits the owner against the dog in a misinformed attempt to be dominant by using very physical and even abusive methods, creating an adversarial human-pet relationship, and adding stress to an already tense household.

Physical punishment that some owners attempt also has little use: dogs that bite are usually very anxious and punishment can make their aggressive behaviors worse. Effective punishment is also difficult for the average pet owner to administer correctly. Lastly, punishment doesn't teach the animal(s) alternate behaviors.

Still common to sibling rivalry cases is the notion of identifying an "alpha" dog and supporting that dog's status in the group. Pet owners who have tried this approach often report an increase in tensions. As many behavior counselors report, this "preferential treatment" often results in the appointed "alpha" becoming a bully, making life miserable for other individuals in the group.

Pet owner education is critical to the success of behavior modification programs, and this starts with early assessment and prevention.

Early Assessment

Note: If the dogs are already fighting, especially over a long period of time, the client may have lost their chance to teach appropriate group living behaviors, and may need to exert "damage control" only. Part II will explore options for those situations.

Although a case can easily be made that all households should employ training with the goal of teaching individuals appropriate group living behaviors, early assessment can alert the pet owner to potential problems and motivate them to accelerate training in order to maintain peace.

The most important factor to assess is the individual dog. Each individual is unique in its behavioral plasticity or rigidity, ability or lack thereof to recover from stressors, bite inhibition, bite threshold, age, sex, size, and play skills. Next, evaluate the interaction of each individual involved. Consider their past history, who they are as an individual, and the number of individuals that are together.

Additionally, breed-specific traits can make certain breeds more predisposed to conflict with littermates or other dogs. A particular breed's purpose and function, baseline arousal levels, and early onset of aggression (earlier then five weeks of age for most domestic dogs) are critical elements in assessing a particular dog's potential for sibling rivalry.[4,5,6,7] More study is needed on this issue; however, many trainers and behavior counselors mention terriers, for example, as a common breed or breed type involved in sibling rivalry contests.

The following are some common characteristics and/or behaviors that might indicate that a particular dog may warrant proactive management, monitoring, and training.

- Same-sex individuals

- Same-age individuals

- An individual reaching maturation, e.g., 18-24 months of age

- Siblings

- Play behavior

  - Dogs who don't respect cut-off signals from others

  - Dogs who appear to enjoy bullying or harassing others

  - Dogs whose play quickly results in a high-arousal level

  - Resource guarding toys, water bowl, or other individuals during play

- Density (number of dogs and/or people in a small space)

- Breed predisposition (e.g., terriers)

- Excitement levels

- Under-socialized individuals

- Asocial or proximity-sensitive individuals

- Resource guarding overall

Keeping the Peace

Early identification of potential conflict is critical. Equally important is early intervention. The list below contains some of the more common strategies for owners who hope to avoid sibling rivalry.

- Implement a "Say Please" or "Nothing in Life is Free" work program in which each dog earns food, praise, and other valued resources by performing sits, down, stays, or any other cued behavior.

- Train impulse-control behaviors, put them on cue, and practice them often. These include sit stay, down stay, leave it, wait, etc.

- Practice ad-hoc impulse-control opportunities throughout the day. These include ensuring that dogs politely wait for you to pass through doorways, move out of your way when you walk into their space, remain quietly tethered while you are otherwise occupied, etc.

- Read and implement the training exercises in *Feeling Outnumbered? Living in a Multi-dog Household* by Drs. Patricia McConnell and Karen London. This small book is jammed full of great impulse-control exercises that teach dogs to be "patient and polite" instead of "pushy and rude." For example, "Belle of the Ball" reinforces one dog who waits patiently while the owner interacts with another dog.

- Get help from a competent behavior counselor at the earliest signs of trouble.

PART II

In Part I the biological role of sibling rivalry, characteristics of social groupings, and the importance of early prevention were addressed. Unfortunately, most owners of multiple dogs do not understand the importance of implementing many of the strategies and exercises presented in Part I. Often trainers and behavior specialists are called in to help only after several fights have occurred between housemates, some of them incurring critical injuries. Determining the severity of such cases and choosing training strategies starts with educating clients and assessing the risk involved.

Client Education

There are several key educational points to cover with clients. They include:

- **Approach aggression with an open—and objective—mind**. It can be very difficult for people to separate their feelings for their dogs from the situation at hand. For example, if a younger dog is challenging their older dog, the feelings they have for the older dog may influence how they deal with the upstart youth, not realizing how their interactions with each dog can influence stress in the household. Aggression should be viewed as a temporary emotional state elicited by a combination of threats, resources, and behavioral options in a given individual that may be predisposed genetically or by experiences and uses aggression as the only effective strategy per situation and context.

- **Know what is "normal" and what is not**. Many owners do not know the difference between normal (appropriate and in context) aggression and abnormal aggression (maladaptive and inappropriate per situation and context). Before addressing the owner's or dogs' body language, behavior counselors should educate owners about what is normal and what is not from a big-picture perspective. For example, one might describe how Dog A, who has a valuable item, might lower his head and give a low growl when Dog B approaches. Dog B retreats. This is normal and appropriate. Conversely, Dog B might simply enter the room where Dog A is relaxing with a bone, and Dog A leaves his bone and charges 45 feet across the room and attacks Dog B, causing punctures and lacerations. This would be considered abnormal aggression.

  Interesting reading by Dr. Karen Overall about canine communication can be found at www.jazzpurr.org/letlive/overallabstract.htm. Both Dr. Overall's paper and Jean Donaldson's *The Culture Clash* are excellent sources of information for owners.

- **Observe their dogs' body language**. Maintaining harmony with multiple household dogs requires good observational skills, good interpretation of behaviors, and their intentions. We can help clients build their observational skills through watching dog behavior on video. Being able to pause, rewind, and play at various speeds helps to see the very covert and subtle precursors to escalation. Making a list of the variety of behaviors—not an interpretation of them—helps clients become better observers. For example, such a list might include ears forward, body posture with weight forward, tail up, tail tucked, but would not include interpretations, e.g., submissive, dominant, angry, happy. The goal is to increase clients' ability to be objective observers.

  I have my clients view my copy of Dr. Suzanne Hetts's video, *Canine Body Language*, and I provide them with the workbook that goes with it. I also assign homework to videotape their own dog for five minutes and then to write up what they see with ONE body part. As they get proficient with observing that body part, then I add a new body part and continue to build their observational skills in that manner.

  Another exercise for owners is for them to take a still photo of their dog while playing and then place tracing paper over the image and trace the outline of the dog's posture, an idea from colleague Gretchen Foster. This makes weight shifts more apparent to them. They can also videotape their dog in a highly reactive situation, and then replay using freeze-frame review, it's best if they view it once in real speed, then watch it two more times—once in slow speed, then in fast speed. This can highlight many things owners may miss when watching the event in real time.

- **Create individual ethograms**. An ethogram lists and describes each of the dog's behaviors. Creating an ethogram helps owners learn to observe a behavior rather then to project their interpretation of the behavior.

  Owners should list the behaviors in context, e.g., location, proximity to other individuals or valued resources, spatial type of environment, time, light, previous behaviors, and which individuals were present. This helps to identify protracting warnings so that they can become better at proactively refereeing and managing conflict. Not all owners have the desire to study and observe behavior to this degree, but for those who do, it can be an invaluable tool.[1] See sidebar "Sample Ethogram."

Assessing Risk

Trainers and behavior specialists who choose to work on cases of sibling rivalry should make sure that they have the experience to work with these cases because the potential for injury is high for both dogs and humans. Key factors affecting successful outcomes include:

- **Client compliance**. Is the client able to live a life of strict management, training/behavior modification, and deal with the underlying stress that often results from worrying about what the dogs are going to do if management lapses or the program fails? Behavior specialists who work on these cases cite this as the most critical success factor. If the client cannot implement the management protocols or find the time to commit to advance training with each dog, the fighting will likely increase.

  A client's ability to commit to a program will, in some part, be affected by the effects of the fighting on the overall quality of life for the entire family. For example, if one dog is being stalked by another, and is afraid to be anywhere near the stalker, is it reasonable to expect the dog being stalked to live in that manner for any length of time? Will management protocols put undue burden on some members of the human family, and is that acceptable to everyone involved? These are difficult questions for which answers may not be immediately apparent, but they should be posed. As a professional, it is our job to assess the overall picture of the family unit and to discuss with clients the challenges ahead. Counseling on rehoming should be included in discussions, as well as euthanasia if it applies.

- **Age on onset**. When aggression is displayed from a very early age, it might be an indication that one, or more than one individual, has anxiety issues with coping with its environment. Depending on how early "inappropriate aggression" started, a genetic predisposition (e.g., resource guarding behaviors) may be at its root. Aggression could also stem from an early traumatic event dealing with being in close proximity to other dogs. Early onset might also shed some light on a dog's early life experiences, e.g., dogs who are semi-isolated tend to develop maladaptive behaviors, be more hyper-active, exhibit compulsive behaviors, and develop social deficits such as inappropriate play skills, reactivity to excitement, lowered threshold for tolerance, and an inability to cope with low-level stimulation. The earlier the fighting began, the harder it can be to change.[2]

- **Predictability of outbursts**. Specific triggers such as resource guarding can be more easily managed, and training targeted for such specific triggers, than if the triggers are more diverse, plentiful, or hard for the owner to identify.

- **Severity of fights**. What has been the severity of the fights and has the severity escalated over time? The more severe the fights, the harder it will be to change behavior. What is the danger level to humans and to other family pets? Is this an acceptable level of danger? Putting dogs at risk of severe injury is not acceptable to most people.

- **Duration of condition**. Over what period of time have the fights occurred? If the fights (or underlying tensions) have been going on for several months or years, the behaviors are more entrenched and, thus, more difficult to change.

- **Frequency of fights**. What has been the frequency of fights? Breaking up fights once every few months is much different from fights that occur weekly. Practicing the art of fighting will result in fighting as a learned behavior. Learned behaviors are harder to change than ones in the earlier stages of behavior acquisition.

Risk Assessment Tools

Suzanne Hetts, PhD, has a questionnaire tool (see "Assessing Risk Factors Index" below) that gathers information about the onset and history of the behavior whether the behavior is generalized or happens in particular contexts, whether the behavior is unpredictable, does the aggression cause injury, if the dog is easily interrupted and redirected, and so on.

Dr. Ian Dunbar's bite index (see below) is another great tool to use when assessing the danger to owners who choose to attempt behavior modification. Cases with the best prognoses are when: a) there are few fights and few, or no, injuries; or b) there are frequent fights but still few, or no, injuries. Level 1 or Level 2 bites indicate that one or more of the dogs have good bite inhibition. Cases with good bite inhibition have a better prognosis than cases where the fights are either a) frequent with serious injuries; or b) infrequent with serious injuries. A serious injury would be considered a Level 3 and above, using Dr. Dunbar's bite index.

Each behavior counselor should decide which bite levels they are comfortable working on, as well as considering the legal and liability factors involved with high risk cases. For some behavior counselors, anything above a Level 3 is referred to a veterinary behaviorist, certified applied animal behaviorists (CAAB), or other professionals with extensive experience evaluating and working on cases that have involved serious injury.

Integrated Approach

To change behavior there are three environments that need to be modified to the best of our abilities. These are: 1) the physical environment; 2) the behavioral environment; and 3) the pharmacologic environment (veterinary assistance required). These three environments impact the animal as if they were one; however, if one environment is disturbed or agitated, we often see changes in the others. [3]

Managing, adding, subtracting, and manipulating certain aspects of these environments can modify an animal's behavior. The following is a list of the environments and samples of elements that can be manipulated within each. (Note: This integrated approach applies to any behavioral problem, i.e., not just sibling rivalry.)

Physical Environment

- perceived or actual spatial considerations
- visual stimulation
- olfactory

- auditory
- other animals
- relevant objects
- fences
- background music
- time accrual or time exposure
- toys
- beds
- baby-gates
- drag leashes
- head-collars
- body harnesses
- noise interrupter

Behavioral Environment
- individual or social environment (possible interaction)
- social group
- social stress / conflict
- arousal level of individual (easily triggered)
- excitement levels in the presence of the individual
- time accrual or time exposure

Pharmacological Environment
- medication (drug therapy)
- dietary changes
- lack of exercise
- altering or not altering the animal (spay/neuter)
- disease

The Behavior Modification Program
Once a determination has been made to pursue a behavior modification program, several key elements should be implemented and/or understood by the client:
- Proactively manage the environment and the individuals.
- Minimize high-arousal situations.

- Crate train so the dogs can be relaxed in crates. Relaxation is an important element in reducing stress.

- Remove all valuable resources from the environment.

- Use baby gates or crates to separate dogs when not supervised or during times likely to cause rivalry, e.g., existence of high-valued items, feeding time, returning home with one dog, etc.

- Keep dogs in separate parts of the house.

- Keep dogs on tethers and on-leash or draglines (and head halters) during any interaction.

- Select appropriate individuals to interact with each other while others are confined.

- When you leave with one dog, confine individuals so that when you return you avoid a potential high-arousal situation.

- Acclimate dogs to head-collars and muzzles if required for safety of others.

- Be keen observers of body language. Early identification of impending aggression is critical.

- Have the aggressor wear a bell. This makes the other dogs aware of his/her location. It also helps owners be more aware of what's going on in the house, helping them be a little more attentive to their dogs and the situation.

- Implement a work program. Make all dogs work for calories, attention, exercise, and affection.

- Implement step-by-step impulse-control training. Train individual dogs to reliable behaviors first then together as a group, e.g., down/stay, leave it, wait, etc. (See *Feeling Outnumbered: Living in a Multi-dog Household* by Dr. Patricia McConnell and Dr. Karen London for specific exercises.) Train to the point of mastery.

- Accustom the dogs to tethers. Tethering should not be a punishment, but a management and/or training tool.

- Teach a retrieve. This is a proactive management behavior that can be used to redirect a dog's path (i.e., cue the retrieve to redirect the dog away from another dog). Teaching a retrieve and relinquish to low-level resource guarders can also reduce anxiety levels as well. That is because responding to a cue helps switch the dog to a cerebral cortex "performance" function. But caution needs to be used due to the risk inherent in using this technique in a real conflict. An experienced trainer is required to ensure accurate and early interpretation of body language, as well as precise timing of the cue to avoid provoking an aggressive interaction between the dogs.

- Teach positive emotional responses. Use classical counterconditioning to elicit a positive conditioned emotional response from the dogs (e.g., see Fido, get something really, really tasty).

- Do not let the dogs "work it out." This allows the dogs to learn to either be a better aggressor or become victimized, and may induce chronic stress/anxiety in the group or between specific individuals.

- Don't support the "top dog." This can be a dangerous strategy. "Preferential treatment" can result in the "top dog" becoming a bully or more of a bully than it was before, as well as increasing tension and fights in the household.

- Have a planned response for when there is a fight.

- Have some noisemakers handy for interrupting a fight.

- Have leashes ready to catch individuals.

- Have eye-hooks (tethering locations) in the walls so that you can tether individuals as you separate them (or put them outside or in separate rooms).

- Have a slip board handy to separate the individuals in a safe manner.

- Have water sources (e.g., squirt guns, hoses) or citronella spray to interrupt spats and/or fights.

- Respond to protracted warnings early. Use distractions or cue alternative behaviors, e.g., sit, down, come, go to your bed, get your toy, walkies, to redirect the dogs.

- Avoid yelling or physical punishment. Positive punishment adds to the stress level and can potentially create a negative association between the dogs. It can also teach the animals that the owner is part of the stimulus package, i.e., suppression of behaviors when the owner is around, but as soon as the owner is out of the room, aggression escalates. An owner who uses verbal and physical punishment is really putting that animal in a "pressure cooker," a time bomb waiting to explode.

- Manage and coordinate interaction. As described throughout this article, owners need to have specific strategies in place for which dogs get to be together and under which specific conditions.

Conclusion

Sibling rivalry is a very difficult behavior to live with on a daily basis. Trying to modify the dogs' behavior requires a lot of commitment from the family and since the aggression may never be 100% resolved, the risk of future incidents is high. Management is a critical component in limiting incidents, but management is like treading water: it takes care of immediate needs but doesn't resolve any underlying causes. The bottom line is to keep everyone safe.

The two main variables that predict success are the frequency-damage ratio and the owner's education, understanding, and ability to implement the program. If the frequency-damage ratio is high and the client compliance low, it will be a very challenging situation to live with and modify. The more dogs living in a given household, the higher the likelihood that conflict between a pair will occur. It has been reported that most females start fights, and that the pairing of females are the most frequent gender combination to be in fights.

Behavior modification should include desensitization, counter-conditioning, and training reliable impulse-control exercises. Owners should be warned before a program starts that short-term results don't guarantee a long-term fix. Owners often get a false sense of security when they see improvements and relax their standards for management and treatment protocols, leading to another incident. Don't let them gamble with progress. Frequent follow-up by behavior counselors, in person and by phone, should be an integral part of these cases. ❖

Sample Ethogram

Resting: no movement, eyes closed, occasional body tremors (leg movements), occasional vocalizations

Freeze: no movement, eyes open, erect posture, stiff muscles, shallow breathing

Hard eye: eyes open, non-wavering gaze, stare, limited blinking

Vertical lip retraction: vertical displacement of the front lips that exposes canines and/or front teeth only

Horizontal lip retraction: horizontal displacement of the commisure (corner of lips) to expose back molars

Defensive posture: flexed limbs, ears and tail down, lowered body, weight shift in hind legs, slight round in back

Offensive posture: rigid standing, ears and tail up, erect body, weight shift forward over front legs

Lip licks: brief tip-of-tongue exposures, three to four times in a row

Lizard flicks: similar to lip licks, but with more frequency and more intensity associated with higher arousal/threat

Assessing Risk Factors Index
(*Pet Behavior Protocols*, AAHA Press, Lakewood, CO, 1999, p. 181. Used with permission from Dr. Suzanne Hetts, PhD)

The greater the number of "yes" answers, the higher the risk the dog poses.

1. Is this a long standing problem, rather than a recent change of behavior?

2. Is the aggression or threatening behavior generalized to many different stimuli or contexts?

3. Is the behavior unpredictable—i.e., is it rarely possible to determine when the dog is likely to bite or threaten? (Is it true even after the owner has been educated about what to look for?)

4. Does the behavior consist primarily of aggressive behavior that has caused injury, rather than threats or inhibited bites?

5. Is it difficult to get the dog to stop or inhibit the behavior?

6. Does the aggression or biting occur without observational warnings prior to the behavior?

7. Are one or more of the family members afraid of the dog?

8. Does the dog respond intensely to relatively minor triggers—i.e., Does he have a "10" response to a "2" stimulation?

9. Is the family's lifestyle such that it is difficult to supervise the dog or control his environment (denying access to potential victims, muzzling in certain situations, etc.)?

10. Is the family's commitment or ability to follow through with treatment recommendations questionable?

Dr. Ian Dunbar's Bite Index

Level 0: No bite inhibition information or history.

Level 1: No contact of skin or clothing. Growls, snaps, and lunges. Harassment but not skin contact.

Level 2: Dog bites but does not puncture the skin, tooth contact, this includes a tooth scratch ... 95% of all dog bites. These are usually unintentional bites, accidents.

Level 3: One to four holes in the skin, a puncture is considered a triangular hole with a curved entry point, from the canine—can include multiple bites; the holes must be less than 1/2 the length of the canine tooth, with tears in one direction only as a result of movement. These are not deep injuries. You can get serious injuries that are bruises only. Motion/movement can escalate the level of injury. These can take up to four to five days to heal.

Level 4: Deep punctures must be more than 1/2 the length of the canine tooth, with lacerations (black bruises that are up to six inches in diameter) or slashes in both directions from the puncture (the dog bit and shook his head). These dogs do not have a high rate of rehabilitation. Training recommendations are given out in triplicates—owner, trainer, vet. Animal is not allowed in public without muzzle.

Level 5: Multiple level 4 bites. Deep punctures—can include multiple-attack incident. Euthanasia advice given as the animals have a high risk of re-injury.

Level 6: Death of victim or flesh consumption.

References
PART I
[1] Sherman, CK., Reisner, I.R., Taliaferro, L.A. & Houpt, K.A. "Characteristics, treatment and outcome of 99 cases of aggression between dogs." *Appl Anim Behav Sci* 47: 91-108, 1996.

[2] Mock, D.W. & Parker, G.A. *The Evolution of Sibling Rivalry*. Oxford University Press, 1997.

[3] Hamilton, W.D. "The genetical evolution of social behavior." *J Theor Biol* 7:1-16 and 17-52, 1964.

[4] Frank, H & Frank, M.G "On the effects of domestication on canine social development and behavior." *Appl Anim Ethol*, 8, 507-25, 1982.

[5] Frank, H & Frank, M.G. "Comparative manipulation-test performance in ten week old wolves and Alaskan malamutes: a Piagetian interpretation." *J Comp Psychol*, 99, 266-74, 1985.

[6] Zimen, E. "Ontogeny of approach and flight behavior towards humans in wolves, poodles and wolf-poodle hybrids." In *Man and Wolf*, ed. H. Frank, pp. 275-92. Dordrecht, The Netherlands: Dr. W. Junk Publishers, 1987.

[7] Serpell, J. & Jagoe, J. A. "Early experience and the development of behavior." *The Domestic Dog* pp. 80-102. United Kingdom: Cambridge University Press, 1995.

PART II
[1] www.msu.edu/course/lbs/158h/snapshot.afs/manual/AnBehav.pdf www.marietta. edu/~biol/introlab thogram.pdf http://asstudents.unco.edu/faculty/radams/Ecology2005/Labs/Lab2/Ethogram.doc

[2] Lindsay, Steven, R. "Adaptation and learning." *Handbook of Applied Dog Behavior and Training, Vol. 1*. Ames, Iowa: Iowa State Press, 2000.
Lindsay, Steven R. "Aggression between dogs sharing the same household." *Handbook of Applied Dog Behavior and Training, Vol. 2*. Ames, Iowa: Iowa State Press, 2001.
Lindsay, Steven R. "Neurobiology and development of aggression." *Handbook of Applied Dog Behavior and Training, Vol. 3*. Ames, Iowa: Blackwell Publishing, 2005.

[3] Overall, Karen. "Treatment of behavioral problems." *Clinical Behavioral Medicine For Small Animals*. Mosby, Inc.: St. Louis, MO: pp. 274, 1997.

Recommended Reading

Aloff, Brenda. *Aggression in Dogs. Practical Management, Prevention and Behavior Modification*. Wenatchee, WA: Dogwise Publishing. (pp. 369-379), 2002.

Horwitz, Debra. *Aggression between household dogs*. Atlantic Coast Veterinary Conference, 2001.

Horwitz, Debra. BSAVA *Manual of Canine and Feline Behavioural Medicine*. Quedgeley, Gloucester: British Small Animal Veterinary Association, 2002.

Lindsay, Steven R. *Handbook of Applied Dog Behavior and Training, Vol. 2*. Ames, Iowa: Iowa State Press. 2001.

Lindsay, Steven R. *Handbook of Applied Dog Behavior and Training, Vol 3*. Ames, Iowa: Blackwell Publishing, 2005.

McConnell, Patricia & London, Karen. *Feeling Outnumbered? How to Manage and Enjoy Your Multi-Dog Household*. Black Earth, WI: Dog's Best Friend, Ltd., 2001.

Overall. Karen L. "Interdog aggression can strike with deadly consequences." *DVM Newsmagazine*. Jan 1, 2002.

Overall. Karen L. "Interdog aggression: What are the warning signs?" *DVM Newsmagazine*. April 1, 2002.

Overall. Karen L. *Clinical Behavioral Medicine for Small Animals*. St. Louis, Missouri: Mosby, Inc., 1997.

When the You-Know-What Hits the Fan: Dealing with Difficult Housetraining Issues
Teoti Anderson, May/June 2006

Did you ever notice that dog trainers spend a lot of time discussing dog waste? Where it is, how often it appears, if it's normal, how to clean it up...to a group of dog trainers, this is casual dinner conversation.

We know housetraining a dog isn't rocket science. Realistic expectations, proper scheduling, confinement, supervision, consistency, a proper training program, and patience are all keys to a successful housetraining program. Remember, however, that our clients' dogs don't live with us. They live with people who don't usually talk about dog pee at the table. People who are sick and tired of finding messes on the carpet. And for the people whose dogs have especially challenging housetraining issues, they may be getting sick and tired of Fido altogether.

Is It Behavior or the Body?

Dr. Mary Fluke, DVM, of Mallard Creek Animal Hospital in Charlotte, NC, says some pet owners will think to consult her first. She says, "The astute person notices a change in behavior and thinks, 'Gosh, why is my dog doing this? I wonder if something is wrong? I think I'll call the vet!'"

Other clients notice there's something amiss, but don't realize it's really a problem. So the behavior continues for some time. Mary adds, "Eventually the dog comes in for another reason altogether and the elimination problem gets mentioned in passing. I discover that the dog has had bladder stones for months and months, or is diabetic or something like that."

Dr. Fluke shares some physical ailments, conditions, and medications that can cause a dog to pee more than usual:

- Urinary tract infections

- Bladder stones

- Bladder tumors

- Any disease that can make a dog drink more water than normal—diabetes, kidney disease, liver disease, thyroid problems, and adrenal disease.

- Diuretics and drugs like prednisone and theophylline—these cause dogs to drink more, therefore increase urination.

Mary also explains that diet changes can cause problems. She says, "I've seen dogs who were changed to food that was saltier start urinating more because they are drinking more, so keep diet change in mind."

When you're working with a dog that has persistent housetraining issues, it's a good idea to recommend a trip to the veterinarian to rule out physical problems first.

Tough Cases

What if you've ruled out physical problems, and are now faced with a dog that persistently eliminates in the house?

Margaret Johnson, CPDT, of the Humaner Trainer in Austin, TX, had such a case with a Yorkshire Terrier who belonged to a retired couple. The dog came from a puppy mill and had free reign of a huge house. She had a long history of eliminating wherever and whenever she pleased.

Margaret explains, "These people stopped going on vacation because they couldn't take her with them nor could they leave her alone. They said, 'She'd just scream if we left her.' They got up when she said, which was about an hour or two before they'd prefer to get up. They fed her when she said ... you get the picture."

Margaret helped the dog by helping the people first. "I started by asking them how their lives would be different if life were 'ideal' with the dog," she says. "When they defined that, I asked what would be acceptable—what's the least they could live with and be happy. Then, I outlined how we could get to ideal by starting with acceptable."

She helped the couple make small changes, including how they interacted with the dog and set up their household. Margaret adds, "The house had a very open floor plan. They didn't understand how to partition off areas so the dog couldn't just 'go' everywhere. That may seem very simple and obvious to us, but it's not to many people."

Margaret says the clients never did make it to "ideal," but they were thrilled with the progress they did make. She says, "The dog is now housetrained, and so are the clients. They can sleep through the night, they can go on vacation, and they say the dog seems happier, too."

Challenging problems don't always deal with urination. Janice Patton, MEd, CDBC, CPDT, CC-SF SPCA of A Real Friend Dog Training Inc. in Austin, TX, once worked with a Beagle who persistently pooped in his crate. She began with her usual protocol—getting a properly sized kennel, switching kennel types from what he was used to, establishing a feeding and potty schedule. None of this worked, until one day she realized what the problem really was.

"He was eliminating to get out of the crate," Janice says. "When he had done it in the past, the owner had taken him out of the crate so she could clean it. Then she'd put him back in, at which time he would promptly eliminate again." The Beagle had learned that messing his crate was his ticket out!

Janice had to teach him a new routine. She explains, "What finally worked was him only getting out of a clean, dry crate. So if he eliminated in the kennel, we would take dog, kennel, and all outside and wash the crate, open it, dry it, and not let him out. We'd give him an hour or so and if the crate was dry, we let him out with a party!" The Beagle successfully learned how to stay in a clean crate.

The Client's Perspective

If a dog trainer comes home and her dog has pooped in his crate, what does she do? She dons a pair of latex gloves, examines the poop thoroughly, then disposes of it or bags it for the vet, with a label. To our clients, this probably seems ridiculous!

When a client comes home and her dog has pooped in his crate, she's likely to think it's really gross and unfair. If her dog has had ongoing housetraining issues, her anger is going to increase accordingly. She's going to lose patience with her dog quickly, and she may come to feel that it's better to just start over with a new dog than to have the carpet professionally cleaned once again.

Can you relate to your client's frustration? What a pet dog owner is willing to put up with may be a fraction of what you're willing to endure. Even if you personally think her reaction is out of proportion, it's important to acknowledge and respect your client's feelings. She has every right to be upset. Cleaning up after dogs who continually eliminate in their crates or in the home is unpleasant and exhausting. And if you ignore or dismiss your client, she's likely to think you don't care about her or what she's going through. Then she won't listen to your training plan, no matter how brilliant it is.

When your clients complain, listen to them carefully. What are their underlying concerns? Here are a few my clients have shared over the years, along with some ideas for helping them better cope with their frustration so you can tackle the problem together:

- **They're tired of coming home every day to the same mess**. Put together a cleaning kit for your client. It can be inexpensive —paper towels, cleaner, rubber gloves. Put it all in a bright bucket, and include a treat just for the client, such as peppermints (they're sweet, and they smell good!). Be sure to give the family lots of encouragement as they work through your program, and praise them for even the smallest successes.

- **They're tired of cleaning their dog over and over**. Share tips on bathing and grooming their dog. You can even make part of your lesson all about training the dog to enjoy bathtime. Try working out an arrangement with local groomers to offer discounts to your client (you may be able to work out a mutually rewarding marketing relationship). Try a gift of soothing hand lotion for your client. If you acknowledge the fact she's working her hands raw in bathing her dog every day, you're showing respect and recognition for her efforts.

- **They worry the dog will never get better**. Contact them in between lessons and ask how they're progressing. Sometimes something as simple as you asking how they're doing is enough to make your clients feel as if they're not alone with their problem.

Even if the dog's main issue is housetraining, try expanding your lessons to include family manners exercises, which will make him easier to live with overall. Toss in a few tricks lessons, too. If the dog is acting adorable and they're having fun training him, they are less likely to give up on him! If the dog is in a group class, try using the dog as a demo for an exercise in front of the class (make sure you set him up to succeed!). Many students feel a sense of pride when you choose their dog for a demonstration. And if the family can see him succeed with you, it can give them hope for his progress.

In order for dogs to successfully live with humans, most of them are going to need to be housetrained. Therefore, it's important for trainers to understand the possible underlying causes of persistent housetraining issues. But it's also critical we listen to our human clients so we can better understand their perspectives. If you can manage both, you'll be helping the entire family. ❖

A Case Study: Separation Anxiety

Lore I. Haug, Edited by Terry Long, March/April 2005

Case Information

Name:	Caruso
Age:	1.5 yrs
Species:	Canine
Sex:	Castrated Male
Color:	Black
Breed:	Labrador Retriever Mix

History

Presenting complaint:	Separation Anxiety
Vaccines:	1/20/04 Bordatella, Rabies, DHLPP
Operations:	Castration
Prior illness:	none known
Medications:	Sentinel monthly, 80mg Clomicalm once daily
Other animals:	none
Environmental history:	Primarily indoor, but with access to dog door to go outside
Diet:	Science Diet Adult Beef and Rice, 2 cups a.m. and 1 cup p.m.

Physical Exam

Temperature:	101.7
Heart Rate:	68
Respiration Rate:	36
Weight:	57#

Description of abnormal findings: No abnormal findings

Caruso was acquired at approximately one year of age from a shelter. Immediately, the dog began destructive chewing when alone, particularly when the wife was gone. Shortly after this, the referring veterinarian placed the dog on 80 mg Clomicalm once daily. The destruction stopped for a few days and then resumed at a frequency of one to two times per week. The current frequency is the same, but whereas before the dog targeted one item for destruction, now he tears up multiple items. These typically include pillows, furniture, personal belongings, and household items.

The owner has a crate for Caruso, but he has never been locked in it. The dog will voluntarily enter the crate at times. Toys and food-related enrichment items are left for the dog and he will play with these and eat the food. The dog does not routinely destroy barriers or try to escape the house although, when the owner is home, if she closes a door between herself and the dog, he will scratch at it.

When the owners are home, Caruso will solicit play and sometimes lie quietly on the floor. He does follow the wife around the house, and jumps on her frequently and wraps his front legs around her body. Other behaviors directed toward the wife include: biting at her hands and pants, blocking her path of movement with his body, biting at her purse and keys when she picks them up, barking at her, jumping in her lap when she is sitting down, and barking and raking at her with his paws when she is asleep in bed. Caruso does not do these behaviors to any significant degree with her husband.

Caruso has had some informal basic training and is fairly responsive to basic commands. He is walked daily for two miles.

Behavioral Observations

Caruso was very friendly and forward during the consultation. He immediately approached to greet us. He would sit readily on command and eagerly took food treats. If I sat down on the stool, he would push up against me looking for food treats. The dog was responsive to my body blocks, but was somewhat persistent in repeatedly invading personal space.

Caruso would occasionally rest on the floor near the husband. He also would jump up and put his forelegs on their laps, particularly the wife. I asked the wife to body block the dog away from her. He became a little more respectful of her space, but then began jumping on her every time she sat down. She would stand up and push him back (body block). The dog would jump on her and grab her with his forelegs. On the ground, he would mouth at her hands, arms, and pants as she herded him away. Once he backed away, she would sit, but he would immediately jump on her again. Her attempts to protect her personal space excited the dog.

Questions:
1. What is/are the significant problem behavior(s)?
2. What are the differential diagnoses for each of these?
3. What is your final diagnosis/diagnoses?
4. What historical or observational findings support your diagnosis?
5. What management steps would you recommend?
6. What modification steps would your recommend?
7. What is the prognosis for this case?

Presenting Problems

1. Chewing household objects in owner's absence.

   Differential Diagnoses:
   a. Separation anxiety
   b. Separation-related disorder
   c. Destructive chewing
   d. Reaction to external environmental stimulus (e.g., territorial invasion)

2. Jumping on people (including grabbing with forelegs).

   Differential Diagnoses:
   a. Unruliness
   b. Dominance-related aggression
   c. Play behavior

3. Biting at wife's hands, clothes and personal objects.

   Differential Diagnoses:
   a. Separation-related disorders
   b. Separation anxiety
   c. Dominance related aggression
   d. Play aggression/behavior
   e. Attention seeking behavior

4. Barking and raking at owner.

   Differential Diagnoses:
   a. Attention-seeking behavior

Diagnosis

1. Separation-Related Disorder

2. Destructive Chewing

3. Unruliness

Caruso was diagnosed with destructive chewing, separation-related disorder, and unruliness. Classic separation anxiety in the strict definition refers to a dog that has developed a hyper-attachment to a particular individual. This is a pathological condition. These dogs show signs of arousal, hyper-vigilance, and anxiety when separated in any way from that individual. These symptoms can include pacing, panting, trembling, urination/defecation, anorexia, and salivation. The dogs also show anticipatory signs of anxiety even before separation occurs. Some dogs are destructive and typically this is targeted primarily toward barriers (doors, windows) and personal items. The dog's primary goal is to reestablish contact with the attachment figure.

Caruso does show some of these symptoms; however, he is not anorexic nor does he target barriers with his destruction. He destroys a random assortment of objects. In addition, dogs with true separation anxiety do not typically show marked response to clomipramine within one to two days. Their behavioral symptoms are relatively constant (although they may wax and wane to some degree) rather than occurring intermittently.

Caruso's destructive response is more a release for his frustration at not being able to access the wife. He does not actually attempt to escape the house or show escape behaviors. His behavior when the owners are home is attentive but also bossy and controlling at times. When the wife is not home or she is separated from him, he is unable to monitor her if he so chooses.

The jumping, "hugging" (which is an abbreviated mounting behavior), and grabbing/mouthing are generally unruly behaviors. Caruso is rather pushy and assertive with the wife, although he is not aggressive. The context of the behaviors, as well as the sequence of the interaction, rule out play behavior as the primary issue.

Management Steps Include:

- Try to avoid leaving Caruso home alone. Consider doggie daycare for now or leaving him with a friend or relative.

- The wife should avoid putting herself in situations where Caruso tends to jump and get bossy.

- Caruso should not be allowed to get near the wife at night when she is sleeping.

- The owners should avoid allowing Caruso to follow them everywhere. If the owner goes in the bathroom, she should shut the door. If she goes into the bedroom to get something, she should shut the door while she is in there. Ignore him the entire time. The owner's attention should be focused on the task at hand, not on the dog.

- For the next two weeks, the owner should try to interact with Caruso only during training sessions or to provide for his basic needs. All interactions should be constructive. The wife should refrain from actively greeting the dog at all when she returns home. There should be no specific "hello." Her first interaction with the dog should be a command of some type, and that serves as her "hello."

Modification Steps Include:

- Begin adapting Caruso to being confined in the crate. Start with very short periods and put some type of enrichment device (e.g., Kong™ toy with food in it) in the crate with him.

- Caruso should receive his entire daily ration of food during training sessions or in an enrichment device.

- Continue working on basic training with Caruso. Caruso should learn good responses to voice cues for at least sit, down, come, and wait/stay. He should learn to do these from a distance of 10-20 feet. Caruso should also learn to "play dead" lying on his side with his head flat on the ground (as one type of relaxation exercise).
  - The owner should begin enforcing personal space. Caruso should not invade that last 12-18 inch perimeter around his/her body without specific invitation. This invitation comes only if he is already being polite and calm.
  - The owner should never interact with the dog directly (e.g., giving a cue or proceeding with a training exercise) unless the dog is outside the 12-18 inch perimeter.
  - The owner should use body blocks when the dog does invade personal space, especially to jump or to try to prompt the owner for some type of resource (e.g., attention, food, toys).
- Begin a deference protocol.[1] The goals with this program include the following:
  - To help the owner learn to manipulate his reward systems.
  - To condition the owner to be aware of how to maintain control over all interactions with him.
  - To teach Caruso self-control and "emotional maturity."
- Begin using body blocks to help with the jumping and pushy behavior.
- The dog was fitted with a Gentle Leader™ head collar for additional control, especially to help with the jumping behavior and some of the unruliness.
- Caruso should be rewarded frequently for calm and polite behaviors.
- Begin working on the relaxation protocol1 and massage exercises.
- Begin the D/CC[2] exercises for graduated departures once Caruso has completed the above exercises.
- Teach Caruso a "go to mat" command.
- Clomicalm was continued at 40mg twice daily. I would not have considered this dog a candidate for drug therapy; however, since the medication had reduced the dog's motivation for destruction to some degree, it was continued for a short time while the owner implemented management and modification steps.

Prognosis: Good to excellent.

Follow Up

The jumping and pushiness were dramatically reduced within 36 hours of the consultation. Within one week the dog was voluntarily leaving the wife's side to go outside or rest in another room. His greeting behavior was more polite and controlled.
❖

References:

[1] The deference and relaxation protocols are adapted from Dr. Karen Overall's protocols (B-1 and B-2) from Overall, Karen L. *Clinical Behavioral Medicine for Small Animals*. St. Louis, MO: Mosby, Inc., 1997.

[2] Desensitization and counter-conditioning.

A Case Study of Impulse Control

Lore I. Haug, Edited by Terry Long, May/June 2006

Case Information

Patient:	Kiri
DOB:	Four years old
Species:	Canine
Breed:	Golden Retriever
Sex:	Female/Spayed
Color:	Gold

History

Presenting complaint:	Dog aggression
Operations:	Ovariohysterectomy at one year of age
Prior illness:	Occasional ear infections
Medications:	Heartgard, Frontline Plus, Tresaderm PRN (as needed) for ear infection, Glucosamine/ Chondroitin/MSM two tablets daily, Omega 3 FA 1000 mg. BID, multivitamin daily
Environmental history:	Mostly indoors (a house), crated at night
Household:	Two adult women (Angela and Katie), no children, few visitors
Diet:	Science Diet lamb and rice
Other animals:	Amie, seven-year-old female spayed Golden Retriever; Erica, six-year-old female spayed Golden Retriever; Ricki, one-year-old female spayed Golden Retriever; and Tara, recently deceased 13-year-old female spayed Golden Retriever.

Chief Behavioral Complaints:

1. Dog-directed resource guarding: food or food substances, toys and non-food items, some locations (e.g., dog bed)

2. Easily over-stimulated (becomes highly aroused). Arousal occurs rapidly and is excessive for the context. Triggers include sounds, lights, toys, and hose/sprinklers.

3. Fearfulness of novel objects such as a yardstick, new sounds, or lights. Often difficult to distinguish this reaction from excitability/frustration.

4. Aggression when taken by collar to move her away from a guarded resource.

Behavioral History

Kiri was acquired at one year of age from a rescue organization. She was in poor condition including a fractured tail, thin body condition, and poor socialization. She demonstrated various compulsive-like behaviors including incessant retrieving and ball focus, constant pacing, and chasing/focus on shadows/lights.

The owners took her on as a foster, but decided to keep Kiri as they felt the average owner would not be able to deal with the dog's energy level and behavior issues. For the first few days, Kiri was tethered to Angela to encourage bonding, facilitate housetraining, and keep her away from the cat. After several days, Kiri began guarding Angela from the other dogs.

When Kiri first came to live with Angela and Katie, she paced constantly and was never still. They started crating her whenever they were sitting down and now when she is put into a crate, she calms instantly. This is one of the few times that she voluntarily calms herself. Despite intermittent play sessions with the other dogs (after an acclimation period where she did not appear to know how to play), walking her five miles a day, and training sessions, Kiri never seemed to tire.

She did not seem to have many canine social skills. Tara began to play with her and Kiri began showing some normal play behavior after these interactions. Eventually some of the other dogs began to play with her intermittently in the beginning. However, by the time of the consult, the other dogs generally attempted to avoid Kiri. Kiri does play with the new puppy, Ricki. Currently Ricki is the only dog that typically shows social behavior to Kiri.

Immediately upon coming into the home, Kiri began guarding resources such as food, stool, emesis (vomit), toys, and some locations from the other dogs. She would then, and still does, often swallow items (e.g., socks, gloves) to keep other dogs from getting them.

The first incident of dog aggression happened after a few days of bonding with the owner. Kiri attempted to attack Tara, the oldest Golden, whenever Tara would approach the owner.

Another major incident occurred when Tara was being fed in her crate. Angela walked into another room and Kiri opened the crate and attacked Tara for the food. Angela pulled her off and Kiri growled. There were only minor lacerations on Tara's neck.

The major incident that prompted the consult was on the morning of Sept. 11. The owners woke up early for a bathroom break, everyone went out and Tara seemed normal. They went back to sleep for about an hour and woke up to find Tara on the floor next to the bed screaming and Kiri was on top of her growling and gripping the underside of her neck. There were feces behind Tara on the floor and a small amount of urine. Tara died immediately after. There were no punctures on her and only a small tuft of fur had been pulled out. The suspicion was that Tara may have become agonal or had a seizure and Kiri attacked her at that point due to Tara's bizarre behavior.

Kiri has attacked Erica over a piece of food on the floor and over an empty food bowl. Kiri also bullies Amie, following her and trying to posture to her or challenge her. On one occasion, Amie stood her ground and postured back to Kiri after Kiri had been badgering her for a while. The dogs then got into a scuffle that resulted in several small lacerations to Kiri's head. Amie had no injuries.

In general, Kiri is the dog that is injured in a fight even though she is not the smallest dog. Kiri has postured toward every dog except the puppy, Ricki.

Kiri also is overly excited with noises and lights on walls. She will bark and pace trying to catch the lights. She is also coprophagic.

Kiri will also show aggression (growling, snarling) when someone grabs her collar to interrupt a behavior or tries to remove her from a guarded resource. She has never actually bitten either owner.

When Kiri becomes over-stimulated, she may lash out at one of the other dogs especially if she is frustrated or thwarted in some behavior. Kiri also becomes aroused and aggressive during meal times. She is crated in the living room during food preparation times, but often shows explosive outbursts of aggression in the crate during this time, especially when she sees another dog.

Kiri will interact well with other dogs outside the home and at the agility ring even in the presence of food or other rewards. She is very friendly with people, including strangers.

Kiri has had extensive training, as both owners are involved in competitive sports such as agility. Initial training was extremely difficult as Kiri would become anxious and agitated during class. They note that it has taken an extensive level of work to achieve Kiri's current state of behavior in the home. Eventually she began showing great focus and response during training. She is highly focused during competitive situations.

Aggression seems to escalate if one of the owners is out of town, particularly Angela. Kiri has a closer relationship with Angela than Katie.

Physical Exam

Temperature:	101.8 F
Heart rate:	70 bpm
Resting rate:	18 bpm
Weight:	50.3 lbs

Description of Abnormal Findings

No significant findings

Behavioral Observations

Kiri jumped up and greeted the student and clinician upon entering the room. She was calm during her physical exam. She spent most of the consult sitting or lying near the owner. She was very responsive to obedience cues from the owners. She did not react to environmental stimuli outside and generally appeared calm and well behaved.

Questions

1. Develop a problem list and a differential diagnoses list for each problem.

2. What medical conditions, if any, could play a significant contribution to the dog's problems?

3. Determine the degree to which you feel the dog's reactions appear to fall within the bounds of "normal."

Presenting Problems and Differential Diagnoses

1. Resource guarding

   Differential Diagnoses:
      a. as component of "dominance" (inter-dog) aggression
      b. primary resource guarding

2. Aggression to household dogs (non-resource related)

   Differential Diagnoses:
      a. Dominance/status

3. Aggression when grabbed by the collar

   Differential Diagnoses:
      a. Fear
      b. Conflict/"Dominance"
      c. Redirected

4. Constant pacing and failure to calm down

   Differential Diagnoses:
      a. Anxiety (e.g. Generalized Anxiety Disorder)
      b. Stereotypic pacing
      c. Compulsive disorder
      d. Hyperkinesis

5. Eating of non-food items

   Differential Diagnoses:
      a. Primary Pica
      b. Component of resource guarding
      c. Nutritional issue
      d. Attention-seeking behavior

6. Rapid arousal

   Differential Diagnoses:
   a. Impulse-control disorder

   b. Hyperkinesis

   c. Neurologic/neuro-mental disorder

7. Hyper-responsive to sounds

   Differential Diagnoses:
   a. Neurologic/neuro-developmental disorder

   b. Impulse-control disorder

   c. Fear/anxiety

8. Hyper-responsive and chasing of lights/shadows

   Differential Diagnoses:
   a. Neurologic/neuro-developmental disorder

   b. Impulse-control disorder

   c. Compulsive disorder

   d. Stereotypic disorder

   e. Attention-seeking behavior

Possible contributing medical issues

1. Hypothyroidism

2. Neurologic disease

   a. Neoplasia (cancer)

   b. Infectious (distemper, Rocky Mountain Spotted Fever, Erhlichia, Lyme)

   c. Protozoal (Toxoplasmosis, Neospora)

3. Nutritional

   a. Food allergy, food intolerance

   b. Elemental nutrient deficiencies

4. Seizure-related disorder

   a. Epilepsy

   b. Infectious (e.g. distemper)

5. Hyperkinesis

Diagnostics Performed

Complete Blood Count (CBC): Neutropenia (low white blood cell count). Recheck values one week later were similar. Further monitoring was recommended to determine if these values are normal for this dog.

Urinalysis: Kiri's urine specific gravity is low (1.008). Although this value is not necessarily abnormal, it is unusual for a healthy adult dog. Recheck values one week later were within expected limits.

Chemistry panel and electrolytes: No significant findings. Thyroid results within normal limits.

Diagnosis

Kiri's behavior is clearly abnormal. She demonstrates an inability to relax and self-regulate. She reaches arousal easily and in response to a wide variety of environmental stimuli. She is hyper-vigilant, generally irritable, and has an obvious impulse-control disorder. Although an animal's environment always plays a role in its behavioral expression, Kiri's issues are also environmentally independent indicating an inherent physiologic/neurologic dysfunction.

Kiri has an obvious neurologic/neurophysiologic disorder. She demonstrates activity levels excessive for her age, breed, and level of training/exercise. Additionally, her agitation and hyper-reactivity is pervasive and crosses almost all contexts and multiple stimuli. Her reactions are disproportionate to the situation. The other adult dogs in the home have essentially ostracized her. When multiple socially normal dogs shun or actively avoid a patient, this speaks volumes about the patient's level of abnormality. Additionally, despite over a year of appropriate training and household management by experienced owners, her behaviors have been minimally mitigated. When dealing with physiologic abnormalities, it is often difficult to determine whether such abnormalities are acquired or congenital/developmental. This is particularly true when no information is available about the dog's puppy history.

Although Kiri's thyroid results were within normal limits, some clinicians might classify her as "suboptimal." However, there is little scientific data to support the notion that so many dogs are hypothyroid rather than hypothesizing that our reference values may be what are erroneous. If Kiri is truly thyroid normal, even nominal supplementation may exacerbate her aggression, irritability, and hyper-reactivity. At the time of the consult, trial thyroid supplementation was not considered as a first-line intervention.

Although neoplasia and infectious disorders can cause a number of the symptoms seen in this dog, due to the duration of the problem, they are unlikely. With the exception of distemper virus, Kiri could not harbor an infection for three years without the signs progressing to more obvious neurologic deficits. Early distemper virus infection can cause lifetime alterations in neurologic function (usually manifesting as seizures); however, this is difficult to diagnose and no specific treatment is available. For these reasons, further diagnostics for distemper were not performed.

Little is currently known about the myriad of ways in which elemental nutritional deficiencies may affect behavior in any specific individual, particularly dogs. Diet can play a subtle but important role in behavioral management. Again, there are no straightforward diagnostic steps that can determine if dietary issues are a component. We are left to rely on some degree of trial-and-error manipulation of the dog's diet.

Although seizures are frequently listed as a cause of aggression, this scenario is actually rather uncommon. Additionally, Kiri shows a variety of behaviors that, although individually could be attributed to a seizure disorder, when taken together make such a disorder unreasonable as a diagnosis.

Hyper-kinesis was considered as a possible disorder. Kiri demonstrated a number of symptoms often associated with such dogs, including difficulty focusing, inability to relax, incessant pacing, aggression, impulse control problems, stereotypic behaviors, and a general irritability/arousability. Although Kiri was very calm during the consultation, this was after over a year of intensive training by experienced owners. Additionally, individuals with hyper-kinesis often show improved focus and composure initially in novel environments. In the canine literature, elevated peripheral sympathetic tone (increased heart rate, respiratory rate, dilated pupils, etc.) is listed as diagnostic criteria. However, in human medicine these parameters are not part of the diagnostic picture. This is a neuro-chemical disorder. As noted above, Kiri did not exhibit elevated sympathetic tone during the consultation. (Her heart rate was actually rather low for a dog in a veterinary clinic.) When evaluating dogs for possible hyper-kinesis, I do not use peripheral physiologic measures as an essential part of my diagnostic criteria, but instead depend on behavioral criteria. Definitive diagnosis is based on drug trial with stimulants such as methylphenidate (Ritalin®) or d-amphetamine.

Outline initial recommendations for intervention

- The owner should continue management steps to ensure the safety and welfare of all the dogs in the home.
    a. Keep the dogs separated around resources.
    b. Keep Kiri under close supervision around the other dogs, on leash when necessary.
    c. Attempt to avoid letting Kiri near other dogs during excitable situations.
    d. Consider experimenting with dietary changes such as natural foods, raw foods, and/or low protein/low corn diets.

- Continue basic training.

- Adapt Kiri to wearing a muzzle for as-needed situations. Consider also desensitizing her to a head collar.

- Begin the Deference Protocol1 to continue to reinforce calm, focused behavior, with specific emphasis on:
    a. Response to commands when given.

b. Remaining calm, polite and focused (making eye contact) throughout the interaction.

    c. Remaining aware and outside of personal space perimeters of both humans and other dogs.

- Begin Relaxation Protocols1, including massage or TTouch.

- Reward specific "de-stressing" behaviors such as sighing and shaking off.

- The owner was given information on the Anxiety Wrap™.

- Dog Appeasing Pheromone™ (DAP) diffusers were dispensed to be placed in areas where the dogs spend a lot of time.

- More targeted desensitization/counterconditioning exercises for specific triggers such as resources, noises, lights, etc., can be incorporated into the program after she has completed foundation exercises and her physiologic/neurochemical issues have been more adequately addressed.

- Although Kiri was a potential hyper-kinesis candidate, a drug trial was not performed at the consultation. We elected to start with a selective serotonin reuptake inhibitor (SSRI), specifically fluoxetine (generic Prozac), for several reasons. First, methylphenidate is a Class II scheduled drug making it both difficult to acquire and subject to the legal interventions and scrutiny associated with such drugs. SS-RIs, particularly fluoxetine, have been used safely in dogs for many years and for extended periods of time. This class of drug is typically the treatment of choice for dogs with impulse control disorders. A number of studies in humans and non-human primates have demonstrated that impaired impulse control appears related to reduced levels of 5-hydroxyindoleacetic acid (the primary metabolite of serotonin) in the brain and cerebrospinal fluid (Coccaro, 1997; Fairbanks, 2001; Mehlman, 1994). Additionally, I personally have had more success treating aggression cases with SSRIs versus tricyclic antidepressants. These drugs are also used in the treatment of some cases of human ADHD. Lastly, SSRIs are generally less likely than tricyclic antidepressants (TCAs) to interfere with future thyroid level testing. Kiri was prescribed 10 mg. of fluoxetine by mouth once daily for 14 days to then be increased to 20 mg. once daily.

Initial Follow Up

Initial follow up two weeks after the consult showed that the general training was going well. Kiri was making progress with the muzzle and relaxation tasks; however, her attempts to attack Erica were increasing and several of her other behaviors had worsened. Indeed, the owner felt that the more time she spent training Kiri the more belligerent the dog became to the other bitches. Kiri and Erica were being kept separated at all times. Kiri's over-reactivity to sounds and her pacing had improved by 50%; however, her agitation/aggression toward the other dogs and her general fearfulness had worsened by 60%. The owner was instructed to discontinue fluoxetine to determine if the drug was contributing to the dog's increased agitation. One month after the consult, Kiri was switched to sertraline (generic Zoloft) at 25 mg. once daily. Although sertraline is a slightly less potent reuptake inhibitor than fluoxetine, it also has dopamine reuptake blockade, has few drug interactions, and tends to have a low side-effect profile. Three days after starting the medication, the owner again noticed an increase in the dog's agitation and reactivity, even more pronounced than while she was on fluoxetine. By the tenth day, the owner described the dog as "manic." Sertraline was discontinued.

Why, if Kiri reacted adversely to fluoxetine, was she placed on sertraline, a drug in the same class? While both of these drugs are SSRIs, meaning their primary mechanism of action is blockade of the reuptake of serotonin from the synaptic cleft, each drug in the class has variations in potency and actions on other receptor classes. Thus an individual may respond differently to one drug versus the other even though they are in the same drug class.

At this point Kiri was placed on a methylphenidate trial at ten mg. twice daily, which was then increased to 15 mg. three times daily based on improvements in her behavior, but the short duration of action of the drug. While on 15 mg. three times daily, Kiri's overall reactivity improved 40% and her sound sensitivity even more so. The owner noted a greatly improved ability to connect with the dog verbally and in the dog's reactivity to outside stimuli. Her impulse control also improved. Combination drug therapy will most likely be instituted at the dog's next re-check.

Ten-Week Follow Up Visit For Kiri

1. Due to continued aggression noted between Kiri and Ricki, efforts need to be made to keep them separated as much as possible. When it is necessary for one of them to pass the other in a kennel, the kenneled dog should be cued to sit or lie down calmly. Using a Treat 'N' Train™ device might be helpful for remotely rewarding the dogs during such situations.

2. The owner will begin using the Gentle Leader™ on Kiri. The muzzle can be fitted over the Gentle Leader when necessary. Previously, they did not feel Kiri would have allowed them to put the Gentle Leader on her routinely. They now think she may.

3. Try slowly switching Kiri to a new diet. Some dogs physiologically respond better to one diet or another. This is a matter of trial and error for the most part, but start with some type of "natural" diet that is low in cereal by-products, colors, and preservatives. Some examples of these are: raw diet, homemade diets, California Natural™, Nature's Variety™, etc. Stay away from any type of performance diet that is very high in protein and/or calories. Keep her on the diet at least four weeks before determining whether it has helped. Also stay away from any commercial dog treats such as Snausages™, Beggin' Strips™, etc. Use healthy table food or commercial dog rolls such as Natural Balance for dog treats.

4. Keep working on small areas of self-control and relaxation. For example, from now on, the command "sit" and "down" should include silence. If she is barking while sitting, the owner should not reward the behavior.

5. Introduce a more intensive use of bridges into her training. The owner can teach both a terminal bridge (which means the behavior is over) and an intermediate bridge or Keep Going Signal (KGS). The use of both of these bridges will allow the owner to give Kiri more continuous feedback about her progress toward the goal behavior. The KGS gives her second-by-second information.

6. Kiri's behaviors must be shaped in small increments since she has short-duration focus and self-control. If she is asked to inhibit her behavior (e.g., down- stay) for longer than she is capable, she will break from the behavior and likely be even more agitated than if the owner had released her earlier than necessary. The release (terminal bridge) is actually very important because it gives the dog a moment or two to "de-stress" from the labor of the required behavior, before putting her back on task.

7. Introduce more target training. We discussed how the owners could use target training to assist in toweling Kiri after a bath by teaching her to target her front feet onto a small platform (e.g., a two-by-four). She also must remain standing still in order for the owner to "reward" her by continuing the toweling process. If Kiri moves, the owner should stop touching her, and re-cue her onto the target. Once she is on target, she gets the KGS while the owner begins toweling. At first the owner should only towel a small section of her body before giving her the terminal bridge and allowing her to come off target. Then the owner can re-cue her and do another section. Over time the owner can towel larger portions of her body before giving the terminal bridge.

8. Continue to work on the relaxation/settle exercises.

9. Anytime Kiri is calmly resting, reward her. Frequently reward any inactivity and the lack of jaw popping, etc.

10. Because Kiri often bolts away in agility when the owner even briefly breaks focus on her (e.g., to look ahead to the next obstacle), the owner should begin teaching Kiri to stay focused on her when she is not giving Kiri direct eye contact. She can get Kiri's attention, look away briefly, and immediately reward Kiri while the owner's eyes or head is still turned away (but while the dog is still looking up at her). Slowly increase the amount of time the owner is looking away before rewarding Kiri. The owner can progress to turning her body all the way around, slowly walking past Kiri, and/or walking directly away from Kiri. With these latter maneuvers, the owner may need a mirror to make sure Kiri is still watching her. The owner may also need another person to give the bridge signals during and at the end of the behavior; however, the reward should come from the handler.

11. We discussed the controversy about "sub-optimal" thyroid status in dogs. We started Kiri on a two-week trial of low-dose thyroxin supplementation. Kiri was started on 0.2 mg thyroxine twice daily. After three days, the owner reported that the dog's behavior had deteriorated. The owner journaled the dog's behavior in relation to various experimentation with the thyroid dose (from 0.2 mg to none at all) over the next several days. The association between the relapse and the thyroxine appeared real and not just an unrelated down cycle in the dog's behavior. Thyroxine was discontinued.

12. 14 weeks post initial consult, Kiri is stabilized on 15 mg methylphenidate every eight hours. She remains fearful of noises, but her ability to focus and filter out environmental stimuli has improved greatly. Kiri and Ricki continue to be reactive to each other in the house, but the owner is able to walk them together when away from the house. Kiri also continues to have problems maintaining focus when walking/heeling with the owner at agility. The owner can continue working on training the dog to stay focused without eye contact. The owner can also experiment with teaching the dog to target to a spot on her arm or leg when walking at heel to encourage the dog to maintain focus. A trial of clomipramine 5 mg twice daily will be instituted to try to further reduce the dog's reactivity and noise sensitivity.

Additional Discussion

A detailed discussion of hyper-kinesis and Attention Deficit Hyperactivity Disorder (ADHD) is beyond the scope of this article; however, Corson et al first documented hyper-kinesis in the dog in a case study in 1976. Various animal models have been developed in the course of research on human ADHD. Dogs with hyper-kinesis do show a number of symptoms similar to ADHD and their response to stimulant drugs such as amphetamine supports a similar, although possibly not identical, pathogenesis. Although there is some inconsistency in the studies, research on ADHD in humans generally supports the theory that this disorder is related to a catecholamine dysfunction (Faraone, 1999). Neuropsychological and neuroimaging studies implicate an abnormality in the frontal and subcortical regions of the brain (Faraone, 1999). The frontal lobes are involved in planning, organization and execution of higher behavioral functions. Additionally this area is associated with impulse control and inhibition of emotional responses and primitive behaviors (e.g., prey drive).

Pharmacologic therapy for ADHD in humans, and hyper-kinesis in dogs, is centered on two major classes of drugs: stimulants and TCAs. Drugs in these classes block the reuptake of norepinephrine and also increase availability of dopamine to varying degrees. Depending on the particular drug, the latter effect occurs either by direct agonist properties, increased release, and/or reduced reuptake from the synapse. SSRIs have also been used successfully in a number of ADHD cases.

Although this case is ongoing and incomplete, it does demonstrate a few important issues regarding drug therapy. While drug therapy can be an important adjunct for patients with certain disorders, it should not be undertaken without a clear understanding of the desired goal and the pharmacodynamics and kinetics of the drugs. Additionally, pharmacologic intervention should not be undertaken in the absence of a behavior modification program; it should be part of a comprehensive approach.

Pharmacologic intervention is the last topic I discuss with any client. The bulk of the consultation is spent outlining management and modification steps; the topic of potential drug therapy is not mentioned until the very end of the consult. Many clients come to a consult with strong feelings regarding the use or avoidance of drug therapy as part of their dog's program. Clients must be educated on the advantages and disadvantages of such intervention. Owners must be willing to maintain close contact with the prescribing doctor and/or behaviorist to monitor response and potential side effects. Clients also must understand that most drugs require a number of weeks of consistent dosing before peak therapeutic effects are evident. Additionally, they must have a clear understanding of, and motivation to establish, adequate safety measurements in the dog's environment. Although increased aggression is uncommon in a carefully chosen drug intervention, it is a real possibility. In cases of aggression it is imperative that the owner can ensure the safety of involved humans and animals if such an adverse reaction occurs.

While some counselors feel that drug intervention should only occur as a last resort, it is important to remember that some animals have underlying physiologic abnormalities that interfere with acquisition of target behaviors. Until these are addressed, no meaningful progress will be made. Withholding pharmacologic therapy only prolongs recovery and increases the client's frustration. Kiri's owners had made notable progress in controlling her behavior; however, further improvement will be dependent on trying to correct underlying neurochemical abnormalities.

As in human medicine, there often is some degree of trial and error in choosing the best pharmacologic treatment for dogs. Various individual and behavioral parameters should be taken into consideration when choosing a class or specific drug for initial therapy. ❖

Definitions

Neoplasia. Cancer.

Impulse-control disorder. A group of disorders where an individual acts on an impulse and therefore engages in a behavior that may be risky or harmful, but that he/she cannot resist; an inability to inhibit a behavioral response even when that response may put the individual in a dangerous or risky situation.

Compulsive disorder. A disorder characterized by exhibition of an apparently purposeless behavior to the extent that it interferes with the individual's normal functioning. The behavior may or may not be ritualistic or repetitive (i.e., stereotypic). The behavior originally may have arisen during situations of conflict or frustration, but has become emancipated from that context.

ADHD (Attention Deficit Hyperactivity Disorder). A disorder in humans characterized by a variety of symptoms associated with inattentivity, hyperactivity, and impulsivity. Various subtypes exist but are usually designated under the umbrella term ADHD.

Hyper-kinesis. A term used to designate animals that show symptoms analogous to human ADHD including hyperactivity (above and beyond normal for the animals age and breed/species), inability to focus, and impulsivity. Various other symptoms are typically present, including aggression, stereotypic behaviors, agitation, learning deficits, etc.

References

[1] The deference and relaxation protocols are adapted from Dr. Karen Overall's protocols (B-1 and B-2) from Overall, Karen L. *Clinical Behavioral Medicine for Small Animals.* St. Louis, MO: Mosby, Inc., 1997.

[2] Desensitization and counter-conditioning.

Coccaro, E.F. "Central serotonin and impulsive aggression." *Brit J Psychiatry*. 155: 52-62, 1997.

Corson S.A., Corson E.O., Arnold E.L, & Knopp W. "Animal models of violence and hyperkinesis." G. Serban & A Kling (Eds.) *Animal Models of Human Psychobiology*. (pp. 111-139). New York: Plenum Press, 1976.

Fairbanks, LA., Melega, W.P., Jorgensen, M.J., Kaplan, J.R. & McGuire, M.T. "Social impulsivity inversely associated with CSF 5-HIAA and fluoxetine exposure in vervet monkeys." *Neuropsychopharm*. 24:370-378, 2001.

Faraone, S.V., Beiderman, J. "The neurobiology of attention deficit hyperactivity disorder." D.S. Charney, E.J. Nestler & B.S. Bunney (Eds.) *Neurobiology of Mental Illness*. (pp. 788-801). New York: Oxford University Press, 1999.

Mehlman, P.T., Higley, J.D., Faucher, I., Lilly, A.A., Taub, D.M., Vickers, J., Suomi, S.J. & Linnoila, M. "Low CSF 5-HIAA concentrations and severe aggression and impaired impulse control in non-human primates." *Am J Psych*, 151:1485-1491, 1994.

A Case Study: Resource Guarding, Conflict Aggression, and Fear Aggression

Lore I. Haug, Edited by Terry Long, September/October 2005

Case Information

Name:	Randall
Age:	10 years
Species:	Canine
Sex:	Castrated Male
Color:	Liver/White
Breed:	German Shorthaired Pointer

History

Presenting complaint:	Aggression when Randall is kenneled or cornered
Vaccines:	Current
Operations:	Castration, March 2000
Prior illness:	Heartworm treated with Immiticide™, July 1999
Medications:	Heartguard and Advantage monthly
Environmental history:	Randall lives in an outdoor run during the day and is allowed to run on the 3/4-acre lot during the day. At night he is kenneled indoors.
Other animals:	14-year-old castrated male cat and 14-year-old spayed female cat.
Diet:	Science Diet™ Senior Large Bites

Physical Exam

Temperature:	100.6
Heart Rate:	126
Respiration Rate:	34
Weight:	71#

Description of abnormal findings:

Nuclear sclerosis bilat; moderate dental tartar; lean body condition; no other significant findings.

Behavioral History

Randall spent the first nine months of his life at a veterinarian's house. The veterinarian socialized Randall at his vet clinic with other animals and people. Randall then spent the next three years with a man who purchased the dog from the veterinarian. The dog lived primarily in a kennel situation. This man had a woman train the dog for hunting. After a year and a half, the owner had a heart attack so for the next year and a half Randall was alone in a kennel. Randall then spent another nine months within another hunting-dog kennel. The current owners picked up Randall from this kennel and took him to their home. They have had him for five years.

Randall was purchased to be used primarily as a hunting dog. He has been trained by two different trainers. Mr. Smith claims that neither trainer used harsh or cruel methods to train their dogs, but the dog is conditioned to an electronic shock collar. During hunting trips, Randall has not shown aggressive behavior to either Mr. Smith or his hunting companions. However, when he is kenneled at night in the hotel room, he will growl at Mr. Smith's hunting companions. Randall will also start to growl and bark if he is in his kennel in the back of the truck and anyone other than Mr. Smith starts to approach him.

Randall spends the majority of his time in an outdoor 15' x 35' run. The area is well shaded and he has access to fresh water. He is given Nylabones™ to play with during the day. When supervised, he is allowed to run free on the ¾-acre lot. Outside of his run, Randall seeks attention from everyone and will allow people in the yard to pet him. He is often walked down the neighborhood street and is usually greeted by several of the neighborhood children. Randall is normally very friendly and allows the children to pet him.

Randall's aggression is manifested primarily in confined areas such as his crates and the kennel run in the yard. When loose in the yard, he will growl and snarl at people who look over the fence, including Mrs. Smith. He also growls if Mrs. Smith puts her face too close to his, hugs him, or leans over him. There was one incident when the dog was allowed to "hang out" with the family all day in the yard. Towards the end of the afternoon, however, Randall suddenly seemed to turn on Mrs. Smith, barking and growling at her.

Randall will also growl and bark if he feels cornered in the yard. Often he will start to dig a hole near the corner of the house. If Mrs. Smith or her brother starts to approach Randall, he begins to growl and snarl.

During the evening, Randall is placed in a crate in the house for the night. The crate is in the living room next to the fireplace and Mr. Smith's recliner chair. Randall is able to view people entering and exiting the room from three directions. When Mrs. Smith is talking to Mr. Smith in the kitchen and Randall can see them, he starts to growl. When they both get up from the couch to go into the kitchen, Randall starts to growl even if neither of them is talking. When Mrs. Smith enters the room, he starts to growl. If woken during the night by anyone entering the room, Randall immediately starts barking and growling and this lasts for several minutes. This has gotten so bad that Mrs. Smith wants Randall to spend the night in his outside run. Randall seems very protective of his kennel area, and Mr. Smith is the only person allowed to approach the kennel to let Randall out. Mr. Smith is also the only person who feeds Randall in the morning and evening. Randall does occasionally growl at Mr. Smith around the kennel, but this happens much less frequently than it does with anyone else.

When Randall is asleep and Mrs. Smith walks into the room where he is (whether he is in the crate or not), he startles and then comes at her barking and growling. This behavior is also directed at Mr. Smith, but with less intensity. The owners feel that part of this behavior is a reaction to being startled. To avoid this, Mrs. Smith first tries to wake Randall by saying, "Coming, coming, coming," before entering the room; however, this has not aborted the behavior. There was one incident when Randall was sleeping on the tile floor outside of his kennel while Mr. Smith was watching television. Mrs. Smith entered the room with a pillow to sleep on the couch. Randall awoke and came at Mrs. Smith barking and growling. His face actually bumped the pillow that she was carrying.

Randall normally gets along with the cats and wants them to play with him. However, if Mrs. Smith starts to pet the cat while rubbing her face on the cat's face, Randall will start to growl (even if he is in his crate).

In an attempt to correct these behavioral issues, Mrs. Smith has always tried to announce her presence to Randall so as to not startle him, and then offers him treats. If they verbally reprimand him for growling while he is in his kennel, he immediately will begin to destroy items in the kennel such as the bedding.

Mr. Smith is the only person who feeds the dog. The dog has not shown aggression to him during this context; however, Mrs. Smith feels that the dog would show aggression to her if she approached while he was eating. The dog did growl once at a nephew who came near the dog while he was eating in his kennel.

Randall is relatively responsive to commands, but he has never been taught to sit and has only been introduced to the down command. The gun dog trainers told the owner to never teach the dog to sit or down as these were "dominating" commands to give the dog, and it might interfere with his pointing/hunting behavior.

Although Randall shows intense aggressive displays, he has never bitten anyone.

Behavioral Observations

Randall was quiet in the exam room. He immediately approached the student when the student entered the room and did not show any signs of aggression. When the clinician entered, the dog immediately approached, wagging his tail and his ears up. He moved into her space when she had treats although she was ignoring him. He also tried to put his head up on the counter to try to reach the treat container.

During the consultation, Randall would periodically walk around the room investigating each person and then would return to the corner by the computer console (the spot furthest from any person) to lie down. During the demonstration exercises, Randall seemed anxious and displayed marked submissive/appeasement behaviors including licking of the lips, raising his paw, avoiding eye contact, and tensely laying his ears back. These behaviors were shown first to the clinician during demonstrations of personal space, but were then shown to both owners as well. Mrs. Smith noted that the dog shows these behaviors to her during almost all interactions at home. Mr. Smith felt that the dog does show him more confident/relaxed postures at home most of the time, but wasn't sure of the percentage.

During all the demonstrations, the dog would intermittently disengage from the person and cross to the opposite side of the room. He would then either move a short distance back toward the person, or remain on the other side of the room until encouraged to return. Overall, he showed some level of discomfort in social engagement, even with his family members.

Randall was easily fitted with a Gentle Leader™ headcollar while being distracted with food.

Questions

1. Develop a problem list and a list of differential diagnoses for each problem.

2. Mrs. Smith is very apprehensive about this dog. She asks if the dog is likely to actually bite her in the future. What do you tell her?

3. Based on the information provided, how would you gauge the dog's prognosis?

4. Develop a management and modification program.

Presenting Problems

1. Growling over food

   Differential Diagnoses:
   a. Food aggression/resource guarding
   b. As component of conflict/dominance-related aggression

2. Growling while in crate/kennel

   Differential Diagnoses:
   a. Fear aggression
   b. Territorial aggression
   c. Conflict aggression
   d. Resource guarding

3. Growling when hugged, petted, or leaned over (by Mrs. Smith)

   Differential Diagnoses:
   a. Fear aggression
   b. Conflict/dominance-related aggression
   c. Pain-induced aggression

4. Growling when disturbed while resting.

   Differential Diagnoses:
   a. Fear aggression (startle component)
   b. Conflict/dominance-related aggression
   c. Irritable aggression

Diagnosis

1. Resource Guarding

2. Conflict Aggression

3. Fear Aggression

This case demonstrates to some degree the difficulty in placing categorical labels on aggressive dogs. While some dogs obviously fit into a specific diagnostic label (e.g., fear aggression, territorial aggression), others do not. Many cases are more complicated than even this one.

While resource guarding is relatively straightforward, the diagnosis of conflict aggression (previously often referred to as "dominance-related aggression") is less so. This dog routinely shows marked appeasement/submissive signaling to humans, including the owners. Appeasement signals are displayed to prevent or abort conflict. The more marked the displays, the more potential conflict the animal perceives. If the dog is routinely showing notable conflict appeasing signals to the owners (or other persons), then the dog is routinely perceiving potential conflict during the interactions. In general, the more intense the display, the higher the level of the dog's apprehension. Passive submission, in particular, indicates a higher level of actual fear versus active submission. ("Passive submission" includes postures such as rolling onto his side or back and remaining motionless. It probably indicates a greater level of fear than active submission (Schenkel, 1985). "Active submission" includes postures such as the dog remaining upright and actively moving and approaching the recipient.)

Randall has been showing these aggressive displays the entire five years the owners have had him. These problems most likely started before they acquired the dog. He has demonstrated great bite inhibition to this point and that is not likely to change at ten years of age. However, it is possible that age-related disorders such as arthritis or cognitive dysfunction could alter the dog's tolerance level and lower his bite inhibition to some degree.

The prognosis for improving these behaviors is guarded to very good. Many dogs with conflict aggression respond rapidly to alterations in the way the owners interact with the dog. Resolving the kennel aggression toward Mrs. Smith while the dog is outside will most likely take the longest time because it is one of the most consistent and intense of his behaviors. (Additionally, unless the owners don't put Randall in the kennel at all, or Mrs. Smith never goes out in the yard, it will be hard to confine their encounters to structured training sessions only. This means there is risk of triggering the behavior just during the course of a routine day; therefore allowing the dog to continue practicing it.)

Diagnostics Performed

No medical diagnostics were performed during the consult visit. However, a complete blood count, blood chemistry, thyroid panel, and a urinalysis are recommended for geriatric monitoring purposes.

Medications Prescribed

A DAP diffuser was dispensed to be placed in the house, alternating between the living area and the room where the dog's crate is. The hope is that the diffuser will reduce the dog's stress/anxiety to some degree, especially when he is crated in the house. (The Dog Appeasing Pheromone—DAP—is a calming pheromone.) No other medications are indicated at this time.

Initial Management and Modification Recommendations

Randall has been diagnosed with resource guarding, fear aggression, and conflict aggression. Randall has spent most of his life in a kennel situation and his interactions with people have been highly specific to the training/hunting environment. Randall did receive a lot of socialization, but it was only at the vet clinic and the clinic owner's home, so the socialization experiences were highly restricted.

This program focuses on two basic concepts:

1. Liberally and frequently rewarding appropriate behavior.

2. Preventing, ignoring, or neutrally interrupting inappropriate behavior.

It is very important that the owners remain calm around the dog. In every situation, ask this question: Do I like this behavior? If the answer is "yes," then reward the dog. If the answer is "no," decide whether the behavior should be ignored (Is it attention seeking?) or neutrally interrupted with the leash. See "Neutral Interrupt" below.

Management

Control the environment: This involves controlling the dog's environment to avoid placing him in situations that trigger the behaviors we are trying to change. The more the dog practices these reactions, the more habitual they become and the harder it will be to change them.

- Avoid the use of the kennel whenever possible. Allow Randall to run in the yard often, under supervision in order to avoid having him growl and snarl at people when he is in his run.

- Do not lean over or hug Randall. This is an invasion of his personal space and he is uncomfortable with it. Affectionate behavior should be kept to patting, rubbing, and praising if he appears to enjoy these interactions.

- Move the indoor crate to a more private area such as a spare bedroom to avoid growling behavior when people enter the living room.

- Feed Randall his entire daily ration of food during training sessions. Mrs. Smith can toss Randall pieces of his food each time she passes by him throughout the day.

- Environment enrichment should be provided for Randall as well. Although he is a senior, he still enjoys playing and the owner should provide more play toys for the dog.

- Put the DAP diffuser in the living area or the room where the dog's crate is.

Training

- Continue basic training.

Behavior Modification

- Begin a structured interaction ("Deference") protocol.[1] The goals with this program include the following:
  a. To condition the dog to watch the owners and look to them for direction in how he should behave in any situation. He should learn to ask permission before engaging in certain behaviors or activities.
  b. To help the owners learn to manipulate his reward systems.
  c. To condition the owners to be aware of how to maintain control over all interactions with the dog.
  d. To teach the dog self-control and "emotional maturity."

The following steps were discussed as important aspects of implementing this program. This process is easy in theory, but is one of the more difficult steps to do because it must be implemented in every interaction the owners have with the dog. The dog must be behaving appropriately (in relation to their goals) and respond to a simple or complex cue before they provide him with any rewards. These include petting, talking to him, eye contact, food treats, his dinner, going outside or coming inside, going for a walk, having his collar put on or taken off, playing with a toy, etc. They are establishing a bargain with the dog: They will follow through with their end of the bargain only if the dog meets his end of the bargain. There are several criteria the dog must meet:

  a. He must be responsive to a command that the owners give such as sit or down.
  b. He should remain calm, polite, and focused (making eye contact) throughout the interaction.
  c. He should remain outside their personal space (a 24-inch perimeter) unless they specifically invite him to invade it.
  d. The dog also should not be permitted to persistently lean or press against them.
  e. Ignore him or walk away from the dog in response to attention-seeking behavior. Wait until he is behaving in a more relaxed, polite manner and then make a point to pay attention to him at those times.

2. Randall should be trained to wear a soft nylon muzzle. Randall should also wear his Gentle Leader™ at all times when the owners are home. The Gentle Leader and houseline will allow them to interrupt inappropriate behavior and move him safely.

3. The owner was instructed to teach the dog a hand-targeting exercise. See "Hand Targeting" below. This exercise has three purposes:

   a. It allows the owners to move him without having to physically touch him;

   b. It gives the owners a relatively easy way to try to refocus him when he is distracted or fearful; and

   c. It is an additional way to counter-condition him to having hands reach out near him.

4. They should begin working on the Relaxation Protocol.[1] This is a counter-conditioning exercise designed to condition the dog to remain relaxed around various stimuli.

5. Mrs. Smith is to start counter-conditioning exercises to her approach.[2]

6. Exercises were outlined to countercondition the dog to remain calm in his crate or outdoor kennel when approached.

7. The owners were also given a handout on a Food Aggression Protocol. However, it is possible the food aggression will spontaneously improve in response to the above exercises and changes.

Prognosis

Fair to good. ❖

Helpful Definitions

Presenting problems. Identification or listing of problems presented by the owner and those identified during exam and history.

Differential diagnoses. A list of possible causes for each presenting problem. In the final analysis, there may be more than one diagnosis. An example would be "barking" as a presenting problem, with attention-seeking and excitement listed as differential diagnoses.

Neutral Interrupt. A verbal interrupter cue such as "Quit that!," is given to the dog, and then the client immediately walks over, picks up the drag line or leash, and takes the dog away from the stimulus. Then the dog is given an alternative behavior (e.g., lie down quietly). The dragline or leash is not jerked; rather, the leash just allows the owner to safely move the dog or stop the ongoing behavior (e.g., the dog jumps on someone; the owner uses the leash to pull the dog off the person).

Hand Targeting. Start by putting your open palm about four to six inches from the side of the dog's nose. Most dogs will almost reflexively turn toward it to investigate it. Click/treat. The hand is removed after the click. Repeat this multiple times on both sides of the dog's head. Once the dog starts getting an idea of the behavior, begin moving your hand further away in two to four inch increments. Work "round the clock," offering your hand in different orientations to the dog's head. The goal is that the dog will eventually target from any orientation and from up to ten to fifteen feet away from the owner. We want the dog to learn to follow the hand so the owner can walk away and have the dog follow.

References

[1] The deference and relaxation protocols are adapted from Dr. Karen Overall's protocols (B-1 and B-2) from Overall, Karen L. *Clinical Behavioral Medicine for Small Animals*. St. Louis, MO: Mosby, Inc., 1997.

[2] Desensitization and counter-conditioning.

Schenkel R. "Submission: Its features and functions in the wolf and dog." *Amer Zool.* (7) 319-329, 1967.

A Case Study: Human-Directed Aggression

Barbara Davis, Edited by Terry Long, January/February 2007

Case Information

Dog's Name:	Stinky
DOB/Age:	Two years
Breed:	Shih Tzu mix
Sex:	Male/neutered
Color:	Black and white

History

Presenting Complaint:	Human-directed aggression
Operations:	Castration at age eight months
Prior Illnesses:	Demodex from age six weeks to six months
Medications:	None
Environmental History:	Mostly indoors (house), yard time for play/exercise
Household:	Two-parent home; son, age 17; daughter, age 12; daughter, age 8
Diet:	Eukanuba Lamb & Rice, free-fed, commercial dog treats
Other Animals:	None

Chief Behavioral Complaints

1. Human-directed aggression. Client documented 26 separate bite incidents (twelve Level 1 bites, four Level 2 bites, six Level 3 bites, one Level 4 bite). There are more beyond this, but they can't recall all the details.

2. Doesn't respond to obedience cues, especially around distractions.

3. Door-dashing, running away, won't come back.

Behavioral History

Stinky was acquired at six weeks of age from a pet shop, an "impulse purchase." He was this family's first pet although the parents had small dogs and cats growing up. The family's expectation of Stinky was that he'd be small, travel easily, low maintenance, no issues, good with kids, and an all-around good companion.

At his initial veterinary exam Stinky was diagnosed with demodex and was treated almost continuously until he was six months old with ivermectin, antirobe drops, cephalexin, ophthalmic ointment, Clavamox, and Dermcaps. Client reports Stinky was very "mellow" as a young pup, and they did not experience any of the usual puppy behavior problems (biting, chewing, hyperactivity, etc.). Because of the demodex, the client followed the veterinarian's advice and kept Stinky mostly at home until he was six months old.

Once Stinky was medically released, the family enrolled Stinky in obedience class. Stinky wasn't comfortable in class, and mostly hid behind his handler or barked and lunged at other dogs. They dropped out after week four of the six-week class because the mother found collar corrections problematic: the choke chain got caught in Stinky's curly coat, and bits of dog hair would be yanked out.

Stinky was more responsive to his obedience cues outside of class and did better with practice at home although by eight months of age, the family decided they were having problems with door-darting. Stinky would regularly manage to shoot out the open door and would not return; they'd have to chase him to get him back.

Stinky's escapes and failure to respond to obedience cues were attributed to his being intact so he was neutered at about nine months. After a few months, the door-darting problem was getting worse and other issues (including the early bite incidents) were developing. When Stinky was a year old, he was re-enrolled in the obedience class. The correction problem was addressed by using a larger gauge chain and keeping Stinky's coat groomed short around his neck. Although Stinky performed better this time and finished the class, his family had to participate at a greater distance than the other families because of Stinky's barking and lunging at other dogs. At graduation, the instructor suggested enrolling Stinky in more advanced training using a shock collar to help get his behavior "under control," but the family declined.

Because of Stinky's behavior (barking and lunging at other dogs, strangers, bicycles, skateboarders, etc.), the family quit taking him for walks. He was unable to accompany his family on picnics and camping trips. As a result, most of Stinky's time was spent in the house or in the backyard. His exercise came mainly from fence-fighting with the dogs next door (his family interpreted this behavior as play), charging the front fence at passersby, and running laps around the pool, barking, as the kids played in the water.

Stinky also started charging the front window of the house, barking and growling as people walked, skated, or biked by.

Stinky's family is very socially active, and the home is frequently a center for kids and friends, pool parties, sleep-overs, barbecues, scout meetings, and other activities. Rather than welcoming friends and visitors as the family had hoped, Stinky greeted arriving guests with growling, lunging, and barking.

Eventually, Stinky's access to the front door had to be restricted with baby gates to prevent him from charging people as they came and went, and also to keep him from dashing out the door. Even though he was no longer able to reach the door, any activity at the front door would launch Stinky into ever-increasing spells of wild barking, growling, and circling, sometimes for ten or more minutes. On occasions when multiple guests arrived over time, Stinky might engage in this behavior continuously for 45-60 minutes.

Finally, Stinky's greeting behavior became so unacceptable that he'd be put away in an upstairs bedroom when visitors were expected. Although this helped some, Stinky would still act out when the doorbell rang.

The biting incidents began when Stinky was nine months old. Many of the 26 documented incidents were preceded by some period of high excitement, which might include the arrival of visitors, a door-darting adventure, chasing around the swimming pool, or a fence-fighting session. A few involved a human attempting to remove a "stolen" object from Stinky's mouth, three involved a human moving Stinky from one of his favored resting places, and one occurred when a family member startled Stinky awake with a hug.

The family tried having visitors offer Stinky treats by hand, but Stinky mostly refused to accept them. If he did take a treat, he'd move a few steps away and drop the food on the floor uneaten.

After every bite incident, Stinky was verbally reprimanded (usually screamed). In some cases, Stinky was allowed to retreat to another room, in other cases he was chased, caught, and put outside or confined to another room. On two occasions he was "scruffed," and he was spanked on a few others.

By the time Stinky's family sought professional help, the biting problem was serious enough that if it could not be improved significantly soon, the dog would be euthanized.

At my request, Stinky was examined by their veterinarian with the behavior issues presented as the reason for the exam. There was a basic health exam, blood work and urinalysis; no remarkable findings were reported nor obvious physical or biological causes for the behavior identified.

Observations

On the initial consult I rang the door bell and was immediately greeted by the mother, who led me into the dining room. Stinky began barking, lunging, and growling when the doorbell rang and continued for about 15 minutes (although I asked that Stinky be put away twice during that time, I was assured that he would "calm down in a minute," so he remained behind his baby gate for the first half of the meeting). Even after Stinky settled down, he continued to watch me constantly from the staircase landing, growling occasionally, pacing, and then eventually lying down. Because Stinky is small, black, and covered in dense, curly hair, reading his face from across the room was a challenge, but his gross body language was rigid. Sitting up, he'd position himself to face me, but slightly off-center, with his face turned partially away, but always watching. Lying down, Stinky would turn his back part way to me, but keep his head turned so that I was always in sight.

After about 90 minutes, I asked the family to attach a dragline to Stinky's collar and remove the baby gate, which the mother did. Stinky charged out of his area into the dining room, stopping short when he felt the dragline, but then continued to approach me. As he got within five feet or so, Stinky slowed down, crouching, and took a few slower steps forward with his head lowered, growling a bit, then retreated, backing away. I didn't look at him, and he repeated this behavior twice more.

As he retreated for the third time, I tossed a bit of beef dog food over his head and behind him. He went to investigate, found and ate the food, turned and began approaching again. I tossed another treat over his head, and he ate it. Stinky's next approach was slower, but he wasn't crouching. I tossed more meat behind him, and now he scurried to get it. After a few more iterations, he was standing next to my chair sniffing my pants leg; I dropped some treats on the floor, which he ate readily. I ignored him and Stinky sat quietly next to my chair for the next few minutes.

Using the treats, I was able to lure Stinky to sit and down several times. After just a few minutes, he was offering behaviors on his own. Before our training session was over, Stinky appeared more relaxed (less rigid spine, softer "eye," voluntarily sitting/lying at my feet, and a cessation of staring, panting, and barking/growling) and engaged (remaining in close contact with me, actively offering behaviors, and soliciting attention by pawing at my foot/pants leg). This was quite a contrast from our initial introduction. He remained relaxed throughout the session, but again "went off" (explosive barking, lunging, growling, circling, and pacing) as I approached the door to leave.

Assessment

Stinky's family had kept some excellent records and worked hard as a team to compile a detailed behavior history.

Stinky lives in an almost constant state of emotional arousal, at or near threshold, practically awash in triggers, including:

- Door knocking
- Doorbell ringing
- People coming or going through the front door
- Appearance of strangers
- People moving past the front window
- Kids playing in the yard
- Kids playing/splashing in the pool
- Dogs barking next door
- Kids playing next door
- People walking past the front fence
- People approaching his favorite resting places
- Other dogs
- Cars, bikes, skateboards
- Swimming, splashing in the pool

Negative indications/factors that likely contribute to the behavior issues:

- Early health issues
- Primary socialization deficit
- Incomplete/ineffective prior training
- Possible negative associations with some trigger stimuli (e.g., other dogs, strangers)
- Lack of social structure (from the dog's perspective)
- Casual and unstructured lifestyle of his family
- Some ambivalence from the family (balancing concern for liability versus euthanasia)

Positive indications were:

- Owners have taken an organized approach to identifying and enumerating the issues
- Owners have expressed a genuine commitment to work the program, at least for the short term
- Stinky is relatively young and otherwise healthy
- Stinky appears very trainable; his emotional response to me changed markedly within a short period of time (90 minutes). I assessed him as a ready subject for a systematic counter-conditioning program, as well as for training other necessary behaviors

Consult #1 - Intervention Recommendations

The objective is to manage Stinky's environment to reduce his overall stress and the opportunities for bites to happen. If we can't achieve several weeks of bite-free behavior, Stinky will be euthanized.

Stress Reduction/Behavior Management Program

- Use a dragline to control Stinky's door-dashing
- Use a dragline to gently remove Stinky from favored resting places (human beds, sofa)
- Keep Stinky away from the pool when it is in use
- Do not permit Stinky to fence-fight with neighbor dogs
- Crate Stinky at night
- Block Stinky's access to the front window

- Create "safe zones' for Stinky (identified as the bedroom crate, the family room dog bed, and an exercise-pen in the study).
- Confine Stinky to a safe zone away from the action when company comes. Make sure he has some busy work to do (e.g., bully stick, stuffed Kong) to distract him
- Confine Stinky to a safe zone when he is not supervised to minimize his accidental exposure to triggers

Deference Program

- "Say please by sitting"
- Scheduled feedings of 10-15 minutes duration
- No gratuitous treats

Information Provided

- Anxiety Wrap™
- Kong toys
- Dog Appeasing Pheromone (DAP) (Comfort Zone™)
- Alternatives to current, commercial dog food

Instructed/Demonstrated

- Basic attention exercise (eye-contact)
- Name recognition
- Trading games/object exchange (drop it)
- Lured sit (just for fun)

I suggested getting Stinky at least one brisk 30-minute leashed walk daily, during odd hours if necessary, to reduce his exercise deficit.

Consult #2

No bites have occurred in the past three weeks. Dad has gotten Stinky out for a brisk 30-45 minute walk almost every day during evening quiet time. A reduction in frequency and intensity of Stinky's outbursts when encountering people and other dogs on walks was noted.

Family reports success using Stinky's safe zones. Stinky barks less when he hears other dogs barking outside, but still "goes nuts" if someone comes to the door. They have not tried an Anxiety Wrap or DAP.

Stinky has not been in the yard when kids are playing, swimming in the pool, or when the neighbor's dogs or kids are out. Stinky now comes off the furniture easily with the dragline. No door-dashing incidents have occurred.

Scheduled feeding plan is not 100% (Mom gives in sometimes if Stinky doesn't eat readily).

Stinky still doesn't give up stolen items readily, but the family is practicing attention and object exchange exercises.

Identified and Prioritized Triggers and Issues:

1. Doorbell rings or someone knocks

2. Dad or big brother approaching Stinky in his favored resting places

3. Barking/lunging at people/dogs while on walks

Instructed/Demonstrated (To Parents)

- Desensitization/counter-conditioning (DS/CC) procedure (open bar/closed bar) for doorbell/door knocking, including how to vary the intensity of the stimulus

- DS/CC procedure for dad/big brother approaching Stinky's favored resting places

Information Provided

- Defensive strategies when meeting strangers and dogs on walks (emergency u-turn).

Consult #3

Four weeks later: no bites. Scheduled feedings are on track. Stinky sleeps comfortably crated through the night. Stinky's doorbell reaction is greatly reduced. Stinky ate his dinner in the presence of a visitor a few nights earlier. Stinky responds to off cue about 75% of the time and when he doesn't, he comes off willingly with the dragline.

Stinky still needs work on door stimuli, as well as relinquishing stolen objects. Client expressed preference for working on poolside triggers.

Instructed/Demonstrated

- Taught mother DS/CC procedure for door bell/door knocking in the room closest to the door, with volunteer children simulating entrances and exits.

- Taught mother DS/CC procedure at the pool gate and for activity in and around the pool. Family kids and their friends helped by engaging in various levels of activity in and around pool.

- Taught mother additional trading game (structured tug o'war).

Consult #4

Three weeks later: no bites. Stinky barks a few times at the doorbell or knocking, but stops right away. Stinky has stopped reacting to the pool gate, but still needs some work on activity in/around the pool. Stinky now gets two walks daily, as Mom added a short morning walk. Stinky eats full meals immediately, and sits to request everything. Mom noticed Stinky sitting quietly by the kitchen door watching the pool guy, something he used to react to. Stinky may begin fence fighting with the dogs next door, but now disengages when called indoors.

Priority issues are now door-dashing and coming when called.

Instructed/Demonstrated

- Taught mother basic "stay" using positive reinforcement. We were able to move this exercise to the living room, and practice adjacent to the entryway. Before the visit was over, we had incorporated door knocking, doorbell ringing, and many other distractions.

Follow up

This is a current case, so follow up by phone is ongoing, and some additional at-home visits are likely. As Stinky gets more comfortable in social situations outside the home, enrollment in a basic positive reinforcement manners class is also recommended.

Stinky responded rapidly to a friendlier home environment where his overall stress levels have been reduced and the home is more dog-friendly. The owners' ability to change their preconceived attitudes about Stinky had been a significant concern initially, but their compliance level has been excellent. Although Stinky may never become a social butterfly, the probability he'll be able to live out his life happily in this home is reasonably high. ❖

Medical and Alternative Interventions in Behavior Modification

Given the recent advancements in veterinary care and the testing and development of drugs that can be used for dogs, the modern dog trainer needs to be up-to-date with trends in medical care. With most behavior problems, for example, one of the first steps a trainer needs to take is to rule out whether there is a physiological reason for the behavior that can be treated medically. Even in cases where training and behavior modification is called for, there may be medical treatments, drugs, nutritional supplements, or new alternatives like Bach Flower Essences that can be use in solving the problems. Read about some of the latest trends that dog trainers should be aware of as they tackle behavior modification cases.

Medical Evaluation of the Behavior Patient

Lore I. Haug, Edited by Terry Long, March/Apr 2007

Cases are often presented to us where we are at a loss trying to decide whether an animal has a behavioral problem or a medical problem. This approach is much like trying to decide whether a behavior problem is nature versus nurture, or the dog versus the owner. All of these are pointless arguments. An individual's genetics, behavior, and physiology are so intimately entwined as to make them inseparable as discreet components. This article will explore a variety of behavioral-physiological interrelationships.

The first "symptom" of any disease process is a change in the animal's behavior. Additionally, alterations in an animal's behavior, especially those that we would consider poorly adaptive (e.g., compulsive disorders) or associated with stress, produce changes in the animal's physiology and homeostasis, some of which become permanent. Humans and animals undergo changes in hypothalamic-pituitary-adrenal (HPA) axis, immune competency, and gene transcription in accordance with environmental influences that affect their behavior.

A veterinary examination should be part of every program when an animal presents to any professional with a behavior problem. This evaluation serves to identify medical issues that may contribute to the behavioral presentation, as well as to identify changes in the animal's health status as a result of the behavioral problem.

When an owner presents his or her animal to a veterinarian for a medical evaluation of a behavior problem, the worst thing the veterinarian can do is dismiss the owner's concerns for such an evaluation. Similarly trainers do their clients a disservice if they tell an owner, or imply to the owner, that the dog does not need a veterinary evaluation because the animal's problem is "just behavioral."

If for no other reason, these evaluations should be done so the owner has the peace of mind that he or she has addressed that step. Inappropriate behaviors are manifestations of underlying problems whether they are primarily psychological or physiological. Just as scratching is not a disease, aggression is not a behavior problem per se. Scratching is a symptom of an underlying pruritic condition just as aggression is a symptom of an underlying issue (e.g., fear, territoriality, conflict). Behavior problems should be addressed in a comprehensive way by evaluating the animal's environment, diet, exercise routine, social relationships, and physiological (medical) status. Although disease processes are not the direct cause of most behavior problems, diseases or chronic illnesses will certainly affect the expression of the behavior issue (and usually in a negative way).

Medical triggers should be highly suspected: 1) in very young animals; 2) in senior animals showing the onset of a new behavior; 3) when there is a sudden onset of a new behavior or a sudden change in the status of a pre-existing behavior; and 4) when the behavior truly appears unpredictable in context, frequency, and/or intensity. Medical evaluations, a minimum database at the least, are also necessary if pharmacologic intervention is being considered. In some cases, a comprehensive diagnostic evaluation is beyond the owner's desire or resources; however, such evaluations should still be discussed and offered to the client. There are limitations to our knowledge and diagnostic capabilities, so while many animals may have "neurologic" or neurodevelopmental problems causing their behavior issues, we currently may be unable to diagnose them.

Applicable diagnostic tests will vary with the age, breed, and symptoms of the animal. Generally, most of our cases have at least a Complete Blood Count (CBC), chemistry panel, and thyroid panel (for dogs over one year and middle-aged to older cats). Suspicion of infectious disease may indicate a need for titers; however, titers are often an unreliable way to diagnose actual infection particularly for rickettsial diseases and viral disease in dogs. The specificity and sensitivity of any individual test should be determined before recommending the client spend money on such a test. In some cases, symptomatic treatment for a suspected infection (e.g., doxycycline for suspected rickettsial infection) is the preferred approach. Brain imaging is indicated in neurologic disease unless a metabolic or toxic cause is suspected. Magnetic resonance imaging (MRI) is generally superior to CT for assessing soft tissue structures; however, high-quality CT machines can also give excellent images. Imaging delineates macrostructures only and will not identify aberrations on the cellular, neurochemical, or molecular level. Abnormalities in the latter structures can sometimes be identified with techniques such as functional MRI or PET scanning; however, these imaging modalities are not currently available to veterinary patients. Diagnosis of neoplasia outside the brain and spinal cord is generally done by some form of imaging such as radiography and/or ultrasonography. Some masses can be aspirated or biopsied for cytologic examination.

The quality of any test or procedure is only as good as the lab and personnel that run it and the proficiency of the person who evaluates the results. There is much misinformation in the public sector about the usefulness and validity of certain diagnostic tests. Tests should be evaluated based on concrete data rather than just personal or anecdotal experience or opinions.

It is important for professionals and owners to understand that treatment of an underlying medical issue, even if it was the inciting cause for an aberrant behavior, may not resolve the behavioral presentation. Learning plays a role in every behavioral issue and long-standing behavior patterns, in particular, may persist even when the inciting cause is removed. Additionally, animals with neurodevelopmental disorders and early alteration in HPA axis responsiveness will always show some level of persisting abnormality (e.g., sensitizing the HPA axis to hyper-respond to stress and threat signals) although behavior modification and appropriate pharmacologic intervention can help normalize the animal on a neurochemical level.

Aggression Disorders

Aggression is affected by a variety of physiologic problems including disease and drug administration. The trigger for the aggression can indicate areas of concentration. For example, a dog that is aggressive when being handled around its head and neck may need careful otoscopic examination, oral examination, and evaluation for cervical spinal pain. In young animals with aggression, other etiologies to consider include: congenital neurologic disease (e.g., lissencephaly, hydrocephalus), portosystemic shunt, storage diseases (although rare), infectious disease (viral—FeLV, FIV, FIP, canine distemper; protozoal—Toxoplasmosis, Neospora; Rickettsia—RMSF, Ehrlichia, Borrelia, Bartonella), and toxins. Of these, the most commonly identified are congenital neurologic disease, particularly hydrocephalus, infectious disease (CDV in dogs and FIP or FIV in cats), and portosystemic shunts.

Middle-aged to older animals should be evaluated for: osteoarthritis, endocrine disease (hyperthyroidism, hypothyroidism, and hyperadrenocorticism), neoplasia, primary neurologic disease (neoplasia, GME, necrotizing encephalitis, Feline Ischemic Encephalopathy, parasitic brain migration, seizures (uncommon as a cause of aggression)), infectious disease (viral, protozoal, rickettsial, fungal), ocular disorders (cataracts, PRA, uveitis), hyperkinesis (also rare), and Cognitive Dysfunction. Acute or chronic pain also frequently plays a role.

Drugs that have commonly been implicated in inducing or exacerbating aggression in dogs and cats include glucocorticoids, phenylpropanolamine, theophylline, benzodiazepines, acepromazine, and excessive or unnecessary supplementation with thyroid medication.

Anxiety Disorders and Phobias

In very young animals, serious anxiety disorders, fears, and phobias are likely to be related to neurodevelopmental issues, prenatal and postnatal stress, socialization deficits, and learning events. However, congenital disorders (hydrocephalus, portosystemic shunts) and infectious disease (distemper, feline viruses, rickettsial, protozoal) can influence the animal's behavior and development (as mentioned above, sensitizing the HPA axis to hyper-respond to stress and threat signals).

In adult animals, infectious disease, endocrine disease, chronic pain (e.g. spinal pain, intestinal cramping) and neurologic disorders can mimic or worsen anxiety states. Some episodes of spontaneous panic may represent limbic system (i.e., temporal lobe) seizures. Hyperadrenocorticism can readily mimic or worsen an anxiety disorder. Corticotrophin Releasing Factor (CRF) directly activates the anxiety centers in the brain. Although CRF is suppressed in hyperadrenocorticism, states of acute or chronic stress increase CRF levels. ACTH has been shown to increase stress grooming in rodents and glucocorticoids themselves are also anxiogenic.

In cases of nocturnal anxiety/restlessness (including nocturnal vocalization in cats), cognitive dysfunction should be considered along with deficits in sensory perception (olfaction, audition and/or vision). Hyperthyroidism in cats is a common cause of nocturnal activity and vocalization. Other intracranial neurologic disorders will affect behavioral adaptability. Additionally, animals with osteoarthritis often become more painful at night and have difficulty finding a comfortable place to rest. Seizure disorders and sleep disorders may also cause restlessness, vocalization and, less commonly, aggressive outbursts.

Inappropriate Elimination

In cats, by far the most common factor contributing to inappropriate urination is sterile cystitis and other lower urinary tract disease. In young cats, pain (and abrupt litter changes) due to declawing surgery can trigger house-soiling. Primary urinary tract disease, including urolithiasis, pyelonephritis, and incontinence can trigger or contribute to urine housesoiling, as can any disease process leading to polyuria/polydipsia. Prostatic disease in dogs can lead to increased urine marking. For fecal house-soiling, especially in cats, the clinician should consider food intolerance/allergy, inflammatory bowel disease, irritable bowel syndrome, constipation/megacolon, parasitism, neoplasia (e.g., alimentary lymphosarcoma), metabolic disease (renal, hepatic, pancreatitis), endocrine (hyperthyroidism), pancreatic insufficiency, and other malabsorption syndromes. Geriatric onset house-soiling in cats is almost always associated with an identifiable disease process.

Repetitive Behaviors and Excessive Grooming

Repetitive behaviors include stereotypies and compulsive disorders manifesting as fly snapping, excessive licking (of self and/or objects), hair pulling/grooming, tail chasing, spinning, self-mutilation, shadow/light chasing, hind-end checking, flank sucking, wool sucking, and pica, among others. The great majority (over 75%) of cats with excessive grooming have an underlying dermatologic issue causing or contributing to the problem. A large percentage of these cats have food allergy, flea allergy, and/or atopy, although parasites such as Demodex are also identified. This is also true for dogs with acral lick dermatitis (ALD). ALD has also been associated with underlying arthritis (or other sources of pain) and neoplasia (soft tissue or bone). In cats, hair pulling is sometimes associated with Feline Hyperesthesia Syndrome (other symptoms include tail chasing, vocalization, bouts of frantic running, and aggression). There is a medical etiology for any repetitive behavior that responds to steroid administration.

Dogs with tail chasing or spinning should be screened for spinal cord disease (IVDD, cauda equina, neoplasia, neuropathies), central neurologic disease (hydrocephalus, infectious, neoplasia, encephalitides, storage diseases), anal sac disease, and urogenital tract problems. Seizures are a potential differential for any form of repetitive behavior particularly tail chasing, shadow chasing, episodic excessive licking, and fly snapping. Neuropathic pain or paraesthesias are probably linked to a significant number of tail chasing, spinning and self-mutilation cases; however, diagnosing these often is problematic. In many cases sequential drug trials with steroids, pain medications

(NSAIDs, opioids), and anticonvulsants are necessary for diagnosis of some of these disorders.

Hyperactivity Problems

Hyperactivity problems are typically related to management (lack of enrichment and exercise) and training (inappropriate and/or inconsistent punishment) issues. However, there are a few disease processes that can contribute or trigger hyperactive behavior. Hyperthyroidism (primarily cats, but also dogs with inappropriate supplementation) and drug administration (PPA, theophylline, etc.) are not uncommon causes. Hyperkinesis is a notable, although rare, cause of hyperactivity and other behavioral manifestations. Cognitive Dysfunction and general brain aging are often associated with nocturnal restlessness. Food allergies and food intolerances have been associated with hyperactive behavior as well. Central neurologic disease, including seizures, portosystemic shunts, and toxins (lead) may also be causes.

In summary, trainers should encourage clients to work closely with their pet's veterinarian during any behavior modification program. Similarly, veterinarians should not dismiss a client's concerns about potential physiologic contributions to the pet's behavior. Running appropriate diagnostic tests is both good medicine and good business. ❖

Internet Resources

- www.dacvb.org (for board-certified veterinary behaviorists)

- www.avsabonline.org (for non-boarded veterinarians with an interest in behavior)

Glossary and Abbreviations

ACTH: Adrenocorticotrophic Hormone
CBC: Complete Blood Count
CDV: Canine Distemper Virus
CRF: Corticotrophin Releasing Factor
FeLV: Feline Leukemia Virus
FIP: Feline Infectious Peritonitis
FIV: Feline Immunodeficiency Virus
GME: Granulomatous Meningoencephalitis
HPA axis: Hypothalamic-pituitary-adrenal axis
IVDD: Intervertebral Disk Disease
NSAID: Non-steroidal anti-inflammatory drug
PET scan: Positron Emission Tomography scan
Polydypsia: excessive drinking
Polyuria: excessive urination
PPA: Phenylpropanolamine
PRA: Progressive Retinal Atrophy
Pyelonephritis: infection of the kidney
RMSF: Rocky Mountain Spotted Fever

Impulsivity and Behavioral Disorders

Lore I. Haug, Edited by Terry Long, Published in Two Parts,
May/August 2007

PART I

Editor's note: This is the first in a two-part series about impulsivity. Part I discusses what we know about impulsivity from studying, for the most part, non-canine mammals such as humans and rats. Part II will address how to identify impulse control disorders in dogs and subsequent behavior modification options.

Introduction

Your first case of the day is a cute eight month old Labrador Retriever that just can't sit still for longer than two seconds during the training session. She bounces all over, won't focus despite high-value treats, and bites at your hands when you touch her. She doesn't seem to grasp the lessons. Her owner says she is always hyper. As you prepare for your second case, you notice the dog is an equally cute three-and-a-half-year-old male neutered Bassett Hound. His owner is also exasperated because the dog, Barney, is easily distracted during training and out on walks, still jumps on visitors, and mouths at her hands when she tries to pet him. He likes dogs, but has gotten into several scuffles after running up to strange dogs and jumping on them in his exuberance. You figure that most likely, just as with the first dog, Barney has had little to no training, poor socialization, and spends most of his day locked in a crate except for a 15-minute walk around the block in the evening.

Then the truth comes out. Barney came from a good breeder, started puppy class early, and had plenty of appropriate socialization to other dogs and people. He is exercised regularly and spends most of his day with his owner. He has consistently been in training for two years. Maybe Barney just has an incompetent owner. However, it is more likely that Barney has an impulse control disorder.

Impulsivity plays a major role in various human (and increasingly in animal) behavioral conditions. There are no clinical studies specifically evaluating impulse control in dogs; however, there are a variety of studies in humans, non-human primates, and rodents from which we can reasonably extrapolate some useful information.

Definition and Subtypes

Exactly what is "impulsivity"? There are a variety of definitions and subtypes, but most sources agree on the basic principle of a failure to inhibit—either consciously or subconsciously—a behavior that is often harmful to the self or others (King, 2003). For animals the risk to self is most critical, as most animals, and certainly dogs, do not possess the cognitive sophistication to pattern their behavior based on its effects on a conspecific's risk of injury.

219

Impulsivity can be broadly divided into two categories: 1) cognitive, in which the individual is overly quick to respond on cognitive tasks or has an inability to inhibit behavior that interferes with long term goals or plans (e.g., putting money away for retirement versus spending it now); 2) a behavioral type in which there is an inability to inhibit responses that may be dangerous (e.g., picking a fight with someone bigger and meaner than you are). (Hinshaw, 2003)

Impulsiveness is related to a lack of behavioral inhibition. It exists on a continuum rather than being an either/or characteristic. Nigg (reviewed in Hinshaw, 2003) proposed three forms of inhibitory processes:1) a form related to fear of punishment, 2) a form related to fear of novelty; and 3) an executive form. The latter type correlates with cognitive impulsivity and the former two types are associated with behavioral impulsivity. It is important to realize that behavioral impulsivity typically represents subconscious reactions (partial or complete absence of cognitive input). All of us have met someone that did something dangerous or unwise and when prompted as to why, the person responded, "I don't know," or "I could not help [stop] myself." These types of reactions are particularly relevant to dogs, as I would suggest that all of their impulsive actions fall into this category.

As previously mentioned, impulsivity is a factor in a variety of behavioral disorders in humans including Antisocial Personality Disorder, Intermittent Explosive Disorder (IED), and Attention Deficit/Hyperactivity Disorder (ADHD) (King, 2003). It also has been studied in association with criminality, aggression (Retz, 2004), and suicide. Impulsivity has received particular attention in patients with ADHD and spontaneous acts of aggression as it is a core feature of these disorders.

Although hyperkinesis in dogs appears analogous to ADHD, it is quite rare. Research on ADHD children and the rodent model, the Spontaneously Hypertensive Rat (SHR), help clarify the interactions between rewards and behavior and between attentional processes and behavior. ADHD patients and SHR rats will choose small, immediate rewards over larger, delayed rewards in delay-of-reward tasks. In Sagvolden's study (1992), larger delayed rewards had less control over SHR behavior compared to wild type (WT) rats. SHR rats were more influenced by the small immediate rewards. This implied that SHR rats may be more sensitive to other smaller, but more immediate, reinforcers in the environment (which are too weak to control behavior in WT rats). This could explain the distractibility and apparent inattentiveness of patients with ADHD and impulsivity. In terms of working with our canine patients, it also provides a potential explanation for dogs that have difficulty learning target behaviors in the face of seemingly high value rewards. If the training process is not broken down into very small steps and if the reinforcement rate is not kept high and rapid, these dogs are "lost to the environment" so to speak. This emphasizes the need to start such dogs in as distraction-free environment as possible.

Impulsivity and Aggression

Impulsive behavior often presents co-morbid with aggression. Similar to humans, canine aggression is a serious public health concern as well as a strain on the human-animal bond. Research in human violence generally recognizes two broad categories of aggression: a proactive-planned-premeditated type and a reactive-impulsive-hostile type (Keele, 2005; Retz, 2004). Studies investigating the latter type in particular show promise in helping us understand and more effectively treat similar behavioral presentations in dogs.

Intermittent Explosive Disorder has special relevance to many of our canine cases. Unfortunately there is a relative paucity of research on this specific condition in humans. IED is defined by impulsive-aggressive behavior. In a study by McCloskey et al. (2006), a group of IED patients was given a TAP test (see sidebar below) and compared with normal controls, patients with Axis I disorders, and patients with personality disorders. IED patients set higher initial shock levels, set higher mean shock levels, and were six times more likely to set the extreme shock level versus all other groups. Most notably, the IED patients were highly reactive to even low levels of provocation (and responded "aggressively"). IED patients also rated higher on general anger and hostility scales versus the other groups. In a study by Best et al. (2002), IED patients exhibited impaired recognition of facial signals for "anger," "disgust," and "surprise." When shown neutral faces, these patients were more likely to interpret them as showing "disgust" and/or "fear."

Anger and aggression variables in humans correlate negatively with psychosocial functioning in numerous studies. That is, humans scoring higher in scales for anger/hostility and aggression demonstrate poorer efficacy in social relationships and social functioning compared to those people that score lower on such scales. The behavioral profile of IED patients sounds remarkably similar to the dogs we see with "explosive" aggression. These dogs also sometimes have difficulty integrating into social units whether they be canine or human.

Neurobiology of Impulsivity and Reactive-type Aggression

There is a vast body of literature consistently linking impulsivity with serotonin dysregulation. Serotonin (5-HT) is the primary neurotransmitter involved in behavioral inhibition, particularly in the context of threat or punishment (Hong, 2003). Studies in non-human primates, rodents, suicide victims, and people exhibiting acts of unplanned violence show decreased levels of CSF 5-HIAA, the primary serotonin metabolite. It is too simplistic to state that impulsivity is related to a deficiency of serotonin. The 5-HT effects on impulsive behavior vary with the type of 5-HT receptor as well as the area of the brain in which it is activated. For example, drugs that stimulate one type of 5-HT receptor improve performance on delay-of-reward tasks, whereas drugs that stimulate a different type decrease performance on this task (Keele, 2005).

The neurobiology of aggression is even more complex. Even in rodents, there is no simple relationship between aggression and biophysiologic variables (Krakowski, 2003). There is evidence to link 5-HT depletion with increased aggression, but this effect is difficult to isolate from 5-HT's effect on impulsivity and social behavior (5-HT tends to improve both), but even the latter effect depends in part on the animal's social status to start with. Reisner et al. (1996) found decreased CSF 5-HIAA in dogs with dominance aggression versus non-aggressive dogs. Additionally, dogs which did not warn before biting and reacted with an intensity out of proportion to the level of "threat" had the lowest levels. 5-HT may be especially linked to violence/aggression associated with states of high emotional tumult (Krakowski, 2003).

This makes particular sense when the role of the amygdala is considered. There are dense concentrations of various 5-HT receptors in different parts of the amygdala. (The amygdala is also highly innervated by other neurotransmitters as well.) The amygdala is part of the temporal lobe, an area of the brain with a low seizure threshold. Partial seizures of the temporal lobe can trigger feelings of fear, as well as irritability, anxiety, and anger (Keele, 2005). If a "hypersensitivity" developed in the amygdala such that subseizure thresholds of neuronal excitability existed, the individual could present with emotional disturbances. This hypothesis is supported by the fact that anticonvulsant medications improve the aberrant emotional states that exist between seizures in human patients with epilepsy. If dogs develop a similarly excessively hyper-responsive amygdala, this might explain the behavioral profile of the classically "reactive" dog. The dog's amygdala may be overreacting to stimuli that have even low potential for threat or to stimuli that appear suddenly—sudden environmental change. Essentially, the amygdala sends a lot of false alarms that activate the fight-flight system and the regions of the brain responsible for vigilance, attention, anxiety, and fear. If there is concomitant serotonin dysregulation, this might prevent the amygdala and associated neural systems from returning quickly to baseline.

Research also shows strong support for abnormal function in the frontal lobes as one mediator of impulsivity. Frontal lobe deficits or hypofunction are consistently identified in patients with various types of impulse control disorders. Parts of the dopaminergic system in the midbrain (nucleus accumbens) also appear to be involved in deficits in impulse control (Winstanby, 2005). This part of the brain contributes to the reward recognition system.

PART II

The insight that research has given us into the biological basis of impulsivity offers suggestions for approaches to dealing with this problem in dogs although options for treating dogs with impulse control deficits are far more limited than those available for humans. Cognitive Behavior Therapy is a popular and successful treatment for a variety of psychiatric conditions; however, it is not a modality available to us as dog trainers.

Genetics

Many psychiatric disorders in humans and animals have a heritable aspect, and for some the heritability is quite high. The trait of impulsivity, as a component of many of these behavioral presentations, is also influenced by genetics. This means, like other heritable traits, impulsivity can be modified in careful breeding programs. In many cases, impulsivity may be confused with motivation and excitement. For example, a dog that is difficult to hold back from performing a task at an inappropriate time may be perceived as highly motivated when, in actuality, the dog has an inability to refrain from performing the behavior. In the course of breeding for better performance, we should not confuse the two. By far, the majority of dogs produced intentionally or unintentionally ends up in pet homes. One of the major factors for relinquishment of pet dogs is unruliness. If we are to do dogs a service, breeders should recognize that moderate to high behavioral inhibition is a highly desirable trait for the average dog.

Early Intervention and Training

As an inborn element of the animal's behavioral profile, characteristics of impulse control problems should be evident early in development. Aspects of the individual's behavior will reflect this. In a study by Alessandri (1992) of preschoolers with and without ADHD, 74% of the exchanges between the ADHD children and the teacher consisted of verbal reprimands and redirections of the children's activities. Thus, there was an increased level of negative affect interactions between ADHD children and adults compared to normal children. ADHD children were less cooperative and also less socially interactive with peers.

Puppies with impulse control problems will also show difficulty with task attention and, similar to ADHD children, may have more fragmented and less structured play behavior. They also may have poor social interaction with both conspecifics and humans. Impulsive puppies are more difficult to manage and train, and thus can be highly frustrating to their owners. Similar to the children described above, many of these puppies will have a high prevalence of negative interactions with their human family members as the families attempt to deal with the puppies' frustrating behavior. This sets up a downward spiral in the health of the human-animal bond: as the humans become more irritated with the puppies, the puppies' competence at social interactions with humans also declines and the relationship develops a higher degree of anxiety. It is crucial that animal professionals identify these puppies as early as possible in order to set up programs to assist owners in dealing with them. Many of these puppies, with proper guidance, will develop into excellent companions.

These dogs need intensive daily "coaching" and micromanaging of their behavior to reduce reinforcement of behaviors that arise due to deficits in executive planning and decision making. Management is an essential element in any successful training program, but it is particularly crucial for dogs with impulse control disorders. Puppies should be confined in safe environments when not under direct supervision. When out of these areas, the puppies need direct visual supervision and the owner/trainer must be willing to be actively training during this time to ensure suitable reinforcement.

Additionally, training sessions for dogs with impulse control disorders, especially those that exhibit symptoms suggestive of an ADHD-like condition, should minimize environmental distractions and contrasting reinforcement options. These puppies may not initially do well, or make much progress, in a puppy class. The bulk of their progress is likely to occur at home when the owner can train in a small distraction-free area. Owners should not be discouraged if their puppies "act up" in class more than other puppies. These points apply to adult dogs as well.

Reinforcements should occur in quick succession to the target behavior even if a bridge signal is being used. Additionally, a high rate of reinforcement will reduce the likelihood of the animal being sidetracked by competing environmental reinforcements. Sagvolden et al. (1992) demonstrated that low reinforcement intervals equalized response patterns of Spontaneously Hypertensive Rats (SHR) with those of control rats. In other words, SHR rats did not demonstrate hyperactivity of responses when reinforcement ratios were high.

In dogs this means the trainer must be well-prepared to start and continue a training session. It is advantageous to use a bridge to quickly mark the target behavior, but it is also important to deliver the primary reinforcer rapidly after the bridge. Repetitions of the behavior should occur in quick succession to each other to allow maximum density of reinforcement and minimize the chances of the dog attending to some other stimulus.

Although exercises for self-control are important, the animal's developmental stage should be taken into consideration. Even normal puppies have difficulty with impulse control because inhibitory circuits in the brain are not fully developed. As the animal ages, more strict criteria can be placed on self-control tasks. Furthermore, sufficient "moving" exercises should be interspersed with stationary self-control tasks. Animals with impulse control disorders should not be "forced" to be calm or show inhibition at all times. Doing so will increase the animal's frustration level significantly and only make training more difficult. Because these animals truly cannot "hold themselves back" empathy and patience must be a significant part of the trainer's or owner's toolbox. As with any task, criteria for self-control should be raised slowly and in accordance with what the animal is likely to successfully achieve.

Exercises that emphasize inhibitory control are essential. Particular attention should be paid to how the animal performs a behavior. Neurobiofeedback has shown some promise in altering brain wave activity and behavior patterns in humans with ADHD. Although this is not a modality available to us with dogs, we can attain somewhat similar effects by reinforcing the animal when it is in certain physiologic states (i.e., high states of relaxation). By reinforcing for certain body postures associated with relaxation, the body can be conditioned to achieve those states more frequently. This is a matter of maximizing the use of classical conditioning during operant training. Thus, "sit" means rump on ground, closed mouth, relaxed muscles of face and body, and slowed breathing pattern. While all of these could be considered operant behaviors (as the animal can voluntarily perform all of them), the physiologic changes that occur in response to the latter two are not. Eventually, relaxed muscles, lowered heart rate and respiratory rate, etc., become classically conditioned to the "sit" cue and the sit position.

Typically, when people list exercises useful for teaching impulse control, we end up with a long list of stationary exercises such as sit, down, stay, settle on a mat, etc., and some exercises that teach dogs to refrain from a potential reinforcement (e.g., "Leave it"). While these are all valuable for enhancing impulse control, the actual exercise is not as important as how the animal performs the exercise. Impulse control exercises are about teaching the animal to retain focus and inhibit actions that deviate from the ultimate behavioral goal no matter what that behavioral goal may be. This means that even heeling and retrieving can be impulse control exercises. Nevertheless, exercises that require the dog to focus directly on the handler ("deference" exercises) and exercises that require the dog to refrain from choosing a behavior with immediate reinforcement in exchange for one with a larger delayed reinforcement ("Leave it") may have particular relevance for impulsive dogs.

Nutrition

There is considerable controversy over the effect of nutrition/diet on hyperactive behavior even in humans. In some studies, ADHD children appear to show some improvement with diets reduced in sugars and "additives," while in others they do not. Many of these studies are poorly done, but even those that are more rigorous show equivocal results. No studies to date have been done in dogs regarding hyperactivity and nutrition. Impulsivity itself has not been linked to diet. Nevertheless, it may be useful to investigate diets that could boost serotonin synthesis in the brain. Diets high in tryptophan (the amino acid precursor) as well as Vitamin B6 (a cofactor in serotonin synthesis) would be reasonable to try. Ironically, tryptophan availability is often higher in carbohydrate-rich diets (with the exception of corn) than those high in protein. There are purported links between food allergy and hyperactivity in dogs, but again, these have not been documented in any controlled manner. Essentially, dietary effects on behavior are variable and unpredictable. Finding a diet that may improve a particular behavioral presentation is a matter of trial and error, but is an avenue that an owner can explore.

Pharmacology

Many individuals feel strongly about the use of adjunctive psychopharmacological agents in the treatment of behavioral disorders. There is ample evidence that such interventions may prove quite useful in these cases. Pharmacological interventions for impulse control disorders fall into three broad categories: stimulants, serotonin modulators, and mood stabilizers.

In terms of impulse control disorders, stimulant medications are used almost exclusively for ADHD (or hyperkinesis in dogs). They are highly successful in improving performance on attentional tasks and decreasing activity in subjects with ADHD although not all individuals respond to such medications. Evidence suggests that children improve as much on stimulant medication alone as they do when being treated with both stimulants and cognitive behavioral therapy.

Because of the well-documented link between serotonin and behavioral inhibition, a variety of impulse control-related conditions respond to medications that affect serotonin receptors. These include selective serotonin reuptake inhibitors, some tricyclic antidepressants, and some specific serotonin agonists. These drugs are likely working in several areas in the brain, but particularly on receptors in the amygdala and in the frontal cortex.

Given the information suggesting amygdalar hyperreactivity in some individuals, the third class of drugs may prove reasonable. Mood stabilizers and anticonvulsants may reduce neuronal excitability in the amygdala. These drugs include carbamazepine, gabapentin, and phenobarbital. In dogs, phenobarbital does occasionally increase aggression. Additionally, carbamazepine has been used in some cases, but overall has not shown high efficacy for treating aggression problems in dogs. However, this class of drugs may still hold potential for certain cases or as newer forms of these medications become available.

Summary

Impulsivity is a key element in a number of psychiatric disorders in humans; similarly, it appears frequently in a number of canine problems. Research is progressively elucidating more about the neurobiology of impulse control disorders, which should help us intervene in a more comprehensive and effective manner. ❖

The TAP Test

The Taylor Aggression Paradigm is a laboratory measure of retaliatory aggressive behavior. The subject competes against a fictitious opponent in a reaction-time game where electric shock is administered and received. Before the task begins, each subject selects a starting shock level to administer to the fictitious opponent should that person be slower than the test subject. Retaliatory aggression is measured by having the fictitious opponent select increasing shock levels for the subject to receive. This is considered provocation, and the subject is then able to adjust his/her own shock level to administer to the opponent in retaliation.

Glossary of Terms

5-HIAA: 5-hydroxyindoleacetic acid, the primary metabolite of serotonin.
5-HT: 5-hydroxytriptamine (serotonin).
ADHD: Attention Deficit/Hyperactivity Disorder.
ASPD: Antisocial Personality Disorder.
Axis I Disorders: Clinical disorders such as depression, bipolar disorder, schizophrenia, etc., but not including personality disorders.
BPD: Borderline Personality Disorder.
Comorbid: Pertaining to two diseases which occur together, such as ADHD and depression.
CSF: Cerebrospinal fluid.
DA: Dopamine.
IED: Intermittent Explosive Disorder.

Mediator: a substance that brings or facilitates some action or process in the body.
NE: Norepinephrine.
SHR: Spontaneously Hypertensive Rat, an animal model of ADHD.
TAP: Taylor Aggression Paradigm
WT: Wild Type rats, used as controls in rodent studies.

References

Alessandri SM. "Attention, play, and social behavior in ADHD preschoolers." J*rnl Abnorm Child Psychol*. 20 (3): 289-302, 1992.

Best M, Williams JM, Coccaro EF. "Evidence for dysfunctional prefrontal circuit in patients with an impulsive aggressive disorder." *Proc Natl Acad Sci USA 2002*; Jun 11; 99(12): 8448-53, 2002.

Coccaro EF. "Intermittent Explosive Disorder and Impulsive Aggression: The time for serious study is now." *Curr Psych Rep*, 6: 1-2, 2004.

Hinshaw SP. "Impulsivity, emotion regulation, and developmental psychopathology: Specificity versus generality of linkages." *Ann NY Acad Sci*, 1008: 149-159, 2003.

Hollander E, Evers M. "New developments in impulsivity." *Lancet*, 358: 949-950, 2001.

Hong HJ, Shin DW, Lee EH, Oh YH, Noh KS. "Hypothalamic-pituitary-adrenal reactivity in boys with Attention Deficit Hyperactivity Disorder." *Yonsel Med Jour*, 44(4): 608-614, 2003.

Keele NB. "The role of serotonin in impulsive and aggressive behaviors associated with epilepsy-like neuronal hyperexcitability in the amygdala." *Epilepsy & Behav*, 7:325-335, 2005.

King JA, Tenney J, Rossi V, Colamussi L, Burdick S. "Neural substrates underlying impulsivity." *Ann NY Acad Sci*, 1008: 160-169, 2003.

Krakowski M. "Violence and serotonin: Influence of impulse control, impulsive and aggressive behaviors associated with epilepsy-like neuronal hyperexcitability in the amygdala." *Epilepsy & Behav*, 7:325-335, 2003.

King JA, Tenney J, Rossi V, Colamussi L, Burdick S. "Neural substrates underlying impulsivity." *Ann NY Acad Sci*, 1008: 160-169, 2003.

Krakowski M. "Violence and serotonin: Influence of impulse control, affect regulation, and social functioning." *J Neuropsych Clin Neurosci*, 15: 294-305, 2003.

McCloskey MS, Berman ME, Noblett KL, Coccaro EF. "Intermittent Explosive Disorder-integrated research diagnostic criteria: Convergent and discriminant validity." *Jour Psych Res*, 40: 231-242, 2006.

Reisner IR, Mann JJ, Stanley M, Huang YY, Houpt KA. "Comparison of cerebrospinal fluid monoamine metabolite levels in dominant-aggressive and non-aggressive dogs." *Brain Res*, Apr 1; 714 (1-2): 57-64, 1996.

Sagvolden T, Metzger MA, Schiorbeck HK, Rugland AL, Spinnangr I, Sagvolden G. "The spontaneously hypertensive rat (SHR) as an animal model of childhood hyperactivity (ADHD): Changed reactivity to reinforcers and to psychomotor stimulants." *Behav Neural Biol*, 58: 103-112, 1992.

Sagvolden T, Metzger MA, Sagvolden G. "Frequent reward eliminates differences in activity between hyperkinetic rats and controls." *Behav Neural Biol*. 59: 225-229, 1993.

Winstanley CA, Theobald DEH, Dalley JW, Robbins TW. "Interactions between serotonin and dopamine in the control of impulsive choice in rats: Therapeutic implications for impulse control disorders." *Neuropsychopharm*, 30: 669-682, 2005.

Behavior-Modifying Drugs: Indications for Use

Karen Sueda, Edited by Terry Long, Published in two parts,
September/December 2007

PART I

When addressing behavior problems in companion animals, the foundations of any successful treatment plan are behavior modification and owner education. However, there are some cases that are not responsive to training alone. In these situations, behavior-modifying medication may help facilitate the training process and allow it to proceed at a faster pace. For some frustrated owners and stressed dogs, drugs can mean the difference between life and death.

Like any training aid, drugs must be used properly and with careful planning and consideration; otherwise, they can do more harm than good. Before considering referral for drug treatment, it is important to determine what goals you hope to achieve by using medication as well as understand the risks and limitations involved. Medication is not indicated in every case. For trainers, choosing which cases may benefit from drug intervention is more important than being able to select which drugs to use.

Understandably, trainers often find it difficult to determine when to refer clients and their dog to a veterinarian for drug treatment. Clients are often instructed to "talk to their vet" with the hope that the veterinarian can make recommendations and prescribe the correct medication. However, some veterinarians do not have experience treating behavior cases or prescribing behavior-modifying medication. This situation is frustrating to everyone involved and can lead to serious health-related and legal consequences. Fortunately, there are veterinarians who specialize in treating behavior problems who can provide guidance in these situations.

The two articles in this series are presented to provide trainers with information and general guidelines to use when they consider referring clients to a veterinarian for behavior-modifying medication. Part I discusses the pros and cons of using behavior-modifying medication, legal aspects to consider, and when and to whom trainers should refer. In Part II a general description of the different classes of medication and which behavior problems may benefit from certain types of drugs will be provided.

Two categories of "drug use"

Drugs treat behavior problems in two different ways. First, "conventional" medications such as antibiotics, pain medication, and steroids are used to treat underlying physical conditions that may cause or exacerbate behavior problems. If a dog's house soiling problem is caused by a urinary tract infection, antibiotics may "cure" the inappropriate elimination by treating the infection. Similarly, addressing concurrent medical problems may help the dog feel more comfortable and decrease his stress, thus increasing his tolerance to behavioral triggers. For example, a dog that is aggressive when disturbed while resting may snap less frequently if his arthritis is treated with pain medication.

The second way drugs treat behavior problems is by altering the brain's neuro-chemistry, thus directly addressing the psychological basis for the behavior. These behavior-modifying medications are prescribed specifically to treat perceived "mental disorders" such as anxiety, aggression, or compulsive behavior. In humans fairly little is known regarding the direct cause-effect relationship between the brain's neurochemistry and behavior; even less is known in dogs.

Several clinical studies have been performed with canine patients and do show that medication improves certain problematic behaviors. However, the field is still very new and much of the information we have regarding drug use is based on experience and knowledge gleaned from the human field. Additionally, there is much individual variation in dogs' responses to medication. This should be kept in mind when counseling clients regarding medication usage.

Why use drugs?

In an ideal world, medications would "cure" behavior problems. However, this is rarely the case. "Magic pills" do not exist and medication does not eliminate the need for compliance with a behavior modification plan. It is important to inform owners of this fact since they may mistakenly believe that drugs will improve their dog's behavior with minimal effort on their part.

Rather than "curing" behavior problems, the main indication for using medication is to reduce the intensity, frequency, or duration of the unwanted behavior so behavior modification can occur. Medication and training should work synergistically. By decreasing anxiety, aggression, or impulsivity, drugs allow the dog to be more receptive to training, thereby accelerating the learning process. For example, dogs exhibiting separation anxiety that were treated with clomipramine (Clomicalm™) and behavior modification improved three times faster than dogs treated with behavior modification alone (King et al, 2000).

In severe cases, medication may be necessary to allow behavior modification to begin. For example, a dog that is extremely fearful may hide and refuse treats. At this stage, counter-conditioning is impossible and desensitization or habituation, while feasible, would take some time. Owners may become frustrated waiting to see progress; in a rescue group or shelter, life-or-death decisions may hinge on how quickly the dog responds to treatment. In the meantime, the dog's quality of life is poor at best. Medication may decrease the dog's anxiety enabling him to emerge from hiding and take treats, thus providing a small "window of opportunity" for training to begin.

Medication is also useful when triggers are unavoidable or unknown. In many cases, owners do not seek help for thunderstorm phobic dogs until storm season. Training helps, but setbacks occur each time the dog panics in association with rain, wind, thunder, and lightning. Drugs can help keep the dog calm during and between storms, minimizing the negative association (Crowell-Davis, et al., 2003).

Medication can also be considered if "training roadblocks" are encountered, i.e., although progress was initially made with behavior modification alone, further improvement seems impossible to achieve. Medication can be "added in" anytime during the training process and may decrease a dog's anxiety, aggression, or impulsivity just enough for training to make further improvement possible.

Why NOT to use drugs

The main reasons not to use medications are because they do not improve or are not indicated to treat a particular behavior problem. Efficacy information comes from laboratory and clinical studies as well as personal and anecdotal experience using medications. Since the fields of veterinary behavior and veterinary psychopharmacology are relatively young, there is still much to learn. More will be said regarding which behavior problems are amenable to drug therapy in the next article.

All behavior-modifying medications have side effects. While some are specific to the individual medication, most drugs can cause sedation, vomiting, diarrhea, and changes in appetite. Severity can range from non-existent to profound. Dogs vary widely in their sensitivity to each medication and individual reactions are difficult to predict. It is beyond the scope of this article to discuss the specific range of side effects for all behavior-modifying drugs. However, it is important to note that anxiety, agitation, and/or aggression have been reported as adverse effects for all commonly used behavior drugs. It is prudent to caution owners that their dog's behavior may worsen and to take extra safety precautions when first starting medication. Having their dog on medication should not lull owners into a false sense of security.

Administration of certain medications may be contraindicated due to the presence of certain health conditions or drug interactions. For example, tricyclic antidepressants (TCAs) such as amitriptyline and clomipramine should not be used (or used with caution) in dogs with heart conditions as these drugs can cause changes in heart rate, rhythm, and blood pressure (Crowell-Davis 2006). Animals taking TCAs may benefit from additional monitoring before and during anesthesia.

Drug interactions, while not common, can be life threatening. Monoamine oxidase inhibitors, such as Anipryl™ (selegeline) and amitraz (used in some tick collars and mite treatments) should never be combined with selective serotonin reuptake inhibitors (SSRIs) (e.g., Prozac™, Paxil™, Zoloft™) or TCAs. Serotonin syndrome, characterized by seizures, mental changes, fever, and death, could result. Other medications can also alter a dog's ability to metabolize behavior-modifying drugs, or vice versa. Ketoconazole, used to treat fungal/yeast infections, can impair the breakdown of TCAs, which can build up to toxic levels.

Many over-the-counter herbal or homeopathic medications are available to treat behavior problems. These products may contain ingredients that can also cause drug interactions. Concurrent administration of tryptophan or St. John's Wort and SSRIs can also lead to serotonin syndrome (Mealey 2002). Since owners often fail to mention homeopathic medications when asked what drugs their dog currently receives, it is important to question them specifically regarding the use of supplements and over-the-counter products.

Once SSRI or TCA administration is started, it may take several weeks for a response to be seen. This can be frustrating for owners who are seeking more immediate improvement. While benzodiazepines (e.g., Valium™, Xanax™) possess a rapid onset of action (i.e., minutes to hours), they do not last as long, nor are they recommended for long-term use due to the development of tolerance and physiologic dependence.

In humans, approximately one-third (33%) of patients do not respond to any given antidepressant (Stahl, 2000). While similar animal studies have not been performed, dogs do not always respond to the first medication they are placed on. Several medications may have to be tried before an improvement is noted. In addition to taking time, this can be both financially and emotionally taxing to owners.

Legal aspects

Benzodiazepines, which include Valium™, Xanax™, Klonopin™, Serax™, and Ativan™, are controlled substances and have the potential for human abuse. Since canine dosages are typically much higher than dosages used for humans, clients may obtain large quantities of these drugs through their veterinarian. If drug abuse is suspected, then these medications should not be recommended or prescribed.

At the time of publication, only three behavior-modifying medications have received FDA approval for use in veterinary patients: Clomicalm™ (clomipramine) and Reconcile™ (fluoxetine) for separation anxiety in dogs and Anipryl™ (selegiline) for canine cognitive dysfunction. Because FDA-approved drugs do not exist for most behavior problems, medications are frequently dispensed "extra-label." Extra-label usage indicates that the drug is being prescribed in a manner other than indicated on the manufacturer's label and that tests may not have been conducted to prove that it is safe or effective when used in that manner. Although behavior problems have been successfully treated using extra-label medication for years, clients should be informed that extensive laboratory and clinical trials have not been run in most cases.

Non-veterinarians, including trainers, should never diagnose behavior problems or make specific drug recommendations, even if a veterinarian asks them to, since this could be construed as practicing veterinary medicine without a license. If you believe that a client's dog would benefit from behavior-modifying medication, recommend that they discuss the possibility with their veterinarian. This leaves the diagnosis of the behavior problem and drug treatment decisions, including drug choice, in the hands of the veterinarian.

When to Refer

Cases should always be referred to a veterinarian if there is suspicion that a disease process may be causing or contributing to a pet's behavioral problem. Please refer to Dr. Lore Haug's excellent article "Medical Evaluation of the Behavior Patient" (page 214).

There is no absolute right or wrong time to consider drug therapy. When to refer clients will depend, in large part, on your own experience and "comfort level." More experienced trainers may have had success with similar cases without using medication; trainers who don't work with aggressive dogs may refer cases sooner than trainers who see many aggression cases. Since medication can reduce anxiety, aggression, and impulsivity, allowing behavior modification to proceed at a faster rate, there is some benefit to referring clients sooner rather than later. This may avoid future frustration or using medication as a "final option."

The following is a list of conditions for which I recommend considering referral to a veterinarian for drug treatment:

- Behavior is "abnormal." The behavior itself may be unusual or be unexpected for the dog's age, breed, history, etc. Because "odd" behaviors may also be caused by physical ailments, a thorough physical examination is very important. (Examples: "fly-snapping" or tail-chasing; sudden behavior change in an old dog).

- It is difficult to start behavior modification. Either the dog is too anxious or reactive to begin training (e.g., a dog with generalized anxiety) or triggers are unavoidable or unknown (e.g., a dog with separation anxiety has to be left alone while owners are at work).

- You have hit a "training roadblock" and are having difficulty making progress using behavior modification alone.

To Whom to Refer

As mentioned in the introduction, a general practice veterinarian may not have much experience treating behavior problems or prescribing behavior-modifying medication. As such, the veterinarian may not feel comfortable making recommendations and/or the client may wish to seek the advice of someone with more experience. Additionally, if clients are insistent about using medications or there are unusual circumstances surrounding the case (e.g., legal issues), then referral to a specialist is warranted.

Ideally, referral to a board-certified veterinary behaviorist should be recommended. Veterinary behaviorists have completed two to three years of additional post-graduate training in clinical animal behavior, passed a qualifying examination, and have had years of experience treating behavior problems and prescribing behavior-modifying medication. A list of boarded veterinary behaviorists can be found at www.acvb.org.

Unfortunately, there are only 42 board-certified veterinary behaviorists in the world at the time of publication. If a board-certified veterinary behaviorist is not practicing in your area, a list of veterinarians with a special interest in behavior can be found at www.avsabonline.org. Since the experience level of these veterinarians varies, clients should inquire about the level of training in behavior and number of cases they have seen.

Veterinarian-to-veterinarian consults may be available for clients who are not able to see a veterinary behaviorist or veterinarian with a special interest in behavior. The client's general practice veterinarian can consult with a behavior specialist and obtain behavior modification and/or drug recommendations for the patient. Obviously, this is not ideal; much information is lost in translation because the veterinary behaviorist is not able to observe or examine the patient in question.

Summary of PART I

When prescribed and used appropriately, drugs can work synergistically with a well-formulated behavior modification plan. However, like any training aid, they are not appropriate for every case. Clients should be well-informed of the benefits and risks associated with using medication and referred to a well-qualified veterinarian who can work with the two of you to achieve a better quality of life for their dog.

PART II

Placing a dog on drugs is never innocuous. As discussed in Part I, the benefits of drug use must always be weighed against the risks. This includes the possibility that medication can cause or worsen a patient's anxiety or aggression. Clients considering drug therapy must be very committed to working with their pet since finding the right medication and waiting for it to take effect can be frustrating. Additionally, they must understand the importance of continuing behavior modification exercises while their pet is on medication; drugs alone are unlikely to resolve the behavior problem. Ideally, the client, trainer, and veterinarian should work as a team to closely monitor both therapeutic and adverse effects.

This article covers categories of behavior-modifying medication most commonly used in veterinary medicine and which behaviors are best suited to drug therapy. It is not intended to be a "crash-course" in veterinary psychopharmacology, nor replace consultation with a veterinarian or veterinary behaviorist.1 Only licensed veterinarians can legally prescribe medications. Trainers are advised not to make specific medication recommendations to clients, but refer them to their veterinarian if they feel behavior-modifying medication is needed.

Neurotransmitters and Drug Classes

An extensive review of neuropharmacology is beyond the scope of this article. However, a brief discussion of how behavior-modifying medications work may aid in understanding why medications are used to treat specific behavior problems.

In general, psychoactive medications act to increase or decrease neurotransmitter levels in the brain. Neurotransmitters are substances that are released by one neuron that can either excite or inhibit neighboring neurons. Through their action on neurotransmitter levels, behavior-modifying drugs can modulate the activity of specific brain areas. The most commonly used behavior medications affect one or more of the following neurotransmitters: serotonin, norepinephrine, gamma-aminobutyric acid (GABA), dopamine, and acetylcholine.

Serotonin. Many behavior-modifying medications act to increase serotonin levels. Decreased levels of serotonin are associated with anxiety, panic, phobias, depression, obsessive-compulsive behavior, and food cravings in humans (Stahl 2000a). Additionally, serotonin also affects aggression (Crowell-Davis & Murray 2006a). Lower levels of a serotonin metabolite were found in dogs exhibiting dominance-related aggression (compared to non-aggressive dogs) (Reisner et al.1996) and in monkeys exhibiting more violent forms of aggression and decreased impulse control (Mehlman et al. 1994).

Norepinephrine. Decreases in norepinephrine have been associated with impaired concentration and decreased attention, depression and fatigue in humans (Stahl 2000a).

GABA. GABA is the major inhibitory neurotransmitter in the brain. Increasing GABA levels results in decreased anxiety, sedation, muscle relaxation and seizure suppression (Stahl 2000b; Crowell-Davis & Murray 2006b).

Dopamine. Dopamine is involved in reward-related behavior and decreased levels are found in patients with Parkinson's disease (Stahl 2000c).

Acetylcholine. Decreases in acetylcholine lead to constipation, dry mouth, drowsiness, and blurred vision (Stahl 2000d).

Behavior-modifying drugs most frequently used in dogs can be divided into four classes:

- **Selective Serotonin Reuptake Inhibitors (SSRIs)**—As their name implies, SSRIs specifically target serotonin with minimal affect on other neurotransmitters. This helps to decrease side effects that may occur with other medications. SSRIs include Reconcile® or Prozac® (both fluoxetine), Paxil® (paroxetine) and Zoloft® (sertraline).

- **Tricyclic antidepressants (TCAs)**—TCAs increase serotonin and norepinephrine, the degrees to which depend on the specific drug. For example, clomipramine is more selective for serotonin compared to amitriptyline. TCAs also decrease acetylcholine, resulting in more frequent side effects. TCAs include Clomicalm® (clomipramine) and Elavil® (amitriptyline).

- **Benzodiazepines**—Benzodiazepines increase GABA and are rapidly absorbed into the bloodstream, making them especially good at treating seizures and acute anxiety. Unfortunately, their effects are short-lived (hours).There are many benzodiazepines; Valium® (diazepam), Xanax® (alprazolam), Klonopin® (clonazepam), and Serax® (oxazepam) are often prescribed.

- **Monoamine oxidase inhibitors (MAOIs)**—These medications also increase serotonin, norepinephrine and dopamine levels. Therefore MAOIs should not be taken with SSRIs or TCAs since such combinations may result in dangerously high neurotransmitter levels. Caution should also be taken when giving MAOIs with other medications (please see the first article in this series). Anipryl® (selegiline) is an MAOI used to treat canine cognitive dysfunction.

Behaviors Amenable to Drug Use

Although each case must be assessed on an individual basis, scientific studies have shown that medications are likely to facilitate the treatment process for some behavior problems, but not others.

- **Fear and Anxiety**. Drugs that increase serotonin or GABA, including SSRIs, TCAs, and benzodiazepines, have anti-anxiety properties. Therefore, anxiety- or fear-related disorders often have the highest rate of treatment success with drug intervention.

   a. **Separation Anxiety**. Both Reconcile® and Clomicalm® have received FDA approval for the treatment of canine separation anxiety. Both drugs showed comparable rates of improvement (70-80%) after eight weeks of treatment (Reconcile—Simpson et al. 2007; Clomicalm—King et al. 2000).

   b. **Thunderstorm Phobia.** Over 90% (30/32) of dogs with thunderstorm phobia showed some improvement with a combination of clomipramine and alprazolam (Crowell-Davis et al. 2003).

   c. **Generalized Anxiety.** In a retrospective study, 67% (27/40) of dogs with generalized anxiety disorder that were treated with fluoxetine showed improvement while 50% (6/12) showed improvement after treatment with paroxetine (Reisner 2003).

   d. **Other Behaviors That May Be Amenable to Drug Therapy.** Although clinical trials have not been performed, other behaviors that occur secondary to fear or anxiety may also benefit from drug therapy. These include fear of specific triggers (e.g. fear of strangers or other dogs, objects, or situations), urine marking, and noise phobias.

- **Compulsive Behaviors**[2]. Repetitive behaviors such as fly-snapping and tail-chasing are thought to occur secondary to stress and anxiety (Luescher 2003). Medications, such as fluoxetine and clomipramine, are used to treat humans with OCD as well as dogs with compulsive disorders.

   a. **Acral Lick Dermatitis (ALD).** In several studies, dogs with ALD exhibited improvement when placed on fluoxetine (Wynchank & Berk 1998; Rapoport et al 1992; Stein et al 1992).

b. **Compulsive behavior (various).** In a study of 51 dogs diagnosed with various forms of compulsive disorder (e.g., ALD, spinning, pacing, flank-sucking, checking rear end, chasing lights, air biting, etc.), treatment with clomipramine was effective, but not curative, as compared to placebo (Hewson et al. 1998).

- **Canine Cognitive Dysfunction (CCD).** Anipryl® (selegiline) is FDA approved and marketed for the treatment of CCD, an age-related disorder characterized by changes in sleep-wake cycle, loss of housetraining, disorientation, and altered interactions with people and other pets. In clinical trials, approximately 80% of dogs exhibited improvement in clinical signs after 30 days of treatment (Campbell et al. 2001).

- **Aggression**. Treatment of canine aggression with psychoactive medication has produced equivocal results. This is likely due to the fact that there are many underlying causes of aggressive behavior.

    a. **Human-directed aggression**. Many dogs once thought to be "dominantly aggressive" actually exhibit a great deal of anxiety and fear. Therefore, aggressive dogs may benefit from increased serotonin levels, which reduce anxiety and impulsivity. In one study, nine dogs diagnosed with "dominance aggression" showed a reduction in aggression scores while being treated with fluoxetine as compared to placebo (Dodman et al. 1996). However, in another study, dogs treated with clomipramine did not exhibit a significant reduction in aggressive behavior as compared to placebo (White et al. 1999). Dogs did not undergo concurrent behavior modification in either study. The importance of behavior modification was demonstrated in a prospective trial of 12 dogs diagnosed with dominance-related aggression, fear-related aggression or both; treatment with amitriptyline and behavior modification did not significantly differ from treatment with behavior modification alone (Virga et al 2001).

    b. **Interdog aggression.** Although large studies have not been conducted, case reports have reported successful treatment of interdog aggression with fluoxetine (Overall 1995; Dodman 2000).

Behaviors Unlikely to Benefit from Drug Therapy

Normal behaviors such as destructive or escape behavior secondary to boredom, "unruly" behaviors (e.g., jumping up, pulling on leash), and predatory behavior are unlikely to be significantly affected by medication. Therefore, before referring clients to their veterinarian for drug therapy, you must determine the underlying motivation for the dog's behavior. For example, treatment with an anti-anxiety medication may be essential for a dog that is destructive because of separation anxiety, but would be worthless in treating an under-stimulated, bored dog.

Learned behaviors, such as barking for attention, that have been purposefully or inadvertently reinforced will also not respond to pharmacologic intervention. Medication may initially appear to work since many drugs cause sedation for a few days to weeks. Typically, these effects are short lived and result in recurrence of the problem behavior as the sedative effect wears off.

Owners frequently complain of "hyperactivity" and "attention deficit disorder" in their dogs. True hyperactivity or hyperkinesis is extremely rare; these dogs cannot settle down and possess elevated heart and respiratory rates at rest. While hyperkinetic dogs benefit from treatment with methylphendate (Ritalin®), most dogs thought to be "hyperactive" by their owners are simply under-stimulated. The best treatment is consistent, daily mental and physical activity to channel their behavior into more acceptable avenues.

Drug Selection

Anti-anxiety medications can be divided into two groups: drugs that are fast-acting, but only last for a few hours and drugs that may take weeks to reach peak effect, but last longer. Benzodiazepines are in the first category (fast-acting/short duration) while both SSRIs and TCAs are in the second (slow-onset/long duration).

When contemplating whether the drug choice is appropriate, ask yourself the following questions:

- How long does the dog remain fearful or anxious?
- How often do triggers occur?
- Are there specific objects or events that trigger their fear? Are triggers avoidable or unavoidable (predictable or unpredictable)?
- Is the dog aggressive?

1. **How long does the dog remain fearful or anxious?** If the dog is anxious most of the time, a long-duration medication should be used. To achieve a "steady-state" anxiolytic effect, longer-lasting medications only require once or twice daily dosing. To achieve the same effect, shorter-duration drugs must be dosed two to four times a day and run the risk of more adverse effects with frequent, daily usage.

2. **How often do triggers occur?** The more frequent the trigger, the greater the need for a longer-lasting medication. When triggers are frequent and occur regularly (e.g., encountering strangers), continuous administration of a longer-lasting medication is most beneficial. If the trigger occurs infrequently, such as fireworks, than a shorter-duration medication may be given on an "as needed" basis to avoid daily, long-term administration. There are several options when triggers occur frequently during one particular time period. If the overall time period is short—for example, owners taking a car-phobic dog on a road trip for a week—then fast-acting/short-duration medications are preferable to slow-onset/longer-lasting drugs since the latter may take weeks to reach peak effect. If the overall time period

is long—e.g., thunderstorm season lasting several months—then longer-lasting drugs may provide more constant relief. A fast-acting/short-duration medication can be "piggybacked" with the longer-lasting medication to provide a more rapid anti-anxiety effect or if a stronger anti-anxiety effect is needed during more severe thunderstorms.

3. **Are there specific objects or events that trigger their fear? Are triggers avoidable or unavoidable (predictable or unpredictable)?** Triggers that can be identified and predicted can be avoided to some degree. Practicing good avoidance techniques while implementing behavior modification and training may decrease the need for daily medication. For example, owners should avoid taking dogs that are fearful of car rides on unnecessary trips while they implement a systematic desensitization and counter-conditioning plan. On those few occasions when a car ride is necessary (e.g., trip to the veterinarian), a fast-acting/short-duration medication may be appropriate. However, if triggers are unknown/unavoidable/unpredictable, a long-duration medication may be beneficial so anxiety-relief is "on board" all the time. This is especially important if the dog is frequently fearful.

4. **Is the dog aggressive?** Clients must be warned that all behavior-modifying medications run the risk of increasing aggressive behavior through disinhibition. This is especially true with benzodizepines, which may increase impulsivity (Thiébot 1985). Crowell-Davis (2006) states, "Generally, lacking good clinical guidelines as to the specific aggression situations in which benzodiazepines might be helpful or risky, they should be avoided or used with extreme caution in cases involving aggressive animals."

The Trainer's Role in Drug Therapy

• **Identifying Problems**. Trainers are often the first person to recognize the presence of a serious behavior problem. Inexperienced pet owners may not realize that their dog's behavior is abnormal or potentially dangerous. Encourage owners to take their dog to their veterinarian to rule out medical problems. If necessary, they can discuss drug treatment with their veterinarian. (Please see the first article in this series for indications for drug use).

• **Source of Knowledge**. Behavioral medicine is a relatively new discipline and is not yet taught in all veterinary schools. Although many veterinarians seek out information through continuing education courses, they may not have extensive clinical experience in this field. Even though you may have more experience treating behavior cases, avoid diagnosing behavior problems or making drug recommendations (even if the veterinarian asks you to). Instead, delicately recommend that the veterinarian consult with a board-certified veterinary behaviorist or another veterinarian with behavior experience. If another veterinarian is not available, refer them to veterinary textbooks such as the *Handbook Of Behavior*

Problems of the Dog and Cat by Landsberg, Hunthausen, and Ackerman (2003) or *Veterinary Psychopharmacology* by Crowell-Davis and Murray (2006).

- Inappropriate Recommendations. If you or your client feel that an inappropriate drug recommendation has been made, ask your client whether his or her veterinarian:

  a. Diagnosed a behavior problem? Drugs should only be prescribed after a history has been taken and an accurate diagnosis made.

  b. Discussed why a certain medication was selected? There may be medical, behavioral, or financial reasons why a specific drug was prescribed.

  c. Discussed the pros/cons/side-effects with the client?

  d. Did the client express his or her concerns to their veterinarian?

In some cases, it may be beneficial for you (the trainer) to speak directly to the veterinarian. This should be done only with your client's permission since the pet's medical records are confidential. In some cases, the client may not be communicating their specific concerns to the veterinarian or the veterinarian may not be aware how the drug is affecting the dog's behavior and training regimen. Again, avoid making treatment recommendations, even if asked.

Finally, a second opinion may be needed. If one is available in your area, I recommend seeking the advice of a board-certified veterinary behaviorist or veterinarian with a special interest in behavior. These doctors typically have more clinical experience working with behavior cases than general practitioners and may be able to recommend alternative behavioral or pharmacologic treatments.

Summary

In addition to facilitating the training process, drug therapy can benefit a large number of dogs that cannot be successfully treated with behavior modification alone. However, drugs are not indicated in all cases. In order to maximize success, a good trainer must be able to recognize what behavior problems are amenable to drug treatment and discuss the pros and cons with their clients. ❖

References and Recommended Reading

[1] For more in-depth information, I recommend the book *Veterinary Psychopharmacology* by Sharon Crowell-Davis and Thomas Murray.

[2] Since we cannot definitely determine whether animals exhibit "obsessive" behavior (i.e., defined as having recurrent, persistent, and unwanted thoughts), the diagnosis "obsessive-compulsive disorder" is not typically used in veterinary medicine.

Campbell S., Trettien A., Kozan B. "A non-comparative open label study evaluating the effect of selegiline hydrochloride in a clinical setting." *Vet Therapeutics.* 2:24-39, 2001.

Crowell-Davis S.L., Seibert L.M., Sung W., Parthasarathy V, Curtis T.M. "Use of clomipramine, alprazolam and behavior modification for treatment of storm phobia in dogs." *JAVMA.* 222:744-748, 2003.

Crowell-Davis, S.L. "Tricyclic antidepressants." *Veterinary Psychopharmacology.* (pp. 179-206). Iowa: Blackwell Publishing, 2006.

Crowell-Davis, S.L., Murray, T. Introduction. *Veterinary Psychopharmacology.* (pp. 3-24). Iowa: Blackwell Publishing, 2006a.

Crowell-Davis, S.L., Murray, T. "Amnio acid neurotransmitters: glutamate, GABA, and the pharmacology of benzodiazepines." *Veterinary Psychopharmacology.* (pp. 25-33). Iowa: Blackwell Publishing, 2006b.

Crowell-Davis, S.L., Seibert, L.M., Sung, W., et al. "Use of clomipramine, alprazolam and behavior modification for treatment of storm phobia in dogs." *J Am Vet Med Assoc.* 222:744-749, 2003.

Dodman, N.H. "Behavior case of the month." *J Am Vet Med Assoc.* 217:1468-1472, 2000.

Dodman, N.H., Donnelly R., Shuster, L., et al. "Use of fluoxetine to treat dominance aggression in dogs." *J Am Vet Med Assoc.* 209:1585-1587, 1996.

Haug, L.I. "Medical evaluation of the behavior patient." *The APDT Chronicle of the Dog.* March/April. (pp. 13-16), 2007.

Hewson, C.J., Luescher, A., Parent, J.M., et al. "Efficacy of clomipramine in the treatment of canine compulsive disorder." *J Am Vet Med Assoc.* 213:1760-1766, 1998.

King, J. N., Simpson B.S., Overall K. L., et al., The CLOCSA (Clomipramine in Canine Separation Anxiety) Study Group. "Treatment of separation anxiety in dogs with clomipramine: results from a prospective, randomized, double-blind, placebo-controlled, parallel-group, multicenter clinical trial." *Appl Anim Behav Sci.* 67:255-275, 2000.

Landsberg, G., Hunthausen, W., Ackerman, L. *Handbook of Behavior Problems of the Dog and Cat. 2nd Ed.* Edinburgh: Saunders, 2003.

Luescher, A.U. "Diagnosis and management of compulsive disorders in dogs and cats." *Vet Clin Small Anim.* 33:253-267, 2003.

Mealey K.L. "Clinically significant drug interactions." *Compendium.* 24:10-22, 2002.

Mehlman, P.T., Higley, J.D., Faucher, I., et al. "Low CSF 5-HIAA concentrations and severe aggression and impaired impulse control in nonhuman primates." *Am J Psych.* 151:1485-1491, 1994.

Overall, K.L. "Animal behavior case of the month." *J Am Vet Med Assoc.* 206:629-632, 1995.

Rapoport J.L., Ryland, D.H., Kriete, M. "Drug treatment of canine acral lick: an animal model of obsessive-compulsive disorder." *Arch Gen Psych.* 49:517-521, 1992.

Reisner, I.R., Mann, J.J., Stanley, M., et al. "Comparison of cerebrospinal fluid monoamine metabolite levels in dominant-aggressive and non-aggressive dogs." *Brain Res.* 714:57-64, 1996.

Reisner, I.R. "Diagnosis of canine generalized anxiety disorder and management with behavioral modification and fluoxetine or paroxetine: a retrospective summary of clinical experience (2001-2003)." *J Am Anim Hosp Assoc.* 39:512, 2003.

Simpson, B.S., Landsberg, G.M., Reisner, I.R., et al. "Effects of Reconcile (fluoxetine) chewable tablets plus behavior modification for canine separation anxiety." *Vet Therapeutics.* 8:18-31, 2007.

Stahl, S.M. "Depression and bipolar disorders." *Essential Psychopharmacology: Neuroscientific Basis and Practical Applications. 2nd Ed.* (pp. 135-197). New York: Cambridge University Press, 2000.

Stahl, S.M. Depression and bipolar disorders. *Essential Psychopharmacology: Neuroscientific Basis and Practical Applications. 2nd Ed.* (pp. 135-197). New York: Cambridge University Press, 2000a.

Stahl, S.M. Anxiolytics and sedative-hypnotics. *Essential Psychopharmacology: Neuroscientific Basis and Practical Applications. 2nd Ed* (pp. 297-334). New York: Cambridge University Press, 2000b.

Stahl, S.M. Psychosis and schizophrenia. *Essential Psychopharmacology: Neuroscientific Basis and Practical Applications. 2nd Ed* (pp. 365-400). New York: Cambridge University Press, 2000c.

Stahl, S.M. Classical antidepressants, serotonin selective and noradrenergic reuptake inhibitors. *Essential Psychopharmacology: Neuroscientific Basis and Practical Applications. 2nd Ed.* (pp.199-244). New York: Cambridge University Press, 2000d.

Stein, D.J., Shoulberg, N., Helton, K., Hollander, E. "The neuroethological approach to obsessive-compulsive disorder." *Comprehensive Psychiatry.* 33:274-281, 1992.

Virga, V., Houpt, K.A., Scarlett, J.M. "Efficacy of amitriptyline as pharmacological adjunct to behavioral modification in the management of aggressive behaviors in dogs." *J Am Anim Hosp Assoc.* 37:325-330, 2001.

White, M.M., Neilson, J.C., Hart, B.L., Cliff, K.D. "Effects of clomipramine on dominance-related aggression in dogs." *J Am Vet Med Assoc.* 215:1288-1291, 1999.

Wynchank D., Berk, M. "Fluoxetine treatment of acral lick dermatitis in dogs: a placebo-controlled randomized double blind trial." *Depression and Anxiety.* 8:21-23, 1998.

An Overview of the Bach Flower Essences

Don Hanson, March/April 2006

Like many people, I was initially very skeptical of complementary and alternative medicine and treatments such as Bach Flower Essences. Having an engineering/science background, I found it difficult to deal with the concept that complementary medicine could not always be explained by science. It wasn't until one day when I had one of those "a-ha!" moments that I discovered they might be a subject worthy of further study. My moment began with a client who had a dog with mild separation anxiety. Our discussion revealed: 1) the dog was mildly destructive when left home alone; 2) the clients were concerned about the dog's emotional state, but not what was being destroyed; 3) they were uncomfortable with the idea of using any drugs such as Clomicalm, but were open to natural remedies; and 4) in my opinion, the couple was unlikely to have the time or motivation to follow my standard behavior modification protocol. They were very busy and the problem was just not severe enough to cause them to take action.

I wanted to help these people and their dog, but was uncertain how to proceed. Based upon their comments it was obvious that my normal treatment plan, Clomicalm from their veterinarian and a behavior modification protocol, was not going to be acceptable. I asked if they had heard of Bach Rescue Remedy™. I explained that I had limited knowledge of flower essences, but that I had been looking for a natural, anti-anxiety treatment for one of our dogs, and had done a little research on this product and had heard of many people who had great success using Rescue Remedy. I provided them with dosage guidelines, and sent them to the local health food store to buy a bottle (since this was before we sold the Bach Flower Essences at our store).

Approximately one week later my clients called and told me that after giving the dog Rescue Remedy for a week, all separation problems had resolved! The clients indicated that they had made no changes in their routine, were not treating the dog with anything other than the Rescue Remedy, and had done no behavior modification. They reported that their dog was no longer showing any signs of stress when left alone and all destructive behavior had ceased. While this is only anecdotal evidence, it was enough to convince me that I needed to learn more about Bach Flower Essences.

Most of the information I will be presenting in this article is based upon anecdotal evidence. Because it is not based upon statistical research and the scientific method, anecdotal evidence is often dismissed by the scientific community, yet the following is a prime example of the role and importance that it plays. As early as the 1700's, sailors were fed limes as a way of preventing scurvy. This practice was based strictly on anecdotal evidence. It wasn't until 1932 and the discovery of vitamin C that the scientific method was able to prove why limes and other citrus fruits helped prevent and cure scurvy. Fortunately, no one stopped sailors from eating limes because scientists had not completed a study demonstrating that eating limes cures scurvy. Anecdotal evidence is often the first step in the discovery of new methods and ways of thinking.

Bach Flower Essences fall into the realm of complementary and alternative medicine along with Chinese medicine and acupuncture, herbal medicine, aromatherapy, homeopathy, and others. You will not find vast numbers of studies proving scientifically and/or statistically that these modalities work, yet much of the world's population, including many scientifically trained physicians and veterinarians, use these modalities with great success on a daily basis. While my engineering background initially caused me to be very close-minded about complementary medicine, I have seen first hand, with myself, pets, friends, family, and clients, how complementary modalities do heal.

A few studies have been published on the use of Bach Flower Essences with people. These studies concluded that they were effective in treating clinically depressed patients[1], safe and effective when used with children for a variety of disorders[2], and effective at reducing stress.[3,4]

What Are the Bach Flower Essences

The Bach Flower Essences are all natural, very dilute solutions made from spring water, an alcohol preservative, and the parts of specific flowers. They are used to help balance the emotions and bring about a state of equilibrium in living organisms, and have been successfully used with people, animals, and even plants. Bach Flower Essences are listed in the Homeopathic Pharmacopoeia of the United States (HPUS), have been issued with National Drug Code (NDC) numbers by the Food and Drug Administration (FDA), and are sold as over-the-counter homeopathic products in the United States.

Although the Bach Flower Essences are listed in the HPUS and are prepared at a 5X homeopathic dilution (0.00001 gram of active substance per milliliter of tincture), they are not considered homeopathic medicine. While they are prepared from plant material, they do not fall in the same category as herbal medicine. The fact that we refer to them as "essences" suggests to some that they are aromatherapy—the use of essential oils and other aromatic compounds from plants to affect someone's mood or health—which they are not. Flower essences fill their own unique niche in the arsenal of complementary medicine. Like homeopathy, Chinese medicine, acupuncture, and Reiki, the Bach Flower Essences work at an energetic level in the body. This class of complementary therapies is usually called vibrational medicine. In his book, *A Practical Guide to Vibrational Medicine*, Dr Richard Gerber, a physician, describes vibrational medicine and the Bach Flower Essences thusly:

> Vibrational medicine is based upon modern scientific insights into the energetic nature of the atoms and molecules making up our bodies, combined with ancient mystical observations of the body's unique life-energy systems that are critical but less well understood aspects of human functioning. Bach believed that his flower remedies would not only neutralize negative

emotional—and mental—energy patterns but also infuse positive vibrations associated with specific virtues into an individual such as the virtues of love, peace, steadfastness, gentleness, strength, understanding, tolerance, wisdom, forgiveness, courage or joy.

The Chinese call this energy Qi, homeopaths call it vital force, and Dr. Bach called it "positive vibrations." While we cannot currently use scientific instruments to measure any of these forms of energy, many believe in their healing ability. There are many entrenched in the world of orthodox, traditional medicine who would say it is unwise to use a method of healing when we do not completely understand how it works. This is why there has been resistance to complementary medicine by many modern scientists. Yet, our knowledge of many medicines accepted by the traditionalists is equally sketchy. Aspirin, found in most household medicine cabinets, has been commercially available since 1899, yet scientists only began to understand how aspirin worked in the 1970's. Buspirone (Buspar) is a commonly prescribed drug for certain anxiety disorders. The National Institutes of Health MedlinePlus database contains the following citations for Buspirone:

> Buspirone is used to treat certain anxiety disorders or to relieve the symptoms of anxiety... It is not known exactly how Buspirone works to relieve the symptoms of anxiety.

Considering that Bach Flower Essences can also be used to treat anxiety and do not have the side effects of Buspirone, I believe consideration of the Bach Flower Essences would be a smart choice.

There are a total of 38 different Bach Flower Essences, 37 made from specific flowers, and one made from the water of a spring believed to have healing properties. Each essence is used to treat a specific emotion or state of mind such as fear, anger, apathy, etc. These are all emotions that most people can readily identify in themselves and in other people, and with training can also identify in animals. These emotional states and their corresponding essence are all described in *The Twelve Healers and Other Remedies* by Edward Bach. Dr. Bach's goal was to create a system of medicine that was simple enough that people who become familiar with the essences through his publications could identify their negative emotional state, select the corresponding essence and thus treat themselves.

The Bach Flower Essences may be used individually or in combination. Rescue Remedy is the only combination remedy prepared and sold ready-made; it contains five essences and is typically only used for emergencies or extremely stressful situations when the subject is in a state of mental or physical shock, terror, or panic. It should not be used as a replacement for veterinary care, but it is often used as a complement to traditional treatments. I know of many people who use Rescue Remedy to calm themselves before trips to the dentist and who also use it with their pets before trips to the veterinarian. I always carry a bottle in my briefcase and car, so it is available in case of an emergency or accident.

The Bach Flower Essences are very safe. The only contra-indication is hypersensitivity to any of the ingredients. Since the botanical component is so dilute, a reaction is very unlikely. Grape alcohol is used as a preservative, so the essences may be unsuitable for those sensitive to alcohol.

Bach Flower Essences are not used to treat physical disease, but rather the emotional state of the patient. They can be used to help resolve fear and anxiety, anger, grief, and many other emotions. Common sense and numerous research studies have shown how stress can have a negative impact on the immune system.[5] Anything that we do to reduce or relieve stress, including use of Bach Flower Essences, has the potential to positively affect our immune system and thus aid in maintaining physical health.

History of the Bach Flower Essences

The Bach Flower Essences were discovered by Dr. Edward Bach, a Welsh physician practicing medicine in the early 1900's. Trained in conventional allopathic medicine, Dr. Bach observed that his patients' recovery seemed to have as much to do with their emotional health as it did with any physical condition. Those in a positive emotional state recovered quicker.

Dr. Bach's area of expertise was bacteriology, but as he became more intrigued with the emotions of his patients, he started to study the work of Dr. Samuel Hahnemann, the founder of homeopathic medicine. Homeopathic medicine emphasizes treating the "whole" patient including their emotions and mental state, rather than focusing exclusively on physical symptoms. As a result of his research, Dr. Bach developed seven nosodes to treat intestinal disease. A nosode is a homeopathic remedy made from a pathological specimen. The Bach nosodes are made from bacteria found in the bowels. As Dr. Bach began to use the nosodes with his patients (which are still in use today), he observed that he could select the appropriate curative nosode for his patients based solely on their emotional state.[6]

While Dr. Bach was very satisfied with the positive effects of homeopathy, he was concerned that many of the typical homeopathic remedies were made from toxic substances (bacteria, Belladonna, Mercury, Arsenic, etc.). He was convinced that if he were to devote his efforts to searching among the wonders of the natural world, he would find non-toxic medicines that would have a similar effect. In 1930, Dr. Bach left an extremely lucrative private practice in London, and started on his quest to find what would become known as the Bach Flower Essences. During the next six years he would discover and successfully use the same 38 essences that we use today.

My Journey with the Bach Flower Essences

After my "a-ha!" experience, I enrolled in the Dr. Edward Bach Foundation's practitioner training program. The foundation offers two training tracks; one for those who wish to use the essences with people and one for those who wish to use them with animals. You must complete the first two levels of the human track before applying for the animal program. My level one and two human classes each involved two days of study in Boston, MA. These classes provided an in-depth review of the 38 essences and their use. The level two class included case studies and an overview of counseling techniques.

I completed my animal training at the Natural Animal Centre in the United Kingdom, the only place where the animal courses are currently offered. This training involved a two-day, three-day, and four-day class and readings to complete at home in between sessions. (www.bachcentre.com/found/animal.htm) The classes covered the essences as well as animal behavior and emotions, and counseling techniques. While we focused on canine, feline, and equine behavior we also studied turtles, rabbits, pigs, and other species. At the conclusion of the classes there is both an oral and written exam. Upon passing the exam, I had to successfully complete a series of case studies and a field study, before qualifying as a Bach Foundation Registered Practitioner Animal Specialist.

Since completing my qualifications in December of 2003, I have been using the essences with almost all of my behavioral clients. I have found them especially useful in treating many of the fears and phobias seen in pets. If a client's veterinarian has recommended a prescription drug, I advise the client to continue to use that drug in conjunction with the Bach Flower Essences. One of the nice things about the essences is that they can be used with other treatments, including homeopathy, without interference.

The Evaluation Process

My standard behavioral evaluation asks clients to complete my behavioral and emotional questionnaires. This is followed by an interview at which we also observe and evaluate the pet. I almost always do evaluations with a colleague who assists, takes notes, and documents behaviors while I talk with the client. The Bach Foundation Code of Practice requires that I have a veterinary referral before recommending specific essences and that I actually observe the animal's behavior. When working with clients that are unable to bring their pet to my office in Maine, I review video of the pet's behavior and work with the client and their local veterinarian or behavior specialist.

At the conclusion of the consultation, I provide the client with a behavior modification protocol as well as a combination of essences for their pet's specific emotional profile. I usually use both behavior modification and Bach Flower Essences because it has been my experience that the use of the essences can shorten the amount of time for a given behavior modification protocol. One of the biggest problems with behavior modification is getting the pet's guardian to comply with the protocol. If the essences shorten the amount of time required it's a win-win for the guardian and the pet. In these cases I cannot prove the essences helped resolve the issue; however, I have also treated some cases only with essences and have seen dramatic results.

I continue to have "a-ha!" moments with the essences. For example, last year I was treating a dog with severe resource guarding issues, some of the worst I have ever seen. Seven days after treatment with the essences, and prior to beginning any behavior modification, the client sent me an e-mail noting "profound changes" in the dog's behavior. I had them continue with the essences and behavior modification due to the severity of previous incidents, but the dog has never again exhibited any guarding behavior and has become more engaged with her guardians. The behavior modification protocol we used involved safely identifying the items that were considered valued resources, managing the environment to prevent uncontrolled access to those items, and gradual desensitization to the loss of those items. While there is no scientific evidence to demonstrate that the Bach Flower Essences caused this dramatic change in this dog's behavior, if I look at the dog's behavior, the essences selected, and the short time in which the change occurred, I believe it makes a very strong anecdotal case for the use of Bach Flower Essences.

I do not have a set of standard combinations of essences used for specific problems (e.g. separation anxiety, resource guarding, show dog formula, etc.) as each pet must be evaluated as an individual. Two dogs, each with separation anxiety, may be treated with entirely different combinations of essences. I remain in contact with the client and meet with them as the situation requires. At times I treat both pet and guardian, as often the pet is feeding off the guardian's emotions. In almost all cases, the problem is treated as a chronic problem rather than an acute issue or passing mood. For chronic behavior problems, essences should be administered at least four times per day.[7, 8]

The Bach Flower Essences are not the proverbial "magic bullet." While the two cases I have summarized showed dramatic improvement within a week, treatment typically takes longer. Depending on the issue being treated, the length of time the problem has existed, and the clients compliance, issues may start to resolve in anywhere from two weeks to a year. I have found the essences typically help to accelerate the behavior modification process and therefore help improve client compliance. If clients start to see results, they are more likely to continue with the behavior modification protocol and the administration of recommended essences.

Tips on Using Rescue Remedy

Bach Rescue Remedy, the most well known of the Bach Flower Essences, is a combination formula created specifically for addressing stress in emergency or crisis situations. The essences used in this formula help with trauma and shock (Star of Bethlehem), terror and panic (Rock Rose), hysteria or loss of control (Cherry Plum), impatience and agitation (Impatiens), and faintness and stunned feelings (Clematis). It is usually only used for acute or emergency situations, but can be used for treating chronic conditions, when appropriate. It can help after an accident or in any situation that causes extreme anxiety, nervousness or terror. Rescue Remedy often has an immediate calming effect, and is safe, gentle, and non-toxic. It may be taken as often as needed without fear of overdosing.

Rescue Remedy is not, however, a magic, instantaneous solution for long standing behavioral problems. While it can be helpful in reducing the stress and anxiety of a timid animal, it will not make them into a gregarious, "gotta love everybody" dog. Nor will it remove your pet's natural instincts, although it can help your pet to adapt those instincts to its environment.

When dealing with sudden behavior changes, you should arrange for a complete medical evaluation by your veterinarian to rule out any physical or medical reasons for the behavior change before trying Rescue Remedy or any of the other Bach Flower Essences.

How to Treat Your Pet with Rescue Remedy

Rescue Remedy is usually administered by mouth, diluted in spring water. A little goes a long way, because it is not necessary to use it directly from the stock bottle you purchase. If you wish, when you purchase a stock bottle, you may also buy an empty 30 ml eyedropper bottle to be your treatment bottle. To prepare the treatment bottle for use with your pet, do the following:

1. Fill the treatment bottle ¼ full with vegetable glycerin, brandy, or vodka to act as a preservative. If you choose not to use a preservative, you must refrigerate the treatment bottle.

2. Fill the remainder of the bottle with spring water (do not use tap water). Dr. Bach specified spring water because he felt it was natural, unlike tap water which can be loaded with chemicals.

3. Put four drops of Bach Rescue Remedy in the treatment bottle. You will treat your pet from this bottle.

Treating for an Acute Condition or Emergency

An acute situation might be a visit to the veterinarian or groomer, a thunderstorm, a dog fight, or a seizure. It is something that happens suddenly and rapidly affects your pet's emotional state.

Place four drops of the mixture from the treatment bottle on your pet's gums or tongue or on a treat or small piece of bread. Alternatively, you may apply the mixture to the paw pads, nose, belly, or ears. The remedy will be quickly absorbed from these areas.

If you see no improvement in 20 minutes, administer an additional four drops.

References

[1] Masi, MP. "BFE treatment of chronic major depressive disorder." *Alternative Therapies in Health and Medicine, Vol. 9 No. 6,* 2003.

[2] Campanini, M. "Italian medical study of 115 patients." *La Medicine Biologica; Anno XV, n.2, Aprile-Guigno,* 1997.

[3] Cram, J. "Two double-blind scientific studies of flower essences and stress." *Flower Essence Society*, 2001. www.flowersociety.org.

[4] Walach, H. & Rilling, C. "Efficacy of Bach-flower remedies in test anxiety: A double-blind, placebo-controlled, randomized trial with partial crossover." *J Anxiety Disord UK*. 15(4) July-August, 2001.

[5] Segerstrom, SC & Miller, GE. "Psychological stress and the human immune system: A meta-analytic study of 30 years of inquiry." *Psychol Bull*, 130, 4., 2004.

[6] Howard, J. & Ramsell, J. *The Original Writings of Edward Bach*. The C.W. Daniel Company, Ltd., England, 1990.

[7] Bach E. *The Twelve Healers and Other Remedies*. The C. W. Daniel Company, Ltd., England, 1933.

[8] Product Information and Usage Guidance Sheet, Nelson Bach USA Ltd., Wilmington, MA., www.bachfloweressences.co.uk, www.bachcentre.com.

Class Tips and Curriculum

Teaching a good group training class is an art many trainers aspire to. How you keep the attention of several dogs and owners for an hour, help them learn new skills in a highly distracting environment, and make the experience enjoyable so that clients return each week for the next lesson are essential skills that every group trainer must master or they won't stay in business for long. The articles in this section feature tips on working with special age groups such as senior citizens and children, and how to provide instruction that owners understand and maintain over time, and what to do if you have the dreaded class where nothing seems to work quite right! Specialty dog classes for small breed dogs and fearful dogs are presented, as well as ideas for keeping your classes fresh and entertaining by adding Rally, freestyle, agility, and games to your curriculum. Finally, an article on dog training in Japan gives us a new take on how other cultures train their dogs using dog-friendly, science-based methods.

First Impressions

Terry Ryan, July/August 2005

Over the years our school has tried different strategies to come up with the "perfect" pet dog training curriculum. We're not there yet! Recently we've been particularly concerned with the first experience clients and dogs have with our program. Success breeds success. That first "real" lesson needs to be a good one. Immediate success will lay the foundation for continued enthusiasm and the future effectiveness of your instruction. What is the definition of success and how do you get there? Revisit your archive of student profiles. Planning your curriculum to meet the actual needs and requests of your students is step one. Step two is to put those goals into exercises broken down into easily attainable steps.

Most instructional formats include a pre-class orientation of some sort. In the briefest form the orientation is a chat over the phone or written information provided before the class begins. Some schools have a people-only orientation as the first class. Others start right out with the dogs in attendance. Is there a right or wrong answer to the question, "Should dogs be invited to the first class meeting?" This needs to be your own opinion based on the goals you have for your students and your style of teaching. Once I was asked why I conducted our first pet dog class without dogs. My answer was, "So that the very first class meeting is a positive learning experience." Another instructor I respect was asked why she always had dogs attend the first session. Her answer was, "So that the very first class meeting is a positive learning experience."

I believe people need a bit of knowledge before they train their dogs. I use the analogy of the horse and rider. If a horse isn't trained and a rider doesn't know how to ride, they might get into trouble. A few lucky ones will ride off into the sunset and live happily ever after, but the others might experience a rough ride. People-only orientation provides an extra chance to help owners avoid mistakes that are sometimes irreversible.

Our school's curriculum is a 30-year work in progress! Currently the entry level to our pet dog training program is called Pet Dog Manners I (PDMI). It's a seven-week course for dogs over 14 weeks and their families. If you're wondering how we handle younger puppies, see "Legacy's Puppy Head Start" below. PDMI is a behavior and training class. In the early days when we made the change from more traditional obedience classes, the "behavior" and "training" classes were separate! The behavior option was presented as a short course on canine body language, the science of learning, and an overview of humane methods to change unwanted behavior. It preceded the training class, which taught the mechanical skill of establishing and reinforcing basic behaviors along with a variety of practical and easy relationship exercises. It was (in my opinion) a brilliant combination except, not many people signed up for the behavior option! I was disappointed. I began to notice that during the training course, the people that had questions or stayed after class for extra help were, for the most part, those who did not attend the behavior option. This confirmed my opinion of the value of the people-only foundation class. I eventually became brave and decided there would be no option. It was one class, a behavior and training class. Period. I simply called the behavior portion "orientation."

Currently Legacy provides a 90-minute people-only orientation, followed by six weekly 50-minute sessions. We strive to keep our orientation relevant, immediately useful, and somewhat entertaining. We incorporate learning theory and mechanical skill into audience participation exercises. This information is supplemented by demonstrations, a few 90-second video clips, and a notebook of illustrated handouts. PowerPoint slides are shown on a blank wall at the front of the room. Each point in the orientation is depicted by a line drawing, photo, or graph. Written words are rarely used, but if so, they are kept to one or two key words. The focus is on the live presentation, which involves toy and real dog demonstrations. If you don't use a computer, flip charts or reusable clear vellum posters can be prepared. Regardless of form, the visual aids help the student retain information. The aids also keep the presenter on track and your school's orientation standard. The student notebook supplements the information given at orientation and during the weekly lessons. The handouts in the notebooks are coded with a drawing. When the instructor mentions a particular exercise during orientation, the drawing on that handout comes up on the PowerPoint presentation to help the student identify this resource material in their notebook.

We conclude by demonstrating a few "settling-into-class" exercises we will coach them to do with their dogs at the beginning of next week's class. Finally, we play our "goodbye" music, but invite anyone with more questions to stay on after the music ends. This musical interval allows those that are satisfied to politely go home on time rather than sit through more questions. ❖

Legacy's Puppy Head Start

Research and common sense have taught us the value of providing early, quality experiences for puppies. We have been offering puppy classes in one form or another since the early 1970's. Our first puppy classes were modeled after Milo Pearsall's Kindergarten Puppy Training format. Our current puppy class is offered twice a week, free of charge. When we receive an inquiry about classes for a puppy under the age of 14 weeks, the pup is invited to register for the next Pet Dog Manners I class. While they are waiting for that class to begin (we start new PDMI classes every few weeks) the puppy is eligible to attend our Puppy HeadStart. This drop-in program insures that puppies never have to wait more than a few days to begin classes. There is no minimum age requirement. In addition to the regular PDMI registration policies, the pup's veterinarian needs to provide written permission for the pup to attend. The drop-in classes are held on different days at different times to increase the chance that families can squeeze one or both sessions into their weekly schedule.

Avoiding the Impact of Biases When Considering Published Information

John Buginas, September/October 2007

Every day dog trainers are barraged by Web pages, magazines, seminars, colleagues, and advertisers seeking attention. Choosing which ideas to use or pass on to clients is critical. Choosing wrong can harm dogs, clients, and the community; at the very least, it wastes time.

Most information has a bias, intentional or otherwise. A bias can be dangerous if it causes you to act without thinking.

This article discusses how to recognize biases in published material in any form. A subsequent article will discuss a way to review information to reduce impact of bias.

Sources of Bias

Biases are difficult to avoid. The most obvious biases come from the author and publisher. Readers bring biases too because we are human.

Author and publication biases

When considering an author, follow the money. Authors writing for money have a boss. If your paycheck comes from a company producing dog-appeasing pheromones, they may not be honest about the effect of dog-appeasing pheromones on dog behavior.

Money isn't the only source of bias. A veteran trainer may give good advice, but could have a vested interest in a favored approach. They may filter evidence and conclusions to support their own approach to training. Vested interests can be more powerful than money in a field with clearly defined camps such as dog training.

Consider the publisher. Anyone producing printed or video material is restricted by space; even people publishing personal Web pages have limited time and must choose what to publish. Biases will have a role in what they select—people putting up their own pages are not motivated to or required to present alternate views. Biases show up in what the author decides to write about, as well as what the author chooses to leave out.

Sensational stories drive magazine sales and profits. In a study looking at the front page of the *New York Times* regarding coverage of causes of death (AIDS, automobiles, cancer, homicide, suicide, airline crashes), articles about airline accidents outnumbered other causes. Adjusted to a per-death basis, airline accident articles appeared sixty times more than AIDS and eight thousand times more than cancer.[1,2] The airline industry is subject to distorted coverage similar to what we encounter daily about dog bite statistics.[3,4]

Advertisers pay publishers to display advertising. Publishers hesitate to publish articles that could offend advertisers. Classic examples are newspaper publishers who don't place articles about air crashes next to airline advertisements or about gas-guzzling cars next to stories about rising gas prices. Publishers can't be expected to encourage readers to take a critical view of advertised products.

Organizations that own Web sites or magazines can have a vested interest in a particular point of view.[5] You might expect different training tips in *The APDT Chronicle of the Dog* than *Gun Dog* magazine. Both groups have a distinct point of view.

Be wary of Web sites featuring one product. They may seem news-oriented, but many are advertisements in disguise, like late-night TV infomercials. Their publishers know tricks to show up high in search results and make content seem believable. This is especially true with health and nutrition sites featuring one product and a "buy me now" button on every page. It's possible for a manufacturer to publish balanced information; it's unlikely their site will be balanced.

Many single-product sites feature endorsements by veterinarians or doctors and technical-sounding writing. Be skeptical. Businesses and advertisers are bound by Federal Trade Commission guidelines on truth in advertising and fairness, but the government can't review every Web page.[6,7] The First Amendment prohibits prior restraint—all policing must be done after publication. Policing may never happen unless a consumer complains.

While publishers and businesses are bound by truth in advertising laws and are required to be able to back their claims, most Web pages don't fall under these laws because they aren't advertising.[8] The FTC has no clout internationally.

Blogs, Internet groups, and e-mail discussion lists are often home to outspoken advocates of a point of view. People participate for personal, financial, or professional motivation. You may get information you won't get anywhere else, but there may be a reason. Such content is usually not edited—readers have less consumer protections than with traditional media. These sites may show up high in search results—be careful.

Even when articles are backed by research, consider the funding. A 2003 analysis of 200 beverage industry studies shows "funding source was significantly related to conclusions" and that studies funded by industry were almost eight times as likely to be favorable than studies funded outside of the industry.[9]

Looking Within

Not all biases come from authors and publishers; some come from within the reader.

For thousands of years, humans lived in small groups. We gathered food, hunted animals up to the size of a SUV and faced dangers from fast running predators. Our ability to perceive large and small things is shaped by this history.

In the past, if a tiger ate ten of thirty people in a village, it was good to take notice and avoid tigers. Those who didn't were eaten.

Today, we are exposed to instant news from around the world, but we still see it through the eyes of a village dweller. When dogs kill 10 people out of 300 million we see a potential threat; this is made more menacing by disproportionate media coverage. As a society, we are irrationally afraid of dogs.

Our nature makes us suckers for fear-inducing news and advertising. We are suckers for lottery tickets.[10] We simply don't understand very large or very small probabilities. The world has changed; we just haven't caught up yet.

As humans we make interpretations of things we can't perceive. This simplifies things, but interpretations can be wrong. We believed the sun revolved around the Earth before telescopes proved otherwise.

We trust authority. This can be efficient…each generation doesn't start from scratch. Trust can be exploited when authority figures are paid to pitch a product or technique.

We believe new things. When someone yelled "TIGER," it was good to act fast—doing so brought more offspring. The $4.7 billion nutritional supplement industry preys on this tendency, producing new products monthly to combat modern day tigers, often without much research.[11] The FDA lacks funding to police nutritional products and does not require proof of "structure based claims."[12]

These traits helped our ancestors avoid being eaten; but acting quickly may not always be in our best interests today.

When reading new material, remember—you don't need to act right away. We are not faced with many tigers today—holding back on the "buy" button may be the best choice. Acting quickly can waste time, money, and lead to poor treatment of dogs when we are influenced by bias.

When considering new material:

- Follow the money.

- Beware about vested interests.

- Watch out for brochure-ware.

- Find out who funds the research.

- Use http://scholar.google.com or research-backed information.

To help overcome biases we have because we are humans:

- Be careful when reading or watching the news. Global media can distort perception by making rarely or infrequently occurring events seem likely.

- Look for information based on observation and not interpretation.

- Consider that authority figures may be biased.

- Examine new information carefully.

Finally, many biases are so strong that we cling to them in the face of conflicting evidence. It's good to be aware of these biases when we make critical decisions. ❖

References

[1] Barnett A., Wang A. "Passenger-mortality Risk Estimates Provide Perspectives About Airline Safety." *Flight Safety Digest*, Vol. 19 No. 4, pp 1, 2000.

[2] Reid, W., PhD. *Don't Panic*, Harper Collins, pp 341-342, 1996.

[3] Curtis, T. PhD. Air Safe Foundation Web site. *Airline Accidents and Media Bias: New York Times 1978-1994.* Retrieved March 2007 from: http://www.airsafe.com/nyt_bias.htm

[4] Bradley, J. *Dogs Bite: But Balloons and Slippers Are More Dangerous.* James & Kenneth Publishers, 2005.

[5] United States Government Department of State Web site. *Global Issues: Media & Ethics – Understanding Media Watchdogs.* Retrieved March 2007 from: http://usinfo.state.gov/journals/itgic/0401/ijge/gj05.htm

[6] Federal Trade Commission Web site. *FTC Policy Statement on Unfairness.* Retrieved March 2007 from: http://www.ftc.gov/bcp/policystmt/ad-unfair.htm.

[7] IBID.

[8] Federal Trade Commission Web site. *Frequently Asked Advertising Questions: A Guide for Small Business.* Retrieved March 2007 from: http://www.ftc.gov/bcp/conline/pubs/buspubs/ad-faqs.htm.

[9] PLoS Medicine Web site. *Relationship between Funding Source and Conclusion among Nutrition-Related Scientific Articles.* Retrieved March 2007 from: http://medicine.plosjournals.org/perlserv/?request=get-document&doi=10.1371%2Fjournal.pmed.0040005.

[10] Boing Boing Web site. *Psychology of bad probability estimation: why lottos and terrorists matter.* Retrieved March 2007 from: http://www.boingboing.net/2006/06/17/psychology_of_bad_pr.html.

[11] Mindbranch Web site. *Nutritional Supplements in the U.S.* Retrieved March 2007 from: www.mindbranch.com/Nutritional-Supplements-R567-609/.

[12] United States Food and Drug Administration Web site. *Dietary Supplements: Overview.* Retrieved March 2007 from: www.cfsan.fda.gov/~dms/supplmnt.html.

Size Matters

Laurie Williams, January/February 2006

The minute Barbara Johnson walked into the room her apprehension and nervousness was apparent. She clutched little Pipsy tightly to her chest, and in turn the little Maltese held on for dear life. As Barbara got closer to the ring she stopped and pondered which spot she should take; the one next to Bo, the energetic black Labrador Retriever who was serenading the class and using his owner as a spring board, or next to Thor, the quiet Shiloh Shepherd whose eyes were fixated on Pipsy as if she were a snack! Barbara chose neither. Instead, out the door she went and the next day her message requesting a refund was left on the trainer's voicemail. She never returned.

Unfortunately the above scenario happens all too often and many toy breed and smaller sized dogs reach adulthood missing out on crucial positive training and socialization experiences during their critical stage. We all know the benefits of providing puppies with these positive experiences in a safe environment. That's why most puppy kindergarten classes have an age cap of 16-20 weeks along with minimum vaccination requirements to ensure the health and safety of all participants. But maybe age and immunizations shouldn't be the only considerations. For Mrs. Johnson, putting little two-and-a-half pound Pipsy in such close proximity to 40-pound Thor or 25-pound Bo in perpetual motion just didn't seem plausible, and her concerns are shared by many other small dog owners. As trainers and canine behavior educators, it is our responsibility to address these concerns and take a look at things from their perspective. Fortunately many of us are doing this and acknowledging these concerns by implementing classes specifically for toy breeds and small dogs. "Tiny Tots" and "Mighty Mites" classes are sprouting up everywhere, facilitating a more pleasant learning experience for small dog lovers and their pets.

Changing Misconceptions

Let's face it, tiny dogs have gained the reputation of being snippy, yappy, ill-mannered, and downright untrainable. They're often referred to as "ankle biters," "rats on a leash," and worst of all, "not real dogs." Is this reputation earned? In many cases, yes, but just like their human counterparts, these spoiled brats didn't just happen. Most often they are unwittingly created by the very people who claim to love them the most. "He doesn't need any training. When he's bad, I just pick him up!" Yes, a tiny dog owner actually said this to me. Like many others, she felt training a tiny dog was pointless. Therefore our first task is to spread the word that small dogs are not prone to bad behavior. They are taught to be this way by their owners continually reinforcing these behaviors and overlooking problems that would otherwise be intolerable in a larger dog. Driving this point home is not easy. While it is our job to educate, walking up to a person and telling him his pride and joy is a monster and he is Dr. Frankenstein, isn't exactly the way to fill up classes! As the old adage says, actions speak louder than words. Showing the benefits of proper socialization and training for small dogs, rather than telling owners about them, can be so much more effective. Adding a "Tiny Tots" class to your training schedule could be the perfect opportunity to dispel the myths and misconceptions and demonstrate how well a small dog can do when given the opportunity to learn.

Unique Challenges for Small Dog Classes

Are little dogs really just big dogs in smaller packages? In some ways they are, but little dogs do come with their own unique set of training challenges. Taking this into account, implementing a class exclusively for small dogs involves more than merely changing the class name on the schedule. While class objectives and behaviors introduced could remain the same, modifying training methods and paying more attention to certain issues could lead to greater success and customer satisfaction.

Potty Training. How often have you heard it said that smaller dogs are nearly impossible to potty train? It is very likely that much more attention to potty training issues will be expected in a toy/small dog specific class. Often toy dog breeders will not relinquish a puppy to his new home until he is over 12 weeks of age. By this time the puppy may have spent the majority of his time in newspaper lined play pens learning to master the three P's—peeing, pooping and playing! Re-training these puppies not to soil the areas where they sleep, eat, and play can be a struggle for the new owners. The opportunity to address these concerns in a class with others who share and understand their plight can be very comforting.

Socialization. Acquiring a puppy older than 12 weeks of age often leaves a new owner with less time to work with the puppy during the critical socialization period. Naturally, a four-month-old Golden Retriever puppy who has been in his home for two months and has been exposed to many more sights, sounds, people, places, and objects will be better socialized than the four-month-old Chihuahua who has only been in his new home for two weeks. The Golden Retriever might begin puppy kindergarten with much more confidence and be ready to socialize with a vengeance. One thing is certain—thrusting the Chihuahua into a class with much larger dogs and allowing them to pounce all over him would hardly be a positive experience. Allowing the Chihuahua to remain huddled in the corner alone or cradled in his owner's lap wouldn't be the answer either. In a "Tiny Tots" class, the introduction to new things, strangers, and other dogs can be handled safely and delicately, resulting in a much more positive experience for the small dogs, and their owners as well.

Oh My Aching Back! We spend a lot of our time addressing dog safety in our classes, but what about handler safety? Expecting a handler with a five-pound dog to spend the better part of an hour repeatedly bending over is unreasonable. In the past, that handler may have been encouraged to take a seat on a chair or on the floor, but may not have felt comfortable being the only one doing so. In a "Tiny Tots" class, new behaviors can be introduced with all the participants sitting in chairs or on mats on the floor. Or better yet, a raised surface such as a grooming table could be provided and participants could take turns practicing with their pups. Training techniques for sits, downs, and stays with a dog on a chair or couch and leash walking using a target stick can be demonstrated.

In the interest of safety, it's not uncommon for some trainers to allow adult toy breed dogs in regular puppy classes. Given the vast developmental differences, this may not be such a good idea either. A five-year-old re-homed Yorkshire Terrier in his first obedience class may not be so eager to interact with an enthusiastic Boxer puppy. Subsequently, he could very well give that unsuspecting Boxer a nice little bite on the nose to remember him by. This wouldn't at all be fair to the young puppy who just wanted to play. As a result, the Yorkshire Terrier gets labeled as dog aggressive and the Boxer puppy learns little dogs are not nice. Both dogs lose.

The benefits of implementing toy breed and small dog exclusive classes are clear, and with five out of ten of the most popular breeds of dogs (according to 2004 AKC registrations) being toy/small breeds, the need is certainly there. A quiet, well mannered three-pound dog walking nicely on a loose leash with his head and tail held high is an impressive sight. And if that dog was trained at your facility or in one of your classes, there's no better advertisement than that. More importantly people will see that training their little tike is not only possible, but can be safe, fun, and enjoyable as well. ❖

New Kids On the Block: Using Rally and Freestyle to Add Variety, Fun, and Skills in Basic Pet Classes

Julie Flanery, May/June 2006

As pet owners, many of our clients are generally not clamoring to train their dog for the obedience ring. Their primary objective is to have a well-behaved family pet. Rarely, in the past, has the pet owner been drawn to the traditional dog sport of ring obedience. Entries in obedience trials have consistently dropped over the past several years. In the meantime, sports such as agility, flyball, and disc dog, have gained steady popularity and increases in participation. And much of that increase is from the pet owner, rather than the dog fancier or obedience enthusiast. The popularity of these "off-leash" sports has fueled the acceptance and momentum of positive reinforcement training. And now we are able to add two new dog sports to that list that not only encourage the use of positive reinforcement training but in some venues, require it.

Rally Style Obedience, or Rally-O, was first developed by Bud Kramer in 2000. Kramer was concerned about the drop in popularity of traditional obedience and wanted to bring a more realistic or "everyday" approach to the obedience exercises to encourage a greater interest in obedience training. This "real life" approach included the use of encouragement, verbal praise, and reinforcing the dog in a timely and enthusiastic manner as the handler guides the dog through a course of obedience skills. The skills vary by course and level, much like agility courses. The APDT was the first to embrace this new dog and handler friendly sport and within a couple of years, AKC followed suit, realizing this was a way to encourage people to try traditional ring obedience. This has led to a dramatic increase in entries at AKC events. More importantly, it has helped to continue the momentum in the traditional obedience world to more positive reinforcement techniques and less use of compulsion or correction-based training.

Canine Musical Freestyle, or simply freestyle, sometimes called "dancing with your dog," was first seen in Canada in the late 1980's. It quickly spread to Europe and then to the U.S. About ten years ago, we started seeing the first freestyle competitions on the East coast. The sport was slow to grow here in the U.S., until 1999, when Patie Ventre founded the World Canine Freestyle Organization, embracing the pet owner with their motto "Dancing with Your Dog is Fun for You and Your Pet." Though defined slightly differently by each venue, freestyle combines tricks with obedience and sets it to music to form a choreographed routine between dog and handler. Other freestyle venues include the Canine Freestyle Federation and the Musical Dog Sports Association.

The common thread in both of these sports is that they exemplify the bonding and teamwork between the dog and handler while, at the same time, exhibiting the complex behaviors that can be taught using positive reinforcement training. As a competitor in both of these sports, I can tell you neither is easy. Both require extensive training and handling skills to succeed. But they also keep the process of training lively and fun, giving dog and handler an enjoyment in continuing the training process beyond basic skills. Both sports also cover the gauntlet of expertise, from the beginner to the advanced participant. The beginning levels are basic enough for everyone to enjoy and the advanced are challenging enough to capture the attention of those wishing to take it to the limit.

In my pet classes, I often draw on these sports to add variety and skill level to class exercises. Rally exercises, with their turns and close proximity between dog and handler, encourage attention and heeling skills, while honing communication, teamwork and enjoyable interactions with your dog. Freestyle adds fun tricks and maneuvers such as spins, circles, and weaving between the handler's legs, giving students an exciting reason to practice. In addition, training freestyle behaviors gives handlers the opportunity to "show off" to family and friends, building confidence in their ability to train using non-traditional methods. An added bonus is that both sports teach skills on the left and front sides of the handler. In freestyle, the dog is also taught to work on the right side of and behind the handler and even at a distance from the handler, helping to advance student skills and opening up the possibility of participating in the dog sport arena.

Rally Exercises That Can Be Included in Pet Classes

My favorite Rally exercises to help the student learn to aid the dog while walking on leash are the cone exercises of "straight figure eight" and "serpentine." With four cones laid in a straight line, six to eight feet apart, the handler's job is to maneuver the dog between the cones without touching or knocking them. The instructor's job is to teach the handler how to use reinforcement, body language, and verbal praise to help the dog succeed and do so without using the leash for manipulation. In Rally, deductions are taken for tight leashes. As the dog and handler succeeds, the instructor can raise or modify criteria; for example, increased animation or changes of pace.

Before working the dog through the cone exercises, it's fun to have handlers pair up and each take turns at being the dog. Even though the person playing dog knows exactly the task at hand (stay close to your handler on the left and traverse the line of cones), he still finds it difficult to remain in position as the handler changes direction. A new appreciation and empathy toward the dog and the importance of communication and rate of reinforcement becomes apparent.

I start this exercise using chairs instead of cones. It's much harder to knock a chair than a cone and the chair acts as a guide, giving a greater level of success to both dog and handler. Once the dog and handler are comfortable with traversing the cones, they can advance to the "off-set figure eight" exercise. The dog and handler team walk around a pair of cones set six to eight feet apart in a figure eight pattern. Placed about ten feet apart, opposite the X of the figure eight, are two "distractions," usually toys or food. The student's job is to maintain the focus of the dog while traversing the figure eight with the nearby distractions. This encourages owners to take their pet dogs out into the world, having practiced how to maintain control in distracting environments.

In Rally-O there are several "Call Front" exercises. These start with the dog walking in heel. He is then asked to come to the front position and sit. The handler is allowed to walk a couple of steps back to encourage the dog to come to him. The dog is then asked to return to the left of the handler by going either left or right, and then to either sit or continue forward, depending on the rally exercise. There are enough variations in the "Call Front" rally exercises to make a rousing game of Simon Says!

The "call front - 1, 2, 3, steps backward" exercise gives the new handler built in repetition. When combined with a high rate of reinforcement, it helps build the dog's understanding of "come." In this exercise, with the dog walking in heel, the handler calls the dog to sit in front and then takes one step backward, calling the dog again to come sit in front. The handler repeats this with two steps back and then three steps back. In class, students are to reward every correct response. The 1, 2, 3, step exercise builds a nice progression of reinforcement for slightly more distance with each additional step.

Behaviors Taken From the Sport of Canine Musical Freestyle

Simply adding music to your classes can make classes more relaxed and fun. You can choose specific songs for specific exercises such as Jackson Brown's "Stay," ("Staaay, just a little bit longer"), or James Taylor's "Walkin' My Baby Back Home." Have music playing as students enter and leave the classroom. Music playing in the background can help relax handlers and relaxed handlers help to create relaxed dogs. I'm always looking for new ways to reduce the inhibitions of the students in class in order to encourage animation and interaction with their dogs.

Most of my classes are taught using lure-reward methods. One of the first things a student needs to learn when using a lure is how to elicit the behavior, fade, and eventually eliminate the lure, placing the behavior on a verbal cue. When I first started teaching, I used "sit" to teach this skill. The students were instructed how to lure the dog into the sit, and after several repetitions, fade the lure to a hand signal and then pair a verbal cue to the behavior. I found that many of the dogs coming into a basic class would already automatically sit when presented with food. The student didn't have a chance to lure the dog as it was already seated by the time the treat got to the dog's nose. While this is an admirable trait in a dog and can be used to explain to the student about reinforcing offered behaviors, it didn't teach the student how to elicit a behavior through luring or how to follow through on the process of placing a behavior on a hand signal or verbal cue.

My solution: I now use "spin" to teach these skills. Spin is a behavior most dogs don't know when starting a basic class. It is a moving behavior that is easily taught with a lure and one that initially requires an exaggerated hand signal that can be made visibly smaller. And, after the first class, the student now has a fun trick to share with family and friends. Spin is a trick that many dogs appear to find enjoyable and can be used as a reinforcer for other behaviors or for students to use during play-breaks while training new or more difficult tasks.

There are several freestyle moves where the dog passes between the handler's legs. These include weaving between the legs, crossing through the legs to bring the dog onto the other side of the handler, or having the dog travel a figure eight pattern around the handler's legs. Most dogs, once taught, enjoy these exercises as do their human counter-parts. I often have students tell me how fun it was to walk down the aisles of their favorite pet supply store with the dog weaving between their legs!

To help build speed in the recall, as the dog is running toward the student, rather than having the dog come to a sit in front, have the student toss a treat between his legs, landing behind him for the dog to chase. After a few repetitions, have the dog come into the front position and sit for the reward instead. Alternating between the two adds variety and enjoyment for both the dog and handler. This fun game also increases the dogs comfort level for tricks such as weaving between the handler's legs or performing a figure eight around the handler's legs. Tossing treats through the legs for the dog to chase and eat will help eliminate any concerns.

Getting into heel position doesn't have to be boring! To add a little flare and fun, from the front position or the recall, have the dog go through the handler's legs and then quickly turn to their right to come up into heel. For the pet owner, how the dog gets onto the left side isn't an issue. Getting the dog to heel doesn't have to resemble formal obedience finishes. You can perform this exercise with the dog coming up onto the handler's right side as well. When combining the two, you've taught a new trick, a figure eight around the handler's legs, giving ample fun to practicing "thru heel" and "thru right."

Another game to practice and proof stays is "circle me, circle you." Teach the dog to circle around the handler repeatedly with the use of a food or toy lure. Then the dog is placed in a sit-stay and the handler circles around the dog. If the dog succeeds, he is rewarded and released, and then the handler "stays" and the dog circles around the handler. Chasing a toy around the handler's legs is a fun way to reward the stay and release the energy the dog was controlling during the stay. Getting to practice the "circle around the handler" trick can act as a reinforcer for the handler as well, for practicing the stay (a little bit of Premack Principal at work on the handler).

You can add pizzazz to the basic skills of sit, down, and stays by teaching a freestyle trick that requires practicing the basic skill. When a student is teaching tricks, they are so involved with their dog that they may not even realize that they are reinforcing basic obedience skills. For example: The class thinks they are teaching the dog to lift a paw, when in reality, they are practicing sit on cue, duration in the sit and use of a release cue. Practicing "roll-over" requires repeating and reinforcing the down. The by-product of the handlers increased reinforcement and interaction with the dog is increased attention skills from the dog. When adding freestyle behaviors to practice basic obedience skill, time flies by so quickly that at the end of class students often linger behind to continue to interact and work and play with their dog.

Conclusion

With the increase in pet friendly dog sports such as agility, Rally, and freestyle; and the huge number of pet owners now seeking a greater degree of interaction and stronger bond with their dogs, it makes sense that we will continue to see new sports that encourage greater involvement from the owner and greater skill from dog and handler. In developing these new sports, trainers were thinking outside of the box in terms of what our dogs are capable of learning and how to teach some of these skills. As pet obedience instructors, it's up to us to think outside of the box to increase student skills and teaching in a way that keeps both students and their dogs begging for more! ❖

Children in Obedience Class: When to Allow Them and How to Keep Them Safe

M. Cecilia Saleme, Published in two parts, July/October 2005

PART I

With good reason, many trainers do not encourage parents to bring their children with them to obedience classes. If they are not well-behaved, children not only cause disruptions to the class, but they can also pose a safety risk around unruly dogs. Nevertheless, there are many benefits to allowing children to attend obedience classes with their parents. By including children in my classes and setting appropriate guidelines and expectations from the beginning, I have found the following to be true:

- Together, the owners retain more information and, in the end, the dog benefits. It's best for all adult family members to attend, but since many parents have trouble getting babysitters, having them attend with well-behaved children may be the best option.

- Children learn to respect dogs. What's more, children—who are like sponges for learning—can often retain more information than their parents. On more than one occasion, I've had a parent approach me and tell me their child caught them in a mistake and called them on it with a comment such as, "Mommy, that's not the way the teacher said to do it." Score one for the kids! This shows that they are not only learning, but that they want to do what's right for the dog.

- Children ask questions. There is a lot to be said for the "innocence" of children. Of course, they keep us honest too, lest we be left feeling like an unclothed emperor!

Guidelines for Including Children

So, how should one go about incorporating children into a classroom full of untrained dogs? As in any classroom situation, rules are essential. I recommend explaining the rules at the first class meeting, and reminding the students (young and old) as needed throughout the course.

Ages Four to Ten. I allow well-behaved children, ages four and up, to attend classes. However, children under the age of ten are not allowed to work the dogs in class. Occasionally, with nice-tempered, smaller dogs, I may allow a child as young as eight to work a dog, but I make certain that the parent is closely supervising.

Ages Ten to 13. For children ages ten to 13, I closely monitor their work with the dog, and make certain the parents are supervising and assisting them as well.

Ages 14 to 17. High school students (ages 14-17) can usually be given more leeway, but I do require that every under-aged child have an attending adult present in the class. I've had parents try to drop off young teens, intending to return after class to pick them up, but I do not allow the teens to stay in class alone. Unsupervised children present a tremendous liability, as this puts the trainer in charge of the child.

Of course, as a trainer, it's up to you to use your discretion. I've had particularly unruly dogs in class that I insisted be handled only by adults. Only you can determine what is appropriate for a particular dog and handler in a class, and where a liability may outweigh potential benefits.

Classroom Rules

1. Only one person is to work the dog on any particular exercise. This prevents siblings (and partners) from trying to work with a dog simultaneously. I explain to them how confused a poor dog can become with commands coming from multiple people at the same time, and I stay alert for potential conflicts of this sort.

2. No interaction is allowed with other dogs in the class without my permission and the permission of that dog's owner. I make them ask me first because, as we know, many dog owners are not entirely aware of their own dog's temperament. The key is to avoid increased liabilities while teaching the children to learn respect for all dogs.

3. Leash work is only for adults. Except in cases with older children and smaller dogs, I only allow the adults to do the loose-leash walking work. With older children and teenagers, I may allow them to walk the dogs, but I insist that the parent supervise very close by.

4. Absolutely no running around or horseplay! This may seem obvious, but to some children (and some parents) it is not so. There are many ways to keep children entertained and engaged in the classroom in order to keep them from becoming disruptive.

5. The trainer is in charge. The ground rules and class logistics must be agreed to by all the attendees before the actual class work begins. It is essential to build rapport with the parents and receive their agreement, so if a child should become disruptive, I have their permission to correct the child. Parents often appreciate this because the authority of a "teacher" often carries more weight than mom and dad outside the home. Although my instinct now is to avoid reprimanding someone else's child, when I am in my "teacher" role—a position of authority, even for the parents—I'll readily do so and I've not had many challenges from parents. Oftentimes, the parents will even reinforce what I've said with something like, "She's right, dear, you can get hurt if you run around like that past the dogs."

Handling Children's Questions

To make certain that the often copious questions from children do not become a disruption, it's a good idea to remind all the students to raise their hands only when you call for questions. I do this both before and after each exercise to give everyone a chance to ask clarifying questions. I also ask for questions at the beginning of each class session, in case anyone had problems in the previous week. Many children love to raise their hands and ask questions, so by giving instructions as to when to do so, you can avoid unnecessary interruptions by curious children.

Some children do tend to ask irrelevant questions. Occasionally, I'll have a child in class who just likes to talk. In such cases, I'll tell them that I can answer their particular question—or listen to their exciting anecdote—after class. Sometimes they remember to ask again, but often they completely forget their comments. Whatever you do, don't disregard possible questions from youngsters. Remember that they can ask relevant and important questions that others may be too embarrassed to ask. In one lesson about teaching dogs how to sit for petting, a child asked what to do when his dog jumped up on him. I was surprised that the parents hadn't asked this, but it gave me a great opportunity to explain, in detail, how to teach dogs not to jump up, as well as how a child should behave around a dog.

It has been my experience that appropriately incorporating children into dog training classes not only strengthens the family/dog relationship, but provides trainers with an additional opportunity to teach children how to be safe around dogs. Trainers can take advantage of this opportunity to teach children how to properly approach dogs, how to ask permission before petting any dog, and other important dog safety tips.

PART II

Incorporating children into your dog training classes offers many potential benefits, including the opportunity to teach children to be safe around dogs, allowing both parents to attend all classes, and improving the family/dog relationship. Adherence to the following three principles will help make your class a success.

- Explain age appropriate guidelines at the first class.
- Go over classroom rules.
- Build rapport and receive agreement from parents on guidelines and rules before the class begins.

Now, we will explore ways in which to effectively integrate children into your classes to maximize learning and minimize potential problems.

Be Aware of Liability Issues

Before incorporating children into your training classes, be aware of the insurance and liability issues. Be sure to have both parents sign a release of liability waiver, and check your insurance policy to be certain that they would be covered in the event of an accident. And naturally, safety must always come first.

Fighting Boredom

A child-friendly curriculum includes hands-on dog and child interaction and simple language for the younger set. With children, as with dogs, boredom can spell disaster when they begin to look for ways to entertain themselves. When teaching a class that includes children:

- Make a point of explaining things in a manner in which children can understand.

- Be sure the lessons are clear. Stop on occasion to ask the kids if they understand what you mean. This is also a good time to check in with the parents.

- Use examples from your own childhood or stories for the children to relate to depending on their ages.

Exercises for Children and Dogs

Once you have their attention, your work with the children has only just begun. Keeping them involved in the training is a key to maintaining their interest and making certain that they do not become a nuisance in class. Children can be included in the following exercises during a puppy or basic obedience class.

1. **Name Game.** A precursor to the recall, this exercise is very easy even for young children.

   a. Have the child call the dog's name and give him a treat as soon as he looks over. In the beginning classes, this is a first week exercise that the entire family can work on. By teaching the children to give the treat as soon as the dog's head turns, they are also learning about timing. This is especially helpful as training progresses.

   b. With very young children (under six years), watch closely to make certain that they are not inadvertently playing the "keep away" game, pulling their hand away when the dog tries to take a treat. This is very common with young children who are fearful of a dog's mouth. This unintentional movement can cause a dog to become mouthy or pushy as he tries to leap for a treat before it goes away. If you see this happening, stop the game and tell the parents that they should be the ones to practice this exercise until the child is more comfortable giving treats to the dog.

   c. Additionally, teach the child to give the treat from the middle of the palm of a wide open hand, so as to avoid the finger nips.

2. **Puppy Push Ups.** Everyone knows this game: the classic sit-down-sit-down. Encouraging children to be enthusiastic in this exercise can make it fun for dogs and children alike. As the class progresses, tell them to reward only after every several ups/downs instead of after each move. Again, help them with their timing as they reward the dog.

3. **Recalls.** In this exercise, I insist that a parent stand directly behind the child who is calling and rewarding the dog. If there is any uncertainty about the dog getting past the child and parent, put a long-line on the dog for this exercise.

4. **Drop It.** This exercise should only be practiced with low-value toys such as balls or tug toys. Use your professional judgment if you feel that this would be inappropriate with a particular dog.

   a. Teach a typical drop it, showing the treat to the dog and then rewarding when the toy is dropped.

   b. For safety reasons, I tell the children not to touch the item that the dog has dropped unless the dog backs away from it, as with a ball that is to be thrown. (With adults, they pick up the item as the dog is taking the treat, then hand the item back to the dog to initiate the exercise again.)

5. **Fetch.** After the dog learns the drop it command, fetch can be taught. This is an ideal game for children and dogs for a number of reasons:

   • Bonding. The children and dog have an interactive game, improving the child-dog bond, while teaching the dog not to be mouthy with the children.

   • Control. Fetch teaches the dog to repeatedly drop an item for a child in order to be rewarded with the throw. Each time the child tells the dog to drop it, he is being reinforced for obeying the command.

   • Exercise. Children and dogs can often continue to play fetch long after the average adult human has tired or become bored. What better way to exercise an active dog and child?

   With this game, as with every exercise, I closely supervise and insist that the parents always do the same. This is a great opportunity to remind the parents again that dogs and children should always be supervised together.

Homework

Contrary to the popular belief among children everywhere, homework is a good thing. Giving the children exercises that they can practice at home will keep them interested in the classes. It's a good idea to involve the entire family in the homework exercises. Following are some guidelines for the homework assignments.

   • **Short sessions.** I recommend that they work the dog in three to five minute sessions, depending on the dog's and the children's ages.

   • **One person at a time.** Emphasize that only one family member should work the dog at any given session, and make certain that the dog has from 10 to 20 minutes of down time in between sessions. This will allow the children to each get time with the dog while preventing the dog from becoming overwhelmed by multiple handlers.

- **No mixed signals.** Another important rule is everyone in the family must agree on the same verbal and hand commands. I ask families in class what their specific commands are for things such as leave it, drop it, and the release command, to make certain they are all in agreement.

- **Adult present.** In all cases, insist on adult supervision at home. When dealing with gentle, well-socialized dogs and teenaged children, I suggest the children be the ones to feed the dogs, practicing the sit and stay commands before putting the food dish down. Even this should be supervised by the parents. Of course, we know that no dog should ever be unsupervised with a child, but some parents may need to be gently reminded of this in class.

The Advantages

Although it can be more work to include children in dog training classes, the advantages far exceed the inconvenience. By involving the children, the bond can be improved not only with them, but with the parents as well. The dog gains the advantage of having more people to work with him between class sessions, and the learning curve is enhanced. Most importantly, the likelihood of the dog remaining in this "forever home" is greatly improved. ❖

Hoyle for Hounds or Card Games for Canines

Maggie Blutreich, March/April 2005

A recent edition of *Hoyle's Rule of Games* is touted as the "essential family guide to card, board, and parlor games." I leafed through this chunky little paper back recently at my local book store and found a complete absence of card games for dogs! To address that void, I offer you a game we might also refer to as Hounds "according to Hoyle."

Bob Bailey reminds us that, "Training is a mechanical skill." Janet Smith once wrote, "If we want our dogs to be predictable, it is imperative that we are not!" We can all agree that behaviors, regardless of species, tend to pattern, to go on rote, to chain. Dogs and their handlers get bored, anticipate, and become dull. It's not always easy for us to devise random training exercises for our own dogs or those of our clients. Those who compete in obedience or other performance activities might just find Hoyle for Hounds a fun way to relax and hone skills.

You will need a deck of playing cards, preferably those with large, easy to read faces. To play in a class situation, an oversized deck would work best. One person is designated as the dealer. The instructions are rhymed to facilitate memory.

Level One-A

Remove all four suits of cards aces through ten from the deck. This will give you a total of forty cards. Shuffle these cards and place the deck face down. The dealer turns the cards over one at a time. If an odd number turns up (ace, 3, 5, 7, 9), the handler asks the dog to sit and counts off the total appearing on the cards, e.g., "Sit, one, two, three, four, five." If an even number is turned up (2, 4, 6, 8, 10), the handler asks the dog to lie down and counts off the total appearing on the cards, e.g., "Down, one, two."

By the time the total of these 40 cards have been turned, the handler will have asked the dog to sit 20 times for a count varying between one and ten and to lie down 20 times for a count varying between two and ten. These behaviors will be requested of the dog in an unpredictable sequence each time the deck is shuffled. In the meantime, the handler is practicing mechanical skills. The handler/trainer needs only to remember, "Sit on odd, down on even, count the card before leaving." Handlers who can recite a silly poem while cuing, marking, and rewarding the dog's behavior are developing pretty good mechanical skills. In short, they can walk and chew gum at the same time!

Level One-B

The directions for play remain the same as Level One-A with the addition of a chair. Each time a heart or diamond turns up, the handler first sits on the chair before cuing the indicated behavior and counting the number on the card. The three of hearts turns up, the handler sits on the chair, cues sit, and counts to three. "If it's red, you're sitting down and if it's black you're standing. No different than you did before, but slightly more demanding!"

Remember, "training is a mechanical skill" and the four of spades might be next. The handler stands, cues a down, counts to four. "If we want our dogs to be predictable, it is imperative that we are not."

Level One-C

The same simple game plan as the beginning can be elaborated by assigning a compass direction to each of the four suits in the deck. Let's say, clubs are east, spades are west, hearts are south, and diamonds are north. Now the handler must face in the compass direction indicated by the suit of the turned card before cuing the dog. For example, the five of hearts turns up. The handler faces south, cues the sit, counts to five. If Level One-C is played in a class situation, posters can be put at the compass points bearing the direction and card suit symbol. "Clubs are east, spades are west, hearts are south, you guess the rest!"

The difficulty level can be increased by placing four chairs facing the compass points and requiring the handler to sit for the red suits facing the appropriate compass direction before cuing the dog. What we are helping our clients develop is an ability to pick up and follow cues for themselves while training their dogs. Just because it's fun doesn't mean it's easy. Raising the criteria by adding cards and behaviors can be accomplished in several different ways depending on what behaviors the dog has been taught and the client's goals. Here are some possibilities:

Level Two-A

Using the uncomplicated format from Level One-A, add the queens, kings, and jacks back to the deck before shuffling and placing it face down. The game is now dependent on how many behaviors the dog is trained to offer on cue. For example, dogs that stand, play bow, or wave on cue can participate, adding more complicated behaviors. One example might be "Stand for the king, wave at the jack, bow to the queen, show no slack!" This is, of course, in addition to the original, "Sit on odd, down on even, count the card before leaving." A variation on Level Two-A would be to permit the handlers themselves to wave or bow, if their dogs are not yet trained to do so.

Level Two-B

Bring back the chair, and require the handler to sit when a heart or diamond turns up. If it's red, you're sitting down and if it's black you're standing. For example, if the queen of hearts turns up, the handler sits on the chair before cuing the dog to bow.

Level Two-C

Add three more chairs and the compass point criteria.

Level Three-A

In this version, five cards are dealt from the deck and placed face up (a standard poker hand). Following the criteria of Level One-A, handlers as quickly as possible cue their dogs in the sequence the cards were drawn. "Sit on odd, down on even, count the card before leaving." The difference is that a time element has been added.

Level Three-B

Add the chair, and complete the sequence of five behaviors dealt as quickly as possible. The dogs continue to "sit on odd, down on even," while the handlers still "count the card before leaving." However, the handlers now also need to remember, "If it's red, you're sitting down and if it's black you're standing. No different than you did before, but slightly more demanding."

Level Three-C

Continue as in Level Three-B, but with the addition of three more chairs Clubs are east, spades are west, hearts are south, you guess the rest! For the face cards, the play could be "stand for the king, wave at the jack, bow to the queen, show no slack!" A variation, of course, would be to keep with the spirit of a five card poker hand. Got a straight? Big treat for Rover. Dealt a flush? The game is over!

Although Hoyle for Hounds is designed to offer randomized cues and be played on a "personal best" basis, it would be easy to add points for those who might prefer competition. A score of one for each completed behavior with zero for failure to accomplish could be used. Alternatively, the numerical values of the cards turned and the number of behaviors completed could be totaled with small prizes awarded to the highest score. In group play handlers/trainers could ante up with a dog biscuit in order to play a round. The winner of each round keeps all the cookies! ❖

Dealing With Timid Dogs in a Class Situation

Joan B. Guertin, November/December 2006

When called upon to help a client with a dog that is unsure of itself, we hear the dog labeled as "shy." Since most owners seem to indulge in absolute adjectives in describing their pet and its issues, it is up to the trainer to assess each situation on its own merit. Some are extreme cases—those dogs that most likely are not good candidates for a traditional training class. Others are suffering from owner-generated anxiety which a good trainer can deal with in a class situation.

Introducing My PSST Approach to Insecure Dogs

- **Patience**. The main ingredient in training all dogs. However, with dogs with problem behaviors, it is the prime ingredient.

- **Stress**. All reactions, positive or negative, are related to stress. This is true in both the human and animal world. Trainers should be aware of this and deal with the human and four-legged client accordingly. In many situations we may never be cognizant of the actual stressors. However, we have to allow the dog to grow in confidence at its own speed. We must create a safe environment for this process to work.

- **Strategy**. Develop a strategy that allows for growth in small increments. It must not threaten the dog and yet allow for growth while exposing it to real life situations.

- **Training**. Must progress at the animal's speed, not the trainer's or owner's expectations of a timetable! The dog must be allowed to develop a sound comfort zone. This may occur in plateaus. Be ready to move at the dog's speed, not your own! And above all, exert unending patience and gentle interaction!

Lila's Story

PSST grew out of my association with Lila, a thoroughly traumatized, rescued Basenji. Lila came to the attention of a former client with the announcement of a serious puppy mill bust in Florida in the early 1990s. A year later after countless delays and legal gymnastics, Lila, an approximately two-year-old Basenji, was deemed adoptable and joined the home of Ann and Bruce Baker in rural Northern California. It was obvious from the beginning that she had not been socialized and that she was very wary of humans. She did, however, soon learn to trust Cheka, the Baker's resident, very confident, well-trained Basenji.

Enter Common Sense Dog Training

Ann was frustrated with her efforts to socialize Lila. We brainstormed, weighed options and PSST emerged. Ann and I felt comfortable with the plan. At that point, we had nothing to lose and everything to gain.

The first step was to enter Lila in a puppy class. We were working inside a park building with no outside stimulation other than the puppies (all between eight to 20 weeks of age). The area was spacious and the class size was probably 10 to 12 pups.

When Lila appeared agitated in the environment on or off a leash, and showed no desire to engage in free play or to socialize in any way, I suggested Ann put her crate in the play area. For the next six weeks, Lila sat inside her crate in the area while we did class. We didn't force her to do a thing.

When the next series of classes began, Lila attended again. We placed her crate inside the play area. When the pups entered and began free play, Lila emerged from her crate and jumped to the top from where she surveyed class activity for the next six weeks.

At the beginning of the third six-week session Lila came down off of her crate to actually interact with some of the puppies and play with some toys. At this point, Ann began introducing the exercises the other puppies were doing.

By this time, Lila's trust in Ann and Bruce had grown and a relationship was forged. She was a different dog.

Hoping to increase Lila's confidence level, we moved her to the outdoor classes in the park. Not wanting to upset her with the antics of the beginning dogs, we moved her straight into the intermediate class. It was soon evident that Lila liked the structure and that she was so focused on Ann that she was not fazed by the presence of either people or dogs. At home her behavior, was becoming more and more confident.

Lila grew at her own speed. Ann was ultimately patient, never pushing Lila beyond her comfort zone. As I watched the confidence build and the bond strengthen, I commented on a future in competition obedience. Ann, of course, thought I was joking.

Lila crossed the rainbow bridge this past year, a victim of cancer. However, in her brief, tumultuous time on this earth, she survived a horrible puppy mill existence and the inherent fears that went with lack of early socialization.

Ann did compete with her and Lila earned two legs on her CD. Given more time, and better health, Lila would have finished her title. But what she did accomplish, given her beginning, was awesome!

Shy Dogs in Class

Since the days of Lila, I have often brought older dogs in to the less stressful puppy classes to build confidence. Insecure Shelties kept by breeders in kennels while they grow and fail to stay within the height requirements for show, have thrived in this format.

The atmosphere is less stressful than in a regular class. They are allowed off-leash freedom to move around, testing the waters and developing confidence while not being tethered to their often-nervous owners. It is heartening to watch the freedom of growth as they realize that other dogs and people are really pretty OK.

Following are guidelines that I have used successfully over the years in my regular classes in dealing with dogs that many would label shy or timid, but who are merely insecure:

- Following an initial phone call and acquiring some background, it may be beneficial to meet once, in private, with dog and client in order to assess the extent of the dog's temperament problem. This may be in the home to determine what, if anything, the role of the owner may be in fostering the timidity or insecurity. Or, it may be in a neutral location affording a very low stress atmosphere such as at a local park that the dog is familiar with, but not the home where it might be conflicted regarding its role.

- If the dog is really quite normal and feeding off of an insecure owner, I generally have no problem in suggesting that the pair (or the family) join a regular class. Once in that environment, it is relatively easy to supply the type of coaching within the class confines that will increase the confidence level of the owner/family and thus the dog.

- If the dog is nervous in situations regarding bigger dogs or dogs entering too closely into its personal space, I will simply place the dog and handler(s) on an end where they only have to contend with one dog on one side. Be aware that some dogs may react better when dogs are placed on either the right or left, so try both ends in the beginning to place the dog in the least stressful position until such time as the confidence level grows to where its position within the class causes no intimidation.

- If the above dog is one that becomes physically reactive when other dogs are too close, I may move the dog a good distance away from the other dogs, or into a "safe zone," until such time as I can begin moving it in closer until it is integrated back into the class without reaction or incident.

- Another solution to the nervous dog that reacts when other dogs are too near is to erect a blanket/sheet barrier in a corner which allows the dog to be isolated with its people without the ability to make eye contact with the other dogs. Here the dog can learn to focus totally on its owner/handlers. When the barrier is removed, the dog will have a totally new focus and will ignore the other dogs.

- Offer positive encouragement to the owners so that they act confidently and don't feed into their pets' insecurities. Discourage chastising. Encourage focus on the humans. Allow no eye contact with other dogs! This can be accomplished by a turn away from the distraction and having them respond to unwanted behaviors with such comments as, "Silly dog, what are you doing." Keep it light, keep it fun, and don't chastise the dog. Offer lots of praise and rewards for even the tiniest of positive performance. Teach the humans to encourage their dog's eye contact with them.

The important thing to remember is that forcing an insecure dog is an exercise in futility. They need patience. We need to work to reduce their stress. We need to develop a strategy to allow the dog to grow at its own pace and we need to make the training gentle and positive for both dog and owner(s). ❖

When a Senior Holds the Other End of the Leash

Lilianne Merida-Scannone, July/August 2007

Although many of us have chosen a career in dog training because of our love of animals, we soon realize that our "people skills" have to be just as good and sometimes even better, to effectively reach out to the dog at the end of the leash.

There are a growing number of adult communities where I live, so an important percentage of my clients are seniors. Seniors pose a very particular challenge for the trainer. I would like to share some of the ideas I have developed to better help this special clientele.

The emotional aspect of working with a senior client is very challenging. Many buy or adopt dogs or puppies to fill a void left by family that no longer live close to them. In situations in which they live by themselves, the dog may be their only companion. It may be the last tangible link that connects them to a deceased spouse and in many cases it is the dog that keeps them interested in going on with their lives.

Another common situation is when adult children, sometimes seniors themselves, need to bring home their even older parents to live with them. The parents often have to spend most of their time alone in the house with the dog. So training issues arise because they are unable to physically deal with the dogs that are already living in the household.

Physical Limitations That Might Influence Training Ability

Some limitations might be quite evident, such as difficulty in walking. I myself have sometimes found after a couple of very frustrating lessons that the person had hearing problems and forgot to put on his hearing aid! People can be very self-conscious about hearing loss limitation. Asking questions several times during the session will enable you to assess whether they can hear you properly so that you can position yourself closer or talk louder.

Other less obvious, but important limitations are bursitis, shoulder or wrist surgeries, and even strokes that have left the person with minor disabilities. For example, some of my clients have lost finger coordination and cannot hold treats properly between their fingers. Adjustments can be made like feeding larger treats out of the palm of their hands, or if another family member is available, have them assist with the treat delivery. Treats can also be placed in an open container out of the dog's reach, but easily accessible to the senior.

Ask your senior clients to choose on which side they prefer their dogs to walk and they will inevitably choose the side they feel stronger.

Head halters are often very helpful, but extra time needs to be devoted to teaching them how to put it on. I usually have my clients repeat the procedure three or four times to ensure they can "untangle" the head collar. The halter will be useless if they cannot put it on properly at home.

Tone Down the Pace of Your Class

Ideally, a couple of individual sessions are better to start with, but private lessons are usually more costly and many seniors are unable to afford them. If private lessons can be scheduled, keep in mind the pace of these may be nowhere near that of your regular classes. It might be necessary to repeatedly explain the same exercise or behavior modification protocol several times. It is also crucial to have them relay back to you what they understood or perform the exercises for you several times. I give my clients a written handout and write an additional page of detailed instructions. One important difference with seniors is that they feel quite accomplished if they can teach their dog one or two commands per session. Too much homework will overwhelm them and impair their success.

If they form part of a group, take a little extra time to work with them. I might ask them to arrive 15 minutes earlier. This enables me to check that collars and head halters are properly worn. Ask if they brought other equipment we might be using in class, like treats, toys or clickers and make sure they let their dogs relieve themselves in the designated potty areas. I can also work with an overly active dog to help him settle down. Watching their dog perform for me also reassures the clients that there is nothing "wrong" with their dog and motivates them to keep on trying.

Small Talk Can Lead To Great Discoveries!

One important obstacle we need to help our students overcome is their anxiety over a dog's correct performance. Although they enroll in a class because their dogs have a training or behavior issue, they can get so anxious about a dog's lack of attention or failure to perform that it impairs their ability to follow instructions.

You can get them to relax by spending the first 10 minutes in class chatting casually with them. Many seniors are overprotective of their dogs and pamper them as if they were their grandchildren. Asking questions about a dog's origin or their routine may reveal some problems. You might discover they have bursitis or balance problems when you ask them how many times they go for a walk. They could answer that they can't walk their dogs because they pull too much or try to chase squirrels or golf carts and they are afraid to be pulled off balance. What appears to be small talk can result in the source of many interesting details that will aid in preparing a training protocol.

Positive Reinforcement is Very Important for the Human End of the Leash Too!

When training in a group, seniors feel the "pressure" of the other "more able" handler/dog teams. Take special care to reward them by making a positive comment about their dogs as soon as they come to class, during class and when wrapping up the class.

For example, if they arrive with a dog lunging ahead of them you could comment: "His coat is so shiny, did he get a bath today?" and maybe they will respond "Oh no!

It's naturally shiny, we have to take him to the groomer's because he will bite the brush every time we try to groom him." There you go, another training project!

During class you can comment on tiny improvements and phrase corrections emphasizing on the good: "Wow, what a nice tone of voice you used to call Sassy" or "Great! You remembered not to give Molly a treat if she gets up before you have released her," or "Your timing was so much better this time!"

When wrapping up the class and discussing homework, you could say, "You need to work on ..." and immediately focus on something the dog is doing well: "I see lots of improvement with waiting by the door. I am very proud of you, because I can really see you are taking the time to practice every day."

Seniors Can Become a Source for Referrals

Being extra patient and devoting a little more time to your senior clients will reap huge benefits for your business. In this super-fast cyber world, they really appreciate a slower pace. The word spreads around fast in senior communities. Training their dogs is a very important part of their day and they will boast about any tiny progress, command or trick their dog can now perform. "Jake is going to obedience school and we found this wonderful trainer, she is so patient with us, you should take your Daisy there ..."

Most senior communities have an Activities or Event Coordinator. They are constantly looking for new or different activities to offer. You can contact them and volunteer to do a free demo or come over and talk about training or behavior problems. This is a great opportunity to introduce yourself to the community and leave business cards or brochures.

In summary, seniors have special needs and extra time must be devoted to be able to successfully help them train their dogs. But the positive benefits for all involved, the client, his dog and the trainer are certainly worth it. ❖

Dog Training in Japan

Pia Silvani, with Mika Ishiwata, July/August 2007

Every time I visit Japan to work with Japanese trainers, I become more and more enthusiastic about the direction in which this country is heading in the field of dog training and animal welfare. There are 1.2 million registered dogs in Japan at this time. Less than 10% of that population has had some sort of training.

The Japanese have different customs from many Western countries. For example, it is taboo to wear shoes indoors. This holds true for restaurants and other public places, not just private houses. Japanese homes are typically built with tatami (thick mats made of dried straw) or wooden floors. Both types of flooring are easily damaged by dogs' nails. In years past, very similar to the Western world, dogs were kept outdoors for reasons of cleanliness.

The Japanese people are extremely neat and clean. Their cars and homes are immaculate. As a result, most dogs wear clothing year round to avoid shedding. It is not unusual to see a Weimeraner wearing a raincoat, a Labrador in a sweater, or a Samoyed with a t-shirt. Dogs do not ride in cars without their clothing, nor do they enter a public place "naked"! I laugh when I think about how we in America pile dogs into our cars; we make excuses for our dirty car by saying "It's my dog car," and would rather take an antihistamine and sleep with our dog's head on our pillow, than have the dog sleep in another room.

Japanese city dogs live indoors, yet to date, in the country large dogs are still kept outside, tied to a post with a "dog house." The shape of the doghouse varies from a simple wired cage to a fancy designed "house" to match the owner's home.

Moving Forward

Approximately 15 years ago, boarding schools for dogs were becoming quite popular. Typically, they were run by "traditional" trainers. People with purebred dogs sent their dogs away at approximately six months of age. The dog spent three to six months at the kennel where it received training from the professional trainers. During this time, the trainers competed with the dogs, winning championship titles. These "winners" were thought to be the "intelligent" ones in the dog world.

During this time, people had a tendency to look down on mixed breed dogs, thinking they lacked intelligence. The thought behind this was people who owned mixed breed dogs did not have the means to purchase a purebred dog, nor could they afford a boarding school for training. There were—and still are among some people—myths that training should start when the dog is six months of age, and the window for learning shuts down when they are a year old. Fortunately, the owners of mixed breeds never gave up on them since these dogs showed them intelligence and affection, all of which helped to develop a beautiful bond between them.

The manner in which people treat their dogs has changed drastically in the last 15 years. As we all know, Dr. Ian Dunbar has made a big difference in pet dog training in the United States. There are people in Japan who are making the same changes, with great success! Kazuya Arai, Managing Director, and Mika Ishiwata, CPDT, Deputy Managing Director, are co-founders of a company named "DINGO," (Dog Instructors Network of Great Opportunity), a training system planned to help instructors grow their dog training businesses.

A Little Bit of History

Terry Ryan was instrumental in helping DINGO get started about five years ago. She continues to be a special advisor in hopes of helping them continue on with their mission. Annually, DINGO invites leading trainers from around the world to Japan to help with their continuing education programs. Last year, I was honored to become DINGO's Master Instructor Trainer. Each year, I make the long trek—over eight hours—to Japan to work with trainers on many levels. We travel from the north to the south and after two exhausting weeks, we treat ourselves to a nice Japanese spa as we discuss our goals for the next year.

The system that DINGO has developed offers new trainers in the field a step-by-step process in which they can develop their handling skills starting from pre-owner classes to "Master Handling" classes. This can be supplemented with fun activities such as film dog training, swimming, canine musical freestyle, and much more. Much time is spent teaching the novice handlers to better read dogs and understand people.

Kazuya and Mika are now tapping into a greater audience. In addition to their instructor training course, they have developed educational opportunities for pet shops, dog sitters, and programs for day care workers, delivery companies (bite prevention tips), apartment residents, and many more. Their most recent venture is setting up a non-profit network to help shelter workers and people involved in dog rescue groups called "FORWARD" (For the Wellness and Respect of the Dogs). Their goal is to build a networking system to encourage members to work together.

The headquarters has a small staff where they prepare and supply all of the necessary tools for instructors to maintain consistency among trainers. For example, they have developed charts for client records, PowerPoint™ presentations for class orientations, handling test tools, certificates, plastic I.D. cards, and more. Every instructor can download what he or she needs from the Web site and utilize whatever DINGO has developed to help his or her business.

The goal is to standardize the training method and offer the most up-to-date and high quality information to every dog owner (both pet owners and professional instructors), hoping that they will have a better understanding about dogs and improve upon the human-canine bond.

Their methods are reward-based and they are beginning to see a change in how trainers work with people and dogs. As Mika explained, there are not many classes in Japan that focus on reward-based training, so it is an eye-opening opportunity for pet dog owners. What we hear from the clients is that "their pet has turned into a real partner!"

Mika left Japan and started training dogs in England about 10 years ago. Upon her return to Japan, about seven years ago, one of the greatest challenges she faced was finding the right treat for training. Since England was far ahead of Japan in reward-based training, dog treats were difficult, if not impossible, to find in Japan. As training became more and more popular, the treat companies began to expand their offerings. They are still in the process of developing new soft and chewy training treats. Since the sea surrounds Japan, the treat companies have made a variety of treats made from fish, which is an all-time favorite to most Japanese dogs.

DINGO's initial membership was about 40 inside and outside of Japan. In 2004, they had an opportunity to give a short presentation at the APDT Annual Educational Conference. Their membership has increased to over 900, including both pet dog owners and instructors worldwide.

The goal for DINGO is to have more pet dog owners enjoy their best friends! By offering these educational opportunities and fun activities, they are helping the Japanese people find a way to understand their dogs: how to be a better communicator while understanding what their dog is communicating to them; and, most importantly, having fun!

I wholeheartedly support DINGO's dream to help educate all animal professionals. I especially hold true to my heart their dream to keep more animals in their loving homes through motivational training.

I was thrilled to spend my 50th birthday in Japan this year! How many people can say they celebrated their birthday with only a handful of people that speak your language, had a raw fish birthday cake with candles and sake (forget the cake, you can't beat the fish!) and a show given by the trainers? It just goes to show that the Japanese trainers' talent isn't only in dogs! ❖

Making It Stick: How to Provide Memorable Class Instruction

Eileen Udry, Sep/Oct 2006

The vast majority of instruction in the pet dog realm focuses on how dogs learn. Obviously, it is vital to have in-depth knowledge of canine cognition, but the importance of understanding learning from the human end of the leash is at least as important. This article is designed to give pet dog trainers a more complete understanding of how human memory and learning works. I will discuss principles of human learning that can be used by trainers to increase the chances that the information they provide in class and during consultations will remain with students well after the session or class has ended.

I Thought You Had It

Suppose as a dog trainer you've given one of your students a demonstration of how to put an Easy Walk Harness™ on his dog. After you demonstrate, you give your student the opportunity to practice putting the harness on and removing it while you observe and give feedback. First, good for you for realizing that your student will need to actually practice the skills you just showed, not simply see you demonstrate them! Your student, however, may still have trouble remembering how to put on the harness several days later when he wants to walk his dog. Why? The concept referred to as over-learning may be relevant. Over-learning refers to additional practice time above and beyond what it would take to achieve basic mastery of a skill.[1] One rule of thumb says that if it took someone four trials to learn how to do a task, to store the skill in long-term memory, the person should practice the skill at least another 50% or, in this case, two more times. The more steps there are in the skill, the more likely this principle will be relevant. Thus, as a pet dog trainer, to help students retain more of what was practiced in class, it is suggested that you give your students multiple opportunities to practice a newly acquired skill. Of course, you'll want to make sure you are not creating boredom by including too much repetition.

Wait Just a Moment, There

Let's again turn to the example of teaching a client how to put a walking harness on her dog. When you demonstrate this skill you might be tempted to get two dogs with you, putting the harness on one dog (your demo dog) while your student simultaneously watches you and puts a harness on her own dog. This is what motor learning specialists refer to as "concurrent imitation" or in more vernacular terms, "monkey see, monkey do." What research has shown, however, is that using what is termed "delayed imitation" is actually more helpful in terms of long-term retention of how to complete the task.[2] With delayed imitation, as the instructor, you would give a brief demonstration and then pause for a short time (i.e., three to ten seconds) before having the student attempt to recreate the movement. In this brief pause, the student will be more likely to be actively engaged in storing the information in long-term memory rather than simply copying you. It can be noted that having to make the effort to store the information in long-term memory generally takes a bit longer and takes more effort on the part of the students. Sometimes students will start imitating the movement as a demonstration is being given, in which case, it can be helpful to let them know that you first want them to observe the demonstration and then there will be opportunities to practice.

Practice, Practice, Practice

As pet dog trainers, when we think of demonstrating a skill for our students, we often think of having them physically practice the skill shortly after we've demonstrated it. As it turns out, there are several forms of practice and to maximize long-term learning, we should really think about involving all three forms of practice when possible. Practice can include: physical practice, mental practice, and verbal practice. Let's look into each of these in more detail.

Physical Practice

Most instructors are well aware that physical practice—or giving students the opportunity to kinesthetically practice a skill—is a powerful form of learning. Most of us would not dream of only explaining and demonstrating loose leash walking, for example, but never allowing students to actually practice this skill in our time with them. However, a common mistake is for instructors to give too much information to students before giving students the opportunity to practice the skill; in other words, students don't get physical practice soon enough after the demonstration. Research has shown that in the early stages of learning, learners are simply "getting the idea."[3] As a result, in the early stages of learning students benefit from brief demonstrations followed by practice opportunities. More specifically, due to limits in short-term memory capacity, students tend to benefit the most from having the one to three most critical components of the skill explained and demonstrated and having additional demonstrations and refinements provided as their mastery of the skill increases. It can be noted, however, that when instructors shift back and forth between explaining/demonstrating and allowing students time to practice, it can appear a bit chaotic. This is okay. The key is to remember that when relatively short practice sessions are intermingled with demonstrations, long-term learning is enhanced.

Mental Practice

This form of practice is sometimes referred to as mental rehearsal, visualization, or imagery. Mental practice is simply using the mind to create or recreate an experience in the mind in the absence of physical practice.[4] Research has shown that the use of mental practice, in addition to physical practice, is superior for learning as compared to physical practice alone.4 Additionally, mental practice has also been shown to help individuals overcome performance anxiety and is often used by elite athletes for this very reason.[2] Helping students incorporate mental practice in the context of dog training instruction doesn't have to be complicated or time consuming. Using phrases such as "before we begin this exercise, I'd like you to run through it in your mind" can be helpful. This can be particularly useful if you have one or more students in your class who are waiting for another student to complete an exercise.

Verbal Practice

Verbal practice—which refers to having students verbally rehearse information—can be useful in a number of ways. First, you might use it as a way of checking for understanding after you have just described or demonstrated a skill.[5] For example, in the pet dog classes that I'm involved in, we practice an exercise called "Come to the Center." This exercise involves having the handlers and dogs in class form a large circle and gradually bringing the dogs in closer proximity by tightening the circle. As this happens, the principles of classical conditioning are used so that each dog's experience of being in tight quarters with other dogs is a good one. Handlers are instructed to: (a) keep their dog on a short but loose leash; (b) praise and treat their dogs as they move in closer to the other dogs; (c) take only the number of steps designated by the instructor (usually two to four steps); and (d) when signaled by the instructor, to move back to their original spot and remain quiet and neutral with their dog. Because of the number of steps involved in this exercise and the need for students to execute them appropriately, it is one where verbal rehearsal may be especially valuable. Thus, before beginning this exercise, we may ask three to four questions to make sure that all students are aware of the steps and to maximize the chances that the exercise can be done without, shall we say, incident.

Research has shown that verbal practice can be especially helpful for certain individuals. First, we know that information processing abilities can be compromised when anxiety and arousal levels are elevated.[2] Some examples of when anxiety levels might be elevated include: the first night of class with dogs, when someone's dog has a history of being reactive with other dogs and the person is embarrassed by this, and/or when students are not confident about their ability to work their dog in front of other students. Also, from a developmental perspective, we know that children under the age of ten and older adults often have a more difficult time getting information stored into long-term memory. So, using verbal practice is one more strategy you can use to help students get information loaded into long-term memory.

Finally, verbal practice can be a way of cueing students to what their body should look like or feel like during an activity. For instance, students often tend to tighten up on their leash when they are walking a dog, especially if their dog has a history of being reactive. I like using the cue word "cooked spaghetti" as way of encouraging students to relax their arms (or move their arm from being like "uncooked" to "cooked" spaghetti) when their dog is walking appropriately. Experiment with finding cue words that are easy to remember and can easily be repeated by students and you'll improve your chances of providing memorable instruction.

In closing, over-learning, delayed imitation, and the three types of practice (physical, mental, and verbal) can be used to make your lessons stick! ❖

References

[1] Magill, R.A. *Motor Learning: Concepts and Applications (7th. ed.).* Madison, WI: Mc-Graw-Hill, 2003.

[2] Schmidt, R.A & Wrisberg, C.A. *Motor Learning and Performance: A Problem-Based Approach (3rd ed.).* Champaign: Human Kinetics, 2004.

[3] Gentile, AM. "A working model of skill acquisition with application to teaching." *Quest-Monograph* (17), 3-23, 1972.

[4] Coker, CA. *Motor Learning and Control for Practitioners.* New York: Mc-Graw-Hill, 2004.

[5] Ryan, T. *Coaching People to Train Their Dogs.* Sequim: Legacy Canine Behavior and Training, 2005.

Agility to the Rescue!

Sue Sternberg, November/December 2006

I was at an agility trial about a year ago, sitting on the sidelines with some friends, watching the competitors. A woman ran the novice course with her Basset Hound. They ran clean. They were a beautiful team. They were not the fastest team, but they worked well together and they had a lovely partnership. I turned to one of my friends and remarked how well that woman and her Basset ran. My friend (a professional trainer) told me that the woman and her Basset Hound had once been students in her puppy kindergarten classes a couple of years back. In that puppy class, an agility tunnel and a couple of other obstacles were introduced during the last two classes. This pet owner and her puppy got hooked on agility then, and she continued taking pet agility classes and training her dog week after week, and now spends the occasional weekend competing at agility trials.

Agility is perhaps the best thing to happen to dogdom in a long, long time. It can be the instinctive sport for every dog of every breed, mixed and pure. It is the one type of training that encourages the average or inexperienced pet owner to continue training their dog well past graduation from the first class. Agility hooks us into training and working with our dogs; it entices people to learn about handling and body language—human body language—to communicate more clearly with our dogs. For so many dogs, having their owners take them through agility training is finally a way for these dogs to get help. Dogs want and need their owners to have better timing, to be more generous with rewards, to make life more fun, to include them more in their lives, and to give them mental and physical exercise. Agility does all this and much more.

Pet owners sign up for agility not because they're at their wit's end with their dog, and not because their dog is such a problem that without one final try at training, they would "get rid of the dog." Pet owners sign up for agility because it looks like fun. They believe their dog would enjoy agility, and they believe they will enjoy it too.

Pet owners sign up for "obedience" or basic manners classes usually because they are indeed at their wit's end, or because they feel every dog should have a basic foundation with a certain level of training. Following this line of thinking is the concept of a graduation—or an end point to the training. The most common perception by pet owners about basic training and manners is that after a certain period of time (usually six to 12 weeks) the dog is trained, and all that is left is application and occasional practice sessions. Only professional trainers get hooked into training to the point where we desire to, and are motivated to, train our dogs every day for the rest of our lives, just for the sheer fun of it!

What agility has done is motivate the average pet owner to get hooked into permanent training with their dog. Agility offers the average pet owner a hobby; an activity that raises the status of their dog to an integral family member, worthy and deserving of being included in everyday life. Elevation to the status of important family member is the key to a truly successful dog-owner relationship. It transcends temperament and basic manners. Agility is the manifestation of a healthy dog-owner relationship. Every dog deserves to do agility.

What Agility Teaches

Included in agility training is every basic training skill minus walking nicely on leash. In fact, agility training is all about off-lead control, recalls, sits, downs, stays, attention, and leadership. Every important behavior is embedded within an agility class. Plus, as an added bonus, agility teaches dogs to respond to their handlers:

- During arousal and excitement;

- On-leash or off-leash; and

- In the company of other dogs.

And agility offers:

- Physical as well as mental stimulation and exercise;

- The handler's ongoing pursuit of attaining clearer and timelier non-verbal cues;

- A concentrated forum for practicing gentle, non-confrontational leadership skills, as dogs can't do agility without following the cues from their handlers.

A dog can go hiking, play with his toys, and play with other dogs without its owner. A dog cannot do agility without a human. Therefore, agility is a great activity for owners with leadership problems, "dominance" problems, poor timing, and unclear body language. Once the basic obstacles have been taught, the rest of agility is all about the human learning to communicate more clearly, consistently, and in a timelier fashion with their dog.

Agility lessons include a balance between impulse control and freedom. There is access to speed and joy, and then control and limits set at the highest point of arousal and excitement. It includes a fine balance of encouraging physical skills and allowing the all-too-often suppressed detonation of physical ability, athleticism, and desire.

The Pros and Cons of Offering Introductory Agility Classes without Any Prerequisite Training Classes

I teach a lot of short introduction to agility workshops for dogs in shelters. These are dogs that often have no prior training and no bond with their handlers and are truly blank slates. I like the challenge of getting a group of dogs with no prior training to be immediately successful and "hooked" into training.

However, I can see the value of insisting on a basic training prerequisite class before agility. I think it motivates people to take basic training in order to enroll in an agility class. It allows the instructor time to assess the temperament and behavior of the class dogs in a much less stimulating environment. It allows the instructor to identify problem or dangerous dogs before the arousal levels of an actual agility class. But at the same time, I like allowing students to be able to sign up and try agility directly.

There are some important things that need to be included in any introductory agility class, whether it's after a basic course or a stand-alone course. Students need to be taught how to wait in line and maintain their dog's attention. Students must be briefed and prepared to keep their own dog and all the other dogs in the class safe. Nothing should be left to chance. They need to be told where to stand, how to stand, how much leash to allow, where to wait in line, when to move the line forward, and where to go after they've finished a sequence. The instructor must be ever watchful of leash lengths, proximity of dogs to other dogs, personality conflicts between dogs waiting in line—everything. Nothing can be left to chance or luck.

An Introductory Lesson

I start most introductory agility workshops by back chaining a sequence of four obstacles, typically tunnel-jump-jump-table. I teach the table first and with the most repetitions and rewards. I stay down at the table on the far side of the sequence. I have the handler bring the dog on leash to the table, approaching it from the landing side of the third obstacle, in this case jump #3. The dog is allowed to see the jackpot of treats I have placed on the table and then is pulled backwards away from table, and released when he/she is pulling to get to the table. The dog is allowed to work out for himself to jump up on the table and eat. The handler allows the dog to forge ahead to the table with the handler trailing behind on leash. This is repeated many times.

The next sequence is to start with the dog just behind jump #3, and repeat the table sequence, allowing the dog to negotiate over the (very low) jump bar when he's straining to get to the table. The handler tosses the leash over the jump and follows the dog to the table. This sequence is repeated a number of times, gradually allowing the dog to move his starting position backwards until he is held just in front of jump #2.

Finally, while the treats are still plentiful and the dog's appetite still keen, the tunnel is introduced in a position as squished as it can be. I hold the leash and the dog and have the handler move to the exit side, bend down and peek through the hole, but not plug the exit. The handlers are instructed to make eye contact with their dogs only while peering through the hole. When the dog pokes his head in, the handler should give a burst of praise. I hold the dog back, and restrict him from moving to either side of the tunnel. When the dog goes through, the handler grabs the leash, peels back, and offers a generous reward and huge praise.

The tunnel sequence alone is repeated and with each repetition, I stretch out the entrance end of the tunnel, until it is straight and almost completely open.

Before the dog is tired or full, I have the handler hand me the leash while I remain at the entrance to the tunnel. The handler runs down the course to the far end of the table, and loads the table with treats and calls their dog. I will at this point unclip the dog, and allow him to enter the tunnel off-leash.

Almost all dogs are successful at the entire sequence. I recommend using a wing jump (a jump with side pieces attached) for jump #3.

A few things happen:

- This particular sequence allows the dog to access as much speed and momentum as he wishes, regardless of the speed, timing, or skills of his handler.

- Handlers are usually very proud.

- Dogs are off-leash, and under control, without any of the fuss and worry often inherent in the usual maiden voyage off-leash.

- Dogs learn to jump, go through a tunnel, "go on" ahead of the handler, desire the table, and to respond the same whether on- or off-leash.

- Everybody has fun!

Preparing for the Worst and Keeping Everyone Safe

At the start of every class, and multiple times during class and at each subsequent class, I advise handlers on what to do if and when a dog gets loose and out of control. I tell them, if I yell "Loose dog!" those handlers with healthy backs and small dogs will pick up their dogs and turn their backs toward the loose dog. Those handlers with weak backs or larger dogs are to place their dog's head between their legs, so that the dog's butt is to the loose dog, and his head is sticking out behind the handler. These handlers are then instructed to feed their dog continuously until the loose dog is caught.

I continuously remind students of this and practice fake drills every once in a while. I explain quite clearly to each class the risks and dangers agility training can produce, and the importance of being proactive and prepared. I remind students relentlessly that there are two types of dogs: predators and prey.

This set-up keeps the other class dogs safe, and also ensures that the loose dog doesn't get rewarded for his behavior by playing or fighting with any other dogs.

There's Nothing Easy About Teaching Introductory Agility Classes

Instructing introductory pet agility classes can be the most difficult of all classes to teach, second only to the responsibility and knowledge needed to instruct puppy kindergarten or basic manners classes. The pet agility instructor needs advanced agility and competition-level skills and knowledge, but just as important, if not even more, they must know dog behavior and temperament; they must read canine body language well; and must be able to manage students and their often out-of-control dogs in a highly stimulating environment. The pet agility instructor needs to be able to read and assess temperament and diplomatically expel dangerous dogs or dogs not ready for group situations immediately while maintaining rapport with the owner. Helping the dogs that need agility the most, which are so often the least suited for group classes where they must wait patiently while other dogs run around so stimulated, is something we should strive for. ❖

And Then You Punt

Joan B. Guertin, November/December 2005

There was no reason to think that the class on this normal Monday night would be any different from the week before. Of course, it would be expected that by week four, both two-legged and four-legged students would be working better this week than the last. However, five minutes into the class, it was clear that none of the five adolescent pups wanted to be there and all were showing major resistance to doing even the simplest of exercises. As a result, the human team members were becoming extremely frustrated.

Those of us who have trained for a long time recognize the problems inherent in rising stress levels. This is the point where the owner is likely to become exasperated and the force level increases. The natural result is increased resistance from the dog, with legs stiffening, pulling away from the owner who automatically increases tension on the leash. Some dogs merely fold and fall to the ground, becoming dead weight. Thus, nothing positive happens.

This is the point where younger and less experienced trainers tend to freeze. Their lesson plans appear set in stone as is the time schedule. The old pros, however, recognize that this is the perfect time to simply "fall back and punt."

The above scenario actually happened to me recently. It was a class of five adolescents, ranging from a willing Labrador Retriever down to a willful Miniature Pinscher, all in the hands of either first-time owners, beginning trainers, or the admitted cat-person owner of the Miniature Pinscher. So, what do you do? There are 50 minutes left and we want to make sure "they get their money's worth."

In earlier years and prior to the APDT's dog-friendly philosophy, a traditional trainer would have resorted to force. Make the dog do it! Show it that "you are the boss." Now we look for positive solutions.

So, what did we do? First we dug into the store of high-powered motivators, the "killer treats" that the dogs generally don't get at home. I pull from my freezer the liver or cheese that I use in the conformation ring. And, note here that we weren't asking for the moon, we simply were working on some loose leash walking.

The Miniature Pinscher refused to budge. The Labrador Retriever laid down and rolled on her back. The Shih Tzu mix turned its back to the class or kept trying to get "mom" to pick it up. The Corgi just wanted to play and was more interested in the other dogs (who wanted nothing to do with that agenda), and the Standard Poodle figured "if they aren't doing it, I'm not either!"

Even the basic attention exercises weren't working. It was as if, in silent agreement, the pups simply were on strike!

Taking stock of possible outside influences—full moon, pending storm, drop in barometric pressure, high wind (although we were inside), or a stressful weekend—

nothing seemed to offer a reason other than the fact that the dogs simply weren't cooperating. So, I decided to punt!

Punting is merely doing something very different, fun, and offbeat to move both dog and human minds into a different space. On this particular night I opted to teach tricks!

The class had already learned the tricks rollover and crawl. This evening we added chase the tail, sit up pretty, and then I showed them how to exercise the pup while watching TV by sitting on the floor and directing the dog to jump over their legs or under tented legs. Then we pulled out the hoops and began the process of teaching all of the dogs to walk through. We had almost instant success, with just a few trips back and forth to begin teaching the jump. This became a natural opportunity to teach the pups "door protocol" with the "wait, go through, turn, sit, and treat" from the inside/out and outside/in. The pups were finally both mentally and physically back in the room with their owners.

The class time was not wasted. The human owners gained new skills in what I call "engagement." When the interest level is low, it is essential to devise a means to once again engage with the dog. Rather than fostering resistance through force and having to deal with a "clash of wills," simply introduce something new and fun. Once dog and owner are on the same page and sharing an experience, then the learning process moves forward.

And what about the lesson plan? In this case, the pups left happy, the people left relieved and all was back to normal the next week with the dogs all working extremely well on their loose leash walking. And best of all, the people were thrilled! ❖

Business Practices

Once you decide to hang up your shingle and take on clients, it will quickly become abundantly clear that you need more than learning theory and behavioral modification techniques to be successful. Dog training is a business that requires you to be an accountant, marketer, designer, and all-around business owner. This series of articles tackles business topics such as how to market your business effectively and cheaply, understanding dog bite liability, and weaning yourself financially from a part-time training business to a full-time one. If you're thinking of expanding, a discussion of developing and training strong apprentices is a necessary topic. Running a successful business doesn't just depend on your business skills and training knowledge though, it also requires understanding how to take care of one's own psychological health. Two articles that highlight this important ingredient provide two separate solutions—learning to set limits to reduce stress and developing a strong professional network of trainers to provide feedback and support for each other.

Making the Move to Your Own Full-Time Dog Training Business

Veronica Boutelle, September/October 2005

Do you want to work with dogs full-time, but can't see how? Do you train part-time, telling yourself you'll keep the other job just until the training really takes off? It's a common refrain. Coaching and supporting dog training businesses for a living, I've seen every kind of business model and every type of owner, from wildly successful full-timers to weekend hobbyists. Mostly though, trainers work part- or full-time at other jobs, and run a dog training business on the side, hoping it will one day support them. Years of experience have taught me the key differences between trainers that make it as full-time entrepreneurs and those who don't. Read on to see if you have the temperament, skill set, and drive necessary to pull it off. If so, you absolutely can bring a new or part-time business into the full-time realm and make a living doing what you love.

The Magic of Niches

Most successful training businesses have one simple concept in common: specialization. This is particularly important if a lot of trainers operate in your geographical area. When a potential client opens the phone book or scans the bulletin board at the local vet office, what will make you stand out? Trainers who focus on one type of training or behavioral issue, set themselves apart and give clients a reason to call them. If, for example, an owner has a dog with separation anxiety and he sees that a particular trainer specializes in that problem, he is much more likely to call that trainer than the fifteen who advertise generic obedience training. This doesn't mean, however, that the trainer in question will do nothing but home alone training for the rest of her career. On the contrary, satisfied clients refer their friends, who again refer their friends, and only a few of those new clients are likely to be separation anxiety cases. The trick is to get those initial calls so you can begin building the all-important word of mouth.

Think about what you are particularly good at. Working with small dogs? Unruly adolescents? Dog-baby intros? Family training? Look at what other professionals in your area offer. Is there a gap in the market you can fill? Whatever you decide, make sure it is something you enjoy.

Know Where You're Going

Most of us are dog trainers because we love dogs, not business development. When we decide to set up shop, we do the bare minimum necessary: think up a name, file for a business license and other paperwork, have stationery and maybe a brochure printed, and post a few fliers around town. And then we wait eagerly for the phone to ring which would work well in an ideal world with endless demand for our product

298

and next-to-zero competition. But the reality is that setting up and marketing a new business, let alone building a profitable one, requires sustained focus, attention, and action. Simply hanging out a shingle rarely does the job, especially if there are other trainers and services available in your area. It is critical to develop a business plan and actively build relationships with other dog service providers (veterinarians, pet supply stores, groomers, etc.).

Hatch a Plan

Trainers often plan to work part-time until the business takes off. Sound familiar? The problem with this strategy is that it doesn't provide a framework for making anything happen. For that, you need a comprehensive business plan. It doesn't have to be fancy or formal as long as it helps you assess viability and provides guidance as you move forward. Your plan should include goals for the business, a numbers assessment, a marketing plan—your niche and message, image, services, materials, and how you will get the word out—and an overall checklist of tasks and due dates. If you're moving from part- to full-time, decide on a clear set of success indicators (number of clients per month, amount of income, etc.) to help you determine when it's time to leave your other job.

Get Organized

Scribbling notes on the backs of envelopes doesn't often inspire confidence. Worse, it hinders the organization that distinguishes a professional business. As soon as you have more than a few clients, you need to keep solid records, notes, and training plans. Consider preparing a ready-made set of tools (diagnostic flowcharts, interview forms, etc.) to save start-up time and effort.

Establish a Schedule and Routine

One pitfall of self-employment is the lack of a routine. If a flexible schedule without a boss and specific deadlines makes you feel rudderless, working for yourself can be a challenge. It's easy to do little or nothing when you have unlimited time. I've seen trainers struggle for months to do what could have been done in weeks or even days. To keep yourself working toward your goals without losing focus, make a realistic schedule and commit to deadlines. Avoid wasting time by structuring your workdays carefully. What days will you see clients? When will you work on training plans? When will you take care of administrative tasks? When will you spend time growing your business?

Professional Image

A person hunting for a dog trainer might look at the cards pinned up on her veterinarian's bulletin board or at the local dog park. She might do an Internet search. But how does she choose? As mentioned, a trainer who specializes in the issue the client is facing is an obvious route. Another vital decision-making factor, however, is the professionalism, or not, of your business materials. Given a choice, any client is going to pick the business card or Web site that looks professional and established rather than printed at home on the old ink-jet printer. The adage "it takes money to make money" applies here. Putting money and time into the development of a professional business image—logo, message, and materials—goes a long way toward building a broader client base.

Dazzle them. Spend some start-up capital on a professional look. This includes your name and logo design, marketing materials such as business cards and brochures, and any materials you leave with clients—contracts, homework sheets, or client instructions.

Relationships

A hallmark of the successful trainer is to prioritize working relationships, and carefully cultivate and maintain them. Letting one client after another fade into the woodwork is a mistake. Smart trainers follow up with clients, even after their treatment plan has concluded, because staying on your clients' radar screen means you're at hand when a need arises—for them or for a friend's dog. Collegial relationships are equally important. They allow you to keep up with industry standards, exchange best practices, and support each other by brainstorming difficult cases, acting as each other's training assistants and, most importantly, through mutual referrals. A separation anxiety trainer, for example, is likely to receive referrals from other trainers not interested in or willing to take separation anxiety cases if she fosters strong collegial relationships. And she can return the favor when she gets calls outside of her own comfort or skill zone. I've seen many niche-business trainers form strong networks and build prosperous businesses with very little marketing expense.

Follow up with former clients. Take an interest in the progress of their pooch beyond your own involvement. And cultivate relationships with trainers in the area—how might you be mutually supportive? What do you each do differently and might you trade referrals?

Temperament

How comfortable are you with risks? Starting a dog training business takes less capital than most enterprises, but you still run the risk of losing money and possibly failing. It takes tenacity and perspective to face such prospects and still work hard and enthusiastically. I've seen many trainers quit or go back to part-time work long before their businesses could reasonably be expected to succeed.

What is your tolerance for risk? Are you comfortable dipping into your savings or borrowing money? Do you enjoy solving problems? Do you stick with your plans over time? Could you see yourself doing this in five years? Do you enjoy a variety of tasks? If you've answered yes to most of these, self-employment could be perfect for you.

Skills

When you run a small business you have to oversee everything. You may be an excellent dog trainer, but are you ready to be a bookkeeper, accountant, marketing manager, secretary, and office manager? A key to successful full-time business ownership is to recognize your weaknesses and subcontract tasks that confound you or that require expertise you don't possess.

List the skills required to run your business. Then ask yourself: What are you good at? Where do your interests lie? Which tasks can you readily do? Which will stress you, weaken the business, or possibly be left undone? For those skills, get help. Trade skills with a friend or hire a contractor.

The Must-Knows: Taxes and Insurance

Self-employment unfortunately comes with the 15% so-called "Self Employment Tax," but this is off-set by a deduction of almost half that. Still, take it into account before you decide to make the jump to full-time. Also consider becoming a Limited Liability Company. There are many advantages to operating this way, one of which is that LLCs can choose to be taxed as a sole proprietorship or as a corporation. To be sure what tax implications apply to you and what options you have, consult a qualified tax accountant. But don't let these issues throw you. Deal with them up front so you can relax and enjoy your work with the pooches.

For liability insurance, you'll need a policy specifically for your business (homeowners' policies do not cover home-based businesses), but insurance is easy and inexpensive for dog trainers to acquire. For example, if you're reading this, you're probably an APDT member and have access to their group insurance policy. Keep in mind that policies vary on such key issues as whether or not you are covered should a client sue to collect damages for a bite years after you worked with the dog, based on the notion that "I was just following the advice you gave me two years ago!" So be sure to check with your insurance provider about what your policy does and does not cover.

Health insurance is another matter altogether. Many part-timers stay in non-training jobs solely to retain insurance benefits. If that's you, contact an insurance broker to discuss your insurability and consider your options. Then look into becoming an LLC. Some trainers hire employees to qualify for group insurance plans, but this is seldom cost-effective when you factor in other employee expenses, such as time spent on paperwork. A two-person LLC, however, can access the same group insurance plans. So if there's someone you'd like to partner with or you can incorporate a spouse as a silent partner, you can usually form an LLC and get health insurance that way.

Consulting a tax accountant before starting a business or going full-time is always a good idea, because you will know the financial implications ahead of time. Additionally, having a professional prepare your taxes in your first year has major advantages, like avoiding mistakes and relieving stress. But it also provides a model for doing them yourself in subsequent years, and often saves you money because the professionals know of deductions and other details that can benefit you at tax time.

And if you think you might have difficulty procuring private health insurance, talk to an insurance broker before you launch your business.

Will it Work?

Finally, if you're poised to take the plunge, but worry about whether you'll be able to afford electricity, try this simple assessment: Figure out how much you need to live on each year. Be detailed and realistic and don't forget the annual or occasional expenses like taxes, insurance, car repair, etc. Then assess your competition—what are others in the area charging, and what services do they provide? Use this information to determine your own rates. Now estimate a reasonable, conservative number of clients per month and year, being careful to consider seasonal variables. Then do the math— does it add up? If it doesn't, don't give up—go back to the drawing board to see what kind of creative solutions are waiting. Other people are doing it. You can too! ❖

Creativity, Not Cash: Tips on Marketing Your Dog Business

Veronica Boutelle, September/October 2006

The number one rule of marketing is to do it. You can't expect word of mouth if you don't build it. But you needn't take out a loan or pawn your grandmother's jewelry to market your business. In fact, you may not need much cash at all. It's not that money can't be a great help to a marketing plan, but if you don't possess great start-up capital, a little creativity can stand in nicely.

Prepare

First, sit down with a pen and paper and construct two lists. The first will be a list of your strongest skills. What do you do well and enjoy? Are you a good public speaker? A talented small group or one-on-one teacher? How's your writing? What about your planning skills?

For your second list, note all the potential networking resources in your area. Consider your environment. What other dog-related businesses are around? Vets, groomers, supply stores and boutiques, shelters and rescue groups? Oh—and don't forget other trainers, walkers, and sitters, too! They can be a terrific networking resource. What about local activities? Are there dog parks or festivals, adult education or community classes? And what are people reading—any local dailies or weeklies or monthlies? In short, what's going on in your neighborhood?

Get Creative

As you scan your two lists, you're looking for good potential match-ups between your skill set on the one side and the resources or potential networking opportunities on the other. If you enjoy writing, perhaps the local neighborhood monthly would like to run a regular "Ask the Trainer" column? Terrific exposure, at no cost! And so much more effective than running an ad, where you're attempting to sell yourself. A column, on the other hand, establishes your expertise and credibility. You become the sought-after local expert. Or, if you specialize in helping people with puppies and new dogs, wouldn't it be great if the local shelter recommended you to all of their adopters?

Give, Don't Ask

Writing a local column and getting shelter referrals are great marketing goals— but how do you make these things happen?

The trick is to give instead of asking. The typical dog training business marketing plan includes drawing up business cards to post around other dog-oriented establishments. Often we ask the owners if we can put our cards on their bulletin boards or in a holder on their counters. If brave enough, we might even introduce ourselves, talk a little about what we do, and ask for their referrals.

But why should they refer people to you? They don't know you or your abilities, they're busy, and you've given them no reason to want to help you. So rather than asking for help, consider what you might have to offer.

If you'd like to write a regular column in the neighborhood paper, first try offering one article, already written, on a dog topic of broad interest. If you would like the shelter to refer their new adopters to you, put together a free adopter's package of articles or tip handouts the shelter can give to its adopters. (Make sure your name and business information are on all the handouts, and include any of your other marketing material as well!) And maybe they would appreciate some training for their staff—a small series of talks or hands-on seminars. These offerings allow the shelter to get to know you, to come to see you as an expert, and to build loyalty to you. Sure, you can leave your cards on the front counter and hope people pick them up and call, but you'll no doubt receive many more phone calls if the shelter staff is actively and enthusiastically sending adopters your way.

Be Active, Not Passive

One reason these kinds of approaches are much more powerful marketing tools than simply placing materials around town is that they are examples of active marketing—opportunities for clients to interact with your business rather than just seeing it advertised. Instead of picking up a business card, a shelter staff person hands your materials to potential clients while telling them, "You have to call this trainer. She is amazing and can help you fix this problem." If you post a flier on a bulletin board, there is no potential for active interaction between your business and your hoped-for clients. If instead you disseminate a quarterly newsletter to the same places, the people who pick it up have a more interactive experience with your business. Rather than a flier that lists "problem behavior solving" as one of your services, an article in each newsletter can highlight an issue and tell the story of one or more dogs and clients whose lives were changed by training. In that narrative they get to "see" an example of the benefits of training and imagine themselves getting similar help, rather than just reading a bullet point.

Get Started Today

Most marketing takes time to be effective—plan to give your efforts a good six months to determine their usefulness—so make your lists right now and see how many great ideas you can create. Start marketing your business today to generate the clients who will help you spread the word tomorrow.

Case Studies

Hillary

Hillary had been trying for some time to network with her local shelter. The shelter had good standing in the community and was viewed as a source of training and veterinary knowledge, but they did not provide private training services. She knew they were short staffed and thought both she and they could benefit from a referral service. But although the front desk staff had her cards on the counter, it seemed they were rarely given out, and she hardly ever received referrals. Then she offered to help answer the shelter behavior hotline. Together with the behavior manager, she set up a triage system for incoming calls to take pressure off the shelter staff. They determined which calls the staff could easily handle and forwarded the more difficult calls to Hillary. Hillary was careful to limit the time of each call, providing some immediately applicable management advice, then scheduling a consult with anyone interested. The hotline is now Hillary's number one source of clients.

Debbie

Debbie couldn't help notice as she walked her pack of client dogs every day how messy the dog park had gotten—trash, untended piles of feces—it was unsightly and, she felt, gave dogs, dog owners, and dog professionals a bad name. Seeing an opportunity to do something for her community and her dog training and walking business, she worked with the parks department to co-sponsor, organize, and promote a Dog Park Clean Up Day. The park got cleaned up, her business got lots of free press, including an article in the local paper and a short spot on the local evening news, and Debbie got several new clients.

Suzanne

Suzanne believed that an ounce of prevention was worth a pound of cure, especially when it comes to puppies and newly adopted dogs. She wanted to focus her business on getting people and dogs off on the right paw, but how to get the word out? The local shelter did a brisk adoption business, and Suzanne decided to start there. She offered to teach a free adopters' class at the shelter, at no cost to them. She gave the two-hour talk one evening each week, and the shelter scheduled that weeks' adopters into the lecture. Suzanne's talk covered the basics of setting up a home for a new dog, house training, and prevention of common behavior problems, and she always made sure to talk about her private training services as well. Her business grew steadily as she signed up occasional clients at the talks, and found that over time people who had attended her class called as they developed training problems, and often referred her to friends and family as well. ❖

The Magic of Niches

Veronica Boutelle, November/December 2006

What makes you special? One of the most common marketing mistakes trainers make is to generalize. If you're the only game in town, it makes sense to tell potential clients you do it all. But if there are multiple dog pros in your area, what makes a client call you instead of someone else? Don't leave it to chance. Give them a reason to call you by marketing a specialization. Find a niche and fill it well.

Finding Your Niche

First, take a look at what the competition in your area is doing. Consider what you might have to offer that is different. For example, do you prefer working with a particular type of dog, such as puppies or small dogs? Is there a training issue you're particularly good at handling? Who are your ideal clients? Do you have skills from a former career or hobby that might serve as a useful complement to your training? A former school teacher might be especially adept at working with families with children. Experience in the corporate world could open doors to lunchtime or other workplace training programs. Also consider services not currently being offered that could be of use to dog owners in your area. Is there a need for specialty classes such as tricks or behavior workshops focusing on tough behaviors like the recall or loose leash walking? Does anyone offer board and train or owner-absent training options? What about boarding in your home or walking clients' dogs?

How a Niche Works

Marketing a niche gives a subsection of potential clients a reason to call you over every other service provider in your area. These clients then tell their friends and family and co-workers about you, and you begin to build your business. And you can absolutely be a generalist, too. Say you specialize in treating separation anxiety, and your marketing efforts predictably bring you clients with separation anxiety problems. If you help solve those problems, the likelihood is that the client will refer you to friends and family for any training needs they have. Even with a narrow niche focus you can expect a good half of your cases to fall outside your specialty.

Case Studies

Tina

Back in the suburbs, Tina owned a successful home-based dog training and boarding business. After getting married and moving to a small place in a big city, Tina wondered how she would make board and train work. Then she noticed how many small dogs were out and about town—in bicycle baskets, in purses, at the mall, and enjoying sidewalk cafes. Tina built her new business around board and train services for small dogs only. Her marketing plan included networking with local small dog rescue groups, groomers, and high-end doggie boutique stores. Her message of special care for small dogs hit home with small dog owners and she now maintains a waiting list for her services.

Miranda

Miranda was scraping by in an urban market saturated with dog trainers. Though she marketed herself as working with all kinds of obedience and problem behaviors, she found that the cases she most enjoyed were dog-dog aggression issues. She began marketing a specialty working with dog aggression and has found her schedule filling up. For one thing, she's given a segment of dog owners a reason to call her over the many other trainers in her area. She also enjoys the referrals of her fellow dog trainers who do not take dog aggression cases.

Cindy

Cindy burned out working as a veterinary technician in a high-pressure veterinary hospital, and decided to start her own pet sitting business. The number of people already pet sitting in her area intimidated her, but her veterinary technician expertise made her worries unnecessary. She directed her business at owners with older and ill pets, explaining that she would be able to care for both their emotional and physical well being, including administering medicines, IVs, and other required home medical care. She networked with veterinary offices and other pet sitters and was soon overwhelmed with referrals for clients needing special care for their elderly or infirm animals while away.

Gina

Gina found her dog training skills very useful both while preparing her young dog for the arrival of her first baby and after she brought the baby home. She noticed several of the women in her new moms' group struggled with their dogs and babies, and a niche was born. Gina changed the name of her business to Tails & Tots and began marketing to expectant and new moms through groups, pediatricians, and parenting classes at her two local hospitals. She also developed curricula for two public dog training classes, one for expectant parents and one for new parents. Her business is thriving.

Start Today

These dog pros found a way to make themselves stand out—what could yours be? If you're generalizing now and don't hear the phone ringing as often as you'd like, it's time to find your niche. Start brainstorming today, and seek input from friends, family, and past clients on what you do best or what is needed in your community. Once you've made a decision about your direction, amend your cards, brochures, and Web site, to reflect your new specialization. (If you still have a lot of good brochures, you can add a nicely printed paper insert instead of throwing them out.) Re-work advertisements and fliers. And tell your colleagues, clients, and anyone you network with—veterinarians, groomers, shelters, pet supply stores, daycares, and other businesses and contacts—about the exciting new service you're offering. ❖

Do You Suffer From Separation Anxiety?

Brandi Barker, May/June 2005

Do you find yourself staying late after every class to help a client with her dog's housebreaking woes? Are you pre-occupied with the potential danger, liability and ultimate resolution of a client's dog that has bitten a neighbor? Are you re-playing the private session with the client who pushes his dog too far every week in trying to counter-condition separation anxiety, wondering how you will ever get through to him?

The answer may be deeper than stress, burnout, or unique challenges that arise every day. You may be getting fused with your clients to the point that you own their fears, feel their anxiety, and share their burden of responsibility (Fischer, n.d.; Kegan 2001). Fusion is developed when we allow our thoughts and feelings to be generated in reaction to a situation. It can be detrimental when dealing with dogs and their humans.

If you allow yourself to become frantic when a client walks in distraught over an instance of her dog-dog-aggressive dog being rushed up on while counter-condition-ing, you can do a huge disservice to her. You will not be able to look at the level of setback that occurred if you are focusing on your emotion. You will be unable to draw upon your intuition and values to think of the best way to move forward. You cannot communicate clearly when driven by external pressures rather than the distinctive scenario (Pratch and Jacobowitz, 1998).

By taking responsibility for all your clients' woes, you can cause burdens so heavy you may not be able to carry the weight and you may revert to "emotional cutoff." If that occurs and you fail to recognize it, you may revert to guilt, a constant need for approval or building a barrier between you and your clients (Bowen, 1994). If you lack the ability to connect with their concerns, see them as unique, or practice understanding while listening to their issues (Kegan, 2001), you could miss the key component of what is really going on and misdiagnose a behavior.

Too much theory and not enough practice may cause trainers and behaviorists to disconnect from their clients' concerns or not connect at all. This may cause you to give trite responses, not fully listen, or to give impractical advice. Appearing to know everything is not comforting to a client who does not share your extensive experience working with dogs. It is just as dangerous to connect too much with a client as it is not to connect at all.

How do you balance the struggle to pursue your vocation without being too pas-sionate about any one situation? How do you avoid getting so close that you fizzle out and lose the ability to make rational, thoughtful decisions? How do you avoid becoming an "expert" who can't relate to your clients?

"Self differentiation" is the balance between making responsive decisions based on your knowledge, beliefs, and the novel situation without succumbing to emotional reactivity or external pressures (Bowen, 1994; Fischer, n.d.; Pratch and Jacobowitz, 1998). Differentiation of self is being capable of having intentional direction when pursuing thoughtful solutions for clients without seeking some unfulfilled familial need to connect (Bowen, 1994). Here are a few suggestions on ways to be sensitive to your clients' needs while maintaining your sense of self:

1. Establish Your Boundaries

- For classes and private sessions, make sure you communicate the start and end times during orientation. If you continuously exceed the allotted time for legitimate reasons, you may need to reconsider the length of your sessions. If a client always stays after class to discuss a problem, offer an in-person or phone consultation later in the week.

- If you are not mentally alert at 11:00 pm, do not accept a private session at that time. You will regret it and may not offer the same valuable service you would at another time. If you can not find a mutually convenient time, phone and e-mail may help until you can meet in person.

- Do not make yourself available anytime. It can be tempting when starting a business, but if you value your time, so will your clients. You will only become too involved if you hear every detail of every behavior Muffy exhibits every evening. If you feel compelled to keep informed all the time, check messages only every couple hours when you are "off." Try to have at least one day a week that is all yours. The rejuvenation will make you much more alert and conscientious of your clients' needs.

2. Recognize There are Emergency Situations

By stating the above, I do not mean you should refuse to talk with a client whose dog bite caused a child to be hospitalized or who is in the final stages of deciding to re-home his dog. If you limit your reactivity to emergencies only, you preserve your emotions for these truly distraught times and are better equipped to deal with them when they occur. A few ways to handle how you are contacted in an emergency are:

- Have a pager number that you only give to clients when there is a potential crisis.

- Get an answering service that has your home number and can reach you in emergency situations or take messages in non-emergency scenarios.

- Leave a pager number on your outgoing message with the disclaimer "if it's an emergency." If a client pages you with a non-emergency, politely tell her you will return the call as a priority the next business day.

3. Get to Know the Client

- Act as a hunter/gatherer when taking on a new client; seek to understand her learning style so you can adjust your approach accordingly. If you find out her interests, time commitment, and concerns up front, you will be better able to relate and give her realistic advice. It is emotionally consuming when you neglect to take a client's need into consideration. Avoid that reactivity by gaining an awareness of her skill level, knowledge, and handling skills. This will save time, questions, and mutual stress that can cause you both to become too sensitive and miss the meaning of what you discuss.

- Be wary. By learning about your client, you do not have to become her confidante for all of life's problems. You are not there to solve marital issues, but if you know there are major life stresses such as this, it will enable you to better diagnose what might be occurring.

4. Get to Know Other Trainers in Your Area

- Befriend a few trainers to have a support network. I once worked at home full-time and found I was always stressed about work. I had no one who empathized with my dilemmas, offered meaningful advice, or who could seek my understanding in similar situations. You may even develop a referral network if your specialties complement each other.

5. Know What You Know

- It is easy to be seduced by taking on an unfamiliar behavioral situation. The doubt you may have in your advice, energy spent doing extensive research, and the anxiety that follows in between sessions as to what the result might be can be consuming. If you do take on a case that you have never dealt with before, be honest with the client. It is ethical, allows her to decide her comfort level, and allows you the challenge of a new skill if she decides to accept your services.

- Check in with clients in between sessions to make sure you are not blindsided with a catastrophic situation. Send a quick e-mail with specific questions so as not to get into a lot of consultation during the week. This will allow you to be more prepared and less reactive in your sessions if you know things such as: "Have you been successful with the 'watch' cue with other dogs 30 feet away?" "Have there been any situations where you didn't see another dog before your dog did and he became reactive?"

6. Do Not Lose Touch with Yourself as a Fellow Dog Guardian

- Never allow your approach to be blameful or cause additional stress. The client may have indirectly reinforced the behavior she is trying to get rid of, but it will only make her feel worse if you are judgmental. It may cost you a client if you make her uncomfortable.

- By going to the dog park alone, you can remind yourself that not everyone shares your enthusiasm for dog training. It will help you better understand what types of behaviors people tolerate from their dogs.

- Continually humble yourself. By taking classes that are outside your area of expertise, you remind yourself that your approach needs to be in-tune to what the student needs. You also learn a fun new skill while meeting local trainers. I have taken lure-coursing, flyball, agility, and massage classes to keep myself humble as a self-proclaimed "life skills trainer."

- Recognize that you are working through training/behavior issues of your own with your dog(s). If you do not acknowledge your own struggles, you are more prone to hold their drama as your own (Bowen, 1994).

If you are anything like me, you found yourself in this profession because you are infatuated with dogs and committed to helping humans work through the nuances, struggles, and communication gaps that come with living with dogs. Doing frequent evaluations of who you are in your profession, how you relate to your clients, and what skills and values you have will help you to be able to better articulate thoughtful, energetic, and effective responses. It is okay to adore your clients and their dogs as much as you want to help them. Just do not let their problems become yours, or you will be unable to help them in a meaningful way. ❖

References

Bowen, M. *Family Therapy in Clinical Practice*. Northvale: Jason Aronson, 1994.

Fischer, T.F. (n.d.). Retrieved on August 7, 2004 from http://ministryhealth.net/mh_articles/345_self_differ_essential_healthy_church.html.

Kegan, R. *How the Way We Talk Can Change the Way We Work: Seven Languages for Transformation*. San Francisco: Jossey-Bass, 2001.

Pratch, L. & Jacobowitz, J. "Integrative capacity and the evaluation of leadership: A multi-method assessment approach." *J Appl Behav Sci*, 34 (2), pp. 180-201, 1998.

Taking the Bite Out of Liability

Mary L. Zoller, September/October 2005

When you train, shelter, or adopt out a dog, you may not be aware how vulnerable you are to being liable for injury. Dog bites have reached serious proportions in the U.S. and we live in a society that often uses litigation to resolve disputes.

A 1996 survey by the Centers of Disease Control found that almost five million people are bitten annually[1] and of these, 800,000 need medical attention.[2] Most of the victims are children, the majority of whom are bitten in the face.[3] This public health problem appears to be growing. Over a ten year period, the number of dogs rose by two percent, but bites increased by 33 percent. The property and casualty insurance industry paid $250 million in claims for dog bites in 1995 and $345 million in 2002.

Kenneth Phillips, known in the news as "the dog bite king," specializes in representing dog-bite victims and has written the online legal treatise, *Dog Bite Law*. He appears in a seminar on DVD, describing how dog trainers, shelters, and organizations that adopt out dogs can protect themselves. The seminar covers the five most troublesome legal issues for canine professionals: liability for dog bites and negligence, avoiding liability on your premises, avoiding liability after adopting out a dog, the liability of the client to you if his dog bites you, and special rules for animal control agencies and humane societies. It includes legal documents to protect those working in this profession.

Phillips explains, in most states, you are responsible for a dog if you own it and responsible for your own negligence. You are responsible for such things as failing to prevent an accident you could prevent and taking unreasonable actions, like letting your dog run free in violation of local leash laws. Liability can also be based on deceit, concealing a dog's history, and the action of an agent.

Actions you can take to prevent an accident on your business premises include eliminating blind doorways and walkways, keeping dogs and their handlers apart from other dogs and handlers in class, having a leash or crate requirement, and a contract that can limit liability. If your classes involve free play with other dogs, it is an absolute "must" to have a contract that informs the client that a dog can be injured in class, and waives your liability if an accident occurs. This obviously can affect socialization opportunities for classes that involve free play with other dogs.

Trainers can limit their liability by examining what might make them responsible. For example, overly aggressive marketing of services, including calling yourself a "behaviorist" (which is coming to mean being certified to the public), can be problematic because the court expects you to perform as you promised. In addition, trainers need a contract that requires clients to assume the risk for accidents. Phillips has a model contract he suggests trainers use to insure that all the bases are covered. Likewise, he recommends stating your background up front and limiting the scope of services you offer to time, services, and advice, not outcome. This contract can be sent to clients ahead of your first training session and they should be asked to acknowledge its receipt.

Adoption organizations have a duty to protect potential adopters, and he recommends collecting as much information as possible about the people surrendering the dog, and the dog itself, especially the bite history. He believes a standard temperament assessment should be used and the results should be disclosed to potential adopters along with the degree of socialization, health status, and breed or breed mix. Perhaps it should go without saying, but adoption organizations should not adopt out dangerous dogs. Adopters should sign a receipt saying they received the known information on the dog. An adoption agreement should serve to eliminate misunderstandings and make the new owner assume the risks of future problems with the dog. Phillips also suggests, if you live in a state that has strict ownership laws, don't accept ownership of the dog, but transfer it directly to the owner through a "bailment" agreement.

Preventing Dog Bites

Members of APDT can become knowledgeable about what they need to do to take the bite of out liability, but they can also play an important role in reducing the risk of dog bites. This includes recognizing the risk factors and educating clients on how to prevent bites.

The types of situations that may result in aggression and a bite include:

1. Protective or territorial aggression: directed to strangers who approach the owner or the home of the owner.

2. Predatory aggression: directed to small, quick moving animals and children.

3. Pain-elicited aggression: directed to family or strangers who approach or touch when the dog is in pain or injured.

4. Punishment-elicited aggression: directed to family or strangers who hit, kick or verbally assault the dog.

5. Redirected aggression: directed to family, strangers, and animals who approach or touch the dog when it is aggressive in another context.

6. Defensive or fear aggression: usually directed to family members who approach too quickly or too closely when the dog is afraid.

7. Dominance aggression: usually directed to family members who take something from the dog, pet it, hold it, pick it up, or disturb it while it is resting.[4]

Some risk factors to consider include:

1. Male dogs accounted for 70-80% of the attacks studied and 60% were unneutered males.[5]

2. Dogs from pet stores and puppy mills have a high incidence of dominance-type aggression and defensive or fear aggression.[6,7,8]

3. Inadequate socialization prior to the age of 14 weeks results in higher incidence of fear aggression.[9]

4. Poor health can result in aggression.[10,11]

5. Pain and fear can result in aggression.[5,10]

6. Submitting to the first vaccination after the first eight weeks of life can result in greater aggression.[12]

7. Chaining can result in aggression.[13]

Dog professionals can assist clients in preventing dog bites in other ways. They can teach them how to read a dog's body language for the signals of increasing tension that may lead to aggression and demonstrate methods to calm the dog. They can alert them to the types of situations that may serve as a catalyst for aggression so they can avoid them. In addition, they can identify behaviors that may indicate underlying health problems that may be contributing to aggression and suggest the owner go to their vet for a physical evaluation of their dog.

Trainers, shelter workers, and other dog professionals can advise prospective dog owners about how to select a breed or mixed breed suitable for their lifestyle and the importance of going to a reputable breeder, humane society, shelter, or responsible rescue organization to find them. They can also educate them about the importance of having a temperament assessment prior to adopting or purchasing a dog and requesting all the history available.

Canine professionals can teach bite inhibition as a standard part of puppy classes and educate clients about the importance of early and continuing socialization. Trainers can also discuss with clients potential risk factors that might lead to future aggressive behavior.

Finally, APDT members can become informed about the state and local laws governing dangerous dogs; the way their state defines negligence; home and business insurance requirements; and become involved in making needed changes. They can participate in National Dog Bite Prevention week (mid-May) in their local communities, joining the Centers for Disease Control, the American Veterinary Association, and the United States Postal Service in this public education campaign.

For more information on *A Community Approach to Dog Bite Prevention*, visit www.avma.org. To learn more about *Avoiding Liability When You Train, Shelter, or Adopt-Out*, visit www.DogBiteLaw.com. ❖

References
[1] Sacks JJ, Kresnow M, Houston B. "Dog Bites: How Big a Problem?" *Injury Prev.* 2:52-4, 1996.

[2] National Center for Health Statistics National Hospital Ambulatory Medical Care Survey for 1992-94.

[3] Weiss HB, Friedman DI, Coben JH. "Incidence of dog bite injuries treated in emergency room departments." *JAMA*, 279:53, 1998.

[4] Borchelt, PL & Voith, VL (1982). "Classification of Animal Behavior Problems." *Vet Clin North Am Small Anim Pract*, 12:571-585, 1982.

[5] Voith VL & Borchelt P. *Readings in Companion Animal Behavior*. Trenton: Veterinary Learning Systems, pp. 226, 235, 1996.

[6] Serpell J & Jagoe JA. Early *Experience and the Development of Animal Behavior. The Domestic Dog, Its Evolution, Behavior and Interactions with People*. Cambridge University Press, 1995.

[7] Freedman DG, King JA, Elliot O. *Science: Critical Periods in the Social Development of Dogs, Volume 122*, pp. 1016-1017, 1961.

[8] Scott JP & Fuller JL. *Genetics and the Social Behavior of the Dog*. Chicago: University of Chicago Press, 1965.

[9] O'Farrell V. "Effects of Owner Personality and Attitudes on Behavior." *The Domestic Dog, Its Evolution, Behavior and Interactions with People*. Cambridge University Press, 1995.

[10] Overall K. *Clinical Behavioral Medicine in Small Animals*. Mosby Year Book, Inc. p. 2, 1997.

[11] Campbell WE. *Behavior Problems in Dogs*. Goleta, CA: American Veterinary Publications, Inc. pp. 88, 1975.

[12] Serpell J & Jagoe JA. "Early Experience and the Development of Animal Behavior." *The Domestic Dog, Its Evolution, Behavior and Interactions with People*. Cambridge University Press, pp. 97 et seq., 1995.

[13] Sacks J, Satin RW, Bonzo SE. "Dog Bite Related Fatalities from 1979 through 1988." *JAMA*, 262:489-1492, 1989.

The Selection, Care, and Management of a Training Team

Joan B. Guertin, September/October 2005

A training business is only as good as its results in meeting the needs of clients. Often very good trainers who try to do it all will become overwhelmed and less efficient. A logical solution is to develop a sound working team of apprentices and assistants. A great idea, but where does one start? In this article I'll discuss:

- Finding team members
- The apprentice role, responsibilities, and growth
- Outside study
- Maintaining lines of communication and morale

Building a team doesn't happen overnight and unfortunately, likely candidates don't grow on trees. Luckily, however, prospects are as close as your own training classes! Most of my team members have come from this source. They're the people you notice because of their dedication to training and their good instincts in handling their dogs. They also get on well with other class members, and demonstrate a team mentality. They generally will be the calm, quiet handlers whose personality is well suited to my personal training style.

Inquiries from outside of class should be observed as well. I invite them to bring a dog, and go through a paid class like any other student. This is important for both of us. They can see if they are comfortable with the methods used, and I can get a feel for their skills, adaptability, and compatibility. It also lets my working team offer their input, an important factor. Interestingly, team members have often pointed out a likely prospect from among current students.

On a few occasions, I've brought in trainers with experience who came with their own agendas and could not adapt to my goals and philosophies. Needless to say, these uncomfortable relationships were quickly terminated.

The Role of the Apprentice

Each new team member needs to know their duties and responsibilities. I need to know we are on the same page with our goals and philosophy. It is important for them to know that questions, discussion, and idea sharing are all strongly encouraged. We learn from one another's experiences.

For a new apprentice, it's easy to feel overwhelmed. To help prevent this feeling, I team each apprentice with an experienced assistant. The first skill to learn is the important but simple task of taking roll. If necessary, I'll walk them through the process well before class. They also learn enrollment procedures and record-keeping.

These undemanding duties get an assistant off to a non-pressured start. It also aids them in getting to know the names of dogs and owners. Once class is underway, their job is to observe the class and get a feel for what is happening. Previously they have been in class and concentrating on a dog; now their job is to focus on what I do as an instructor. Certainly a different viewpoint!

I never rush an apprentice. They need time to get comfortable with the entire atmosphere of the class from this side of the learning process. When I see the individual starting to take initiative, and handling the registration and roll-taking comfortably, I will move them to assisting an individual student who is dealing with simple problems. I will be watching for a comfort level that indicates a person is able to step in and take charge. That's when they will start actively assisting me. I don't ask anyone to teach a class until I'm sure they are ready. I might ask a newer helper to teach just one simple exercise until I see that the comfort level and the expertise is there.

In any field, apprentices move along at different rates. Some will be natural teachers and are ready to assist me in a few months, while others may take a year or more. As an apprentice progresses, it is easy to determine individual strengths. One fond memory is of an assistant with strong instincts and skills, but low confidence. Often I would back up and find myself stepping on her. When I asked why she stood so close to me, she observed that it was the best vantage point to be able to "see what I was seeing" when I addressed the class.

This same apprentice would often sidle up close and whisper in my ear regarding something that she was seeing relative to a student. She was catching the actions of the students, she just didn't have the confidence to address them herself. My comment became, "you're right, go help her." And, she did. She soon became a very effective instructor in her own right.

More recently, a treasured assistant in my Missouri classes grew from a very shy, inhibited young woman into one of the most effective puppy trainers I had ever worked with. Brandi admitted to me that she was very uncomfortable with the children that I encourage in class. However, not too long before I moved from Missouri, Brandi conducted a wonderful class in which she effectively engaged the children in one family in working with their puppy during a desensitization exercise. She worked so calmly with the youngsters that I couldn't help feeling a deep sense of pride. Afterwards she admitted that she had even surprised herself!

When I spot someone with a strong one-on-one rapport with both dog and handler, I'll invite her to join me on house calls. This is a great training ground and often the best confidence builder for an apprentice. Once I assign house calls, I will go along on several to observe the actual teaching interaction. It's a method that has worked well for me over the years.

The individual who appears comfortable in the class atmosphere will be asked to teach individual elements of a lesson so that I can observe their teaching skills. After class we will discuss their experience and the results. No one teaches a complete class until my gut feeling tells me they are ready. The ultimate goal is to develop the skills that allow every apprentice to be able to teach. Then I can think about days off for a dog show, or maybe even take a vacation!

Outside Study

Educating new team members is easier than ever. There's a wealth of material available. I inquire as to what the apprentice has read or viewed. We discuss the merits of the material and then expand on the list. I recommend that they read the controversial books as well as the more popular ones; this is helpful for explaining why methodology has changed and the power of gentle, positive, motivational training. Discussion of what is being read or viewed is often part of team meetings so that there is valuable input from other members of the training team. APDT conference tapes are invaluable here!

I encourage apprentices to become involved in volunteering at shelters. Working with dogs with "baggage" is one of the best training grounds for anyone wanting to seriously train. Balancing the "book learning" with development of "hands on skills" is vital in developing well-rounded trainers.

I also recommend attending workshops and seminars. When developing the Northern California team in the late 1980's, there was a wealth of opportunities and we were privileged to be able to work with Ian Dunbar and observe Karen Pryor and Gary Wilkes in action as they introduced their clicker workshops. My team was thrilled to have been able to attend the last workshop that John Fisher presented in the U.S. Living in the Midwest and Texas, these opportunities are fewer and farther between. Many trainers have to fly half way across the U.S. to find educational opportunities other than those offered at the APDT annual conference. Of course, membership in APDT and attending the annual conference is strongly encouraged.

Keeping Lines of Communication Open and Morale High

Regular meetings are vital to a smoothly functioning team. Not every meeting needs to be a production. Our short Saturday meetings, when most of the assistants and apprentices work, allowed us to assess the accomplishments or problems of the day. Often I would introduce subjects such as safety procedures, i.e. how to handle loose dogs should a situation arise.

If longer meetings were required or the entire team needed to meet, they were scheduled away from the training grounds when all could attend. These were the meetings where grievances could be worked through. It also allowed for discussion of the business direction. The team felt comfortable making suggestions relative to changes that could, and maybe should, be implemented. I always took all suggestions under advisement.

At least twice a year we scheduled a social gathering, which included their families. These proved to be great morale boosters.

Summary

The key to maintaining a cohesive working unit lies in making certain communication lines kept open. My job was to make sure they were taught what to do and how to do it. It was also my job to allow each apprentice to grow and realize their greatest potential. Not to produce clones, but well-rounded individuals with strong training skills, a large bag of tricks, and the skill to network. Trainers who could stand alone in their own right. For some, the difficult part will be to keep your ego out of it. Be their mentor, their guide, their resource. Then let them fly! ❖

How to Form a Regional Trainers Group

Susan Smith, March/April 2005

There are several reasons for regional trainers groups, but the two most obvious are education and networking. As we all know, you can't have two dog trainers in the same room and not learn something! Dog trainers are passionate about their work and determined to share and learn. Because most dog trainers work alone, it can be a very lonely business. Regional groups give like-minded people a chance to get together, talk, vent, and learn. No one understands the problems a dog trainer has better than another dog trainer! Additionally, regional groups give the members an opportunity to let each other know what they are doing in their business, which creates an excellent referral network. There are no "rules" for regional groups, however some groups are very successful and we have polled them to see what their secrets for success are.

Why Start or Belong to a Regional Trainers Group?

As stated above, education and networking are two of the main reasons for regional groups. One of the groups polled has a yearly questionnaire the membership fills out so other members know to whom to refer clients. All the successful groups have an educational focus for each meeting. For trainers who have their Certified Pet Dog Trainer (CPDT) designation, regional groups can also offer continuing education units (CEUs). Since each group will work differently, it will be up to the group to apply for CEUs; however, APDT has contacted the CCPDT about CEUs for regional groups and together we have come up with guidelines to help you (see "Guidelines" at the end of the article.)

Another reason for having regional groups is the opportunity to do community service. There are many ways in which regional groups can participate in community activities to help further education amongst the public. Some groups choose a particular group or activity which they focus on; other groups man booths, promote CGC testing, hold classes for local shelters, etc.

Finally, regional groups can help new trainers get off on the right foot. This can take the form of formal education through the group's educational program, the ability to have trainers answer their questions at the meetings, as well as having experienced trainers available that a new trainer feels comfortable calling for help.

How Large Should a Regional Trainers Group Be?

A regional trainers group is comprised of trainers living and working in a specific area. Some groups encompass quite a large area, while others cover a much smaller territory. Generally, the extent of the area that the group will serve will have to do with the number of available trainers in an area. For instance, if you are located in an area that has very few trainers, such as the Catskill Mountains of New York, the actual area your group serves might be quite large. On the other hand, if you are located in a large urban area such as New York City, your area will probably be smaller and only encompass the city, or even a borough within the city, because there are many more trainers within that small area. It is up to each individual group to decide how large they want to be and how large a territory they wish to cover.

How Does One Start a Regional Group?

Most of the groups polled started with a small, core group of members and gradually expanded. This seems to be the most successful way of starting a group—starting small keeps it from becoming overwhelming. If you can find someone to help you get the group started, that will take a lot of the pressure off you—you can divide the responsibilities and have someone to bounce ideas off.

Some of the things to consider before actually starting a group are:

- Where will you meet?

- How often will you meet?

- When and at what time will you meet?

- What will your meetings look like? (i.e., social time, meal, group business, educational program, etc.)

- Will there be food?

- If there is food, how will it be provided?

- Will there be dues?

- Will there be a formal agenda?

- Will there be officers, minutes, elections, etc.?

- Who will be allowed in the group?

    a. APDT members only or all local trainers?

    b. Trainers only or all dog professionals?

    c. Positive trainers only or all methodologies?

- How will you add new members to the group?

- How will you communicate with members?

- Will you allow members to bring guests?

- Will you apply for CEUs?

- If applying for CEUs, will you apply as a group or will each individual within the group apply for their own?

Once you've answered the above questions, you can get started! Remember that most of the successful groups started small—probably between seven to twelve people at the initial meeting. The groups that tried to do too much all at once are the ones that never got off the ground. It may help to have a vision of what the group will be before having the first meeting and then communicate this vision to the core members. The first meeting is a good time to discuss the vision, changing it as necessary. You can then have a vision statement which will help to bring the group back into focus when it begins to wander—which it will probably do at some point! The Carolina Trainer's Forum has a motto that they put at the top of their agenda and cite at the beginning of each meeting.

Once you've got your vision statement and the structure of the group established, you can begin inviting more members. You may want to limit the number of new members so that they come into the group slowly and do not disrupt or fracture the core structure.

What Makes a Successful Regional Trainers Group?

The Member Relations and Communications Committee polled the existing regional groups to see how they started, what their structure is, what types of activities they are involved in, and what they see as their keys to success. Following are the findings from that poll:

- **Where will you meet?** All of the groups we polled met at a neutral location—either at a restaurant, a local shelter, or local training club. The groups all felt that meeting at a neutral location was important—one group actually felt that changing the meeting place from members' homes to a restaurant was the turning point that kept their group alive and successful. One group rotated meeting at members' homes, but this group has since dissolved.

- **How often will you meet?** Most of the groups meet monthly. The Carolina Trainer's Forum meets quarterly, but they encompass a large territory (both North and South Carolina), so they meet less often for a longer period of time. As discussed above, the distance members have to travel will influence the frequency of your meetings.

- **When and at what time will you meet?** The day, time, and length of the meetings varied. The groups all attempt to accommodate their members and have various ways of doing this. One group meets on a quarterly basis and meets mid-morning through mid-afternoon on Sunday. Another meets monthly and has nine lunch meetings and three dinner meetings each year; they feel that most members should be able to make a traditional noon to one o'clock lunch meeting and the three dinner meetings accommodate those who cannot make a lunch meeting. The groups that meet monthly all designate a day they will meet such as the second Friday of the month, first Tuesday, etc., believing that this helps people with scheduling.

- **Will there be food?** If there is food, will it be provided or will members purchase their own? All the groups have food at their meeting. Some groups have a potluck system, while others meet at a restaurant and order off the menu. The group that has since dissolved had someone pick up food (sandwiches, pizza, etc.), the host provided drinks and each member contributed five dollars to pay for the food. Where your group meets will probably determine how the food is arranged. The general consensus is that food is essential for a successful group!

- **Will there be dues?** Only one group collects dues; the rest are not that formal, although they may collect or earn money for special projects.

- **Will there be a formal agenda?** Most of the groups have an agenda that they follow. The agenda is usually sent with the e-mail notice of the meeting. Some groups have a member(s) that is in charge of creating the agenda; other groups ask for ideas at the end of the current meeting.

- **What will your meetings look like?** (i.e., social time, meal, group business, educational program, etc.) Each group structure varies, however they all seem to have a short social period while members arrive, then a meal. Some groups discuss their agenda issues while eating, others carry the social time over through the meal and discuss their agenda items after the meal.

- **Will there be officers, minutes, elections, etc.?** None of the groups have a formal organization with by-laws, officers, etc. One group does collect dues and sends out minutes. All the groups feel that informality is necessary for a successful group. One group has a "red paw" which is used for more active discussions and only the person holding the red paw can speak; however, this is not used all the time—only when things get lively! Most of the groups do not have a formal structure, but feel that having an open, non-judgmental structure helps. All the groups require their members to be civil and polite to each other.

- **Who will be allowed in the group?** This is an important issue and should probably be decided prior to starting the group. Only one group polled limits its membership to APDT members. Some groups invite only positive trainers, whereas other groups invite everyone. The groups that are open to all trainers find that, through attrition, the group is generally comprised of positive trainers. Most groups allowed non-trainers (pet sitters, groomers, etc.) who are in the dog business to join their groups.

- **Will you allow members to bring guests?** Most groups do allow guests at their meetings. Guests are potential new members and being invited to the meeting allows them to get a feel for the group as well as allowing the group to get a feel for the guest.

- **How will you add new members to the group?** Most of the groups allow members to bring guests who may then be invited to join.

- **Will you apply for CEUs?** The ability to receive CEUs for regional group meetings will be an incentive for many trainers to attend meetings. Additionally, the ability to receive CEUs will be very beneficial for those trainers who have a difficult time attending seminars. This will help them maintain their continuing education without having to leave town or spend a great deal of money.

- **If applying for CEUs, will you apply as a group or will each individual within the group apply for their own?** For more information on applying for CEUs, see the guidelines provided in the sidebar below. We would recommend that the group apply for CEUs rather than requiring each individual to do so. Once you've done it a couple of times, you will know what is required and it should be a very smooth process. If each individual has to apply for their own CEUs, the benefit of attending regional group meetings will be greatly diluted.

What type of activities do regional groups have?

Many of the groups participate in community activities. Some of the activities include manning "ask the trainer" booths at local events, CPDT study groups, Rally-O show & gos, and CGC testing for breed clubs. One group is working on training classes for the local humane society; the trainers will be paid and this will be a wonderful opportunity for some of their newer trainers to get experience and new clients.

Within the group meetings there are a variety of fun activities. Depending on where you are located, you might consider field trips—one group went to Sea World for a behind the scenes session with the mammal trainers. Some groups invite speakers and all groups have reports on seminars their members have attended. One group has a regular training challenge; the challenge is presented at the end of the meeting, all members submit their replies in writing, then the topic is discussed at the next meeting. Another has a book of the month that they read and discuss. The Carolina Trainer's Forum plays a variety of games and Barbara Long, Game Master, has been kind enough to share some of them with us:

1. Run through a Rally-O course.

2. Play favorite training games that we use in our group classes such as the "grocery store dash"—this can be helpful because sometimes someone describes a game, but it's hard to visualize how it would work in a class.

3. "Ring, Ring." Take turns answering the phone from "prospective students" and answer their questions. Everyone handles phone calls differently. Some people will do a lot on the phone and others try to keep conversations short and sweet. It is interesting to hear how trainers deal with those "difficult" clients and we have a lot of laughs when we recognize certain types of students. It is also supportive to hear other trainers' frustrations with the more challenging cases.

4. Observe a UKC obedience trial. Each member picks a dog and handler to observe. Watch for calming signals from the dog and how (or even if) the handler deals with them. It is excellent observation training and interesting to hear other trainers' descriptions of behavior and what they noticed.

5. Kids' games. Bop It Extreme is a kid's toy with sounds and shapes. You start it up and as it makes certain sounds you press, pull, and twist the shape that goes with the sounds. It's great for working on your timing.

6. Tanagrams. One person, who knows what the shape is supposed to be, instructs another to lay out the tanagrams in the pattern. You can play it many ways. You can have the instructor talk, but not touch the pieces, give or not give feedback, and have the player talk or not talk. Have people mark down how much reinforcement the player gets from the instructor. It is a great way for us to evaluate teaching styles.

7. Rush Hour is a game with little cars and trucks. You have to move the cars around to get a specific car out of the traffic jam. It's a great game for problem solving skills.

How can I help other regional groups?

If you have a good idea to share with other regional groups, please e-mail the Member Relations and Communications Chair at mrc@apdt.com and we'll include your idea in our information that may go to other groups. Additionally, if you are willing to help a new group get started, please e-mail mrc@apdt.com and we'll list you as a contact on the Web site.

Guidelines to Help Regional Groups Apply for CPDT Continuing Education Units (CEUs)

There are two ways regional groups can apply for CEUs. All methods require the member be present at the meeting and participate in the educational program presented at the meeting. If a regional group applies for CEUs, the group will be required to keep an attendance roll of their meetings, as well as a written outline or syllabus of the educational component of the meeting, which the CCPDT can request at any time.

- **Method #1—Regional Group Applies for Upcoming Meeting:** The regional group designs the educational component of each meeting and submits it to the CCPDT for approval. Please remember that the CCPDT needs up to eight weeks to approve a submission. Groups can plan their meetings as much as a year in advance. Once the meeting has been approved for CEUs, CEU forms can be handed out to members who attended the meeting.

- **Method #2—Regional Group Applies for Completed Meeting:** The regional group recaps the educational component of each meeting after the meeting has been held and submits it to the CCPDT for approval. Once the meeting has been approved for CEUs, the forms can either be mailed by the regional group to the members who attended the meeting, or handed out at the next meeting.

Please be aware that there is always the possibility that CEUs will not be approved for a particular program—group leadership should be certain that its membership understands that all meetings may not qualify for CEUs. For this reason, it is highly recommended that you apply in advance for your CEUs; this way, everyone will know which meetings qualify and which do not.

Groups that apply in advance for CEUs can announce the upcoming meeting on the CCPDT Web site. For more information on the CEU application procedure, please go to the CCPDT Web site at www.ccpdt.org. ❖

Designing a Handout
Sarah Filipiak, January/February 2006

Handouts are a wonderful way to get key points across to your clients. However, creating attractive, professional-looking handouts that your clients will actually read can be a challenge. The following tips will help keep your design-induced stress to a minimum while enhancing the look of your business.

Write It Down

Before you begin designing your handout, write or type the information you would like to include. This will help you narrow your topic and give you a chance to edit the text before it is on the page. Have fun while writing and use humor where you can. My handouts are written in a conversational style. If you enjoy writing the handout, your clients will likely enjoy reading it.

Keep It Short

I find one-page handouts are more useful to my clients than two or three pages, especially if they contain concise information packaged in a useful way (bullets, charts, check lists, etc.). A shorter handout can be tacked to the refrigerator door for easy reference. If you want to provide your clients with additional information, consider posting it on your Web site or announcing in class that the information is available upon request. (This also saves money and paper.)

Keep It Simple

My computer's word processing and design programs are equipped with lots of fun typefaces. Each time I design a handout, I must resist the temptation to try them all. Depending on the program you are using, you may have access to only a few different fonts, or hundreds. Fewer is better, if for no other reason than you will have fewer decisions to wrestle with.

Try to avoid using fancy display fonts, such as ornate script or letters shaped like objects. The finished product will be difficult to read and, chances are, unattractive. Those fonts should be left for marketing gurus to create signs and billboards (and even then used sparingly).

Sans What?

The most important decision regarding fonts will be whether to use a serif font or a sans serif font. A serif is a small line added to the main strokes of a letter, as at the top and bottom of the letter N. A sans serif font does not include these finishing lines, giving the letter a "straight" look.

Here are examples of each:

Serif: Now is the time for all good men to come to the aid of their country.

Sans Serif: Now is the time for all good men to come to the aid of their country.

Assuming you are designing your handout for print use—versus on a Web site—a good rule of thumb is to use a sans serif font (such as Helvetica or Franklin Gothic) for titles and headers, and a serif font (such as Times or Garamond) for the body text.

All in the Family

In most computer programs, fonts are arranged by family. For example, my computer's Times font is available in regular, bold, italic, and bold italic. Each font family is different, and some fonts have variations that look nothing like the original. Sticking within a font family for each type of text you choose is a good idea. The results will look cleaner and more professional.

When I have a series of handouts on the same topic, I use the same font styles and formatting for each handout in the series.

Size Matters

Don't be afraid to use a large font size for titles or headers, provided you skip other embellishments such as italics, bold, or underline. Put space between your headers and text—some word processing programs have automatic formatting you can use.

Body text should be between nine and twelve points in size. Keep paragraphs to four sentences or less. If possible, format paragraphs in block style.

Graphics Are Important

A page of solid, gray text is uninteresting to most readers, and the availability of clip art makes graphics easy to use. If you use a photograph, make sure that the image won't be too dark when reproduced.

Dogs are an obvious choice, especially if you have clear photographs that can illustrate a topic. But characters, symbols, expressions, and dog-related objects can also make a page interesting. Choose art that is relevant to the topic or works well with the layout of your handout.

Give the art you use plenty of room to "breathe"—wrapped text shouldn't be too close to the graphic. In addition, one or two graphics per page is enough; more will give your handout a cluttered look.

Presentation

When using handouts in class, present them during a time when the students can pay attention. I like to give handouts out in the middle of class, following a break, rather than at the beginning or end of class. I find students are busy trying to calm their excited dogs at the beginning of class and thinking about what they need to do at home at the end of class.

Go over the handout with your class briefly, if only to cover key points. The more importance you place on your handout, the more the client will place on it. If the handout didn't include valuable information, you wouldn't be giving it to them. And besides, you spent valuable time designing it! ❖

Marketing Your Rally Classes

Laurie Williams, March/April 2007

A key to bringing successful APDT Rally trials to your area is garnering enough interest in the sport. Therefore the first step is to offer Rally classes that teach APDT Rally exercises. Here is a list of dog people to consider targeting as your participants:

1. **Novice Handlers**. There's nothing like that fresh, wide-eyed, and enthusiastic attitude of a handler who has been bitten by the "bug." This is the handler who perhaps has taken the beginning, intermediate, and advanced pet or family dog obedience classes, has obtained a Canine Good Citizen certificate, and is still looking for more. They've developed a beautiful relationship with their dog and are working nicely, happily, and positively as a team. There was a time when traditional obedience was the only game in town, but those days are long gone. There are presently so many options out there for a team like this. Why should they choose Rally and APDT Rally in particular? Arguably, Rally is one of the most dog and handler friendly of all the current dog sports. Why? First and foremost, handlers are not restricted from praising and communicating with their dogs. In fact, in APDT Rally, praise and communication is not only expected, but encouraged. I feel one of the biggest roadblocks for dogs and handlers entering traditional AKC and UKC novice obedience competitions, particularly those who have used positive, dog friendly methods, are the limitations placed on dog/handler communication and praise. They've trained one way, but have to eliminate most of their methods in order to receive a qualifying score. APDT Rally is one of the few dog sports in which you compete the same way you train—talking to your dog, praising your dog, and reinforcing your dog with food. A handler does not have to become an "alien" in the ring to his or her dog, which provides for a much smoother and natural transition from student to competitor. A Rally course is a great exercise to include with any intermediate or advanced pet or family dog training class. At our facility, we often include a short course of the most basic seven to ten exercises in our Canine Good Citizen classes.

2. **Traditional Obedience Handlers**. Rally is the perfect remedy for a "ring-wise" dog. A dog is considered ring-wise when he appears to already know what is going to happen when he enters the obedience ring, and subsequently starts behaving badly. A dog is only going to behave badly when he associates the ring with bad or unpleasant things. There's no better way to turn a ring experience around than APDT Rally. As stated above, you don't have to become a different person in the Rally ring. You can say and do most of the same things you say and do during your training. Secondly, there is a rule in traditional obedience that prohibits "training in the ring." In between exercises a handler may not do anything that could be construed as training. Essentially that means you cannot ask the dog to

repeat an exercise that has not been performed correctly because this would be training. Not allowing handlers to use corrections, verbal or physical, is a good thing, but even for those who train with positive methods, leaving the ring disappointed and unable to allow the dog to get it right, especially when you know he or she can, is disheartening. In most instances, APDT Rally allows a team to repeat most exercises that have not been performed correctly, giving you and your dog an opportunity to exit feeling good about your performance. There are a few exceptions, such as exercises that receive an immediate NQ if an error is performed (i.e. jump refusals, broken stays, splitting a cone, etc.), but by and large, a team gets the chance to have a more pleasant and positive overall experience with the ring and this could even improve traditional obedience scores.

3. **AKC Rally Competitors**. There is still a huge misconception among AKC Rally competitors that APDT Rally is easier because you can use treats. Therefore the best way to present a Rally class is to keep it non-denominational, or generic, in the beginning. Present both the AKC and APDT exercises simultaneously explaining the differences as you go. Set up both AKC and APDT courses and let your students run through. Many handlers who have attended the class with the intention of competing in AKC trials will often be wooed by the challenge and diversity of the APDT exercises. A surefire way to squelch the misconceptions is to show an AKC Rally competitor any Level 3 exercise!

4. **Agility Handlers and Enthusiasts**. The transition from agility to Rally probably makes the most sense out of all the dog sports. You have handlers who are already experienced with following and directing their dog around a course. And another perk to having agility handlers in your class is they don't mind helping set up courses! It's much easier to get volunteers to help you set up signs and holders that weigh barely more than a piece of paper than it is to get people to help you move A-Frames and teeters!

5. **Canine Musical Freestyle Handlers**. When watching a team following a Rally course I've often thought it looked rhythmic. In fact, if you added music to a Rally run it would almost appear "dance-like." I recently had the opportunity to take my first freestyle class and was pleasantly surprised to see Rally exercises in freestyle (or vice versa), so it all made perfect sense! The two venues use many of the same exercises, often with different names. In freestyle, what is referred to as a "Schutzhund turn" is called a Left About Turn in APDT Rally. Laterals are Moving Side Steps Right. In Freestyle there are 360° and 270° turns, serpentines and spirals. The main difference is the set up and environment in which the movements are performed, but a freestyle-trained dog can become a Rally-trained dog with ease.

As the APDT Rally logo states it really is Rally for all dogs, so use this in your marketing. Truly target all dogs, specifically those dogs (and handlers) often forgotten or excluded from other dog sports and venues. These include:

- **Mixed Breed Handlers**. APDT Rally is one of the true celebrations of the "All-American" dog. A handler with a mixed breed dog can feel at home at an APDT Rally trial because they're not treated like an after-thought, add-on, or reluctant step-child. In fact, I've seen large contingencies of mixed breed dogs at APDT Rally trials in my area, and the number is growing. It would be great to one day see an equal number of All-Americans as purebreds competing!

- **Retired Dog/Handler Teams**. Today our dogs are mostly companions, but we can't forget that dogs were originally bred to work. Senior dogs are often put out to pasture much too soon. Mind you, I write this as my eight-year-old Dalmatian, descendant of coach dogs who were required to accompany horse drawn carriages on 30+ mile stretches, is contently curled up on the sofa in our living room as if it would take a crane to pry him off. But boy you should see him when he walks into the Rally ring! He literally lights up and no one would know he was a day over two. There's nothing like APDT Rally to bring out the spark and adolescence in a senior dog.

- **Physically Challenged Dogs and Handlers**. Dogs and/or handlers with physical challenges are encouraged to participate in APDT Rally, provided the dog is not, and does not appear to be, in pain. I have seen blind dogs, deaf dogs, and dogs missing limbs compete, and compete well, in APDT Rally trials. I have seen wheelchair bound handlers and handlers with canes and walkers maneuvering successfully around a course. These dogs and handlers are not pitied, but are given the respect and admiration they deserve. If necessary, exercise modifications must be approximate to the original exercise, to the best of the dog or handler's ability, and must be approved by the judge in advance.

- **Junior Handlers**. APDT Rally is G-Rated—great for everyone in the family! The Junior Division program is specifically for children ages 8 to 18 who compete on the regular Rally course and Pre-Juniors are children under eight who, accompanied by an adult, compete on shorter, non-regular courses. When I was a child there was an active 4-H club in my community. I was able to participate in many dog activities with them. Unfortunately that is hard to come by these days, so offering an APDT Rally class just for kids could fill this void. In a class specifically for children you can modify the class, allow for their shorter attention spans, and cater to their specific needs.

Market your classes to these groups of people and your classes will not only be full, but you should have continual waiting lists of eager students and happy dogs. ❖

Clients and Community

Dog trainers are members of many different communities—colleagues, dog lovers and owners, and our neighbors in our own locales. This section focuses on these relationships and how we navigate our way through them. Several articles present ideas on how to develop better communication and teaching skills with our human clients, including families with children and learning disabilities. You will read an intriguing examination of our use of terminology when discussing temperament testing with our colleagues, and a discussion of the dog trainer's responsibility to provide accurate information to the community at large on breed specific issues. Rounding out this section is a presentation of the criteria for service dogs and using play to teach owners how to better train and develop their relationships with their own dogs.

A Little Piece of Your Heart

Pat Miller, March/April 2005

One of the most rewarding ways a trainer can give back to his or her community is by volunteering at an animal shelter. It's a win-win situation—dogs benefit immensely from your involvement; the shelter capitalizes on your programs in the public relations and donation/grant arenas; adopters select from a pool of dogs who have been pre-screened for behavior and perhaps learned some basic good manners; the pet-owning public has access to more accurate and effective dog training and behavior information; and it's a great way to increase your name-recognition and market your training/behavior consulting business.

You might think your local shelter would welcome your offer of volunteer assistance with gratitude and open arms. You might be wrong. While some shelter administrators recognize the immense value of working with local trainers, many will shy away from your proposal to volunteer your time and expertise to help shelter dogs, often because they've been burned in relationships with volunteers before. Don't take this personally, if you want to get your paw in the door.

A shelter is a unique culture. Most consist largely of people who care for and about animals, whose actions are often misunderstood and criticized. Shelter personnel quickly learn to insulate themselves from the good intentions of volunteers—it can be more trouble than it's worth to risk the attentions of an outsider who doesn't really understand how shelters work.

When you offer to volunteer, you may find enlightened staff who understand and appreciate all your value. Or you may not. Either way, be prepared to be humble. As much as you know about dog behavior and training, you probably don't know much about shelters, unless you've actually worked in one. If you come in like gangbusters, ready to tell staff all the things they're doing wrong, you'll get a cold reception. If you come in with an open mind, and resist the urge to share what you know, you can gain the trust and respect of staff. Then you'll be in a position to share your knowledge and make a difference to shelter dogs and their future forever homes.

Be prepared to undergo a thorough orientation, observing staff at work in each department of the shelter. If there's no formal program that provides for such training, ask for the opportunity to watch customer service staff at work. Clean kennels alongside animal care workers. Ride along in the field with animal services officers. And yes, spend some time observing euthanasia, so you understand in your heart, not just your head, what happens to the animals who aren't adopted, and to the animal care worker who loses a little piece of her heart each time she says good-bye to another who didn't find a home.

During my 20 years at the Marin Humane Society in Novato, California (ten of those as director of operations), we welcomed volunteers in our Training and Behavior Department, under Department Director Trish King. While an increasing number of shelters recognize the value of incorporating formal training and behavior services as in-house programs, many don't have the resources—or the vision—to do so. Whether the shelters in your area have their own programs or not, there are so many ways your skills as an educated dog training professional can help the shelter, you'll need to be selective, or you won't have any time left for your own business! Following are several examples.

Behavioral Assessments

Volunteer to help and/or train shelter staff to do assessments. The Humane Society of Washington County (MD), where I now volunteer, requires at least one staff person to participate in assessments, so staff has some ownership of assessment decisions. At least two people must be present for assessments, this leaving at least one opening for a volunteer. I assist once a week, and my apprentices are required to do at least 20 hours of shelter behavior assessments.

Group Classes

Write a proposal to teach classes at your shelter. In California, I held classes at the SPCA of Monterey County and the Santa Cruz SPCA. Neither shelter had in-house training programs at the time. Both were pleased to offer my services to their adopters as well as other dog owners. I paid a fee for using the facilities, so the shelters received some revenue. I also gave (and continue to give) a discount for dogs adopted from the shelter.

Training

Help train shelter dogs. At MHS, Trish King and I developed the Good Manners Program, designed to prevent shelter dogs' behaviors from deteriorating during their stay. The program included color coding, which identified "easy" dogs (green means "go!"); moderately challenging ones (yellow means "caution") and difficult dogs (blue, as in "Code Blue!"). Volunteers were also coded—green volunteers could walk green dogs, yellows could walk green and yellow dogs, and blue volunteers could walk all dogs. This ensured that dogs were walked by handlers capable of responding appropriately to reinforce desirable behaviors and discourage undesirable ones. We offered weekly "Good Manners Classes," for which staff and volunteers were invited to select a dog available for adoption to bring to class. This gave volunteers the opportunity to improve their training skills and eventually move up the color scale. It also taught the dogs good manners, increasing the likelihood of success in their new homes. If such an ambitious program is beyond the scope of your shelter or your time constraints, simply walking shelter dogs and teaching them to offer sits as a default behavior can help them get—and stay—adopted.

Behavior

You may prefer not to get involved with a shelter's programs in-house on a regular basis. Time demands, internal politics, and emotional conflicts can make shelter work exceedingly draining. Consider these alternatives: Help staff a behavior hotline. You can return calls from the comfort of your own home (or office) on a flexible schedule. Or offer to be on call to come in and help with particularly challenging assessments or placements. You may be the outside voice of reason when a parent won't listen to shelter staff about the inadvisability of adopting a mouthy, high-energy pup as a companion for her two-year-old toddler.

Events

Events offer you a great opportunity to benefit the shelter, help dogs, and market your business all at the same time. Arrange to staff an "Ask the Trainer" booth at shelter events. Have plenty of business cards, class schedules, and educational handouts available at your booth! Help organize dog games at these events. Musical Sits, Bobbing for Hotdogs, and "My Dog Can Do That" mini-tournaments are sure winners, and give you a chance to showcase your charismatic trainer personality.

There are countless options for volunteering at or with your shelter. You can serve on administrative boards for dangerous dog hearings. Get involved with efforts to rewrite your local animal control ordinances so they are more dog-friendly. Serve on your shelter's Board of Directors. Ask the shelter's executive director for other ways your talents might be of benefit to shelter animals.

Through it all, if you can remember to avoid being an assertive (pushy!) dog trainer, you'll gain an incredible education while providing great benefits to the dogs and dog lovers of your community. But be careful—you might just lose a piece of your heart in the process. ❖

Working with Adults as Learners

Rob Denton and C.J. Bentley, July/August 2005

As children we are lucky. We get to be scientists, mathematicians, musicians, and athletes. We can be anything we want to be. Our primary job is that of "learner." In contrast, it has been said that becoming an adult is a series of giving things up. Eventually, we discover that we are not really scientists, mathematicians, musicians, and athletes. We settle with the knowledge we've gathered and apply that knowledge to a profession.

When it comes to teaching adults, many of us look back to when our primary role was that of learner—when we were children—for clues on how to teach successfully. In many ways we teach the way we were taught. After all, it worked, didn't it? The problem is that adults and children do not necessarily learn in the same ways. Our goal should be to find the most effective way to work with adults in our classes. We must first look at the differences between children and adults when it comes to learning.

When we teach adults, we are working with people with more life experience than children. Adults use that experience as a filter and decide what information they will use and what they will discard. For adults, learning is like a home improvement project. They are looking for the right tool to add to their tool box to accomplish the project. As obedience instructors and behavior consultants, we often see this proven in our customers who have been dog owners before. In some cases prior experience can act as either a motivator or an inhibitor for learning a new skill. What can add to our frustration in attempting to instruct adults is that the same client can have a very different reaction from one skill to another. In many ways the new dog owner is more open to ideas and suggestions than an experienced dog owner.

The good news is that one of the primary motivating factors in adults as learners is change. Marriage, children, divorce, a new home and yes...a new puppy or dog definitely rate as life changes and can be powerful tools in learning.

Key Ideas for Improving Adult Learning

Adults need to know the "why." As a child we all asked our parents why we had to do something and were told, "Because I said so." This approach does not work with adults. We need to be clear on why we are teaching a particular item and what the future use will be. If adults do not see a reason for learning something, they will discard it.

Four key factors for improvement. We all want to see our clients and their dogs succeed. There are four key factors that must be present for this to occur: skill, self-confidence, opportunity to perform, and a supportive environment. Skill is the simplest—they must know how to complete the task and why it is important. Self-confidence is harder, although increased skill will help to build self confidence, as will a supportive environment and the opportunity to perform the new skill successfully. Obviously, all four of these factors are closely related and once they are all in place, you have formed a new skill set that will stay with the client. As we look at self-confidence and supportive environments, it becomes clear what an emotionally risky event learning can be. Take that emotional risk and add a new dog or puppy to the mix (who many owners may see as an extension of themselves) and the potential exists for some fairly large barriers to learning. Keep your clients "in the game" by allowing them to learn in a safe environment where they are able to feel comfortable with the learning process and are rewarded for making improvements—no matter how small.

Beating the Imposter Syndrome. Another challenge that can come with educating adults is your students' feelings that they are not worthy of even being in class, that everyone knows more than they do, and at any moment they will be found out as a kind of fraud. This feeling, known as the "Imposter Syndrome," can rear its ugly head on many levels—in fact, most of us have probably felt this feeling in either personal or professional situations that are new to us. The best way to get past this is to concentrate on providing your clients with many opportunities for success in class. If their dog struggles with an exercise, modify it slightly for them so that their practice is successful. Positive experiences and success are the best cures for the Imposter Syndrome. It can also be beneficial to share the feelings you had when training your own dog. This can help people realize they are not alone with what they're feeling.

Praise, Correct, Praise. One of the simplest things you can do to create a supportive environment in your class it to use "Praise Correct Praise" (PCP). Praise the client for what they are doing correctly, correct them where needed, then have them practice the corrected skill and praise them for the improvement. For example, "Your sit-stay looks really good, now we want to say the word 'sit' just once." Have the client work on getting the pup to sit while only saying the command once and when they're successful, "Great job! That was perfect!" It is the simplest way to create and reinforce the type of supportive environment that can lead to better adult learning.

Understanding that adults' motivation and reasons for learning are different than those of children can help to make the transfer of knowledge much more successful for our clients.

Learning in Children	Learning in Adults
Children are dependent, counting on parents, teachers, and other adults for emotional, psychological, and financial support. They are directed by adults in life.	Adults are self-directed in life and rely on themselves for financial support and setting their own priorities. Adults connect with others for emotional and psychological support, but are primarily self directed.

Learning in Children	Learning in Adults
A child's primary roll in life is that of a learner. They are writers, scientists, and authors. Their role is to learn for later use in life.	Adults see their role as using the learning they accumulated earlier in life to achieve goals as adults. Adults are action and results driven.
Most often children learn what they are told to learn from adults.	Adults treat learning as filling a need—there must be a reason to learn.
Children view formal learning as important because adults say it is.	Adults have very different ideas of what is important to learn based on what they see as a need. Most learning is driven by need: success at work, death of a loved one, new family member, etc.
Children learn within groups at school that are very similar—same age, socioeconomic background, life experiences, etc.	Adults bring a greater degree of diversity to learning—different ages, life experiences, income levels, exposure to education, etc.
Adults and children sense time differently. As we age time seems to pass more quickly.	Adults are more concerned than children about the effective and productive use of time.
Children traditionally have a limited life experience base.	Adults have a much more diverse life experience base related to learning.
In most cases children learn quickly.	As a general rule adults learn more slowly than children, but the transfer of learning is just as effective.
Children can easily adjust their views based on new learning and ideas.	Adults are more likely to use their belief system and life experience to explain away new ideas and concepts.
Motivation is a key factor in learning. Children are generally motivated by external factors, grades, adult praise, peer pressure, etc.	Adults tend to be more motivated internally by feelings of accomplishments, steps toward life goals, and improved self worth.

Learning in Children	Learning in Adults
Children have less life experience to use as a "filter" for the relevance of learning. Since learning is valued for children they are more likely to actively participate in learning.	Adults may have negative life experiences that may lead them to limit their participation in learning. ❖

References

Brookfield S. *The Skillful Teacher.* San Francisco: Josey-Bass, 1990.

Mager R. *What Every Manager Should Know About Training.* Atlanta: The Center for Effective Performance, 1992.

Merriam S. & Caffarella R. *Learning in Adulthood.* San Francisco: Josey-Bass, 1999.

Click Play! Don't Train!

Angelica Steinker, March/April 2005

Are your clients less motivated then you would like them to be? Stop telling them to train their dogs, and start telling them to play. It is often much easier to get them to be consistent when they are having fun. Are you feeling a little bored with your own dog's training? Stop training, and start playing!

According to a personal communication from Dr. Pamela Reid, author of *Excel-Erated Learning*, play is a powerful way of altering a dog's emotional state. Almost all of us desire a dog that is fun, affectionate, and playful. Play is the ticket to a happy dog and more fun in your own life. Many behavior problems can be rapidly resolved using play-training, and clients can get faster results. A win/win situation!

There are several reasons why play is a powerful way to teach your dog behaviors. When rewarding a dog with play, you can make the reward last as long as you want. This is a tremendous advantage. The dog doesn't get full! Maybe tired, but not full.

Rewarding with play can make training self–control quick and easy. While playing with your dog, you can stop all movement and cue the dog to sit. After the dog sits, you can give the release cue and ask the dog to play again. This is a great way to practice sit, and teach the dog self-control at the same time. Politely sitting and holding that position gets the game started again.

A dog who knows how to play can usually be more easily counter-conditioned to ignore stimuli that she is fearful of. Play can be a very valuable tool in teaching a dog substitute behaviors: rather than barking and lunging at the other dog, you instead give me eye contact, and then I click and we play.

Playing rather than training is an easy sell—both the dog and the client have fun. Playing is often more reinforcing to clients than simply dispensing a cookie for a behavior. I admit this isn't scientific, but our clients who play with their dogs report an increase in fun and bonding with their dogs.

Safety First

Use common sense, if the client's dog is fearful, or in any way presents as aggressive, do not attempt playing with the dog. Fear is the basis for much aggression, so playing with a fearful dog is very effective in terms of modifying the fear, but is an advanced training skill. If you are not experienced working with fearful or aggressive dogs, then you will want to pass on play training.

Clients rely on us to assess their dogs. I recommend temperament testing all dogs prior to recommending or implementing play training.

Not all the ideas for games I present may be recommended for all dogs or owners. All games should be on cue, so that the owner can clearly signal the start and end of the game. Do not play a game or recommend that clients play a game, if both the dog and persons will not be safe.

If The Dog Won't Play

Assess why the dog does not play. There are three main reasons why a dog will not play. In some cases, the dog did not learn how to play as a puppy. Puppy mill dogs, pet store dogs, abused, and neglected dogs may never have learned to play, which is tremendously sad. Depending on the genetic make up of the dog, on the dog's resilience, and on the perseverance of the owner, it usually takes a very long time for a dog like this to learn to play. It can take months, but it will be worth all the effort. If the dog takes food, then simply pairing food with targeting a toy is a great start. From there you can shape the dog to pick up the toy, hold it, carry it, shake it, "kill" it, and so on.

The second reason can be that the owner doesn't know how to play. This is also challenging, but fixable. Begin with helping the client to relax and get in a silly mood. Making jokes and kidding around can help loosen clients up. Read the person and adjust to what they need you to be, so you can help them get where they need to be. Observe your client as much as you observe the dog you are training. Once you have created a window of opportunity, expose the client to some fun games that can be played with the dog. Show the practicality of the games so the client can be sold on how fast play-training works and how powerful it is.

Often the easiest problem to fix is when the dog has just never been asked to play. I recently worked with a client who insisted her dog would not tug. Within literally seconds I had the dog tugging. The dog was very tug motivated, but the owner had never been shown how to play tug with a dog. All her attempts at shoving the toy at the dog, or limply dangling it in front of the dog, got her a big yawn. My attitude was silly and my face one big smile, and within minutes the dog was a permanent member of Tuggers Anonymous.

If The Client Won't Play

Just as we shape dog behavior, it is important to shape client behavior. If the client isn't very fun in how she is playing, find the good things about their attempts at play, and reward them. Build the playing behavior just like you build a behavior chain in a dog.

If the client is resistant to play with the dog, model playful behavior: grab a toy, play with the dog, and then demonstrate how willing the dog is to work for you. Explain that this is the power of play and it is an ideal way to establish a reinforcement history very rapidly.

One of our trainers recently worked with a retriever that had been forcefully trained by the previous dog trainer the client had hired and fired. The client noted that the dog would not come to the previous trainer when she called him to her. Our trainer had the dog begging her to give her a cue within minutes simply by playing with the dog and showing the dog that an offered behavior will be reinforced with play. With those kinds of results, it was easy to sell the client on click and play training.

What to Play

Tug! Tug is my all time favorite play training game. Studies have shown that tug does not cause aggression (Rooney & Bradshaw, 2002; Goodloe & Borchelt, 1998). If a non-aggressive dog growls while playing tug, that is usually a play growl. Make your own play growl noises and join in on the fun!

To play tug, evaluate what type of toy movement is enticing to the dog you are playing with. Does this dog like slow toy movements? Does this dog like fast toy movements? Does this dog show interest if you move the toy back and forth? What gets the dog's curiosity going? Entice. Observe. When playing tug, it is critical that the dog has the impression that he could conceivably grab the toy and get a hold on it. If the dog has no hope of being able to get the toy, the game may be over before it ever got started.

When you play tug, it is ideal to move backwards so the dog is moving into you most of the time. There are a couple of reasons for this. Moving backwards makes the tug toy a little harder to get which can be a fun challenge to the dog, and it keeps the dog moving toward you, which is generally a good idea. Think of the recall.

Once the dog grabs hold of the toy, resist the temptation to shove the toy into the dog's mouth to try to get her to grab harder or intensify the play. Instead tease and entice by backing up, but always making it possible for her to grab the toy.

Clearly it is not a good idea to have an elderly lady tug with her Irish Wolfhound, or to pull teeth out of a puppy's mouth when he is too young to have such pressure on his mouth, but aside from these few exceptions, tug is a great game that can help you help clients attain their training goals.

Fetch! Playing fetch is a great way to keep dogs fit and to keep adolescent dogs out of trouble. 20 minutes of fetch a day can sometimes make the difference between being euthanized at animal control or staying in a home. Almost all breeds require daily exercise. Teaching your clients to teach their dogs to fetch cannot only help save lives, it can tremendously improve the quality of the dog's life. Play fetch for life!

Find it! "Find it" is a great mind activating game for a rainy day. If a client is less mobile, it is a fun way for the client to play with their dog. "Find it" can be played by both toy and food motivated dogs quickly and easily. If the dog really enjoys the game, it can be used to reward desired behaviors. Find out what the dog likes and then use it to play. Be a fun detective!

Play, Don't Train

So you have your clients tugging, fetching, and hiding. Now what? Use these games to train. Pair the new games with your clicker. Tugging is an excellent reward for coming when called. Start at a short distance, have the owner hide the toy (no prompting please), call come, and then click and play! Any part of the dog's recall can be clicked: the first step, the half way mark, or the last part. Just choose one part of the recall and click it and reward with tug. As the dog catches on to the game, increase the distance of the recall. Watch the dogs recall at light speed! Wear shin guards, and keep the business cards of a good chiropractor handy.

Playing fetch is a great way to train and proof sit, down, and stand cues. Ask your dog to sit, then throw the toy, then release her to it. Ask your dog to down, pretend to throw the toy several times, then click and feed her steak.

Here are some more games and how I use them. Remember, these are games designed for behaviorally sound dogs and one should be cautious when determining which games to use based on each individual dog's needs and temperaments.

My dog Zoomie loves it if you blow a raspberry on his face. No matter where I am I can always make a raspberry and therefore reward him. Sit! Down! Release, raspberry! Truth be known, Zoomie is a Border Collie. Honestly he thinks my breathing is fun, "oh good she is alive, we can play!" so lest you think only crazy Border Collies can play …

My Min Pin, Turbo, a rescue, loves shoelaces. Lucky me, I am usually wearing shoelaces so I have a toy no matter where I go. Turbo is also obsessed with hair scrunchies, and tugs on them like a rabid fruit bat, so that is another one that is handy. When I got Turbo, who was dumped for barking too much and being too hyper—the precise job description of a Min Pin—he would not play, but today he even tugs on his leash.

One of my favorite games is simply shoving and grabbing at my dogs. Dogs with a good opposition reflex (or balancing reflex) really love this game. The truth is my dogs, my friends, my clients, and I invent new games every day and I lay awake at night thinking about how all my bills might miraculously get paid so that I could just play with dogs all day. Oh wait, that has already happened, I own a dog school that play trains! ❖

References

Goodloe, L. P. & Borchelt, P. L. "Companion dog temperament traits." *JAAWS* 1(4): 303-338, 1998.

Rooney, N.J. & Bradshaw, J.W. S. "An experimental study of the effects of play upon the dog-human relationship." *Appl Anim Behav Sci* 75(2):161-176, 2002.

All in a Day's Work: Including Children with Developmental Disabilities Into Dog Training

Merope Pavlides, January/February 2006

I am standing in the middle of a group of puppy owners, all of whom look just a little overwhelmed. You know that look—the "What have I done?" look. The puppies range in age from 16 weeks to five months and have all been recently adopted from the shelter offering this free class. They yip, they yap, they mouth on their owners and pull on their leashes. All very typical. Also increasingly typical is the conversation I have with one of the owners after class. He tells me that he has a seven-year-old son with a developmental disability. The child and pup are having a great deal of difficulty building a positive relationship. Can I help them?

Developmental Disabilities

This very broad category that includes autism spectrum disorders, cognitive functioning impairments, attention deficit issues, behavioral challenges, and motor skill difficulties—are on the rise. A 2004 study in the *American Journal of Medical Genetics* estimated that 17% of children in the United States have a developmental disability (Rice et al., 2004), while the Autism Society of America notes on its Web site that as many as one in 250 children in this country may have autism. Think about it. Most of us know at least one family dealing with a developmental disability. Was that the case when you were growing up?

As pet dog trainers, we must serve and work with the entire family unit. Sometimes that task is an easy one, as all family members jump on board to learn positive training methods and eagerly work together to educate their dog. More often, even in typical families, pet dog trainers must think carefully about family dynamics and how best to weave the individual personalities into a cohesive dog-supportive unit. Add in the complexity of a developmental disability in the family, and the potential for failure in the interspecies connection can increase dramatically.

When I am asked to help a family such as the one described, I am admittedly nervous—even as a special educator and the mother of two sons with developmental disabilities. Just as each dog we encounter brings an individual set of experiences and behaviors to the table, each child with a developmental disability presents with his/her own set of symptoms and needs. In this particular instance, the boy had both attending issues and glitches in central auditory processing—meaning that it took longer than usual to understand what was being said. He also had a great deal of trouble controlling his impulses; so often, in spite of what he knew about handling a puppy, he was excessively forceful in his interactions with the still small retriever mix. Although sweet in disposition, the dog had grown understandably skittish around the child. She, too, needed behavioral education, as she over-relied on her mouth to get attention. (And in a house with a child with a developmental disability, the dog often doesn't receive attention until he/she engages in inappropriate behaviors, as the parents forget to reinforce calm and quiet bids for interaction.)

As challenging as working with special needs families can be, the potential for tremendous accomplishment is great. Temple Grandin points out in *Animals in Translation: Using the Mysteries of Autism to Decode Animal Behavior* (2005), many individuals with developmental disabilities really have a profound love for and connection with their furry friends. In fact, I credit my house full of loving and forgiving canines with teaching my son with autism a great deal about social interaction. In special needs families the potential for inter-species enrichment is amazing. Dogs can allow a child with a developmental disability to grow and flourish in a truly joyous way. In return, the dog takes on a level of responsibility that enriches his/her life abundantly.

So where do we, as pet dog trainers, start? If the special needs family is interested in obtaining or training a dog specifically to work as an assistance dog, they may do well to look for an appropriate training facility. But, if the family is simply attempting to help their pet dog and child with a developmental disability mesh better, there are a number of ways in which we can help.

Talk to Everyone Openly

The first, and maybe the hardest, hurdle to clear is concern about discussing the developmental disability with the family. Under the weight of political correctness and the heartfelt desire not to offend, we are sometimes hesitant to ask for specific information regarding the child's issues. As a parent, however, I can safely predict that most families will welcome questions that emanate from true concern. Rather than asking for specific diagnostic information, however, it is often useful to first ask if the child has an Individualized Education Plan (IEP) at school. If so, the child is receiving special services of some kind. Asking for further information as to what kind of services the child receives will give you insight into what needs are being addressed by educators. For example, let's imagine that a child's IEP includes speech and language therapy and occupational therapy, but the child is included in general education classes without assistance. Such information tells you that the child probably has little or no cognitive impairment, but has trouble communicating, either in terms of speaking or understanding (maybe both). Occupational therapy services imply that the child may have motor or sensory issues that will impact his/her ease in petting and handling the dog. You now know that you may need to take extra time to talk with the child about how to interact with Fido, perhaps including visuals to help illustrate your points. And you may need to make extra efforts to demonstrate how dogs like to be touched. (I use the cartoon character, Underdog, and accompanying ditty to remind kids to pet their furry friends under the chin and on the chest and sides, rather than the top if the head …)

Depending on the level of the child's involvement, you might even ask if some of the dog interaction techniques can be incorporated into lessons at school. Just as pet dog trainers want lots of ideas in their "toolboxes," special educators often welcome suggestions for helping a child generalize behaviors across environments. A child with autism, for example, may be using social priming to help navigate peer interactions. He/she may rehearse appropriate behaviors prior to trying them out at school through a method developed by Carol Gray (2000) called "Social Stories." In this approach, the child writes—initially with adult help—a script for social interactions. Teachers may be willing to help the child draft a social story for interacting with the family dog, or attending training sessions.

Ask for Permission to Touch the Child While Working With the Family

As dog trainers, we tend to be tactile people. We love to scratch, massage, and rub our canine friends. For children with developmental disabilities, touching a dog appropriately may not come naturally. Yet canine-friendly touch is a valuable skill for them to learn in terms of fostering the relationship with the family pet and in terms of development of impulse control skills. Petting a dog can also be a useful component in sensory integration training. Often the best way to teach this is hand-in-hand, perhaps even practicing first on family members and/or toys. Ask the child's parents if it's okay to touch their child when in their presence. Explain what you are going to do and what you are trying to achieve, demonstrating with a parent's hands if necessary. Working hand-over-hand also allows you sufficient control to insure that the dog is never touched too roughly.

Use Peer Models

Children with developmental disabilities can learn a great deal through peer modeling using neurotypical children. Siblings, neighbor kids, and friends can all help show the child with a developmental disability how to interact more successfully with his/her pet. Peer models will often willingly become "trainer's helpers" and will exhibit remarkable patience and enthusiasm working alongside the child with the developmental disability. Your accomplishment has now tripled: you've taught two children how to interact with and train the dog; you've helped the child with the developmental disability develop peer social skills; and you've given the typical child an opportunity to learn more about children with special needs! Prime the typical child before the session starts to make sure that he/she comprehends how the session will proceed, including that child's parent(s) in the conversation.

Impulse Control All Around

Self-management skills are difficult to learn, both for canines and humans. Of course, this is what we do on a daily basis—we teach dogs to control the impulses that are natural for them and to instead offer us the behaviors we humans find appealing. Apply the same thinking to working with a child with a developmental disability and his/her parents. Instead of focusing on the child's mistakes, develop a plan for what you'd like to see the child do, and teach those skills. Break canine interaction behaviors into the smallest possible components for the child. Keep training sessions short and positive for everyone. If the child doesn't find working with the dog inherently rewarding, find other reinforcers to help increase desired behaviors. And don't forget to praise the parents for stepping back and letting the child learn how to become dog-friendly, rather than immediately jumping in and taking over!

Safe Always

We all know what this means. But the rule when working with animals and children with developmental disabilities is to expect the unexpected, and don't give in to the temptation to push your luck, even just a little! In addition, you may need to help the parents come up with viable ways to insure that the child and dog are always adequately supervised.

Being a pet dog trainer isn't particularly lucrative. Yet it is a career which pays in unparalleled ways. The doggie kisses alone make our emotional coffers overflow. Working with the entire family unit is, I believe, where true job satisfaction lies. Involvement with special needs families can be an especially enriching experience, one which offers incomparable and unexpected bonuses.

I recently began working with a family that adopted an eight-year-old shelter dog. The shelter didn't happen to mention at adoption that the dog had a history of being snarky with children. The family has elected to work with the dog rather than return him, even though the eight-year-old son has a developmental disability with impulse control issues. Interestingly, the dog took to this little boy immediately, and has been nothing but patient. A recent training session gathered together the dog, the son, a young friend with autism, another dog, and the two moms. Whew! With lots of "good listening" and "quiet hands," however, and a big dollop of self-management for all, we had a great time. And we all came away having learned just a bit more about how marvelous the canine-human bond can be. Especially me. ❖

References

Autism Society of America. "Autism facts." Available at http://www.autism-society.org/site/PageServer?pagename=Autism_Facts, 2003.

Grandin, Temple. *Animals in Translation: Using the Mysteries of Autism to Decode Animal Behavior.* New York, NY: Scribner, 2005.

Gray, Carol. *The New Social Story Book.* Arlington, TX: Future Horizons, 2000.

Rice, C. et al. "Public health monitoring of developmental disabilities with a focus on the autism spectrum disorders." *Am J of Med Genet C*, 125C, 22-27, 2004.

This article won 1st place for the 2006 John Fisher Dogwise Essay Contest.

It's Not "Just Semantics"—Words Do Matter

Pamela J. Reid, November/December 2005

What does it mean when we say we are "temperament testing" a dog? What are we really doing? The commonly held belief is that we are revealing the dog's underlying temperament, some pervasive set of characteristics that influences behavior. But are we really getting at temperament or are we simply observing behavior? Some prefer to call the test a "behavior evaluation," viewing the test as an indication of how the dog responds when presented with a particular set of stimuli. What is the difference, if any, between temperament and behavior? Is it just an arbitrary choice of words—is it "just semantics?" Let's look closer at the scientific distinction between temperament and behavior.

Temperament or Behavior?

Behavior is considered to be an expression of temperament. But temperament is more than just behavior. It is presumed to be like "personality:" the product of both raw genetic material and environmental influences. Concepts of temperament and personality are based on the view that there are behavioral styles, enduring dispositions that lead to behavioral constancy over time. To measure personality in humans, researchers examine behavior in a wide variety of circumstances and then look for statistical relationships among the responses. Behaviors that are linked are assumed to reflect an underlying "trait" that leads to similar responses across time and situations. For instance, think of a trait termed "sociability," with an out-going person described as extroverted. This might mean that, in a variety of social situations, an extroverted person is more likely to engage in interactions with both familiar and unfamiliar people. A few studies have taken the same approach with dogs. Recently, Svartberg and Forkman (2002) put dogs through a battery of tests and identified five specific and independent traits: playfulness, curiosity/fearlessness, chase-proneness, sociability, and aggressiveness. They also describe a higher-order continuum they call shyness-boldness. Bear in mind that the findings of such studies are limited by the behavioral tests used and by the dogs tested, as well as statistical decisions about what constitutes a "trait." It is only with studies like this, however, that we can make statements about dog temperament. We can't just jump to conclusions, based on intuition, that certain behavioral responses indicate an underlying trait.

To add even more complexity to this discussion, some traits in people are considered more stable than others. Information about the consistency of a trait is critical if you hope to predict future behavior based on a single observation, like a behavioral test. Furthermore, it appears there are individual differences in overall behavioral stability. Some people behave in a very consistent manner and their future behavior is relatively easy to predict from a small set of observations. Other people are much less stable and it takes a greater number of observations to even begin to get a handle on predicting their future behavior. Martinek et al. (1975) found evidence of individual differences in consistency in dogs. They determined that dogs scoring as extreme on a particular trait were more consistent in their behavior than dogs scoring as moderate. Similar results are found for children: extremely shy and extremely bold kids behave very consistently across various social situations, whereas moderately shy kids are more erratic in their social behavior, depending upon the circumstances. Svartberg et al. (2005) examined the consistency of the five personality traits they identified in dogs by testing the same set of dogs three different times in three different locations, each test separated by about 30-35 days. They found that playfulness, sociability, and chase-proneness were all highly consistent, whereas curiosity/fearlessness tended to increase and aggressiveness decreased across testings.

So here's the essence of the problem we face. We have an unknown dog, in rescue for example, and we want to learn as much as we can about the dog as quickly as possible so we can determine if the dog is adoptable and, if so, to match it with an appropriate family. Can we be reasonably confident that the way the dog behaves on a "test" reflects how the dog will behave in the future? Let's consider an example of human behavior. Suppose we wanted to assess "assertiveness" in people and we decide to do this by observing people's responses to having someone cut in front of them in line. I'm sure this has happened to you before. There are certain people who would never dream of saying anything to the pushy individual no matter what the circumstances. There are also people who couldn't let it go and would always say something. These people are very consistent in their response to this "test" of assertiveness. But then there is the majority: people who vary along a continuum of assertiveness, not at either extreme. Sometimes we stand up for ourselves and sometimes we don't. Suppose we are testing an individual who truly is fairly unassertive, but on the day of our test, gets into a screaming match and swears at the person cutting in line! Maybe the person we are testing got pushed around by his boss all day at work and was at his limit when the person cut in line. Maybe the person we are testing had come from having a drink at the bar and he was less inhibited at the time of the test. Maybe the person we are testing was already late for an important appointment and desperately needed to get to the front of the line as quickly as possible. Certainly you can recognize that observing the person on this particular day with this particular test of assertiveness would give you a distorted view of the person's real nature.

Imagine instead that we are observing an individual who would normally score reasonably high on an assertiveness scale. But on the day of our test, it is a small child or an elderly woman who cuts in front of him and he chooses to refrain from saying anything. Or the person we are testing has just come from having an hour-long massage and is "gelling" so he doesn't care if he has to stand there all day. Or maybe the person we are watching is with his mother and he refrains from saying anything so as not to embarrass his mom. Or maybe the person being tested is in a foreign country and doesn't say anything in response to being cut off solely because he doesn't speak the native language. I recall being reluctant to ask for directions the first day or two in London, England because I was worried that I wouldn't understand the accent!

In this apparently reasonable test of assertiveness, you see how a significant detail can change the situation so dramatically that the person's behavior is not at all representative of his overall style of responding. How do we know the same is not true when we evaluate a dog based on one evaluation on one particular day? We don't know all the internal and external factors that may be impinging on the dog and influencing its behavior at the time of the test. In fact, we don't even know how the previous tests impact the dog's behavior on subsequent tests. So, until we know a whole lot more about the relationship between behavior and temperament in dogs and about the tests we use, I feel that we should be conservative in our claims and choose our words carefully: we are evaluating behavior, not testing temperament.

Changing Behavior

At a conference on shelter dogs, the audience seemed to have a great deal of trouble with the concept of successfully rehabilitating dogs that displayed problem behaviors during the evaluation. The test revealed dogs that responded timidly with strangers, backed away from an approaching woman brandishing a cane, or aggressed toward an interfering person while chewing a bone. It became clear to me that the basis for this skepticism was nothing more than the belief that such behaviors are indicative of temperament and, therefore, inherently unmalleable.

Remember that earlier we defined temperament as the product of both raw genetic material and environmental influences. If that doesn't sit well with you, consider another example of human behavior. I happen to be what most people would label an introvert. In human personality tests, boldness/shyness is considered a behavioral trait. My best guess is that I am genetically predisposed to shyness. I am of Scottish lineage and Scots tend to be hardy people of few words. In addition to the presumed genetic basis, I was also under-socialized as a child. No one would describe my parents as conversationalists. Family get-togethers are characterized by yes-no type questions and lapses of silence. They dread a significant anniversary because they despise parties that feature them as the centers of attention. So my early experiences did nothing to counteract any genetic tendency I might have toward shyness.

Shyness influences my behavior in a variety of circumstances. As a child, I used to hide behind my mom whenever anyone I didn't know spoke to me. In school, I never joined drama or debate club. In university, I never raised my hand to ask or answer a question. I never volunteered to go up to the front of the classroom. I would always opt to write a paper rather than give a presentation. In fact, as an undergraduate, I used to select my courses by first reading the syllabus and rejecting any that required an oral presentation. Never in a million years would I sign up for public speaking. One might be tempted to argue that I wasn't able to do these things; that my genes and early experience dictated I behave this way. However, my life took an interesting turn.

Once I got into graduate school, I could no longer avoid giving oral presentations. I was always terrified, I performed dismally, but I had no choice. I got a bit more comfortable and more proficient as I practiced this new behavior that was so out of keeping with my "temperament." In fact, during my final year, I won an Honourable Mention at a prestigious competition in which I had to present my dissertation research. But, despite all that practice, I would still rather have eaten nails than get up on a stage in front of a group of people!

After I graduated, I followed a career path as an applied animal behaviorist and made two discoveries. The first is that I desperately wanted to share my knowledge of animal behavior and learning with other trainers. I was so passionate about it that I wrote a book. But of course, the written work wasn't enough—people wanted to hear it explained. So I was motivated to give lectures. The second discovery I made was that giving lectures and seminars were financially rewarding. So money was another motivation for taking on public speaking. I studied talented speakers, I read books, I practiced in front of small groups of people, and I worked with a coach. Gradually my skills improved. I still have plenty of room for improvement, but I no longer read from my notes, I no longer fill my sentences with "um" and "ah," and I can even venture out from behind the podium on occasion!

More surprising is that I now genuinely enjoy public speaking. At a conference, I can't wait until it's my turn to get up there and share my stories. Am I no longer an introvert? Of course I still am. That will never change. I still can't make small talk with people I don't know and I'm still a wallflower at parties. But one component of my behavior changed because I was motivated to learn new ways of behaving. If you attempted to rate me on a scale of boldness/shyness from one observation of me lecturing to a large group of people, you likely would arrive at an erroneous conclusion about my sociability.

So now consider how this relates to a dog in the shelter. Suppose you run a dog through a behavior evaluation and you determine that he is asocial, presumably a temperament trait, although you'd need to demonstrate this tendency across both situations and time in order to be fairly confident that this is a stable behavioral pattern. A number of behaviors might suggest asociality. The dog stays at the back of his kennel when you approach. He prefers to explore the room rather than interact with you. He backs away and growls when you reach for him. He becomes rigid when you handle him. He barks and growls when someone approaches him in a threatening manner. Once the dog gets to know a person, he is friendly. Like my shyness, this dog's asociality probably has a genetic basis. That, combined with poor socialization or unpleasant experiences with people, could set the dog up to generally mistrust strangers.

Could this dog learn new behavior patterns that are counter to this general tendency? Suppose you provide this dog with plenty of motivation to interact with new people and give him opportunity after opportunity to practice new social skills? Why would this dog be any different than me learning to give public lectures? He could learn to sit and touch his nose to the outstretched hand of a stranger; he could learn to approach and accept treats from intimidating people; he could learn to enjoy being touched. Would he become a social butterfly? Not likely. He'd probably still be reticent in certain situations, and in a really terrifying predicament, I bet he'd revert back to his old ways, but if he learns to cope with most of the things faced by the average pet dog, he could make a fine companion.

How long would it take to rehabilitate a dog like this? We find that dogs in our shelter often show significant improvement after as few as 20-25 behavior modification sessions. Some require fewer sessions, others demand far more. In the older psychological literature, I found reports of children requiring one to two sessions per day for two months to extinguish a fear of snakes or frogs. With the advent of anti-anxiety medication and health maintenance organizations (HMOs), behavior therapy for people with fears now averages between eight to twenty sessions. A person with anger management problems can learn to control rage in a more normal fashion in as little as eight to ten weeks. Snake-phobic adults can learn to handle a live snake in as few as one session a week for six weeks. Does it take longer to eliminate problems that have a strong genetic basis? There is plenty of evidence that people are predisposed to certain types of fears, such as fear of snakes, spiders, and heights. This makes sense from an adaptive perspective, as these are truly dangerous things. But people also develop fears that don't seem to have an evolutionary history. We fear being in enclosed spaces, being in large spaces, public speaking, meeting new people, and so forth. You'd think that it would be much harder for people to master a genetically predisposed fear, wouldn't you? Well, that's not the case. Indeed, it takes about the same number of therapeutic sessions for a person to overcome a fear of flying as it does to overcome a fear of speaking to strangers. So if we take the leap and extrapolate to dogs, it really shouldn't matter whether we're trying to change behavior that we suspect is linked to "temperament" or not. And devoting 20-25 sessions to teach a dog to enjoy having its body handled or to appreciate people interfering during a good chew on a bone is pretty reasonable.

Conclusions

In summary, there are many unknowns when it comes to dealing with dogs in the shelter environment. We need to acknowledge the limitations of the behavior evaluation and take it for what it is. It is merely a snapshot of behavior at one point in time. It may give you highly valid information that reliably predicts the future behavior of the dog or it may not. Many other factors may come into play. We know that repeated testing or multiple observations across a variety of situations is more likely to provide an accurate reflection of the dog, at least with regard to more stable traits like sociability and playfulness. Fearfulness and aggression appear to be somewhat less consistent over time. So words do matter, because we cannot be sure that when we see a dog behaving in a particular manner on a test that we are identifying its temperament. It is far more appropriate to talk about "behavior evaluations" so we don't imply more than we actually know.

And we need to open our minds when it comes to the rehabilitation of shelter dogs. Again, words matter. Just because we are labeling a dog with words like "fearful," "aggressive," or "asocial," doesn't mean that behavior can't be changed. We know that even highly adaptive, predisposed behavior is amenable to change. The individual is the biggest contributor to whether rehabilitation will succeed. Some dogs will be very resistant to treatment, just like some people, but others will be highly receptive. And, if you do attempt to rehabilitate a dog, acknowledge that nothing happens overnight. It takes time and effort. If you happen to work in a shelter that has the resources to work with problem dogs, recognize that one to two months of work is realistic. If you can't significantly improve the dog in that amount of time, it may not be worth the effort to continue, as other dogs could be benefiting from those resources. This is a judgment call that should be based on the mission of each organization. It is a question of weighing the needs of the many against the needs of the few. There are no right or wrong answers, merely choices that need to be made. But, please, base these choices on sound scientific knowledge, not opinion and intuition. Attend to your words; semantics often have unintended implications. ❖

References

Martinek, Z., Lát, J., Sommerová, R. & Hartl, K. "About the possibility of predicting the performance of adult guard dogs from early behaviour: II." *Activas Nervosa Superior (Praha)*, 17, 76-77, 1975.

Svartberg, K. & Forkman, B. "Personality traits in the domestic dog (Canis familiaris)." *Applied Animal Behaviour Science*, 79, 133-155, 2002.

Svartberg, K., Tapper, I., Temrin, H., Radesäter, T. & Thorman, S. "Consistency of personality traits in dogs." *Animal Behaviour*, 69, 283-291, 2005.

Canine Profiling and the Important Role of Dog Trainers

Mary L. Zoller, July/August 2006

An increasing number of state and local governments are passing laws and ordinances banning or restricting ownership of specific breeds of dogs in an effort to curtail injuries and deaths perpetrated by dangerous or potentially dangerous dogs. While not new, this breed specific legislation (BSL) has continued to gain support and momentum since 1984, when Pit Bulls were banned in Minneapolis, MN and Cincinnati, OH, and later in Denver, CO in 1989. The American Kennel Club (AKC) reports that localities in Delaware, Illinois, Missouri, New Jersey, Ohio, and Oklahoma undertook banning ownership of specific breeds in the last year. The catalyst for these bills is typically a dog bite resulting in a serious injury or fatality that makes headlines. It becomes a problem that elected officials attempt to solve through laws and regulations to alleviate the fears of their constituents.

At the same time, insurance companies are quietly instituting policies to deny coverage to owners of certain breeds under their homeowner's insurance policies on the basis of the numbers of dogs of certain breeds or breed mixes inflicting the bites. The proponents of breed bans use statistics on fatalities and injuries caused by dogs to make the case for such policy decisions and a generalization or stereotype about certain breeds. In a February 2, 2006 article in *The New Yorker* entitled "Troublemakers," Malcolm Gladwell explores whether the basis of these policies are sound by asking whether a ban is based on a stable or unstable generalization? A stable generalization is founded on a thorough examination of many facts and considerations that support the conclusion, while an unstable one uses only a few facts to support the stereotype.

Opponents of breed bans answer that statistics and stereotypes cannot be responsibly used to document the "dangerousness" of a particular breed relative to other breeds. They view them as the canine equivalent of racial profiling.

The Journal of the American Veterinary Medical Association (Vol. 218, No. 11, June 1, 2001) states:

- A dog's tendency to bite depends on at least five interacting factors: heredity, early experience, later socialization and training, health, and victim behavior.

- There is no objective method of determining the breed of a particular dog.

Further, Karen Delise, author of *Fatal Dog Attacks: The Stories Behind the Statistics*, says "the problem exists not within the breed of dog, but rather within the owners who fail to control, supervise, maintain, and properly train the breed of dog they choose to keep."

National organizations and associations representing dog owners and professionals, who are on the front lines combating breed bans, take the position that breed bans are inappropriate and ineffective in addressing the problem of dog bite injuries and fatalities. They insist that policy makers should focus on the larger issues that contribute to the dog bite problem, not on the particular breed of dog who inflicted the bite. These organizations include the American Veterinary Medical Association Task Force on Canine Aggression and Human-Canine Interactions, the Humane Society of the United States, the American Society for the Prevention of Cruelty to Animals and the AKC.

They are working to educate policy makers that the bans fail to take into account the true versus perceived threat, i.e., 10-20 fatalities per year perpetrated by 25 breeds and breed mixes, not hundreds by a few breeds (*JAVMA*). In addition, elected officials need to take into account the contributing factors if they are to craft effective solutions to reduce the number of bites. These factors include the popularity and corresponding number of dogs of a particular breed at a certain point in time (e.g., Dobermans in the past, Pit Bulls today), or in a particular area (inner city versus suburbs); the reasons people choose these breeds (protection and fighting versus companionship); the circumstances under which the bite and attack occurred; the behavior of the victim; the actions of the owner (e.g., tethering the dog, not providing adequate housing, socialization, and/or training the dog to be aggressive); the history of the dog (e.g., health, whether it was selectively bred for fighting or subject to abuse and neglect); and the adequacy of existing laws and regulations and their enforcement.

Moreover, they point out the problems in implementing such policies and enforcing laws and regulations that ban certain breeds and the cost of the ban in relation to the benefits. Fanciers of the Pit Bull visually describe the difficulty of clearly identifying a Pit Bull since this is not a single breed. Ironically, the breed bans may even increase the demand for that particular breed by those who desire aggressive dogs. They may also force responsible dog owners to move to other jurisdictions, where those local governments then feel compelled to initiate a breed ban. Or they may encourage owners to abandon or hide their dogs.

Opponents have an uphill battle in the face of what has become an emotional issue, often fueled by media hype. However, the efforts of a group in Colorado may prove to be instructive for other states and local communities as they seek to counteract growing sentiments in support of breed bans. The Coalition for Living Safely with Dogs, a group of Colorado animal health care, and control professionals, came together because they share the view that while breed bans may reduce people's fears in the short-term, they actually give people a false sense of security, and are not the solution to the socio-economic issues of crime, animal abuse, and ignorance that are at the root of the problem. They offer assistance to municipalities and homeowner associations who want to establish and enforce new or more effective dangerous dog ordinances and regulations and create a common understanding about dangerous dogs. The Coalition also aims to educate owners and the general public on how to live safely with dogs and has drafted legislation to address the issue of dangerous dogs. They offer a list of common questions and answers about why breed bans are not effective and offer alternatives.

In addition, using the approach employed by public health and public safety in addressing specific crime and health problems can be effective in addressing the problem of dog bites. This involves conducting surveillance of dog bites using geo-mapping to determine exactly where and when bites occur as well as collecting qualitative and quantitative information about the dog, victim, owner and circumstances. The Centers for Disease Control and the Texas Department of Health have begun preliminary work that shows promise in developing meaningful interventions and preventing bites.

Even in the absence of good data on dog bites in a community, dog trainers can play an important role in the battle over breed bans. How?

1. Become knowledgeable about bully breeds and how they are different, e.g., quick arousal, or identify experts to whom you can refer clients to understand how to prevent bites, and train and manage these dogs, e.g., breed clubs or rescue groups.

2. Educate owners about why dogs bite, how to prevent bites—especially bites to children—and how to behave if approached by a dangerous dog.

3. Encourage clients to select dogs that are a good match for their lifestyle and where they live.

4. Provide opportunities for clients to socialize their dogs to other dogs and people, educating them about the risks of dog parks and rough play—particularly for bully breeds.

5. Support additional funding for local animal control and training of officers.

6. Volunteer your time to evaluate shelter dogs and their suitability for prospective owners.

7. Promote training and management of dogs along with publicizing and recommending compliance with local ordinances on dogs, perhaps as part of Canine Good Citizen classes.

8. Plan events in conjunction with state or nationally designated weeks to promote responsible dog ownership: e.g., the CDC, AMVA and U.S Postal Service are working to plan events during National Dog Bite Prevention Week, the third week in May, and the AKC has designated the month of September as Responsible Dog Ownership Month.

9. Request a study of the issue prior to your state or local government passing a breed ban and make sure that those with experience in dog behavior and training participate in the study.

10. Enlist public health and public safety organizations in conducting surveillance of this problem so that effective strategies can be employed to reduce dog bites.

11. Identify allies and work with them to provide a clear, coherent message about why breed bans are not effective. Offer viable alternatives for consideration.

12. Support laws or regulations that take a long term, comprehensive approach to preventing dog bites and fatalities and responsible dog ownership.

13. Educate veterinarians and technicians, breeders, and rescue groups about the importance of early socialization and the special management some breeds require.
❖

Selected Resources

American Humane Association, www.americanhumane.org/site/PageServer?pagename=nr_fact_sheets_animal_dog_bite.

American Kennel Club, www.akc.org/clubs/rdod/index.cfm.

American Medical Veterinary Association. A community approach to dog bite prevention. www.avma.org/pubhlth/dogbite/default.asp.

American Society for the Prevention of Cruelty to Animals, "Are Breed Specific Laws Effective?" www.aspca.org.

Breed Education not Discrimination (BEND), specializing in pit bull rescue, training, and education at bendco@comcast.net.

King, Trish. *Bully Breeds: They Are Different.* Video available through www.tawzerdogvideos.com/VIDEO-Index.htm.

Coalition for Living Safely with Dogs, www.colovma.com.

Delise, Karen. *Fatal Dog Attacks: The Stories Behind the Statistics, 2002.* www.fataldogattacks.com.

Pit Bulls on the Web, www.pitbullsontheweb.com/petbull/findpit.html.

Service Dogs Defined

Katrin Andberg, January/February 2006

The government defines a person with disabilities in the Americans with Disabilities Act (ADA) as:

> The term "disability" means, with respect to an individual—(A) a physical or mental impairment that substantially limits one or more of the major life activities of such individual; (B) a record of such an impairment; or (C) being regarded as having such an impairment.

Physical or Mental Impairment

Under the first test, an individual must have a physical or mental impairment. As explained in paragraph (1)(i) of the definition, "impairment" means any physiological disorder or condition, cosmetic disfigurement, or anatomical loss affecting one or more of the following body systems: neurological; musculoskeletal; special sense organs; respiratory, including speech organs; cardiovascular; reproductive; digestive; genitourinary; hemic and lymphatic; skin; and endocrine. It also means any mental or psychological disorder, such as mental retardation, organic brain syndrome, emotional or mental illness, and specific learning disabilities.

Test A: Substantial limitation of a major life activity. Under Test A, the impairment must be one that "substantially limits a major life activity." Major life activities include such things as caring for one's self, performing manual tasks, walking, seeing, hearing, speaking, breathing, learning, and working. A person is considered an individual with a disability for purposes of Test A, the first prong of the definition, when the individual's important life activities are restricted as to the conditions, manner, or duration under which they can be performed in comparison to most people. The question of whether a temporary impairment is a disability must be resolved on a case-by-case basis, taking into consideration both the duration (or expected duration) of the impairment and the extent to which it actually limits a major life activity of the affected individual. The question of whether a person has a disability should be assessed without regard to the availability of mitigating measures, such as reasonable modifications or auxiliary aids and services. For example, a person with hearing loss is substantially limited in the major life activity of hearing, even though the loss may be improved through the use of a hearing aid. Likewise, persons with impairments, such as epilepsy or diabetes, that substantially limit a major life activity, are covered under the first prong of the definition of disability, even if the effects of the impairment are controlled by medication.

Test B: A record of such an impairment. This test is intended to cover those who have a record of an impairment. As explained in paragraph (3) of the rule's definition of disability, this includes a person who has a history of an impairment that substantially limited a major life activity, such as someone who has recovered from an impairment. It also includes persons who have been misclassified as having an impairment. This provision is included in the definition in part to protect individuals who have recovered from a physical or mental impairment that previously substantially limited them in a major life activity. Discrimination on the basis of such a past impairment is prohibited.

Test C: Being regarded as having such an impairment. This test is intended to cover persons who are treated by a public entity as having a physical or mental impairment that substantially limits a major life activity.

What the Law States about Service Dogs

"Sec.36.104: Definitions—Service animal means any guide dog, signal dog, or other animal individually trained to do work or perform tasks for the benefit of an individual with a disability." Through the detailed definition provided by the ADA discussed above, one can fairly easily see what is and what is not a disability in the United States.

Section 26.104 states that the dog "must be individually trained in order to be considered a service dog." This means that owners can train their own dogs should they so choose. Service dogs do not have to be "certified" per se by any sanctioning organization or training school. While many people choose to get service dogs from regional or national training organizations, the law allows for those that choose to put the time and energy into their own dog's training. The law states that any dog being used as a service dog must be able to complete at least one task that specifically helps the disabled individual. For a person in a wheel chair this may be opening the door, picking up objects, or pulling her chair. For a person with a psychiatric disability, this may be getting the person out of bed everyday, bringing them medication at the onset of a panic attack, or getting help during an emergency. For a diabetic or person affected by epilepsy, this may be warning the person of a sugar low or high or warning of an oncoming seizure by pawing, barking, or jumping up on the person. For an autistic individual, this may be helping them stop a stammering session, closing doors, getting specific people by name, watching the person on stairs, or guiding them on the streets from oncoming traffic. The list of tasks may go on and on. Whatever the task, you must be able to demonstrate in some form that the dog does help its owner with life functions and without the dog, their life would be made more difficult.

I also highly recommend that persons with a disability have the disability and the use of a service dog documented by their doctor(s). Having written proof that a person may, and possibly should, be using a service dog at the time they start using the dog may help should they ever run into a legal battle over the service dog.

Picking a Service Dog

When choosing to train a service dog, the most important thing is the actual dog and the temperament and relationship you (or your client) have with the dog. Not every dog can be or should be a service dog. Service work is a very stressful occupation and requires a dog be so dedicated that he will work tirelessly for hours on end taking care of his person.

One of the basic things when looking at a dog is his temperament. A service dog should have an even temperament, meaning that you can do just about anything to the dog or expose him to any stimulus and he will not lunge, growl, snap, or attempt to bite. A service dog can show no aggression, as he would then be considered a danger to both the disabled person and society.

A service dog should be more driven to people than dogs. He will be around people most of the day and see dogs during his work, which he must ignore. The dog/owner relationship is of the utmost importance. If the dog does not want to be with his person twenty-four hours a day, seven days a week, then he is not service dog material. If the dog is adopted from a shelter, take into mind that it may take a few weeks for the relationship between dog and owner to develop.

The dog must also show a desire to learn. He should be energetic, yet not overly bouncy. If the owner works at a job, the dog will be sitting under their desk or chair most of the day. Yet when he is needed, he needs to jump at the chance to work. Finding a dog with that correct balance is a challenge and an art. If the dog is adopted from a shelter or rescue group, it is best for you or the owner to take a knowledgeable service dog trainer along to help evaluate the dog being considered.

A service dog must be physically sound. This means that his hips and elbows should be x-rayed and looked at by a qualified veterinarian. The veterinarian should also check the dog's eyes and knees (patellas) for any kind of deformity or anything that would be detrimental to his work. The veterinarian should give the dog a general check-up, making sure that his heart and lungs are in top shape and that he is not over or under weight.

I feel picking a service dog is still a gut instinct behavior. If you feel this dog may be good service material then he very well may. If you, or the owner, likes the dog, yet still have some nagging doubts, don't get the dog. Remember that relationship is key—the owner and their dog will be working partners and must love and respect each other as partners do.

Indicating That a Dog is a Service Dog in Public

When out in public, most service dogs wear some form of a harness or cape that indicates they are a service dog. Though this is not a legal requirement, it is publicly accepted and most people will respect a dog in a vest as a working dog. Most working dogs also wear a tag on their collar indicating they are a service dog for when they are not in harness yet out in public.

There are a variety of harnesses available on the market. For a hidden disability or psychiatric service dog, I recommend the general service dog vest and patches sold by www.sitstay.com. These vests have two pockets for documentation and emergency information as well as other things that may be needed. They also allow space for patches that say things like, "Service Dog" or "Do Not Pet Me I'm Working." Having the dog labeled in public makes life much easier on both the handler and the dog, keeping those who question at bay. Wolf Packs (http://wolfpacks.com) makes a nice backpack for dogs which allows for carrying even more items on the dog. When using a backpack, be extremely careful to get the dog used to carrying weight slowly in order to train and develop his muscles.

If a mobility or autistic support dog is being used, a more involved harness may be needed that is set up for pulling or guiding. Bridgeport Equipment (www.bridge-portequipment.com) and LDS Leather (www.ldsleather.com) both sell mobility and guide harnesses as well as their attachments such as handles of all lengths. There is also a nylon harness called the Freedom Design Harness™ (www.freedomdesignusa.com), which is very carefully made to support the dog and allows for many specialized attachments, including those not made by the company. ❖

Consulting With a "Full House"

Jen Shryock, March/April 2007

As you approach the front door, you hear the familiar sound of an excited dog, followed by running children. "Mom, the dog trainer is here!" can be heard as the hustle at the door begins. You double-check for your headache medicine and guzzle some water while waiting for the adult to appear and settle the chaos.

If this scenario is all too familiar to you, then it's time for a "full house" consultation makeover! During this makeover, you'll learn how to set your families—and yourself—up for success before, during, and after your consultation.

Working with children, parents, and their dogs can be an overwhelming dynamic for anyone. You need to plan and prepare for these consultations well ahead of time to ensure that they run smoothly. Let's face it—not all dog trainers thrive on the chaos of a full house, so it's important to recognize if this is something you like and do well, or if it may be a situation that sends you running right back out the door. Did I mention that an extra shot of patience helps, too?

The following information will help you through your "full house" consultation makeover—beginning with the initial intake and ending as you walk out the door.

History Taking and Inquiry

Taking a full history prior to entering the home is crucial. It's close to impossible to get questions answered accurately while Mom and Dad are preoccupied with what their children are doing. You'll find that phone and e-mail interviews work best prior to consultations including children. A few questions to consider adding when working with families with kids are:

- Has either parent experienced or witnessed a dog bite? If so, please describe the context. Ask the parents about a bite history, as history does tend to repeat itself. Parenthood is wonderful at helping us heal old wounds. Many parents have no idea how much they are impacted by the "one bite" from their past until they've had a child. Often, they have a stronger vulnerability or even underlying fears about interaction between their child and the dog. Mental imprints can have a strong impact on us without our even realizing it. This is not always true, but it happens often enough to make asking these questions worthwhile.

- What role did dogs play in their childhood? Ask the parents about the role dogs may have played in their childhood, as it offers insight as to what their expectations are and how they may perceive their current dog. Often, couples have not formally discussed this, so they find this question interesting.

Setting Expectations

Discuss your expectations in depth with regard to their children during the consult. Here are some guidelines to follow:

By Age Group

- **Toddlers crawling to age "three-ish."** Ask that another adult be available to supervise the child during the consultation, so that the parents can relax and focus on the material. If the consultation involves aggression toward the child, then make this a requirement. Ask your clients to invite relatives or a childcare provider to attend, as it is also very important for them to be aware of this information. Consistency in supervision and respect for established boundaries is critical for success.

- **Preschool children ages three to five years old.** Include them as much as possible. During the first 5 to 10 minutes, invite them to share their experiences and feelings about their dog. This might include sharing their favorite things or places or showing off tricks. This is an important time to observe the family dynamic between dog, kids, parents, etc. Pay attention to all of the different interactions. Is there tension between parents and siblings? Is one child corrected more than others? How is the dog reacting to your presence as well as all of the interactions going on at that time? When working with more than one child, you may want to carry a timer with you so that each child can have a turn. Offer coloring pages and other activities to help keep them occupied. Once they have had their "share time," you can talk to the parents. Employ the use of games with the whole family to teach basic skills. This is usually a huge hit. Games include hide and seek, controlled fetch, recall game in a circle, etc.

- **School age children ages five and up.** Include the children as much as possible. Do not expect them to be there for the full two hours. You may want to begin by offering information about dog body language. Play "I Spy" by having a checklist of calming and stress signals for the older children to look at and mark off as they see their dog using them, such as licking lips, turning away, yawning, etc. Ask all family members to jot down what might have happened right before their dog offered these signals, and then discuss it. This is a fun and educational way to include the kids while they are learning to recognize subtle signals that dogs offer. Discussing the context helps them to learn how to respond, especially when a dog may need space. The Doggone Crazy™ board game is an exceptionally wonderful tool to use to educate the entire family about calming and stress signals. I always carry this game with me, as it gives the children something to do while I talk with their parents.

Dealing With Uncooperative Children

- Children usually do settle down and participate in one way or another. If a child is not cooperative it is an indication there is a great deal more going on than "dog issues." Children do need to be included in behavioral programs in order for the entire family to be successful in helping their dog. Even participating in a small way is better then nothing.

- Work out a motivational reward system with the parents that will help encourage and empower the child. Occasionally, an apprehensive child may not want to participate due to fear of the dog, lack of confidence, or family criticism. It's important to offer opportunities that will allow the child to immediately be successful when working with you and the dog.

- Family members often have a hard time observing other members participating in exercises without directing or correcting them. This can create stress and tension for everyone involved, especially the dog. It's important to stress that when one person is working with the dog, the others remain quiet and allow the interaction without interruption. Reinforce those children who are listening and observing by offering them a reward, such as a yummy treat, stickers, or paw print stamps. Remember, each situation should be flexible. There may be times when you will want or need to work with only one parent and one child at a time, rather than the entire family.

Your Final Steps

You may want to recommend to the family that they allow the dog to have some "down time" following your session. Usually the dog appreciates the break and the kids will want attention by this time. If this is an aggression case, then I require the dog be given a break. Be alert to the fact that, following a really good session, people tend to let their guard down, which could cause an unintended situation to develop. You will want to recognize this, so that you can help them to avoid it.

"Full house" consultations are both dynamic and rewarding. These tips will help you approach them with confidence and creativity. Preparing ahead of time through history taking via phone or e-mail will get you off to a great start. Discussing expectations ahead of time regarding the role of the children during the consultation will put the parents' minds at ease, as they will know what to expect. Suggesting that the dog have some "down time" when you leave allows the family to regroup and think things over without distractions. These simple guidelines and suggestions will help you and the families you work with make the most of your time and expertise. ❖

Resources

For more information concerning the Doggone Crazy "Family Board Game" and dog bite prevention, please visit the Doggone Crazy Web site www.doggonecrazy.ca.

Safe at Home: What Every Pet Owner Needs to Know

Becky Schultz, March/April 2005

Corky the Yorkie lived across the street from me a few years ago, and his story is short but important. He was purchased from a farm by a busy family with small children that probably should have had a stuffed dog instead of a puppy. Their first complaint was that he was probably going to end up being "too big," and they had really wanted a dog under five pounds. Then the puppy of course jumped up and did some puppy biting with the kids, so they tied him out. He was left unsupervised on the tie-out by the owners, and neighbor kids soon began to entertain themselves by teasing him. My repeated chats with the owners included offers to help train or re-home the dog, but they weren't interested. When Corky began lunging and snapping at the neighborhood kids, I accurately predicted a bite. For Corky, the story was short, because a few months later he was found dead at the end of his tie-out. They didn't do an autopsy, but the owner shook her head sadly, and said it was "probably a brain tumor or something, because that dog has always been crazy."

As a shelter trainer, I've certainly been warped by what I've seen and heard at work. Every day we see cases of neglect and abuse that would curl your hair and confirm your worst suspicions about humanity's inhumanity to our most vulnerable companions. Mostly what really impacts me is that, after 12,000 or more years sharing our lives with canines, most people still don't seem to know very much about them, and frequently this ignorance contributes to dogs ending up in shelters. In a society in which half of all first marriages end in divorce, it shouldn't surprise us that the surrender rate in puppies is often about the same. Some of the surrender studies have suggested that 10-15% of the pet population ends up in a shelter in any given year, and it's estimated that veterinarians lose a similar percentage of their practice to behavior-related problems each year. Working as a shelter trainer has given me an inside view of all these issues and changed the way I train dogs forever.

Considering how long we have been co-existing with canines, it's amazing how much we don't know as a culture. The average person struggles with the basics, including teaching their pet where to eliminate, what to chew, and how to behave in the house. When there's a real problem, people rarely use their veterinarian as the intended first-line resource or consult a trainer.

Virtually none of the dogs surrendered to shelters have received any type of formal training, so these are animals that aren't getting to us as trainers. Either people don't know we're here as a resource, or they don't see what we offer as relevant or salient to their situation. Perhaps we're not offering what they want? Although pet dog training has shifted the focus away from teaching pretty but useless pre-competition skills like square corners and swing finishes, perhaps we should be teaching other things in addition to the basics of sit, down, stay, and come. Here's my list of what every pet owner needs to know and what we can teach them. For every student who comes to classes, there are four to five other dog or puppy owners who do not come to class. Our students become their neighborhood and family experts on pet care and training, so we must teach them well.

Pet Selection

This is entirely an educational piece and it's hard to do, because we all know that puppy breath turns your brains to mush! Everyone who ever had a dog (which means they had one when growing up and Mom took care of it) believes they're an expert, but even people who are trying to do the right thing find themselves unsure about how to get good information. The shelter staff person who talked her 90-year old relative into adopting her foster coonhound puppy, the shelter person who wouldn't allow a family with small kids to adopt an adolescent Labrador Retriever because it "might knock them down," and the breeder who convinced an older couple that their "temple guarding" breed would be great with visiting young grandchildren are all guilty of giving out questionable information to people who trusted them.

A prospective puppy buyer may want to work with a breeder, but doesn't know that puppy-millers also call themselves "breeders" and that there's a world of difference. They think that "farm-raised" is a plus, and that having someone meet them halfway (for cash) is a nice convenience. The English Bulldog puppy buyer with her heart full of excitement was stunned to find out that the puppy she had bought on the Internet was not a female as promised, but a completely different dog. She was overcome by puppy breath and purchased the male puppy brought to her instead, and months later is still waiting for her AKC papers that will never come. Offers of free pet selection consultation and pet parenting classes are a start, but they are notoriously poorly-attended and will reach the people who would do their homework anyway. Pet fairs or a "parade of breeds" event can bring people in for a fun event that can be informative as well as fun. We need to educate ourselves past our own breed prejudices and preferences and look at matching people with a pet that will work for their particular household.

Management

The first thing new pet owners need to know is how to "batten down the hatches" and to use good management tools and practices while they get the training under way. Good management preserves the house and the relationship with a pet, and it does not come naturally to most pet owners. Dog professionals puppy-proof the house and use tools like baby gates, indoor draglines, crates, or exercise pens to save our sanity. But we need to get the message to pet owners that these are great tools for them, too. Gentle Leaders™ are wonderful tools to help prevent puppies from learning to pull, to address puppy biting, and to interrupt barking behavior; in our program, we put them on puppies as young as eight weeks. The puppy study that was published in *JAVMA*, "Evaluation of association between retention in the home and attendance at puppy socialization classes" (Duxbury, Jackson, Line and Anderson, July 2003), showed a 94.2% correlation (p value of 0.008) with Gentle Leader use and retention in the home, so we really encourage their use, especially with our puppy owners. Our students hear us chant our mantra, "Never let them practice it wrong—because they get really good at it!"

One management area pet owners frequently need help with is dealing with the dog in the yard. We try to explain that dogs left alone in the backyard turn into dogs and do doggy things, such as digging to China and barking to hear themselves. It's important to teach pet owners that their yard is just another room in their house, and young dogs need supervision in all rooms until they are trained in that environment.

Another critical management issue is the expectation that in our urban and suburban lives we can safely have our dogs off leash and they'll be okay. Puppy owners are always shocked when their sweet little puppy stops following them around and takes off to explore the world at about five months of age, and we explain to them that the puppy's eyesight has improved and they are developmentally ready to see more of the world than a younger puppy. They must be ready for this and make sure the puppy is not running loose in a non-secure area. We need to teach them how to systematically teach a recall to their pet, rather than seeing this as a moral obligation.

I also include exercise as a management tool, because its judicious use will prevent many behavior problems in dogs, add socialization experiences, and build the relationship with the owner. The mantra, "A tired dog is a good dog!" is so important, and it's a myth that the backyard will adequately exercise the dog. We try to bust this myth.

Early Socialization

The importance of socializing puppies correctly during their first four months of life just cannot be over-sold. As a shelter worker, I see daily the devastating results of keeping puppies in the barn, garage, or even the house, and isolated from other people, places, and friendly animals. You never get that time back. Most of the dogs that come into our shelter as "shy/fearful" are not neglected or abused, but were perhaps a "winter puppy" that came home around the holidays, and kept inside during the winter months, missing their optimal socialization period. Mother Nature ensures that they develop caution about things they haven't seen just about the time that they're ready to range a little farther from their den, so they will approach any potentially dangerous objects carefully. As a culture we forget that Mother Nature doesn't design dogs to live in our homes, but to live in the wild, and that has implications for how we live with and train them. Early socialization includes being handled by people other than family members, going to visit new places, and visiting potentially stressful environments like the veterinary clinic. "Social" visits to the clinic should include being petted, getting treats and being handled without getting poked full of holes or lose body parts!

Dog-Dog Socialization

Another common gap in pet owners' socialization is how to adequately socialize their pet to other dogs. Pet owners don't always recognize that dogs come from "doggy families" and they come to us already knowing how to be dogs, and most of them are very good at it. Most people assume that their resident dog will socialize their new puppy, and what they end up with is a dog that's only good with the resident dogs. A veterinarian called me about a dog-aggression problem with their youngest dog, their fifth. They thought their other dogs would adequately socialize the new pup. While he was fine with those dogs, he was reactive and petrified around new dogs until we muzzled him up and let him play with other friendly dogs. Fixing reactive behavior is a slow remedial process, and it is easier to prevent with adequate socialization in the first four months. We offer additional Puppy Playgroups and a Small Dog Playgroup to our students, and they absolutely love it. Adding play sessions to adult dog classes increases attendance and improves graduation rates. Owners who feel that their pets are having fun at class are less likely to skip class and stay on the couch if they feel they're depriving Fluffy of a fun night out. Trainers can use the play time to narrate what's happening, and educate pet owners about normal dog-dog interactions, different play styles, body language, and dog behavior. Many people forget that their pet is actually a dog, and they're afraid to allow Fluffy to interact with other dogs because they're "afraid of what might happen." Before working at our shelter, my knowledge of bunnies was limited largely to what I learned from Monty Python's killer rabbit in *The Holy Grail* ("He'll bite your head clean off!"), but since learning more about their body language, I'm much more comfortable handling them. Pet owners who get a chance to watch normal dog-dog play in a supervised setting often relax, learn to read their dogs, trust other dogs to not turn into Cujo, and can allow them other play experiences.

Separation Anxiety

A major reason for surrendering pets to a shelter is undiagnosed separation anxiety. The typical dog with separation anxiety (SA) is not the dog that is neglected or left alone for ten hours a day, but is more likely the pet that has never learned to be comfortable being left alone in the first place. They are more likely to come from their litters after twelve weeks, to have always lived with another littermate or resident dog, or to live in a home with a human who is home a lot, such as an at-home parent, retired person, or someone who offices at home. If a wild canine puppy is separated from the pack, he'll distress call and the dam will come and find him. A puppy coming into our homes must learn to exist often as a single pet that stays alone for hours at a time, and we're essentially "warping" that puppy to ensure that it can function in our human households. Puppies that learn this lesson late or don't learn it at all, sometimes end up with what we call "separation anxiety," which is essentially an exaggeration of this normal distress calling, an exacerbation of the panic and anxiety associated with being left alone. Pet owners often think it's very sweet that their dog wants to be with them all the time, and don't see a potential problem with a dog that insists on following them into the bathroom.

As trainers, we really need to get information about preventing SA to pet owners, because they don't know what they are seeing. By the time they surrender the animal to a shelter, pet owners have not recognized that they have a problem until their pet breaks through the thresholds of destructiveness (usually focused on escape, around doors and windows, may come in to a shelter as a "can't confine"), house-soiling (dog is losing bodily functions, happens in an otherwise well-housetrained animal only in the absence of the owners), or excessive vocalization (too noisy, landlord objects, or neighbors report the barking). Until the dog breaks through those major thresholds, many people are completely unaware that their dog is absolutely miserable about being left alone. They may manage it by taking the dog everywhere or stuffing it into a kennel, not recognizing that the dog is in a panic until the dog breaks out of the kennel, soils in the kennel, or refuses to be crated.

As trainers, we need to be able to recognize signs of potential or incipient SA when we get calls about dogs that are barking excessively, having house-soiling accidents, having confinement issues, or being destructive. We need to know what our resources are, and direct these folks to get help sooner rather than later. Once a dog is presented to a shelter with full-blown SA, there is generally nothing that can be done for the dog. If an owner gets help early on, the dog can stay in the home and the prognosis is much better than if they wait.

Nearly every behavior problem can be prevented or resolved easily with early intervention. Early puppy classes keep dogs and puppies in their homes, as do frequent contacts with veterinarians. Issues with adult dogs can still be resolved with our help, but it sometimes takes more time and patience to do the remedial work. Trainers need to recognize that the best "bang for the buck" they have to offer people and their canine companions is to inoculate pets against relinquishment through education and support. ❖

2004 John Fisher Essay: First Place Winner

Contributors

Katrin Andberg is the founder of Maplewood Assistance Partners, Inc., a New England based assistance/service dog training organization. Maplewood Assistance Partners, Inc. offers both facility and owner-trained service dogs, helping its clients with disabilities find and train dogs to match their specific disabilities. More information on the organization can be found at the Web site www.pond-house.com/maplewood.

Teoti Anderson, CPDT, is the owner of Pawsitive Results, LLC in Lexington, South Carolina. She is the author of *Your Outta Control Puppy, The Super Simple Guide to Housetraining*, and her newest book, *Quick and Easy Crate Training*, earned a Maxwell Medallion in the Dog Writers Association of America annual awards competition. She is a former President of the APDT.

Brandi Barker has been an obedience instructor at the Anti-Cruelty Society in Chicago for several years. She is pursuing a master's degree at DePaul University in Developing Behavior Management Practices to Enhance Understanding in Human/Animal Relationships.

Jim Barry, CPDT, CDBC is located in Middletown, Rhode Island. He is co-author of *Positive Gun Dogs: Clicker Training for Sporting Breeds* (Waltham, MA: Sunshine Books, 2007), author of *The Ethical Dog Trainer* as well as the editor of the ethics column for *The APDT Chronicle of the Dog*. Jim conducts private and group field training programs using positive methods. He is the only US trainer certified as an assessor for the Gundog Club. His Web site is www.ridogguy.com.

CJ Bentley, CPDT, is the Business Manager for the Michigan Humane Society Pet Education Center. MHS is a non-profit organization that operates three open-admission shelters with full-service veterinary clinics, is the home of Animals Planet's *Animal Cops: Detroit* series, and touches the lives of over 100,000 animals per year.

Maggie Blutreich, CPDT, is APDT charter member #30, owner of BRAVO! Force-Free Training based in the Charlotte, NC, area where she teaches classes and offers private training consultations. Maggie is an AKC Public Education Coordinator, AKC Canine Ambassador, CGC Evaluator, and an officer in all-breed and breed-specific clubs.

Veronica Boutelle, MA, CTC, owner of dogTEC, coaches new and established dog trainers on starting, running, and growing successful businesses. To learn more about dogTEC's services and training tools, visit www.dogtec.org. Author of *How to Run a Dog Business*.

Jodi Brunson is the owner of the North Bend Farmers Insurance Agency. Competitive obedience is still her first love, and she trains and is involved with her local kennel club.

John Buginas, CTC, CPTD, is an instructor and intern coordinator for the SFSPCA Academy for Dog Trainers and owns Civil Pooch, LLC. John studied the impact of media on society while earning a BA in Mass Communications.

Pamela Buitrago, CTC, CPDT, lives in Ellensburg, WA, where she is a graduate student in experimental psychology, focusing on animal learning. She is also an honors graduate of the San Francisco SPCA Academy for Dog Trainers.

Elisabeth Catalano, MA, CDBC, CPDT is an instructor and behavioral counselor at St. Hubert's Dog Training School in Madison, NJ, where she teaches pet training classes as well as dog-to-dog aggression classes. Additionally, she provides instruction to trainers on learning theory, ethology, instruction skills, and dog handling for PetSMART.

Barbara Davis, CPDT, CDBC is a dog trainer and behavior consultant in Corona, CA. Barbara owns and operates BADDogsInc, specializing in the family pet practice and rescue dog rehabilitation. She is a member of the APDT Think Tank, and currently serves as President of the Golden Retriever Club of Greater Los Angeles Rescue. Barbara's Web site is www.baddogsinc.com.

Pamela Dennison is the author of *The Complete Idiot's Guide to Positive Dog Training, Bringing Light to Shadow: A Dog Trainer's Diary*, and her new book, *How to Right a Dog Gone Wrong: Roadmap for Rehabilitating Aggressive Dogs*. Pam runs Camp R.E.W.A.R.D., her three- to five-day camps for aggressive dogs. Pam's company, Positive Motivation Dog Training is, located in Blairstown, NJ. Her Web site is www.positivedogs.com.

Rob Denton is a volunteer trainer with Michigan Human Society in Rochester Hills, MI. Rob received his M.Ed. in Adult Education and Training from Seattle University and works as a technology trainer and web developer at the law firm of Plunkett & Cooney.

Dr. Ian Dunbar is a veterinarian, animal behaviorist, and dog trainer. He has written numerous books and videos and hosted the popular British television series *Dogs With Dunbar*. He received his veterinary degree and a Special Honors degree in Physiology and Biochemistry from the Royal Veterinary College (London University) and a doctorate in animal behavior from the University of California-Berkeley, where he spent ten years researching the development of hierarchical social behavior and aggression in domestic dogs. Dr. Dunbar is a member of the Royal College of Veterinary Surgeons, the California Veterinary Medical Association, the Sierra Veterinary Medical Association, the American Veterinary Society of Animal Behavior, and the APDT—which he founded. Dr. Dunbar is currently Director of the Center for Applied Animal Behavior in Berkeley, CA.

Sarah Filipiak is a freelance writer, editor, and graphic designer who lives in Athens, OH. She owns Best Pets Dog Training and has a BA in Magazine Journalism from Ohio University.

Julie Flanery, CPDT is the owner of Wonder Dogs in Philomath, OR. She competes in Musical Freestyle, obedience and Rally obedience. In 2001 she was named "Trainer of the Year" by the World Canine Freestyle Organization and is a competition freestyle judge for WCFO. She is an invited presenter across the country giving workshops on Canine Musical Freestyle.

Joan B. Guertin (APDT # 46), the owner of Common Sense Dog Training & Behavior Solutions, is a charter member of the APDT. Her focus is the training of trainers, conducting workshops in developing people friendly class structures (the "Levels Concept"), skills workshops, and conformation workshops for the show dog fancier.

Don Hanson and his wife own the Green Acres Kennel Shop in Bangor, ME where they provide boarding, daycare, grooming, training, behavior counseling, and sell pet food and supplies. He has served on the APDT Board of Directors since 2002, and was President of the APDT in 2007. Don offers seminars on a wide variety of topics including using the Bach Flower Essences with pets. His Web sites are www.greenacreskennel.com and www.bachflowersforpets.com.

Lore I. Haug, DVM, MS, DACVB, CPDT, has been involved with dogs since 1979, participating in competitive obedience, agility, and tracking. Lore graduated from Texas A&M University College of Veterinary Medicine in 1993, completed a residency in behavior from 1999-2002, and became a diplomate of the American College of Veterinary Behavior in 2002. Lore added a master's degree in 2003 and the CPDT in 2004.

Mika Ishiwata, CPDT, is the Deputy Managing Director of D.I.N.G.O. She travels all over Japan to offer seminars and workshops for instructors and pet dog owners. She is also working as an interpreter for overseas dog specialists, and has translated many leading dog training books into Japanese. D.I.N.G.O.'s English Web site is www.dingo.gr.jp.

Stacey La Forge, an attorney, is an instructor St. Hubert's Dog Training School in Madison, NJ. She breeds Tibetan Terriers and is the Secretary and former Rescue Coordinator of the Tibetan Terrier Club of America.

"On Behavior" editor **Terry Long, CPDT,** is a professional writer, dog trainer, and behavior counselor in Long Beach, CA. She provides private and group classes for pet manners, agility, and behavior modification, specializing in clicker training and other reward-based techniques. She is the former managing editor of *The APDT Chronicle of the Dog.* In 2006 her article for the *Chronicle,* "Shape for Confidence" (Mar/Apr), won a coveted 1st-place Maxwell Award for Best Feature in a canine newspaper or newsletter (non-healthcare topic) from the Dog Writers Association of America (DWAA.org). She also authors *Dog World* magazine's "About Agility" column, nominated for Best Magazine Column of 2006 by the DWAA. She can be reached through her Web site at www.dogpact.com.

Eve Marschark has provided sheep herding clinics, private lessons, and boarding training at her farm in Bedminster, PA since 1987. She judges and competes nationally in USBCHA trials. She received her doctorate in Comparative Psychology from Temple University in Philadelphia, PA, and conducts research in human-dog interaction.

Lilianne Merida-Scannone graduated as a biologist in 1980 in her native country, Venezuela, but decided to pursue dog training as a professional career a few years afterwards. She came to live in the US in 2001 and presently resides in Morriston, FL, where she directs Trained Dog Happy Dog, offering obedience, agility, and hydro-exercise rehabilitation.

Jennifer Messer, DVM is a veterinarian working in small animal practice in Ontario, Canada. In addition to routine clinical medicine, she conducts private canine behavior consultations and has implemented an in-clinic puppy parenting program to educate dog-owning clients about puppy behavior and training. She is well recognized as a leader in curriculum development for young puppies, and her comprehensive puppy class program *The Kinderpuppy Course: A Curriculum Manual for Instructors*, available at www.pavski.ca, is being used by puppy class instructors across North America.

Pat Miller, CPDT, CDBC, author of *The Power of Positive Dog Training, Positive Perspectives, Positive Perspectives 2*, and *Playing With Your Dog* is owner/director of the Peaceable Paws training center in Hagerstown, MD, where she offers Good Manners Training Classes, Apprentice Programs, Intern Academies, and Rover Retreats. She is also Training Editor for the *Whole Dog Journal* and writes regularly for that publication, as well as for *Tuft's University's Your Dog, Dog Fancy, Popular Dogs*, and *Bark* magazines. She can be contacted through her Web site at www.peaceablepaws.com.

Nikki Myers is an instructor for DogPACT (Long Beach, CA) teaching agility and pet manners. She is a founding member of the Woof Gang Flyball Club of Orange County (CA) and has traveled across the country to teach at the Iron Dogs Sports Camps. She was a professional groomer for over seven years in a busy Southern

California veterinary hospital, coordinating the puppy daycare program, and starting many puppies on grooming preparation programs.

Trish O'Connor, CPDT is the Animal Training Coordinator for the Dumb Friends League in Denver, CO where she manages the dog training program. She has been instructing dog training classes for several years in both Denver and previously with the Nebraska Humane Society in Omaha, NE.

Merope Pavlides lives in Ellicott City, MD and owns Compliant Canines, LLC and Bea's Barkery (www.beasbarkery.com). She is the mother of two children with developmental delays and author of *Animal-Assisted Interventions for Individuals with Autism*, from Jessica Kingsley Publishers. She may be reached through her Web site, www.compliantcanines.com.

Pamela Reid is a certified applied animal behaviorist and dog trainer. Since 1991, she has held the post of Vice President of the ASPCA Animal Behavior Center, where she works on projects designed to improve the well-being of pets and their people. In addition to many scholarly works (including chapters in *Readings in Companion Animal Behavior, Shelter Medicine for Veterinarians and Staff, Mental Health and Well-Being in Animals*, and *Behavioural Biology of Dogs*), she authored the acclaimed book *Excel-erated Learning! Explaining (in Plain English) How Dogs Learn and How Best to Teach Them.*

Daphne Robert-Hamilton, CPDT, is a graduate of the SF/SPCA Academy for Dog Trainers and works with aggressive dogs. She teaches telecourses through Raising Canine (www.raisingcanine.com), teaches private lessons, and works on behavior cases. She lives in Morgan Hill, CA.

Terry Ryan, CPDT, has been a pet dog class instructor since 1968. She holds workshops for instructors and her newest book is *Coaching People to Train Their Dogs*.

M. Cecilia Saleme, CPDT, is the founder and principal of Canine Higher Learning, www.dogtopiaUSA.com. Counseling owners of dogs with behavioral challenges, she specializes in the family-dog relationship. She also leads dog bite prevention education seminars at libraries and grade schools, and teaches obedience classes at a local pet store. Cecilia lives in Los Gatos, CA.

Becky Schultz, CPDT, is back in private training and behavior practice after six years at a large humane Society. She is the former Coordinator of Animal Training and Behavior Programs at the Animal Humane Society in MN.

Jennifer Shryock, CDBC has a dual degree in Special Education and Elementary Education. Jennifer is the creator of the successful "Dogs & Storks ... The prenatal class that focuses on dogs." She is also a member of www.nationalcanineresearch-council.com and is very active in developing and promoting dog safety programs with www.doggonesafe.com. Her Web site is www.familypaws.com.

Pia Silvani is past Vice President of the APDT and a member of the CCPDT. She routinely lectures around the country and she is the Director of Training and Behavior at St. Hubert's Animal Welfare Center in Madison, NJ. She is author of *Raising Puppies and Kids Together: A Parent's Guide* by TFH Publications and contributor to two new books: *The Dog Behavior Answer Book* by Arden Moore (Storey Books Publications) and *The Dog Trainer's Resource* (Dogwise). Pia travels annually to Japan to work with dog trainers and shelters.

Susan Smith is an active, professional member of the APDT, graduated from the first class held at the San Francisco Academy for Dog Trainers, was in the first group of trainers certified by the CCPDT and is grandfathered into the IAABC. She was named APDT Member of the Year in 2004. Sue is the owner of Raising Canine, www.raisingcanine.com, which provides telecourses for trainers and behavior consultants.

Angelica Steinker, M.Ed., CPDT, CCBC owns and operates Courteous Canine, Inc. She is the author of *Click & Play Agility*, (Courteous Canine Inc.).

Sue Sternberg is a lecturer, shelter owner, trainer, author, and creator of the infamous "Assess-A-Hand." She runs Rondout Valley Animals for Adoptions, in Accord, NY. Her Web sites are www.greatdogproductions.com and www.suesternberg.com.

Karen Sueda, DVM received her DVM degree from the University of California, Davis and completed her Internship at the Veterinary Medical and Surgical Group in Ventura, CA. She returned to UC Davis for her Residency in Clinical Animal Behavior which she completed in 2005. Dr. Sueda taught and saw clinical cases at UC Davis for an additional year before joining VCA West Los Angeles Animal Hospital as their behavior specialist. Dr. Sueda's special interests include canine anxiety disorders, feline behavior and the human-animal bond.

Eileen Udry, PhD, CPDT, has a doctoral degree in human performance and learning. She is involved with pet dog training through Doggone Connection in Indianapolis, IN and is Director of Training and Client Services for Indiana Canine Assistant and Adolescent Network.

Wendy van Kerkhove owns Fresh Air Training which offers growl classes, classes without leashes, private training and small dog play groups.

Janet Velenovsky, CPDT, lives with her husband, Scott, in their (mostly) peaceable kingdom of three cats (Cally, Speedy, and Griffin) and three dogs (Golden Retrievers

Kaizen and Piper, and Border Collie/Papillon mix, Keiko) in Montpelier, VA. Janet is the Training & Behavior Education Specialist for Premier Pet Products. In addition to her membership in APDT, Janet belongs to IAABC, received her Counseling Certificate from the Academy for Dog Trainers at the SFSPCA, attended the DOGS! Behavior Modification course at Purdue University, and volunteers regularly with HOPE Animal-Assisted Crisis Response and local dog therapy organizations. Janet also teaches group classes at All Dog Playskool in Richmond and offers private behavior consultations for dog and cat owners.

"Member Profile" editor **Nicole Wilde, CPDT**, runs Gentle Guidance Dog Training in Southern CA. Nicole is the author of six books, including *So You Want to be a Dog Trainer; It's Not the Dogs, It's the People: A Dog Trainer's Guide to Training Humans; One on One: A Dog Trainer's Guide to Private Lessons*, and her latest book, *Help for Your Fearful Dog*. Nicole presents seminars nationally and internationally, including at the annual APDT Educational Conferences.

Laurie Williams, CPDT, is a freelance writer, owner, and operator of Pup 'N Iron Canine Fitness & Learning Center in Stafford, VA. Laurie has been a professional canine behavior educator and trainer for over 20 years.

Mary Lesli Zoller has her Masters in Public Administration, completed paralegal training in civil litigation, and makes her living as a health policy analyst. She is an aspiring dog trainer and photographer. She lives in Richmond, VA. She is a volunteer for Mini Aussie Rescue and Support, the Richmond Dog Obedience Club, and the SPCA. She is also a member of the APDT Legislative Affairs Committee.

Abbreviations

CPDT. Certified Pet Dog Trainer. Granted by the Certification Council of Pet Dog Trainers. For more information on certification or locating a certified trainer to go www.ccpdt.org

CABC and CDBC. Certified Animal Behavior Consultant and Certified Dog Behavior Consultant. Granted by International Association of Animal Behavior Consultants, www.iaabc.org

CAP1 and CAP2. Competency Assessment Program Level 1 and Level 2. Granted by Kay Laurence (UK), www.learningaboutdogs.com

CTC. Certificate in Training and Counseling. Granted by San Francisco SPCA Dog Training Academy, www.sfspca.org

Index

From Dogwise Publishing
www.dogwise.com
1-800-776-2665

Therapy Dogs: Training Your Dog To Reach Others. Kathy Diamond Davis
Training Dogs, A Manual (reprint). Konrad Most
Training the Disaster Search Dog. Shirley Hammond
Try Tracking: The Puppy Tracking Primer. Carolyn Krause
Visiting the Dog Park, Having Fun, and Staying Safe. Cheryl S. Smith
When Pigs Fly. Train Your Impossible Dog. Jane Killion
Winning Team. A Guidebook for Junior Showmanship. Gail Haynes
Working Dogs (reprint). Elliot Humphrey & Lucien Warner

HEALTH & ANATOMY, SHOWING
An Eye for a Dog. Illustrated Guide to Judging Purebred Dogs. Robert Cole
Annie On Dogs! Ann Rogers Clark
Canine Cineradiography DVD. Rachel Page Elliott
Canine Massage: A Complete Reference Manual. Jean-Pierre Hourdebaigt
Canine Terminology (reprint). Harold Spira
Dog In Action (reprint). Macdowell Lyon
Dogsteps DVD. Rachel Page Elliott
In Search of the Truth About Dogs DVD. Catherine O'Driscoll
Performance Dog Nutrition: Optimize Performance With Nutrition.
Jocelynn Jacobs
Positive Training for Show Dogs: Building a Relationship for Success
Vicki Ronchette
Puppy Intensive Care: A Breeder's Guide To Care Of Newborn Puppies.
Myra Savant Harris
Raw Dog Food: Make It Easy for You and Your Dog. Carina MacDonald
Raw Meaty Bones. Tom Lonsdale
Shock to the System. The Facts About Animal Vaccination... Catherine
O'Driscoll
The History and Management of the Mastiff. Elizabeth Baxter & Pat Hoffman
Work Wonders. Feed Your Dog Raw Meaty Bones. Tom Lonsdale
Whelping Healthy Puppies, DVD. Sylvia Smart

Dogwise.com is your complete source for dog books on the web! 2,000+ titles, fast shipping, and excellent customer service.